IMAGES OF THE NEGRO IN AMERICAN LITERATURE

PATTERNS OF LITERARY CRITICISM

General Editors

MARSHALL McLUHAN
R. J. SCHOECK
ERNEST SIRLUCK

IMAGES OF THE NEGRO IN AMERICAN LITERATURE

Edited by

SEYMOUR L. GROSS

and

JOHN EDWARD HARDY

The University of Chicago Press

Chicago & London

This book is also available in a clothbound edition from

THE UNIVERSITY OF CHICAGO PRESS

THE UNIVERSITY OF CHICAGO PRESS, CHICAGO & LONDON
The University of Toronto Press, Toronto 5, Canada

For my son
JAMES LINFORD GROSS

and

for my daughter
EVE THERESE HARDY

I, too, sing America.
I am the darker brother.

—LANGSTON HUGHES

The Negro is America's metaphor.

—RICHARD WRIGHT

CONTENTS

CONTENTS

INTRODUCTION

SEYMOUR L. GROSS

Stereotype to Archetype: The Negro in American Literary Criticism

Our understanding of any significant movement in human affairs can hardly be said even to approach completeness until the evidence from literature is in. Because writers of fiction and poetry tend to grope for meanings rather than superimpose them—Yeats called this process the "public dream"—literary criticism can bring to the surface what otherwise might lie buried in the culture's subconscious. And this is perhaps even more true for the history of the Negro in American literature than for other cultural phenomena—the Westward Movement or the Industrial Revolution, for example—since so much of that history has been an unconscious, or at least half-conscious, masking of issues that have been contorted by fear, guilt, and rage.

No one, I imagine, would seriously suggest that this three-hundred-year-old American dilemma is fully comprehended by "objective" sociological, political, and economic accounts solely, indispensable as many of these are to an understanding of what Sidney Kaplan has called our national sin. But it is to the literature in which the image of the Negro has cast its shadow that we must also look if we are to find meanings that might otherwise elude us. Alain Locke, certainly one of the great students of the Negro in American life, commented in 1926 that

I doubt if there exists any more valuable record for the study of the social history of the Negro in America than the naive reflection of American social attitudes and their changes in the literary treatment of Negro life and character. More sensitively, and more truly than the conscious conventions of journalism and public debate, do these relatively unconscious values trace the fundamental attitudes of the American mind.[1]

The literary critic, then, in exposing the implications of, say, Melville's *Benito Cereno* or Faulkner's *Light in August*, can offer us ways of knowing that are unavailable, almost by definition, to Herbert Aptheker's *American Negro Revolts* or James Silver's *Mississippi: The Closed Society*.

Walker Percy, in a recent review of seven books on the civil rights movement in the South, had occasion to wonder "what Flannery O'Connor would make of the confrontation of a SNCC militant and a Baptist preacher. The SNCC worker might indeed come off the better, but certainly the encounter would be more complex, more set off in the mysterious round, than the simple adversaries of these books."[2] Such a remark reflects, of course, a novelist's faith in the capacity of the literary imagination to expose moral and psychological complexities in such a way as to act as a brake upon the tendency of history, especially in its more passionate moments, to reduce human experience to manageable simplicities. It is a faith that literary critics share. But having said this, one is led almost immediately into an irony: for the study of the Negro in American literature seems to indicate that he has been depicted more as a stereotype than as a human being, the very opposite of Percy's "mysterious round."

I

Given the history of the Negro in the United States, it is hardly surprising that the concept of the stereotype should dominate the criticism of his image in our literature. Being from the beginning a figure of moral debate and historical controversy, *the* anomaly in a democratic society from whose accusing presence we could not flee except through chromatic fantasies, the Negro has always been more of a formula than a human being. Therefore, until rather recently, studies that addressed themselves to the subject of the Negro in literature have either

[1] Alain Locke, "American Literary Tradition and the Negro," *Modern Quarterly*, 3 (1926), 215.

[2] Walker Percy, "The Fire This Time," *New York Review of Books*, 4 (July 1, 1965), 4.

explicitly or implicitly assumed that their main function was to designate to what degree the particular works under consideration did or did not depict "the truth about the Negro race," which is to say what the critic, as a reflector of his culture, assumed that truth to be.

Studies devoted to the Negro in American literature, either as image or creator, scarcely exist before the twentieth century, and do not flourish until the 1920's, when the Jazz Age's rage for all things Negro gave impetus to the Negro Renaissance, and the 1930's, when a pervasive social consciousness gathered the Negro into the wider sweep of economic interpretations of the Republic. Since 1940, such studies have reached an astonishing volume, predictably having kept pace with the increasing momentum of the civil rights movement.

In the nineteenth century not more than a handful of essays on the Negro and American literature are to be found, and most of these—William Dean Howells' introduction to Paul Laurence Dunbar's *Lyrics of Lowly Life* (1896) is a notable exception—work on the assumption that the Negro falls into a very special, well-understood category; therefore, judgments about any particular manifestation of his presence in a work, as character or author, depend almost wholly upon racial characteristics that are accepted as axiomatic. Julie K. Wetherill, for example, in 1892, takes it for granted that the Negro is "known" since his progress "from barbarism . . . towards civilization [has] been ably handled by the white race." Because he can tell us nothing about himself that has not already been told in the writings of white men, the Negro author should avoid the "didactic and polemical" and work what has been established as his own side of the street: "His fine ear for rhythm should be useful to him as regards poetry, and it is an unquestionable fact that he possesses the story-telling gift, knowing instinctively how to work up to a dramatic climax."[3] It is, of course, the story-telling of an Uncle Remus and the poetry of the "coon song" that the writer has in mind. J. R. Slattery's approval of Phillis Wheatley's poetry, in a pietistic though well-intentioned essay published in 1884, stems primarily from the fact that this Negro poetess so well fits the Uncle Tom syndrome, which the

[3] Julie K. Wetherill, "The Negro as a Producer of Literature," *The Chautauquan*, 15 (1892), 224–25.

writer obviously takes to be the Negro norm. She is pious, grateful, retiring, and civil ("civility is natural to them"). He cites with approval her delicacy in not sitting at the same table with whites even when invited to do so "lest her color offend them," and points out that Phillis didn't marry until all her white friends had either died or scattered—and this marriage, to a Negro, turned out to be unfortunate. He is evidently relieved that her portrait shows in "every lineament . . . the full-blooded negro."[4] But perhaps most revealing of all the nineteenth-century studies is an anonymous essay in *Putnam's Magazine* for January, 1855, entitled "Negro Minstrelsy—Ancient and Modern." Here, the writer finds himself in the uncomfortable position of trying to treat plantation songs with the dignity of scholarly seriousness without inadvertently imputing dignity to the race that composed them. He wants us to accept his assertion that these songs "touched a chord in the American heart which had never vibrated before," but he would not be taken as disturbing the existing stereotype. These melodies represent "the golden age of Negro literature," true, but viewed correctly they reveal limited intellect ("The negro is humorous rather than witty, and his comic songs consist of ludicrous images, instead of witty conceits") and an almost imbecilic incapacity for sadness ("No hardships or troubles can destroy, or even check their happiness and levity"). To forestall any accusations that in praising the art of the Negro ballads he was covertly elevating the race's human capabilities, the writer also includes various patronizing anecdotes about the childish character of the Negro, and ends his essay with several passages of mock-heroic rhetoric ("I have endeavored to discharge my obligations to society fearlessly and sincerely," etc., etc.) to show that despite his interest in the subject no one can accuse *him* of not having a proper sense of the fitness of things.[5]

The nineteenth-century critic, then, approached his subject with every intention of confirming his a priori assumptions about the Negro and his place in American culture. If a disturbing feature now and again edged out from behind the mask that

[4] J. R. Slattery, "Phillis Wheatley, The Negro Poetess," *Catholic World*, 39 (1884), 484–98.

[5] "Negro Minstrelsy—Ancient and Modern," *Putnam's Magazine*, 5 (1855), 72–79.

the culture had fitted to the Negro's face, and that the Negro himself, as Alain Locke has pointed out, agreed to wear "through a sort of protective social mimicry forced upon him by the adverse circumstances of dependence,"[6] then the critic made a quick adjustment so as to leave a smooth and reassuring countenance. Unfortunately, this kind of criticism continued on into the early twentieth century, sometimes in a more subtle manner but sometimes in a manner so blatantly racist that it achieved, unwittingly, parodic proportions.

One segment of twentieth-century studies approached the subject with relative neutrality, being by and large content to catalogue the place of Negro themes and characters in various American authors without paying much, if any, attention to the question of the validity of the handling of the materials or to the biographical and/or cultural factors that produced the depictions.[7] It is possible to accuse these studies of working out of stereotyped assumptions by implication, but one cannot always be sure. In other essays, however, the critics leave no doubt on this score.

John H. Nelson's *The Negro Character in American Literature* (1926), for example, one of the earliest full-scale treatments of the subject, organizes itself critically around such various characterological assumptions as the Negro's "irrepressible spirits, his complete absorption in the present moment, his whimsicality, his irresponsibility, his intense superstition, his freedom from resentment."[8] It follows for Nelson, then, that the "whole range of Negro character" can be revealed in one twenty-six-line sketch by Joel Chandler Harris of Br'er Fox

---

[6] Alain Locke, "The New Negro," *The New Negro: An Interpretation,* ed. Alain Locke (New York, 1925), p. 3.

[7] Examples of such studies include: Elsie C. Parsons, "Joel Chandler Harris and Negro Folklore," *Dial,* 66 (1919), 491–94; Newman I. White, "American Negro Poetry," *South Atlantic Quarterly,* 20 (1921), 304–22; Jeanette Tandy, "Pro-Slavery Propaganda in American Fiction of the Fifties," *South Atlantic Quarterly,* 21 (1922), 41–50, 170–78; Francis P. Gaines, "The Racial Bar Sinister in American Romance," *South Atlantic Quarterly,* 25 (1926), 396–402; Tremaine McDowell's "The Negro in the Southern Novel Prior to 1850," which has been reprinted in this volume, seems to us to be the best of this kind of "horizontal," semi-neutralist criticism of the period.

[8] John H. Nelson, *The Negro Character in American Literature* (Lawrence, Kansas, 1926), p. 23.

and Br'er Mud Turtle. Three years later, in a study of Julia Peterkin's Negroes, Robert A. Law compliments the author for being "first and last a realist" in showing us "the thing as it is"— which is to say, the Negro as "ignorant, indigent, shiftless, immoral." In splendid contrast to Paul Green, who was concerned with "legal and social injustice," Mrs. Peterkin's writings are not inappropriately concerned with a "desire to uplift the negro race," which is composed of "children of nature, primitive in their simplicity" and "in close touch with the beasts of the field." Superstition, repeated extra- or pre-marital "birthins," wife desertion, mindless comedy such as sneezing one's false teeth into a bowl of church lemonade—these "are the warp and woof of negro life," the "naked truth" that the critic thanks the writer for having had the courage to face.[9] But it is perhaps Hyder E. Rollins' "The Negro in the Southern Short Story" in 1916 that comes closest to epitomizing the criticism based on racist assumptions that appeared in this period.

Rollins' premise is absurdly simple: writers who assumed some complex humanity in the Negro, such as Cable; or depicted intermarriage without horror, such as Louisa Alcott; or presented "saintly" figures, such as Mrs. Stowe, are "as ignorant of [the Negro's] real character as they [are] lacking in the fitness of things." Only real southerners can know the Negro and so "it is to their work that one looks for a fair picture of him." The "fair picture" turns out to be the classic paradox of the negrophobe: "the illiterate, happy-go-lucky, good-natured negro" on the one hand, and the brutally phallic "menace to Southern women" on the other. Rollins is charmed by the "realistic" portrayals of Mrs. Sherwood Bonner MacDowell's Sambos, who drop infants into wells to cure them of the "heats" and eat false teeth thinking them ice cubes; he approves Thomas Nelson Page's nostalgic idealizations of slavery "befo de war"; and considers Br'er Rabbit the perfect symbol of "the weakness, the dependence, and the aspiration of the black race." But, he reminds us, beneath the grinning exterior there lurks a mindless savagery (read: sexuality), and he points to the stories of Thomas Dixon, Maurice Thompson, and Sarah Barnwell Eliot for confirmation. Rollins' polemical thrust is capsulized in a statement by a mountaineer in Thompson's "A Race Romance,"

[9] Robert A. Law, "Mrs. Peterkin's Negroes," *Southwest Review,* 14 (1929), 455–61.

which he approvingly quotes (I "translate" the impossible dialect): "It took about a million years to make the white man decent and reasonable, and how the dernation can you expect to take an idiot nigger and make an equal to the white man of him?"[10]

These essays are by white men. But in 1902 a touching volume curiously entitled *Twentieth Century Negro Literature*, the contributors to which were all Negroes, disturbed no waters. None of the contributors to the section of the book on "The Negro as Writer" felt that the function of the Negro writer was to correct the false image of the race promulgated by white literature. Indeed, no one of them even so much as mentioned it as a problem. And why should they? For, as one of them said, "most of the men and women of the race, who have written enough to win public notice, are known to be persons of a cheerful and jovial disposition." Could any Samboist white writer or critic ask for anything more than Walter I. Lewis' assertion that the Negro has "a laughing soul that places a bouquet of joy and sunshine where the somber draping of woe would so often be found"?[11] These writers, it seems, would have agreed with Sherwood Anderson, who, when asked to comment on the depiction of the Negro in white literature, dismissed the whole question as the product of hypersensitivity and incredibly concluded that "I do not believe the Negroes have much more to complain of than the whites in this matter of their treatment in the arts."[12] Certainly, Charles E. Burch, a Negro critic, felt that the Negro had nothing to complain of in William Gilmore Simms since "Simms presented Negro characters honestly"—that is, in describing slaves who were loyal and slaves who slept when they could, Simms was spanning the spectrum of Negro-character possibility in the antebellum South.[13]

[10] Hyder E. Rollins, "The Negro in the Southern Short Story," *Sewanee Review*, 24 (1916), 42–60.

[11] D. W. Culp (ed.), *Twentieth Century Negro Literature* (Toronto, Naperville, Atlanta, 1902), pp. 270–86.

[12] This comment is, practically speaking, the sum of Anderson's contribution to a symposium on "The Negro in Art: How Shall He Be Portrayed?" which ran in the March, April, May, June, August 1926 issues of *Crisis*, the NAACP magazine.

[13] Charles E. Burch, "Negro Characters in the Novels of William Gilmore Simms," *Southern Workman*, 52 (1923), 192–95.

Such a state of affairs could hardly be expected to continue without challenge. The poetry and fiction of Charles Chesnutt and Paul Laurence Dunbar at the turn of the century, W. E. B. DuBois' *The Souls of Black Folk* (1903) and his other writings, James Weldon Johnson's *Autobiography of an Ex-Colored Man* (1912), Benjamin Brawley's literary and social histories of the Negro in 1910 and 1918, Carter Woodson's mighty historical researches that he began publishing in 1915, the founding of such magazines as the NAACP's *Crisis* (1910) and the *Journal of Negro History* (1916)—these, and many more, gave the Negro (and some white critics) a sense of cultural worth and achievement that would no longer allow him to sit complaisantly still for his traditional portrait.

A few months after Rollins' essay appeared, Benjamin Brawley announced the resistance movement: "The day of Uncle Remus as well as of Uncle Tom is over." Not one novel since the Civil War, in his opinion, dealt honestly with the Negro in America. Cable and Harris "embalmed vanishing types"; Dixon and Page manipulated the image of the Negro to confirm their reactionary political intentions; Grace King, Ruth Stuart, Mary Johnston, and Ellen Glasgow all "simply took him for granted as an institution that has always existed and always will exist." To be sure, the idea of a serious Negro figure in literature—one "who is intelligent, cultured . . . and does not smile"—was still "incomprehensible to some people." But a more humanly contoured image of the Negro in American letters had to emerge if literature was not to divorce itself from history.[14] A few years later, William Stanley Braithwaite pointed out the banal superficiality with which the stereotype of the laughing Negro had been handled—"the writers who dealt with him . . . did not see that his humor was a mask for tragedies which were constantly a turbulent factor in his consciousness," reminding one of Langston Hughes's "to keep from cryin',/Ah opens mah mouth an' laughs." Even such well-intentioned twentieth-century authors as Eugene O'Neill in *The Emperor Jones* and *All God's Chillun Got Wings*, Ridgely Torrence in *Granny Maumee*, and Ernest Culbertson in *Goat Alley*, according to Braithwaite, because they were culturally limited to a conception of the Negro as "inferior, superstitious, half-ignorant," could only portray

[14] Benjamin Brawley, "The Negro in American Fiction," *Dial*, 60 (1916), 445–50.

primitivism and so fell far short of a literary rendering of "the immense paradox of racial life."[15]

By the mid-twenties the resistance movement begun in the mid-teens swelled to a revolution, objections to stereotyped characterizations being voiced by white as well as Negro critics. The literary-critical community was no longer willing to accept as inevitable the fact that the majority of white Americans would go on deriving "their opinions of [the Negro] from the 'coon song' and the police reports," as Charles Chesnutt ruefully put it earlier in the century. *Crisis*, for example, in 1926 ran a symposium for five issues on how the Negro ought to be portrayed in American literature. Fred De Armond suggested that it was the white man's inability to take the Negro seriously that kept him from penetrating beneath the "feigned burlesque and mimicry," to see that "all that extravagant deference, feudal manners, and Ham Bone humor is merely a form of guile."[16] Arnold Mulder dismissed the possibility of any white author's adequately portraying the Negro since "the minstrel troupe" and "good old black mammy" types of characterization were too deeply rooted in the white writer's psychology.[17] Randolph Edmonds and Albert Harper ridiculed the excessive emphasis given superstition and voodooism in the depictions of Negroes,[18] as did George C. Morse, who said that "they are legion who believe that if a native band from the jungles of Africa should parade the streets beating their tom-toms, all the black inhabitants of our city would lose their acquired dignity and dance to its rhythm by virtue of inheritance alone."[19] Harold Marley applauded the destruction of the minstrel stereotype in such novels as Clement Wood's *Nigger* (1922) and DuBose Heyward's *Porgy* (1925), espe-

[15] William Braithwaite, "The Negro in Literature," *Crisis*, 28 (1924), 204–10.

[16] Fred De Armond, "A Note on the Sociology of Negro Literature," *Opportunity*, 3 (1925), 369–71.

[17] Arnold Mulder, "Wanted: A Negro Novelist," *Independent*, 112 (1924), 341–42.

[18] Randolph Edmonds, "Some Reflections on the Negro in American Drama," *Opportunity*, 8 (1930), 303–5; Albert Harper, "Whites Writing up the Blacks," *Dial*, 86 (1929), 29–30.

[19] George C. Morse, "The Fictitious Negro," *Outlook and Independent*, 152 (1929), 648–49, 678–79.

cially commending Heyward's understanding of the way the supposedly docile Negro dissembles before the white man.[20]

In announcing the emergence of the "New Negro," Alain Locke, in 1925, predicted the end of the old "unjust stereotypes": "The day of 'aunties,' 'uncles' and 'mammies' is gone . . . Uncle Tom and Sambo have passed on."[21] The "popular melodrama [having] about played itself out," Locke settled down the following year to account for the prevalence of various stereotypes in psychohistorical terms, thus inaugurating a critical strategy that has dominated much of the later criticism of the subject. Basing his analysis of the kind of image that dominated various literary-historical epochs on the unconscious needs and fears of the white race of the respective periods, he showed how the Negro as savage stranger, comic peasant, scapegoat, bogey, or pariah, was not the result of mere literary faddism but was rather the self-justifying "dream materials" of the haunted lower layers of the public mind.[22] Anti-stereotype criticism culminated in the work of Sterling Brown, whose articles and books constitute the fullest exposition of the contention that "the Negro has met with as great injustice in American literature as he has in American life." Thoroughly, painstakingly, Brown showed to what extent the vast bulk of American literature (despite such commendable exceptions as Melville, Twain, Cable, and especially Faulkner) had incarcerated the literary Negro in such tightly restrictive categories as The Contented Slave, The Brute Nigger, The Comic Negro, The Tragic Mulatto, and The Exotic Primitive. These stereotypes, whether flattering or denigrative, all are marked by exaggeration or omission, all agree in stressing the Negro's divergence from white Anglo-Saxon norms, and all are consciously or unconsciously pressed into the service of justifying racial proscription.[23]

[20] Harold P. Marley, "The Negro in Recent Southern Literature," *South Atlantic Quarterly*, 27 (1928), 29–41.

[21] Locke, "The New Negro," p. 5.

[22] Locke, "American Literary Tradition and the Negro," 215–22. See also Walter Daykin, "Negro Types in American White Fiction," *Sociology and Social Research*, 22 (1937), 45–52.

[23] Sterling A. Brown, "Negro Character as Seen by White Authors," *Journal of Negro Education*, 2 (1933), 179–203. This article was absorbed into Brown's *The Negro in American Fiction* (Washington, D.C., 1937) and his *Negro Poetry and Drama* (Washington, D.C., 1937). See also the

It would have been inconceivable to M. J. Moses in 1910, whose ample *The Literature of the South* devoted scarcely two pages to the image of the Negro in southern literature, that so much critical energy would be expended on a problem he didn't believe existed. What, for example, could Moses have made of the cumulative attacks on the "Uncle Remus syndrome," such as Saunders Redding's dismissal of Harris' tales as "skillful and effective misrepresentation, . . . conveying the . . . impression of untaught imagination, ignorance, and low cunning with which [Harris] believed the Negro endowed,"[24] when he had assured us that Harris' Uncle Remus tales had fixed the Negro with such "precision and accuracy" that no one need "venture to trespass upon the ground"?[25] The distance between "accuracy" and "misrepresentation" is the measure of the distance that the image of the Negro had come in the American critical intelligence.

This is not to say, however, that all the battles were over—only that the war was won. Skirmishes on the stereotype line, but in a different style, continued, and still continue. Critical debate has literally raged over whether or not Twain in the ending of *Huckleberry Finn* succumbed to the genteel complacency of the white ruling class and reduced Jim to the stereotyped image of the "stage nigger"; over to what extent, if any, Melville complied with Delano's view of the Negro as frolicsome primitive or Cereno's vision of the black man as Evil; over the degree to which Mrs. Stowe's *Uncle Tom's Cabin* is to be held responsible for the subsequent formulaic depictions of the Negro in our literature; over the question of to what extent Faulkner's Negroes are liberated from traditional southern stereotypes; and so on. But the critical stance had radically and irreversibly altered: the psychological lynching of the Negro through literary stereotyping was no longer to be tolerated by those whose business it was to serve as "ideal

introduction to *The Negro Caravan* (New York, 1941), which Brown co-edited with Arthur P. Davis and Ulysses Lee. Although it does not concern itself directly with the stereotype, Lorenzo Dow Turner's "Anti-Slavery Sentiment in America Prior to 1865," *Journal of Negro History*, 14 (1929), 371–492, is a mine of source materials for the subject.

[24] Saunders Redding, *To Make a Poet Black* (Chapel Hill, 1939), p. 52.

[25] Montrose J. Moses, *The Literature of the South* (New York, 1910), p. 466.

readers" for the literate public. And if this meant subjecting to repeated scrutiny even those writers who had been complimented by earlier critics as being relatively free of literary typecasting, very well, then, the issue was too important to American culture for the critic to be satisfied with tentative assurances. No writer, Charles Glicksberg announced in 1952, who engaged in "rank stereotyping," be it ever so subtly masked or misguidedly eulogistic, could any longer "hope to get away with it."[26] He could no longer get away with it not only because of the alertness to such distortion, but also because modern criticism, with its historical orientation, psychological knowledge, and critically sophisticated procedures for analysis, brought to the problem a capacity for depth of revelation utterly beyond most of the talents of earlier critics. Fiedler on the Negro as Gothic convention, Kaplan on Melville, Howe on Faulkner, Bone on Baldwin (all of which have been reprinted in this volume), as well as, for example, Leo Marx's discussion of "the failure of nerve" in the ending of *Huckleberry Finn*, James Baldwin's attack on "the spurious emotion" in *Uncle Tom's Cabin*, or Philip Roth's scathing exposition of the reverse-stereotyping in Baldwin's *Blues for Mister Charlie* and LeRoi Jones's *The Dutchman*,[27] represent modern criticism of the image of the Negro in American literature at its best—a restless refusal to accept apparently innocent surfaces and an ability to locate those categorical imperatives that inevitably pulse within individual writers and their cultures.

II

The discovery of what the Negro was not did not automatically solve the problem of what he was. To have had it established in literary criticism that the Negro was, in Dunbar's phrase, "more human than African," was a necessary victory, but hardly decisive insofar as a literary image was concerned. In the insistence upon the Negro's similarity to all other men

[26] Charles I. Glicksberg, "Bias, Fiction, and the Negro," *Phylon*, 13 (1952), 127–35.

[27] Leo Marx, "Mr. Eliot, Mr. Trilling, and *Huckleberry Finn*," *American Scholar*, 22 (1953), 423–40; James Baldwin, "Everybody's Protest Novel," *Partisan Review*, 16 (1949), 578–85; Philip Roth, "Channel X: Two Plays on the Race Conflict," *New York Review of Books*, 2 (May 28, 1964), 10–13.

—which had been the rallying cry of the battlers against the literary stereotype—there lay the ironic danger of so bleaching out his personal and cultural identity that he would be stripped of his unique and tragic history, which is to say his particular humanness. "Not to know the Negro on the group and historical level," as Saunders Redding has commented, "is to rob him of his pride and of his rightful share in the American heritage."[28] But this is precisely (although not explicitly) the kind of robbery that was advocated by those critics who demanded that the Negro in literature always be on dress parade, lest an unflattering depiction inadvertently confirm impressions that they had so strenuously sought to overcome and that whites were only too willing to believe in. "The time is more than ripe," wrote Harry Overstreet, "for fiction writers to examine this whole program of [Negro] image-making." Because a portrait of a single bad Negro will inevitably be construed as typical, the writer must "portray the Negro in such ways as to make him respected and liked." Although he acknowledges the validity of depicting Negro characters who have been brutalized by a vicious environment, the remainder of his program is a roster of middle-class respectability: the skilled Negro, the Negro who is a genius or a hero or an effective organizer, the public-minded Negro, the Negro who is shown to be in active and successful partnership with whites in some socially commendable activity.[29]

Most offensive to the critics of this persuasion was the image of the Negro-as-unfettered-child-of-spontaneous-joy generated by both white and black writers of the Negro Renaissance. The emergence of such an image in the 1920's is traceable not only to the Jazz Age's deification of the instinctual in a revolt against the stuffy, ego-constricting respectabilities of what the "flaming youth" of the period chose to call Victorianism or Puritanism; it also reflects the Negro's bitter disappointment in finding in the post-World War I world, contrary to the promises of white America before the war, the same old oppressive conditions still obtaining. "With every avenue of

[28] Saunders Redding, *On Being Negro in America* (Indianapolis, 1951), p. 121.

[29] Harry A. Overstreet, "Images and the Negro," *Saturday Review of Literature*, 27 (August 26, 1944), 5–6; "The Negro Writer as Spokesman," *Saturday Review of Literature*, 27 (September 2, 1944), 5–6, 26–28.

assimilation apparently closed," as Robert Bone has pointed out, there was no longer any motivation for the "conscious imitation of white norms and [the] deliberate suppression of 'racial' elements."[30]

To be sure, at its worst, this image of the Negro as a syncopated inhabitant of *Nigger Heaven* (to use the title of Van Vechten's influential novel) was tawdry, shallow, and commercially inspired. But it was something else as well. For such Negro artists as Langston Hughes, Countee Cullen, Jean Toomer, and Claude McKay, the depiction of life in the black ghetto was a serious attempt to grasp imaginatively their individual and group experiences, especially as these related to their sense of alienation and their glowingly reconstructed (if somewhat fantasized) "African inheritance." Moreover, such works by white writers as O'Neill's plays about Negroes, Waldo Frank's *Holiday* (1923), Sherwood Anderson's *Dark Laughter* (1925), DuBose Heyward's *Porgy* (1925), and Carl Van Vechten's *Nigger Heaven* (1926), whatever their shortcomings, did aid in providing for a more general acceptance of the Negro as a serious subject for literary endeavor.

But the "talented tenth" critics would have none of it, or at least, very little. For them such literature was merely a newer, wilder, more insulting version of the old stereotype of the Exotic Primitive. Benjamin Brawley, who had fought the good fight against the traditional stereotypes, was outraged by the Negro Renaissance and warned that although these writers "protest against the older stereotypes," in their repetitive presentations of pimps, whores, and gamblers, "they will give us new stereotypes hardly better than the old."[31] George Morse found the vision of Harlem as an African cabaret hardly more comforting than the traditional image of the Negro as "comedian, imbecile, or creature of superstition."[32] Walter White deplored "the rut" to which Negro life had been consigned by such works as *Nigger Heaven*,

[30] Robert A. Bone, *The Negro Novel in America* (New Haven, 1958), p. 62.

[31] Benjamin Brawley, "The Negro Literary Renaissance," *Southern Workman*, 56 (1927), 177–80; "The Promise of Negro Literature," *Journal of Negro History*, 19 (1934), 53–59; *The Negro Genius* (New York, 1937), p. 14.

[32] Morse, "The Fictitious Negro," p. 649.

Home to Harlem, Banjo, and *Porgy*.[33] W. E. B. DuBois complimented Jessie Fauset's *The Chinaberry Tree* because it showed the "prim colored society" of a New Jersey town, in contrast to the promiscuity of *Nigger Heaven,* which was "a blow in the face" because it was (?) "a mass of half-truths," and *Home to Harlem,* which merely catered to "that prurient demand on the part of white folks for a portrayal of Negroes of that utter licentiousness which conventional civilization holds white folk back from enjoying."[34] Even James Weldon Johnson, who had earlier defended Van Vechten as "the only white novelist who has not viewed the Negro as a type," came to feel that the image of Negro life in the Renaissance literature, in its exclusive emphasis upon the "picturesque and exotic," had obscured "the fundamental, relentless forces at work" in the racial life of his people.[35] Sterling Brown summed up, in 1937, that the

Harlem school, like the plantation tradition, neglected the servitude. Except for brief glimpses, the drama of the workaday life, the struggles, the conflicts, are missing. And such definite features of Harlem life as the lines of the unemployed, the overcrowded schools, the delinquent children headed straight to petty crime, the surly resentment—all of these seeds which bore such bitter fruit in the Harlem riot—are conspicuously absent.[36]

By 1928, the negrophile movement and its attendant images had reached their zenith; the crash on Wall Street the following year ended the carnival time for America and "sent Negroes, white folks and all rolling down the hill towards the Works Progress Administration."[37] The image of the Negro as represented in the Negro Renaissance, especially in its more jazzy manifestations, was now seen as a bypass, "produced in answer to faddistic demands and hence . . . doomed to neglect after the passing of the Negro vogue."[38]

[33] Walter White, "Negro Literature," *American Writers on American Literature,* ed. John Macy (New York, 1931), pp. 442–51.

[34] W. E. B. DuBois, "Review of *The Chinaberry Tree,*" *Opportunity,* 10 (1932), 88; "Review of *Nigger Heaven,*" *Crisis,* 33 (1926), 81–82; "Review of *Home to Harlem,*" *Crisis,* 35 (1928), 202.

[35] James Weldon Johnson, *Along This Way* (New York, 1933), p. 381.

[36] Brown, *The Negro in American Fiction,* p. 149.

[37] Langston Hughes, *The Big Sea* (New York, 1940), p. 223.

[38] Hugh M. Gloster, *Negro Voices in American Fiction* (Chapel Hill, 1948), p. 195.

III

The proletarian ideology that shaped so much of the thinking of the 1930's could hardly have failed to affect literary criticism concerned with the image of the Negro, since he was clearly the most dislocated and deprived figure on the American economic landscape. The host of social ills he was heir to—crime, poverty, disease—that began to emerge from behind the mask of finger-snapping gaiety made him a natural for the leftist-oriented criticism of the "angry decade," and inaugurated what many critics, at least until very recently, think is his most viable image in literature—protest. This is not to say, of course, that the Negro writer's resentment at being the victim of the most glaring of democratic hypocrisies began in the 1930's; it had been there all along. But whereas before he had to dissemble or gloss or modulate his bitterness, he could now liberate his destroyed dream of equality by identifying himself with all of suffering humanity, black and white. In brief, the depression years gave the Negro both a new way of thinking about himself and an audience that was receptive to explosive narratives of exploitation and oppression.

The party line on Negro art, as described by Wilson Record, whose *The Negro and the Communist Party* is the definitive study on the subject, was patently propagandistic: "It was with the struggle of the Negro nation to achieve its manhood that the Negro artists and intellectuals were to be concerned. Its trials, its tribulations, its sufferings. . . . To select other themes was tantamount to betrayal of the race."[39] The editorial manifesto of *New Challenge*, a radical Negro journal begun in 1937, announced the necessity of depicting Negro life "through the sharp focus of social consciousness" and was backed up by Richard Wright's "Blueprint for Negro Writing," in which he pleaded for "Negro writers to stand shoulder to shoulder with Negro workers in mood and outlook."[40] Two years before, in a speech to the American Writers Congress, Langston Hughes articulated the new revolutionary image of the Negro: by placing himself "on the solid ground of the daily working-class struggle," the Negro writer can "reveal to the

[39] Wilson Record, *The Negro and the Communist Party* (Chapel Hill, 1951), p. 110.

[40] *New Challenge*, 1 (March, 1934), 53–65.

white masses those Negro qualities which go beyond the mere
ability to laugh and sing and make music." The Negro writer
must expose the bigotry in unions, the "sick-sweet" lies of
organized religion, the false leadership of Negroes "owned by
capital," the economic roots of race hatred, and the "Content-
ment Tradition of the O-lovely-Negroes school of American
fiction."[41] On the same occasion, Eugene Gordon and Edward
Clay attacked the "bourgeois" leadership of Booker T. Washington and W. E. B. DuBois and the literary emphases of
Chesnutt and Dunbar for being capitalistic and middle class.
Clay praised Hughes's *Ways of White Folks* for destroying the
"time-honored stereotypes" of the congenitally happy Negro
and the Negro who supposedly fears his white fellow-workers;
several of Wright's radical poems for not mentioning Negroes
("The revolutionary poet has no need to specialize or ever be
racialist"); and William March's *Company K* and T. S. Stribling's *Unfinished Cathedral* for showing the economic basis of
the South's racism.[42] In 1932, V. F. Calverton could say that
"the Negro alone, living in a different world of motivation,
has retained enough of his simplicity and charm and irresponsible gaiety to attract writers for the next generation"; but a
few years later he was complimenting McKay, Cullen, and
Hughes for battling against discrimination and Jim Crowism
and concluding that the Negro is "not interested in forgiving
and forgetting, but in changing, improving, reforming, revolu-
tionizing."[43]

It was not, however, only the doctrinaire critics who were
praising and advocating protest propaganda: a veritable wave
of liberalism swept the critical community. Nick Aaron Ford,
in the last paragraph of *The Contemporary Negro Novel*
(1936), asked himself the rhetorical question: "since the Negro
novelist has not produced even a first rate novel, is he not

[41] Langston Hughes, "To Negro Writers," *American Writers Congress*
(New York, 1935), pp. 139–41.

[42] Eugene Gordon, "Social and Political Problems of the Negro Writer,"
American Writers Congress (New York, 1935), pp. 141–45; Edward Clay,
"The Negro in Recent American Literature," *American Writers Congress*
(New York, 1935), pp. 145–53.

[43] V. F. Calverton, *The Liberation of American Literature* (New York,
1932), p. 147; "The Negro and American Culture," *Saturday Review of
Literature,* 22 (September 21, 1940), 3–4.

justified in laying aside the pretensions of pure artistry and boldly taking up the cudgel of propaganda? Could he not produce much greater results for the cause of his race and bring more honor to himself by open warfare of this nature than by secret subterfuge?" And answered flatly: "I am inclined to think so."[44] Although Harlan Hatcher considered Stribling's novels as having more interest "as social studies than as great fictional works of art," he preferred them to those of the "picturesque" school of writing on the Negro because of Stribling's greater social seriousness.[45] Halford Luccock agreed: "The most significant literature dealing with the Negro [between 1930 and 1940] is . . . that setting forth the Negro in the stress of economic and social conditions, reflecting 'sullen, straight, bitter realism.' . . ."[46] Erskine Caldwell's sympathetic portrayals of proletarian Negroes in the South evoked critical assent, typical of which is Oscar Cargill's remark that "if the treatment of the colored man is ever more humane, we are going to owe a very great debt to Erskine Caldwell."[47]

The list could be indefinitely extended, but it was the impact on the critics of *Native Son* (1940), which is the culmination of the protest tradition of the 1930's and its finest example, that most clearly demonstrates how receptive we had become to an image of the Negro etched in violence, hatred, and revolt. Twenty-three years after the book appeared, Irving Howe beautifully summed up the book's impact:

The day *Native Son* appeared, American culture was changed forever. No matter how much qualifying the book might later need, it made impossible a repetition of the old lies. . . . A blow at the white man, the novel forced him to recognize himself as an oppressor. A blow at the black man, the novel forced him to recognize the cost of his submission. . . . Speaking from the black wrath of retribution, Wright insisted that history can be a punishment. He told us the one thing even the most liberal whites preferred not to hear: that Negroes were far from patient or forgiving, that they were scarred by fear, that they hated every minute of their suppression even

[44] Nick Aaron Ford, *The Contemporary Negro Novel: A Study in Race Relations* (Boston, 1936), p. 102.

[45] Harlan Hatcher, *Creating the Modern Novel* (New York, 1935), pp. 144–45.

[46] Halford E. Luccock, *American Mirror* (New York, 1940), p. 79.

[47] Oscar Cargill, *Intellectual America* (New York, 1941), p. 396.

18

when seeming most acquiescent, and that often enough they hated *us*, the decent and cultivated white men who from complicity or neglect shared in the responsibility for their plight.[48]

In brief, then, Wright took the protest image as far as it could go; and even those who were later to oppose this image, like James Baldwin, were to admit that they were able to go on because of where Wright had allowed them to begin.

IV

Although there were critics (and of course writers) who carried the protest tradition on into the 1940's—and beyond—by the early post-war years the movement had lost most of its vitality and momentum. The reasons for this are, predictably, various. Generally speaking, the growing dissatisfaction with Negro protest literature reflected the wider disillusionment with all forms of social hopefulness. Soured by World War II on all politically utopian dreams of success, criticism met ideal-istic demands, most especially those submitted by the radical naturalists, with a tired skepticism that waved them aside as irrelevant to a culture trying to learn to live with the acceptance of broken promises. Naturally, a critical disposition that ori-ented itself toward "the tragic vision" ("the inevitable betrayal at the heart of things") would not find much viability in any literary program based on the assumption that life's evils are sociologically reversible.

More specifically, as has already been indicated, Richard Wright had so completely embodied the image of protest in his fiction that to follow directly in his footsteps would be to court repetition and anticlimax, especially when those who followed protested not because they were artists but because they were Negroes.[49] Good intentions, James Baldwin wrote in 1949, were not reason enough to forgive violence to lan-guage and incredibility: "It is, indeed, considered the sign of a frivolity so intense as to approach decadence to suggest that these books are both badly written and wildly improbable. One is told to put first things first, the good of society coming be-

[48] Irving Howe, "Black Boys and Native Sons," *A World More At-tractive* (New York, 1963), p. 101.

[49] Bone offers some interesting statistics in support of this contention: of the sixty-two Negro novelists writing between 1853 and 1952, forty published one novel and eleven published two.

fore niceties of style or characterization."[50] More seriously, as various critics warned, Negro protest literature, so far from disturbing the racial status quo, could actually reinforce those very principles of oppression which it deplored. For, in their view, by confining the Negro solely to the hopeless ring of "racial breast-beating," in which the only attitude is paranoia, the only movement is hysterical action, and even the sufferings ironically take on the quality of welcoming punishment for the sin of being black, the net effect is to confirm the assumption of American culture that the Negro is incapable of "sane and cognitive response" and to leave the reader with a pity that is not much different from contempt. Therefore, despite the commendable intention of protest literature, in it the Negro becomes, in however disguised a form, another experientially constricted stereotype, whose agonized choreography in the pit, because it implies that this is his exclusive reality, denies him a *human* destiny even as it moves us.[51] As James Baldwin put it in the now-famous last sentence of "Everybody's Protest Novel," "the failure of the protest novel lies in its rejection of life, the human being, the denial of his beauty, dread, power, in its insistence that it is his categorization alone which is real and which cannot be transcended."

Although there are hints of dissatisfaction with the protest tradition in Ralph Ellison's "Richard Wright's Blues" (1945), it was not until the 1960's, and most emphatically in answer to Irving Howe's energetic defense of the Wright school of Negro writing, "Black Boys and Native Sons," that Ellison articulated what is perhaps the fullest attack on the tradition. Like Baldwin, Ellison felt that the experience of the Negro American had "been distorted through the overemphasis of the sociological approach"; that any attempt to define the Negro "predicament in exclusively sociological terms" would, perforce, short-circuit the exploration of "the full range of American Negro humanity" and obliterate those qualities in the race "which are of

[50] James Baldwin, "Everybody's Protest Novel," pp. 578–85.

[51] William Couch, Jr., "The Problem of Negro Character and Dramatic Incident," *Phylon*, 11 (1950), 127–33; Ira Reid, "The Literature of the Negro: A Social Scientist's Appraisal," *Phylon*, 11 (1950), 388–90; Charles Glicksberg, "Bias, Fiction, and the Negro," 127–35; M. J. C. Echeruo, "American Negro Poetry," *Phylon*, 24 (1963), 62–68.

value beyond any question of segregation, economics or previous condition of servitude."[52]

Saunders Redding once commented that "season it as you will, the thought that the Negro American is different from other Americans is still unpalatable to most Negroes."[53] But not to Ellison, who feels that to deny the special qualities of Negro life in America, its differences, which is to say "its cultural heritage as shaped by the American experience," is to reduce "Negroness" to "a mere abstraction in someone's head," an Invisible Man, as he put it in the title of his famous novel. And this is precisely what the protest tradition does, in Ellison's view, when it insists, for the sake of a militant posture, that unrelieved suffering (the "embodiment of living hell") is the only reality of Negro experience.

> But there is also an American Negro tradition which teaches one to deflect racial provocation and to master and contain pain. It is a tradition which abhors as obscene any trading on one's anguish for gain or sympathy; which springs not from a desire to deny the harshness of existence but from a will to deal with it as men at their best have always done.[54]

Moreover, Ellison insisted, Negro life does not exist solely in the vacuum of a black ghetto but is part of the historical pattern of America and the Western world; for a writer to see it in eccentric isolation is deliberately to reject "the complex resources for imaginative creation" for the easy sanctuary of ideology.[55] Richard Gibson also resented the "conspiracy" to confine the Negro novelist to the protest tradition:

> You are not yet free, he is told. Write about what you know, he is told, and the Professional Liberal will not fail to remind him that he cannot possibly know anything else but Jim Crow, sharecropping, slum ghettoes, Georgia crackers, and the sting of his humiliation, his unending ordeal, his blackness.[56]

[52] Ralph Ellison, "That Same Pain, That Same Pleasure: An Interview," *Shadow and Act* (New York, 1964), pp. 3–23. The piece first appeared in 1961.

[53] Saunders Redding, "The Negro Writer—Shadow and Substance," *Phylon*, 11 (1950), 371–73.

[54] Ellison, "The World and the Jug," *Shadow and Act*, pp. 107–43.

[55] Ellison, "Introduction," *Shadow and Act*, pp. xi–xxiii.

[56] Richard Gibson, "A No to Nothing," *Kenyon Review*, 13 (1951), 252–55.

The ultimate effect, then, of confining the image of the Negro to that of protest is to create a literary version of the political policy of absolute separation of the races.

The reaction against protest was not of course the result of a mere self-propelled swing of the literary-critical pendulum: as always, history itself supplied the momentum. Although no one would be so innocent as to believe that the racial barriers have all crumbled in the past two decades or so, there is no question that the legal advances made by Negroes in the body politic, as well as an increasingly tolerant spiritual climate in the nation as a whole, have altered the terms for the depiction of the Negro in our literature. Arthur P. Davis, for example, while acknowledging the great "creative motivation" in the 1920's and 1930's "when full segregation was not only practised in the South but tacitly condoned by the whole nation," recognized that the time for images of fiery protest was probably past: "As long as there was this common enemy, we had a common purpose and a strong urge to transform into artistic terms our deep-rooted feelings of bitterness and scorn. When the enemy capitulated, he shattered our most fruitful literary tradition."[57] Once again, as when the traditional stereotypes of the Negro were successfully buried earlier in the century, the critical community had to find a new literary image consonant with a changing reality.

One of the first suggestions for widening the base of the image beyond what the protest motif allowed was a shift from the "oppression aspect" of racial life to the conflicts and tensions within the group itself. Such a program, it was hoped, would (unlike the avoidance of Negro characters entirely) ensure the Negro a place in the American cultural framework "without destroying his uniqueness and creative vitality."[58] Blyden Jackson, in an article significantly entitled "A Golden Mean for the Negro Novel," felt that the finest Negro novelists (Petry, Killens, Ellison, Smith) demonstrated how a middle-class Negro organically develops from the Negro masses, which itself is becoming more and more middle class. These works are "Negro to the core," but "one cannot think of them without noticing that the drives they all have assimilated are the drives

[57] Arthur P. Davis, "Integration and Race Literature," *Phylon*, 17 (1956), 141–46.

[58] Charles Glicksberg, "The Alienation of Negro Literature," *Phylon*, 11 (1950), 49–58.

which determine our American middle-class notions of what constitutes an admirable personality." Therefore, he concluded, the duty of the Negro novelist today is to trace the growing assimilation of the Negro to the American middle class.[59] Loften Mitchell, while admitting that propaganda pieces are more apt to soothe consciences, asserted the need for a literature that would deal with Negro business and professional men, historical figures, and family life. Moreover, he pointed out, works that approach the Negro middle class as "human beings may conceivably bring latent prejudices to the fore"; by subjecting white America to "the 'black personality' in a portrait contrary to the traditional concept," they could force into the open submerged aspects of the racial problem.[60]

This "middle-class stance," whose ultimate critical thrust is assimilationist, was, however, repudiated by those critics who refused to accept the implied superiority of white Western-world standards that undergirds the position. Although pride in what John O. Killens calls the "black psyche" has existed in Negro consciousness throughout the last two centuries, the massive irruption of the colored peoples of the world upon the recent scene of history has encouraged the Negro to voice such feelings directly, without recourse to the various masks of apparent conformity traditionally demanded by the white majority. Saunders Redding, for example, contends that the Negro writer has been desperately damaged by accepting the notion—which all the machinery of American life is geared to—that only when he identifies "with the stream of western culture that flows through America" can the Negro author expect to attain to the "privilege of being judged by the standards that prevail among Americans and Westerners as artists and men."[61] But it is in *not* becoming "a real American," in not becoming desensitized to "philosophical and artistic influences that originate beyond our national cultural boundaries," according to Julian Mayfield, that the Negro author can achieve his full power. For

[59] Blyden Jackson, "A Golden Mean for the Negro Novel," *CLA Journal*, 3 (1959), 81–87.

[60] Loften Mitchell, "The Negro Writer and His Materials," *The American Negro Writer and His Roots*, eds. J. O. Killens *et al.* (New York, 1960), pp. 55–60.

[61] Saunders Redding, "The Problems of the Negro Writer," *Massachusetts Review*, 6 (1964–65), 57–70.

the Negro author, ever aware of the disparity between the American dream and the grim realities he knows, "the facade of the American way of life is always transparent. . . . He is indeed the man without a country. And yet this very detachment may give him the insight of the stranger in the house, placing him in a better position to illuminate contemporary American life as few writers of the mainstream can."[62] "My fight," John O. Killens announced, "is not to be a white man in a black skin, but to inject some black blood, some black *intelligence* into the pallid stream of American life."[63] For William Gardner Smith, it is his racial identity that endows the Negro writer with the emotionality and perceptivity that keep him from being "superficial," as most American literature is, and direct him toward those "basic human issues" with potentially great "creative power."[64] It is LeRoi Jones, however, who has taken "the stranger in the house" position to its extremity. (His frenetically angry stance in such statements as "I will destroy America" reminds one of Jules Laforgue's quip—"I'm tired of these Christians; why don't they start eating up the lions?") From the vantage point of his total rejection of America, Jones dismisses Wright, Baldwin, and Ellison, among others, as mere apers of white middle-class life, whose works have taken on the "emotional barrennness" of their model. Insofar as Jones feels that the Negro writer should utilize "the entire spectrum of the American experience from the point of view of his own emotional history in this country, as its victim and chronicler, a man existing outside the boundaries of commercial division or artificial social pretense,"[65] he stands with those critics who find in the Negro's special history the possibilities of unique insight. But insofar as this insight is to be pressed into the service of a disinterested chronicling of doom—"My ideas revolve around the rotting and destruction of America, so I can't really expect

[62] Julian Mayfield, "Into the Mainstream and Oblivion," *The American Negro Writer and His Roots,* pp. 29–33.

[63] Quoted in Redding, "The Problems of the Negro Writer," p. 63.

[64] William Gardner Smith, "The Negro Writer: Pitfalls and Compensations," *Phylon,* 11 (1950), 297–303.

[65] Langston Hughes, LeRoi Jones, John A. Williams, "Problems of the Negro Writer," *Saturday Review,* 46 (April 20, 1963), 19–21, 40.

anyone who is part of that to accept my ideas"—he stands not only apart from those critics but, as George Dennison has suggested, outside of history itself.[66]

V

The image of the Negro in American literary criticism can, finally, be said to have undergone an exquisite reversal in the last one hundred years. For whereas our criticism began by locking the Negro into the fantasy construct of the stereotype, removing him from human consideration to a kind of psychological and moral no-man's land, one recent phase of criticism has interpreted him and his situation as archetypal, as "an image of man's fate," as Robert Penn Warren has recently put it.

Alain Locke, who had an uncanny knack for predicting the literary history of the image of the Negro, as early as 1948 commented that as fiction became less and less a reflecting surface for the face of society and penetrated, instead, to the "crucial inner conflict and anxiety of society itself," the Negro, "as a *symbol* of social misunderstanding," would emerge "as the great tragedy of our time, both nationally and internationally."[67] In the same year, G. Lewis Chandler, although voicing severe reservations about *Native Son*, which, in his view, "boomerangs upon its real purpose and unwittingly returns the Negro to a bestial status where America . . . has tried to keep him," nevertheless sensed that it was possible to view Bigger Thomas as "standing" for all victims of exploitation.[68] A decade later, in *White Man, Listen!* Richard Wright put the matter directly: "Negro life is [all] life lifted to the heights of pain and pathos, drama and tragedy. The history of the Negro in America is the history of America written in vivid and bloody terms; it is the history of Western Man writ small. . . . The Negro is America's metaphor."[69] George Knox, at about the same time, analyzed the fiction of Ellison, Wright, and Faulkner

[66] George Dennison, "The Demagogy of LeRoi Jones," *Commentary*, 39 (February, 1965), 67–70.

[67] Alain Locke, "A Critical Retrospect of the Literature of the Negro for 1947," *Phylon*, 9 (1948), 3.

[68] G. Lewis Chandler, "Coming of Age: A Note on American Negro Novelists," *Phylon*, 9 (1948), 28.

[69] Richard Wright, *White Man, Listen!* (New York, 1957), pp. 108–9.

to show how the Negroes in their works "become grotesque
Everymen," black heroes who serve as the "vehicle of problems
suffered by modern cosmopolitan man generally." The image
of the Negro, he concluded, will find its imaginative consum-
mation when its "unique 'I' will feel rapport with and speak
for the interracial corporate 'We.' "[70] Ester Jackson, more recently, has discussed the relationship of the American Negro to
"the shape of human suffering" in the modern world as manifest in the works of Dostoevsky, Gide, Malraux, Mann, Camus,
and Sartre. The discovery that "an ever larger segment of
humanity seems to share the kind of existence which has been
the lot of the Negro"—alienation from the larger community,
isolation within abstract walls, loss of freedom, a legacy of
despair—has led to a literary view of the Negro as a "prototype"
of the contemporary sense of existential dislocation.[71] How per-
suasive the archetypal view of the Negro has become is perhaps
best evidenced by the large number of critics—too numerous to
name—who have emphasized how the Negro in Faulkner's
work is made, by symbolic extension, to "transcend his sufferings *qua* Negro to emerge to us not as Negro but as man."[72]
The grinning ape of nineteenth-century criticism has become,
then, the twentieth century's "black mask of humanity." It is
something to be grateful for.

[70] George Knox, "The Negro Novelist's Sensibility and the Outsider
Theme," *Western Humanities Review*, 11 (1957), 137–48.

[71] Ester Merle Jackson, "The American Negro and the Image of the
Absurd," *Phylon*, 23 (1962), 359–71.

[72] Robert Penn Warren, "Faulkner: The South and the Negro," *Southern Review*, 1, n.s. (1965), 520.

Traditions

I

MILTON CANTOR

The Image of the Negro in Colonial Literature

Modern scholarship has emphasized that slavery evolved out of the practice of servitude in English America. Colonial society, it is observed, developed a system of slavery which fastened its stigma upon the Negro people. But it should not be assumed that the stigma followed only in the wake of slavery. Rather the slave status of the Negro was worked out within a framework of discrimination. Slavery, as Oscar and Mary Handlin have found, developed uncertainly, and was not legally fixed before 1660.[1] The Handlins' conclusion, however, should not obscure the fact that institutional forms frequently precede their legal cognition, and there is considerable evidence to indicate that the peculiar institution existed *in fact* before it did in law.[2] More important is the underlying assumption of the colonists that the Negro servant—or slave—was of a special inferior status. Since the Negro had been set apart from the first and never treated as the equal of the white settler, free or servant, assurances that the discriminatory word "slave" was rarely

Reprinted from *New England Quarterly*, 36 (1963), 452–77, by permission of the *New England Quarterly*.

[1] Oscar and Mary Handlin, "Origins of Southern Labor," *William and Mary Quarterly*, VII (1950), 203. All ideological aspects of the controversy about the Negro before 1784 are given a first-rate critical assessment by W. D. Jordan, "White over Black: The Attitudes of the American Colonists toward the Negro, to 1784," Brown University doctoral dissertation, 1960.

[2] There is also considerable statutory evidence to support the assertion that chattel slavery began well before it was recognized by statute in the tobacco colonies. *Maryland Archives*, X, 293–96, XLI, 261–62; *Virginia Historical Register and Literary Advertiser*, II (April, 1849); J. H. Russell, *Free Negro in Virginia 1619–1865* (Baltimore, 1913), 34 n.

applied to the Negro in the early decades of settlement are irrelevant: the conclusion derived from this, however—that the Negro servant was the equal of the white—is debatable. For colonial literature touching on the Negro is explicit: the earliest settlers viewed him as different and inferior.[3]

This is not to claim that such literature is abundant or unequivocal; or that the first colonists thought very much or very deeply about the matter. They did not seem to care sufficiently either to justify or to lament the philosophical assumptions of slavery. There was good reason for this: slavery was a tenuous innovation, without roots or tradition, in the first half of the seventeenth century.

References to the Negro, though few and scattered, nevertheless do suggest that a distinct and low status was accorded him. They also demonstrate that the origins of the pro-slavery argument of the next century, as well as the counterattack, may be observed in colonial America. Certainly the advocates of religious conversion of Negro slaves employed arguments which prefigured the shape of Abolitionism. However, there seems to be no organic connection between these movements. Colonial religionists did not attack the institution of slavery, for to do so would have alienated slaveholder supporters;[4] rather, they sought to impress upon masters their Christian duty, the opportunity of the slaves' salvation and the owners' need to care for the souls as well as the bodies of their property. But these same clergymen invariably reminded the slaves of their obligations to their masters. Cotton Mather may have incidentally wished to inculcate piety among the Negroes of Massachusetts, but his primary motive was to increase their usefulness, and he assumed the Negro's inequality and incapacity for freedom.[5]

So widespread was this conviction of inequality that many

[3] A number of laws passed by the Virginia and Maryland legislatures between 1640 and 1650 singled out the Negro for special status. Hening, *Statutes*, I, 146, 257; *Maryland Archives*, I, 80, 233, 342.

[4] Marcus Jernegan, "Slavery and Conversion in the American Colonies," *American Historical Review*, XXI (April, 1916), 511–12. Anglican minister Morgan Godwyn was typical. Critical of slavery and especially of the lack of instruction in the Christian creed for the Negro, "he had no thought, however, of abolishing slavery." Thomas Drake, *Quakers and Slavery in America* (New Haven, 1950), 2.

[5] Vernon Loggins, *The Negro Author* (New York, 1931), 3.

anti-slavery writers acknowledged it.[6] A measure of its universality may be suggested by the assertion of John Woolman. One of the earliest opponents of slavery in English America, he admitted that "the black seem far from being our Kinsfolk" and that they "are of a vile stock." When this champion of conversion and manumission asserted as much, it is hardly surprising that the Middletown Friends would, in 1738, take a stand at least as positive. "Deceased Negroes," they decreed, are "forbidden to be buried within the bounds of the graveyard belonging to this meeting."[7]

There was good reason for the nearly universal stress upon the Negro's low estate. Prevailing opinion had maintained that only heathens could be enslaved by Christians and that, once a slave had been Christianized, he was automatically free.[8] Psychological and economic obstacles, however, stood athwart this tradition. By converting the heathen, first of all, by giving the Negro the rudimentary instruction which inevitably accompanied it, the catechist could only make the slave over in his own image, a repellent thought to the overwhelming white majority. Secondly, baptism might bring freedom and loss of property, a possibility that was anathema to most slaveholders. Finally, there was the fear that conversion would encourage unrest. It would make them "greater knaves" than they were, wrote one southerner, and possibly "result in the cutting of the throats of the baptizers."[9] George Whitefield affirmed as much when he noted the planters' disregard for the souls of their

[6] Anthony Benezet, *Short Account of that Part of Africa Inhabited by the Negroes* (Philadelphia, 1762). See also Nathaniel Appleton, *Considerations on Slavery* (Boston, 1767), 14.

[7] Drake, *Quakers and Slavery in America*, 16.

[8] Jernegan, "Slavery and Conversion in the American Colonies," *American Historical Review*, XXI, 504–6. See also Frank Klingberg, "The African Immigrant in Colonial Pennsylvania and Delaware," *Historical Magazine of the Protestant Episcopal Church*, XI (1942), 128; and Elihu Coleman, *A Testimony against that Antichristian Practice of Making Slaves of Men* (Boston, 1733), 11.

[9] Alexander Hewatt, *An Historical Account of the Rise and Progress of the Colonies of South Carolina and Georgia* (London, 1779), II, 101. Morgan Godwyn, *The Negro's and Indians Advocate* (London, 1680), 61, 117. David Humphreys, *An Account of the Endeavours used by the Society for the Propagation of the Gospel in Foreign Parts* (London, 1730), 5.

property, which he ascribed to apprehensiveness that Christianity "would make them proud and unwilling to submit to slavery."[10] The revivalist continued: "Do you not read that servants as many as are under the Yoke of Bondage, are required to be subject in all lawful things to their masters?" Whitefield then resorted to an ingenious clerical defense of conversion: it would serve as an instrument of control. Christianity, as an Anglican clergyman of anti-slavery views confirmed, "presseth absolute and entire Obedience to Rulers and Superiors."[11]

This viewpoint notwithstanding, there was a basic resemblance between the conversion and manumission movements of the seventeenth- and nineteenth-century anti-slavery agitation. Like the Abolitionists, colonial friends of the Negro postulated two theories: Negro and white were fundamentally equal and the Negro also possessed the divine spark. Equalitarians such as Woolman insisted that "Negroes are our Fellow Creatures. . . . The Parent of Mankind is gracious: His Care is over his smallest creatures, and a Multitude of Men escape not his Notice."[12] Endorsing this sentiment, Thomas Paine held "that all are the work of the Almighty Hand," and that God "has extended equally His care and protection to all."[13] A host of anti-slavery writers agreed—Frederick Dalcho, John Hepburn, Samuel Hopkins, Anthony Benezet, Benjamin Rush, and "Philmore."[14] Faith in the divine nature of man was an essential

[10] George Whitefield, *Three Letters from the Reverend Mr. G. White-field* (Philadelphia, 1740), 15.

[11] Godwyn, *The Negro's and Indians Advocate*, 128 [112]. See also Frederick Dalcho, *An Historical Account of the Protestant Episcopal Church in South Carolina, from the first Settlement of the Province to the War of the Revolution* (Charleston, 1820), 110. Reverend Thomas Bacon, a Maryland Anglican, urged Negro parishioners to submit to "wicked overseers," since there was "no remedy in this world." Thomas Bacon, *Four Sermons* (London, 1753), 32.

[12] John Woolman, *Considerations on Keeping Negroes* (Philadelphia, 1762), 52.

[13] Thomas Paine, "Preamble to the Act Passed by the Pennsylvania Assembly, March 1, 1780," in *The Complete Writings of Thomas Paine,* ed. Philip Foner (New York, 1945), I, 21–22.

[14] "J. Philmore," "Extracts from a Manuscript, intituled, Two Dialogues on the Man-trade, Printed in London, in the Year 1760," in Benezet, *Short Account . . .* , 29. See also Appleton, *Considerations on Slavery,* 3; Dalcho, *An Historical Account . . .* , 110; John Hepburn, *The American Defense of the Christian Golden Rule* (New York [?], 1715), 24; Benjamin Rush,

proposition; to hold to any other would render conversion meaningless. Such was the assumption underlying David Humphreys' claim that the argument favoring Negroes having no soul had *"no foundation in Reason and Truth."*[15] Such was the understanding of the anonymous author of *The Watchman's Alarm*, when he charged that "more than one half those who are owners of these black folk do not care what becomes of the souls of them."[16] Concern for the Negro's soul was shared by numerous travelers, and by a legion of Anglican ministers who had been sent by the Society for the Propagation of the Gospel, the agency which provided the main thrust for conversion in America.[17]

Obviously, the issue of conversion elicited a considerable amount of polemical literature. It ranged from assertions that *"Men*-Slaves and *Women*-Slaves . . . have the same Frame and Faculties with yourselves, and have souls capable of being made eternally happy," to counter claims that Christianity was "too rich a pearl to be cast before negroes."[18] The negative statements presupposed Negro inferiority which, understandably enough, was prerequisite to enslavement. Slavery, after all, could not survive without the assumption that the Negro was special; he *had* to be, otherwise his debasement would be inadmissibly inhuman and unchristian.

The slave's denigration was not always motivated by com-

An Address to the Inhabitants of the British Settlements in America upon Slave-Keeping (Philadelphia, 1773), 28–29.

[15] [David Humphreys], *An Account of the Endeavours used by the Society for the Propagation of the Gospel in Foreign Parts* (London, 1730), 5.

[16] *The Watchman's Alarm* (Salem, 1774), 26. Over a century and a half earlier Cotton Mather, one of the few Puritans to press the cause of conversion, also observed that masters "oppose all due means of bringing their poor negroes unto our Lord." Cotton Mather, *Magnalia Christi Americana*, I, Book III (Hartford, 1855), 581.

[17] Jernegan, "Slavery and Conversion in the American Colonies," 522. See also Frank Klingberg, *Anglican Humanitarianism in Colonial New York* (Philadelphia, 1940).

[18] Dalcho, *An Historical Account . . .*, 110. See also *New American Magazine*, XXV, 1760 [11], 25; [Isaac Skillman?], *An Oration, on the Beauties of Liberties* (Boston, 1773), 74; George Berkeley, *The Works of George Berkeley*, ed. A. A. Luce and T. E. Jessop (London, 1955), VII, 122.

pelling economic reasons or by the desire to maintain the peculiar institution. Spokesmen for the planter aristocracy were not alone in affirming the Negro's spiritual inferiority. New Englanders, too, came to consider the Negro as a species whom it was appropriate to regard in a radically different light from other men. Even such advocates of the Golden Rule as Cotton Mather, after pleading that "thy Negro is thy Neighbour," felt obliged to note his brutishness and "stupidity."[19] More than these judgments were recorded, however. To treat the Negro brutally, it was necessary to find him less than a man; to find him a beast, a thing without a soul to lose. The goal was attainable, since the Negro was *sui generis* from the outset—different in color, language, religion, and appearance.

The transatlantic flow of English opinion, the condition of the Negro in Bermuda, Jamaica, New Providence, and other West Indian colonies, even English culture and folkways, transmitted the notion of Negro inferiority and accelerated his lowering status, although the discriminatory word "slave" was infrequently used. Labor practices on the Caribbean islands provided English America with early examples of discrimination or outright slave status. Information about such practices might reach the colonies through a number of media: newspapers, travelers' accounts, shipmasters' reports, and volumes which described the West Indian labor system. Early literature pertaining to life on the Caribbean islands, such as *Letter from a Merchant at Jamaica* and Thomas Tryon's *Advice to the Gentlemen Planters of the East and West Indies*, though published in England, was circulated in America; and it was apparent to all readers that the servant of black skin in the Caribbean was being discriminated against. Furthermore, this literature, whether emanating from London or from Philadelphia, whether for or against Negro slavery, provided the colonists with the major articles of the pro-slavery creed; and, *pari passu*, as the defense of slavery crystallized, the attack unfolded.

Tryon's work is suggestive. "We are not *Beasts* as you count, and use us, but *rational* Souls," his Negro spokesman avowed. "Can we help it if the Sun, by too close and fervent kisses . . . tinctured us with a dark complexion?"[20] By this inquiry Tryon

[19] Cotton Mather, *The Negro Christianized* (Boston, 1706), 5.

[20] [Thomas Tryon], *Friendly Advice to the Gentlemen Planters of the East and West Indies* (London, 1684), 115.

tells us something of the first line of the slave defense. Black-ness was the Negro's most striking feature, and always had had pejorative meaning for Englishmen. It was the sign of danger, the symbol of baseness and corruption to the men of Shake-speare's day.[21] In Milton's poems, and "Comus" and "The Hymn" serve as two examples, darkness connoted error, ir-religion, evil, or death. Elizabethan dramatic literature was filled with characters like Giovanni, in John Webster's *The White Devil*, who associated guilt and "blacke deedes," or like Aaron of *Titus Andronicus*, a "barbarous Moor" and "foul-spoken coward" who sought "blood and revenge." Macbeth's witches were "secret, black and midnight hags." Surely, colonists might conclude, if so noble a figure as Othello, a prince and a Chris-tian, could be stigmatized as a "thing," the word was appli-cable to victims of the slave trade. Even those who considered black to have some advantages were forced to concede that it detracted from "our ideas of beauty."[22]

Whiteness, on the contrary, symbolized goodness and vir-ginity. It was the ideal color of beauty—for both Elizabethans and colonists. The Negro confessed to the superior beauty of white women, even Jefferson was convinced, by preferring them to those of his own color.[23] A poem instructing Southern gallants how to flatter young ladies, ended with typical advice:

> Her eyes to suns, her skin to snow compare,
> Her cheeks to roses, and to jet her hair:
> And thus, and only thus you'll please the Fair.[24]

Pigmentation, therefore, became the prime stigmatizing fac-tor. The continuous denials of the relationship of slavery to blackness in anti-slavery literature simply measured the degree to which these two ideas were associated. These denials began with the later Puritans. Cotton Mather denied that "the great

[21] C. F. E. Spurgeon, *Shakespeare's Imagery* (New York, 1936), 158. "Every white will have its blacke, / And everye sweet its sowre," is an old English couplet in Thomas Percy, *Reliques of Ancient English Poetry*, ed. R. Willmott (London, 1857), 27.

[22] Rush, *An Address to the Inhabitants of the British Settlements . . . ,* 3.

[23] Matthew Mellon, *Early American Views on Negro Slavery* (Boston, 1934), 106.

[24] *South Carolina Gazette*, July 12, 1735. See also *Providence Gazette*, January 28, 1775.

God went by the *Complexion* of Men, in His Favours to them."[25] Nearly sixty years later, another spiritual leader protested the popular notion that slavery was "connected with the Black Colour and Liberty with the White."[26] With the Revolution, anti-slavery writings proliferated: so did the denials of any organic relationship between slavery and color, as the pamphlets of David Cooper, Charles Crawford and others clearly illustrate.[27]

To be black meant to be a slave and to be a slave meant to be black. But color was not the sum of racial differentiation. There were other factors which were enlarged and reinforced at every opportunity. The racial barrier had to be strengthened, particularly at a time when Negroes were becoming Christians and learning to speak English. The threat of cultural assimilation was met at the threshold—by a theory of socio-cultural inferiority which utilized color, but which also found other criteria. By means of these discriminatory standards, the Negro was established to be very different. "Though in their Figure they carry some resemblence of Manhood," Morgan Godwyn noted, they "are indeed *no Men*."[28] The slaveholders, charged Anthony Benezet, had the conviction fixed "in their Minds, that the Blacks are hardly of the same Species with the white Men, but are Creatures of a Kind somewhat inferior."[29]

The stigmatizing criteria were various. Some observers, mostly of a pro-slavery disposition, ascribed the Negro's inferiority to his background. Life in Africa meant worship of

---

[25] Mather, *The Negro Christianized*, 23.

[26] Woolman, *Considerations on Keeping Negroes*, 29.

[27] E.g., *United States Magazine*, I, December, 1779, 487; Hewatt, *An Historical Account . . .* , II, 101; Charles Crawford, *Observations upon Negro Slavery* (Philadelphia, 1784), 4; David Cooper, *A Serious Address to the Rulers of America* (Trenton, 1783), 8; William Gordon in the *Independent Chronicle*, May 15, 1777.

[28] Godwyn, *The Negro's and Indians Advocate . . .* , 3.

[29] "Philmore," "Extracts . . . , " in Benezet, *Short Account . . .* , 31. Josiah Quincy, Jr., who was less friendly toward the Negro, observed: "The Africans are said to be inferior in point of sense and understanding, sentiment and feeling, to the Europeans and other white nations. Hence the one infer a right to enslave the other." "Journal of Josiah Quincy, Jr., 1773," *Massachusetts Historical Society Proceedings*, Vol. 49, p. 463.

snakes, crocodiles, even gaily colored birds.[30] Hence those who lived on the dark continent presumably existed outside of grace, in a state of religious ignorance as well as backwardness.[31] Comparison was inevitable and some writers were blunt: African Negroes comprised "a race the most detestable and vile that ever the earth produced," while the colonists, conversely, were descended "from worthy ancestors."[32] To extend the parallel: America's Negroes "prove more industrious, honest, and better slaves than any brought from Guinea; this is particularly owing to their Education among the *Christians*, which very much polishes and refines them from their barbarous and stubborn Natures that they are most commonly endowed with."[33]

Such writers emphasized inborn characteristics as the shaping factor. One pro-slavery commentator insisted that the African Negro was guilty of "treachery, theft, stubbornness, and idleness," and that "life at home . . . put it out of all doubt that these qualities are natural to them and not originated in their state of slavery."[34] Thomas Jefferson, who compared the Negro with the Roman slave, after a long commentary on the artistic and intellectual achievements of the latter, concluded that it was nature, not slavery, which produced the distinctions between black and white men.[35] To the contrary, Benjamin Rush asserted, all these "vices which are charged upon the Negroes in the southern colonies and the West Indies, such as Idleness, Treachery, Theft, and the like, are the genuine offspring of slavery, and serve as an argument that they were not intended by Providence, for it."[36]

[30] Griffith Hughes, *The Natural History of the Barbadoes* (London, 1750), 18.

[31] Theodore Parsons and Eliphalet Pearson, *A Forensic Dispute on the Legality of Enslaving Africans* (Boston, 1773), 25–26.

[32] [Arthur Lee], *An Essay in Vindication of the Continental Colonies of America* (London, 1764), 30.

[33] John Brickell, *The Natural History of North Carolina* (Dublin, 1737), 272. See also Parsons and Pearson, *A Forensic Dispute* . . . , 26.

[34] Bernard Romans, *A Concise History of East and West Florida* (New York, 1773), 105.

[35] Thomas Jefferson, *Notes on Virginia*, in *The Complete Jefferson*, ed. Saul K. Padover (New York, 1942), 662.

[36] Rush, *An Address to the Inhabitants of the British Settlements* . . . , 2.

Environmentalism, therefore, could play both sides of the street, and friends of the Negro naturally adopted a hopeful attitude toward his acclimatization. Contrasting the Negro's condition on each continent, they inferred that he was capable of improvement when placed in a more civilized society. "A state of slavery has a mighty tendency to sink and contract the minds of men, and prevent them making improvement in useful knowledge of every kind," claimed Samuel Hopkins; "it sinks the mind down in darkness and despair. . . . No wonder then the blacks among us are, many of them, so destitute of prudence and sagacity."[37]

Hopkins was partially responding to still one more stigmatizing criterion: the Negro was barbarous and, among ancillary characteristics, also was indolent and stupid. No full doctrine of Negro incapacity or brutishness developed in the colonial period, but the seeds of this opinion were scattered broadside. Edward Long, a Jamaican judge, was one of the great disseminators, and his tract of 1714, *History of Jamaica*, revealed the possibilities of anti-Negro thought. "If Labour is so repugnant to the inclinations of mankind in general," he stated, "it is doubly so to the Negro in the West Indies," given his "natural sloth."[38] Fearing the possibility of manumission, he and others played upon public anxieties when they circulated this charge. One anonymous writer phrased the threat bluntly. "If the freemen of the country find it difficult to support themselves and families at the present time," he asked, "is it reasonable to suppose that our slaves, naturally indolent, unaccustomed to self-government, destitute of mechanical knowledge . . . would pay their taxes and provide for themselves?"[39] The obvious answer was negative: the freedman would be reduced to beggary and become a community burden.[40]

[37] Samuel Hopkins, *A Dialogue Concerning the Slavery of the Africans* (Norwich, 1776), 44. See also Parsons and Pearson, *A Forensic Dispute* . . . , 25, and John Woolman, *Journal and Essays*, ed. Amelia M. Gummere (New York, 1922), 338–39.

[38] [Edward Long], *The History of Jamaica* (London, 1714), II, 65.

[39] *New Jersey Gazette*, January 10, 1781.

[40] Long, *The History of Jamaica*, II, 353. See also George Moore, *Notes on the History of Slavery in Massachusetts* (New York, 1866), 106; Lee, *An Essay in Vindication* . . . , 40; *New Jersey Journal*, November 29, 1780; John F. D. Smyth, *A Tour of the United States of America* (London, 1784), 43–44, 48.

American pro-slavery writers, in an effort to confirm the Negro's position as a slave, continually added to these pejorative characterizations. John Saffin of Massachusetts must have labored hard to compress in so few words all the gross anti-Negro sentiments of his day, in "The Negroes' Character":

> Cowardly and cruel, are those *Blacks* Innate,
> Prone to Revenge, Imp of Inveterate hate,
> He that exasperates them; soon espies
> Mischief and Murder in their eyes.
> Libidinous, Deceitful, False and Rude,
> The spume issue of Ingratitude.[41]

It remained for Edward Long, however, and the anonymous author of *Personal Slavery Established by the Suffrages of Custom and Right Reason*, to carry the argument one step further than the traditional anti-Negro animus, for they groped about for scientific and anthropological justifications of slavery. Conjecture about the unity of man furthered their cause. Such speculation was not widespread in colonial America, since its inhabitants had less reason than Europeans to place the Negro in an ordered world of nature; his place already was fixed. But continental thinkers had been pondering upon the gradations of organic life ever since the contributions of Cuvier, Petrus Camper, and François Bernier, all of whom ordered men according to their physical characteristics, and ever since Carolus Linnaeus had, in his *System of Nature*, greatly broadened this approach—by the unprecedented act of integrating man into the animal creation and by throwing him into a separate class of forms—the quadrupeds. Classification was for Linnaeus the vital center of science, and his work, which tended to descriptive categorization of all organic life, seemed to be at odds with the classical conception of the Great Chain of Being. The latter view postulated a hierarchic order that ranged upward without lacunae from inanimate objects to man himself. Linnaeus did not endeavor to rank the various types of men, but the Great Chain of Being offered precisely this opportunity. Some commentators were tempted and, invariably, the Hottentots came out at the bottom of their scale. Since no hiatus in the Great Chain was possible, those on the lowest grade must be in proximity to the highest of beasts. Edward Tyson's study of the

[41] Moore, *Notes on the History of Slavery . . .*, 256.

"orang-outan" established a connection between the ape and the West African Negro. Observations of travelers hardened the philosophical validity of this postulate of scaled creation, and even some anti-slavery writers, such as Morgan Godwyn, assumed the propinquity of Negro and ape.

Samuel Sewall actually prefigured Edward Long's line of attack in his tract, *The Selling of Joseph*. He noted "such a disparity in their Conditions, Colour & Hair, that they can never embody with us and grow into orderly Familes, to the Peopling of the Land; but still remain in our Body Politick as a kind of extravasat Blood."[42] Later observers sought to explain —and to prove—Negro inferiority on scientific and anthropological grounds. Toward the end of the century there were frequent comments on the lips, noses, general features, and the "rank offensive smell" of Negroes.[43] Unlike the literature of the nineteenth century, when Josiah Nott and others were prominent disseminators of pseudo-scientific theories of race, there were only infrequent observations on differences in the shape and size of skulls.[44]

Physiological references usually provided one more intellectual prop under the structure of slavery. On one occasion it had the reverse effect. Dr. John Mitchell of Virginia, seeking to bring clarity to the question of Negro pigmentation, found it only quantitatively different from white skin; it was merely thicker and more opaque, and hence allowed less light to be transmitted.[45] He discarded the commonly held theory of Marcello Malpighi (that black skin was due to black fluid), and established a single scale for all people and a physical basis for their unity. Thomas Jefferson was less certain. He, too, speculated on the question of pigmentation. He wondered "whether

[42] Samuel Sewall, *The Selling of Joseph* (Boston, 1700), 2.

[43] Smyth, *A Tour of the United States of America*, 39. Long noted "their bestial or fetid smell" (Long, *The History of Jamaica*, 353), and so did others: e.g., Richard Ligon, *A True & Exact History of the Island of Barbadoes* (London, 1657), 28; *South Carolina Gazette*, July 17, 1736.

[44] E.g., Thomas Pownell, *The Administration of the British Colonies* (London, 1774), I, 223.

[45] John Mitchell, "An Essay upon the Causes of the Different Colors of People in Different Climates; by John Mitchell, M.D. Communicated to the Royal Society by Mr. Peter Collinson, F.R.S.," *Philosophical Transactions* of the Royal Society of London, XLIII (1744–45). See also Pownell, *The Administration of the British Colonies*, I, 14.

the black of the negro resides in the reticular membrane between the skin and the scarf-skin, or in the scarf-skin itself; whether it proceeds from the color of the blood, the color of the bile, or from that of some other secretion." In any event, the very color as well as ancillary biological data, was friendly to his feeling that there were differences between the two peoples. The Negroes were distinguished by having "less hair on the face and body" as well as by their color. Furthermore, "they secrete less by the kidneys; and more by the glands of the skin, which gives them a very strong and disagreeable odor. . . . They are more ardent after their female."[46] Jefferson, however, was an instinctive equalitarian as well as a faithful adherent to Linnaean classification, thereby endorsing the axiomatic unity of the human species. Nevertheless, he leaned—though uncertainly and ambiguously—toward making an exception to the natural history of Linnaeus and toward acceptance of the Great Chain of Being. He speculated "that different species of the same genus, or varieties of the same species may possess different qualifications."[47]

Edward Long was more confident, arguing with the certitude born of extremism that there was a connection between Negro and ape, which he advanced in terms of the Great Chain of Being. "If such has been the intention of the Almighty, we are then perhaps to regard the orang-outang as,

> —the lag of human kind,
> Nearest to brutes, by God design'd.[48]

Hence he stressed the orang-outang's proximity to man, and, conversely, the debased similarity of the Hottentot. To illustrate their kinship, he cited Tyson, Buffon, and every fragment

[46] Jefferson, *Notes on Virginia*, 662.

[47] "Will not a lover of natural history, then," he inquired, "one who views the gradations in all races with the eye of philosophy, excuse an effort to keep those in the department of man as distinct as nature has formed them." *Notes on Virginia*, 665.

[48] Long continued as follows: "The Negro race (consisting of varieties) will then appear rising progressively in the scale of intellect, the further they mount above the orang-outang, and the measure of it more compleat, and analogous to the harmony and order that are visible in every other line of the world's stupendous fabric. Nor is this conclusion degrading to human nature, while it tends to exalt our idea of the infinite perfections of the Deity." *The History of Jamaica*, II, 371.

of apocrypha on the subject. Orang-outangs ate at dinner tables; they had the same mechanical and intellectual abilities as Negroes; and they were equally lascivious, having "the most intimate connexion and consanguinity" with Negroes, including "amorous intercourse."[49] Moreover, Negroes had "a covering of wool, like the bestial fleece, instead of hair"; and, instead of white lice, they were infested with black lice, like animals. Long did not merely place the Negro below white men, he practically expelled him from the human race.

The logic of the inequalitarian argument led the anonymous author of *Personal Slavery* to similar conclusions. He denied rationality to Negroes and, therefore, emphasized their inability to "have the most distant notions of a supreme being."[50] Like Long, he placed Negroes on the lowest rung of the human scale, directly above the apes. Jefferson, too, accepted the Negro-ape analogue. Negro men, he claimed, preferred white women to black as uniformly as the orang-outangs desired Negro women to females of their own species.[51]

In this manner, the colonial pro-slavery argument was greatly elaborated. The Negro was a beast or beast-like not merely in the rhetorical sense of the term, but in the biological sense. Biology came to the assistance of those who argued against miscegenation.[52] Fear of racial intermixture was widespread in

[49] *Personal Slavery Established by the Suffrages of Custom and Right Reason* (Philadelphia, 1773), 65.

[50] Like Long, this anonymous author also engaged in the game of classifying species. Indeed, he went to the extreme of subdividing "the Africans in five classes, arranging them in the order as they approach nearest to reason, as 1st Negroes, 2nd Orang-outangs, 3d Apes, 4th Baboons, and 5th Monkeys. . . ." *Personal Slavery*, 18. See also "R," *Columbian Magazine*, II (May, 1788), 266.

[51] Jefferson, *Notes on Virginia*, 662.

[52] Racial intermixture was a constant consideration and a constant fear. The phrasing of seventeenth-century legislative measures indicates that sexual union between Negroes and white colonists met with widespread public disapproval. A Virginia law of 1662 provided for a punishment of double the usual fine for "any christian [who] shall committ fornication with a negro man or woman." (Hening, *Statutes*, II, 170.) Maryland law stigmatized as disgraceful those "shameful matches" between "freeborne English women forgetfull of their free Condicion . . . with Negro slaves." (*Maryland Archives*, I, 533–34.) See also Hening, *Statutes*, III, 86–87; *Maryland Archives*, XIII, 307; XXII, 552. In May, 1788, the *Colum-*

the colonial period, and Jefferson's views on the subject were not anomalous. His faith in human equality had caused him to advocate liberty for the black man regardless of the slave's place on the scale of creation. But there was a problem: to give the Negro freedom would remove obstacles to miscegenation and might impair the beauty of white stock. "Among the Romans," Jefferson observed, "emancipation required but one effort. The slave, when made free, might mix with, without staining the blood of his master. But with us a second is necessary, unknown to history. When freed, he is to be removed beyond the reach of mixture."[53] Unable to undertake colonization, or unwilling, provincial assemblies did the next best thing: they passed measures making it clear that "abominable mixture" was unlawful.[54]

The Negro then was permanently bound by biological and anthropological chains. In order to guarantee the viability of his debasement, pro-slavery writers pulled out all stops. Slavery was justified by climatic and economic necessity; by reliance upon history, the Bible, and Providential design. It was argued, in the colonial period, that English America could not be developed without the peculiar institution. White men were physiologically unable to labor in hot climates; Negroes alone had this power. The implications were obvious: Negroes possessed distinct physical traits. Benjamin Franklin speculated that there was "in Negroes a quicker evaporation of the perspirable matter from their skin and lungs, which, by cooling them more, enables them to bear the sun's heat better than whites do."[55] Most commentators, however, did not seek physiological explanations; they simply observed that Negroes became "awk-

---

bian Magazine supposed many African slaves were the offspring of sexual intercourse between Negroes and Hottentots; and that uniquely argued in favor of Negro-white union. The hybrid offspring would be "to the honour of the human species and to the glory of the Divine Being." More often, however, eighteenth-century writers, North and South, expressed fear of "consanguinity." *New Jersey Journal*, December 27, 1780.

[53] Jefferson, *Notes on Virginia*, 665.

[54] Hening, *Statutes*, III, 86–87; *Maryland Archives*, XXVI, 260; XXX, 290.

[55] Benjamin Franklin to John Lining, June 17, 1758, in *The Writings of Benjamin Franklin*, ed. Albert H. Smyth (New York, 1905), III, 449.

ward, ungainly wretches" in cold climates and delighted in "violent heat."[56]

The climatic theory strengthened the view that Negroes were biologically different, and gave it a utilitarian meaning. Frequently the economic-necessity rationalization was joined to this theory. In Georgia, for example, the principal defense of the practice of slave importation combined both arguments: Negro, rather than white labor, was as essential "to cultivation as axes, hoes, or any other utensil of agriculture."[57]

The origins of another nineteenth-century argument developed in the colonial period: the practice of comparing the two labor systems, free and slave. The condition of the free laborer was contrasted to that of the slave and the latter, contended Jonathan Boucher, "were not upon the whole worse off nor less happy than the labouring poor in Great Britain."[58]

[56] *London Magazine*, XV (March, 1746), 127; Hugh Jones, *Present State of Virginia* (New York, 1724), 38. For other instances of literature finding Negro labor essential to cultivation, see Hewatt, *An Historical Account* . . . , II, 120; Ligon, *A True and Exact History* . . . , 28; Edward Long, *Candid Reflections Upon the Judgment* . . . (London, 1772), 13–14; George Milligan-Johnston, *A Short Description of the Province of South Carolina* (Columbia, South Carolina, 1951), 26; Romans, *A Concise History* . . . , 106. Among those who rejected this argument were Anthony Benezet and John Wesley; Benezet, *Short Account* . . . , 15; *The Potent Enemies of America Laid Open* . . . (Philadelphia, 1774), 39–41; John Wesley, *Thoughts on Slavery*, in *A Collection of Religious Tracts*, ed. Anthony Benezet (Philadelphia, 1774), 43. Benjamin Rush denied "that none but the natives of warm climates could undergo the excessive heat and labors of the West India islands." Rush, *An Address* . . . , 8. Arthur Lee, often ambivalent on the subject of Negro slavery, argued firmly that "the free born Briton, in many labours, sustains fatigues," including "the fervid heat of summer." Lee, *An Essay in Vindication* . . . , 42. Edward Tyson, seeking a "scientific" explanation of the Negro's ability to labor in climates unsuited for white labor, concluded that the climatic factor might alter glands which would give a different "humour" (i.e. color) to the skin. Ashley Montagu, *Edward Tyson, M.D., F.R.S., 1650–1728* (Philadelphia, 1943), 213.

[57] Thomas Stephens, "A Brief Account of the Causes that have Retarded the Progress of the Colony of Georgia in America," *Georgia Historical Society Collections*, II, 93. [Benjamin Martyns], "An impartial Inquiry into the State and Utility of the Province of Georgia," *ibid.*, I, 170; P. Tailfir, H. Anderson, D. Douglas, *A True and Historical Narrative of the Colony of Georgia* (Charleston, 1841), 50.

[58] Jonathan Boucher, *Reminiscences of an American Loyalist, 1738–1789* (Boston, 1925), 97. For a denial of the economic-necessity argument,

The Old Testament proved to be an early source of inspiration for anti-Negro writers, an inevitable source considering Puritan reliance upon scripture. New Englanders naturally turned to the Bible when defending slavery. John Saffin, in his refutation of Sewall's tract, justified bondage on the broad ground of Mosaic law. He rested the pro-slavery position on two pillars of scripture, Leviticus 22:44–46 (the divine dispensation to Israel to possess slaves), and 1 Corinthians 13:13–26 (where St. Paul sets forth his philosophy of grades and orders). "By all which it doth evidently appear, both by Scripture and Reason, the practice of the people of God in all Ages . . . , there were Bond men, Women and Children commonly kept by holy and good men, and improved in Service, and therefore by the Command of God, Leviticus 25:44, and by their venerable example we may keep Bondmen."[59] Another writer, after affirming that slavery was "not only known or permitted; but commanded in God's holy word," cited Noah, in Genesis 9:25, 27 in his defense.[60] Under the pseudonym, "Philemon," an

---

see Ralph Sandiford, *A Brief Examination of the Practice of the Times* (Philadelphia, 1729), 64. In an anonymously written essay of 1770, possibly composed by Benjamin Franklin, the author claimed that mine labor was slavery, regardless of the name it assumed: "All the Wretches that dig Coal . . . in those dark Caverns under Ground, unblessed by Sunshine, are absolute Slaves by your Law, and their Children after them, from the Time they first carry a Basket to the End of their Days. They are bought and sold with the colliery, and have no more Liberty to leave their Master's Plantation." Verner Crane, "Benjamin Franklin on Slavery and American Liberties," *Pennsylvania Magazine of History and Biography*, 62 (January, 1938), 9.

[59] He also employed the common argument drawn from Old Testament prophecy, the curse of Canaan (or his father, Ham), by which he distinguished between Negro slavery and the selling of Joseph, one of God's chosen people. Moore, *Notes on the History of Slavery*, 255. "We grant it for a certain and undeniable verity," he continued, "That all Mankind are the Sons and Daughters of Adam, and the Creatures of God: But doth it follow that we are bound to love and respect all men alike?"

[60] He also relied upon Exodus and Leviticus. "Does not *Exodus*, chap. 21, v. 7 shew, that a man might sell his child as a servant . . . ? For the perpetuity of slavery read *Leviticus*, chap. 25, v. 39 to 47." Romans, *A Concise History* . . . , 109. One disputant, in a forensic debate, flatly stated, "The Governor of the universe has, in a certain instance [of the Israelites] expressly tolerated slavery. Nothing was ever by him tolerated but what was agreeable to the law of nature. Therefore—Slavery is lawful." Parsons and Pearson, *A Forensic Dispute* . . . , 30. Richard Nisbet, author of a

unknown tractarian rested his advocacy of the peculiar institution upon Old Testament prophecy relating to the curse of Canaan.[61]

"Philander" and "Philmore," equally unknown, also relied upon the Bible—in order to refute pro-slavery pamphleteers.[62] This reliance suggests that scripture was, before the nineteenth century, a universal source exploited by both sides. Samuel Sewall drew upon it to support his assertion that divine revelation showed equality to be the order of the universe. James Swan, in his *Dissuasion* of seventy years later, judged that "the custom of making Slaves of our fellow men, is expressly against the revealed laws of God ... *He that stealeth and selleth a man, shall be put to death.*"[63]

"God saw fit, for wise reasons," Samuel Hopkins admitted, "to allow the people of Israel thus to make and possess slaves; but is this any license to us to enslave any of our fellowmen?" The reply, emphatically negative, was representative of those who endorsed the argument, "God gave many directions to the

---

pro-slavery tract, asserted that "the scriptures, instead of forbidding it [slavery], declare it lawful." Richard Nisbet, *Slavery not Forbidden by Scripture, or a Defense of the West India Planter* (Philadelphia, 1773), 3.

[61] *Connecticut Journal,* October 22–November 12, 1773; January 1–February 4, 1774.

[62] *Connecticut Journal,* February 11, March 4, 1774. "Philmore" affirmed: "He that made us, made them, and all of the same Clay: We are all the Workmanship of His Hands. . . . He hath given this Earth, in common, to the Children of Men—God gave to Man Dominion over *the Fish of the Sea, and over the Fowl of the air, and over the Cattle, and over the Earth and over every creeping thing that Creepeth upon the Earth.* Gen. i, 26; but not to any one man over another." "J. Philmore," "Extracts . . . ," in Benezet, *Short Account . . . ,* 29. See also Benezet, *A Caution and Warning to Great-Britain and Her Colonies* (Philadelphia, 1767), 29.

[63] James Swan, *A Dissuasion to Great Britain . . . from the Slave Trade* (Boston, 1772), 18. Thomas Paine considered it "shocking" to allege that scripture favored "this wicked practice of slavery." Paine, "African Slavery in America" (1774), *Pennsylvania Journal and the Weekly Advertiser,* March 8, 1775, quoted in Foner, *The Complete Writings of Thomas Paine,* I, 17. For another denial of scriptural applicability, see Godwyn, *The Negro's and Indians Advocate,* 14. See also [George Keith], *An Exhortation and Caution to Friends Concerning Buying and Keeping of Slaves* (New York, 1693).

Jews, which had no respect to mankind in general."[64] Slavery, stated its opponents, might be ordained by divine command only; there was no such justification for it in the colonies.[65] Both sides, however, had recourse to history. "A Whig" of 1780 noted "the practice of holding slaves" was not more offensive than it had been "among the Jews"; and, after favorably commenting on various slave societies, concluded that "all of them have grown and flourished with the pretended accursed thing among them beyond the example of other times."[66]

Articulate clerical opinion often stressed Negro-white equality, at least when it came to their respective spiritual natures. Colonial Congregationalists occasionally did not, it is true. John Saffin, for example, invoked the Puritan theory of election to excuse slavery: God "hath ordained different degrees and orders of men, some to be High and Honourable, some to be Low and Despicable"; some to be masters, "some to be born Slaves, and so to remain during their lives, as hath been proved. Otherwise, there would be a mere parity among men, contrary to that of the Apostle."[67] But other New Englanders, such as Cotton Mather, refused to accept the doctrine of racial categorization and affirmed the basic unity of all men before God.[68]

Among the Friends and kindred sects, Negro-white equality was almost universally emphasized, and Quaker tractarians

[64] Hopkins, *A Dialogue* . . . , 21. John Hepburn agreed; he asserted that "a prophecy of what men will do, is neither a *Command* nor *Permission* to do it." Hepburn, *The American Defense* . . . , 30.

[65] "What the Jews did," declared "A Friend of Justice," "was done by proper authority. They had a divine command for destroying certain nations of people, and for holding in slavery the children of certain strangers, and this command was their justification. But were we, without any authority, to act as they did, what should we have to justify us?" *New Jersey Gazette*, November 8, 1780. See also Anthony Benezet, *The Case of our Fellow-Creatures, the Oppressed Africans* (Philadelphia, 1784), 8.

[66] *New Jersey Gazette*, October 4, 1780.

[67] John Saffin, "A Brief and Candid Answer to a late Printed Sheet, entitled The Selling of Joseph . . . ," in Moore, *Notes on the History of Slavery* . . . , 251–52. Jonathan Boucher also used the predestination argument to the same end. "And when it is considered that, according to the subordination of mankind (which, for the good of all, our Maker has established among mankind), some must toil and drudge for others. . . ." Jonathan Boucher, *A View of the Causes and Consequences of the American Revolution* (London, 1797), 186.

[68] Mather, *The Negro Christianized*, 2–3.

usually buttressed their position by resort to the Golden Rule and its scriptural injunction, "Do ye unto others as ye would wish others to do unto you."[69] The first concerted movement for the abolition of slavery had its origins among the inner-light adherents; and the first protests, those of the Mennonites and the German Quakers, had been composed by writers who were merely pressing the logical implications of their religious creed; namely, its deep substratum of equalitarianism.[70] Beginning in 1688, at the Yearly Meeting at Germantown, Pennsylvania, they groped their way slowly, with growing conviction, toward John Hepburn's simple conclusion of 1715 that the "*making slaves* of them who bear the Image of God" was irreligious, that it could not be reconciled with the Golden Rule.[71] The Keithian schismatics in particular led their less-resolute Quaker brethren to the same conclusion. They recalled that Christ died for all men, and that "Negroes, Blacks and Tawnies are a real part of mankind."[72] Anthony Benezet lamented that "our Duty of Love to our Fellow-Creatures, is so totally disregarded"; so did Benjamin Lay, Ralph Sandiford, John Woolman, and Elihu Coleman, a Nantucket carpenter. They spoke for the entire fraternity of men who devoted their

[69] E.g., David Cooper, *Mite Cast into the Treasury: or, Observations on Slavekeeping* (Philadelphia, 1772), iii; Hepburn, *The American Defense* . . . , 2; Drake, *Quakers and Slavery in America*, 37; [George Keith], *An Exhortation* . . . , 3; Society of Friends, *An Epistle of Caution and Advice Concerning the Buying and Keeping of Slaves* (Philadelphia, 1754), 2. For non-Quaker tractarians who invoked the Golden Rule, see James Swan, *A Dissuasion* . . . , 34; Sewall, *The Selling of Joseph*, 3; Appleton, *Considerations on Slavery*, 12; Elhanan Winchester, *The Reigning Abominations, especially the Slave Trade* . . . *Delivered in Fairfax County, Virginia, December 30, 1774* (London, 1788), 29.

[70] Drake, *Quakers and Slavery in America*, 11. See also Thomas Woody, *Quaker Education in the Colony and State of New Jersey* (Philadelphia, 1931), 270.

[71] Hepburn, *The American Defense* . . . , i. See also Loggins, *The Negro Author*, 5–6; Society of Friends, *An Epistle of Caution* . . . , 2; Woody, *Quaker Education* . . . , 270–71. One student has found that the Quaker attempt "to preach to slaves without bestowing upon them the liberty which inheres in Christianity, betrayed a confusion of ethics common to most seventeenth-century Christians; and their own halfway application of Christian principles to the slavery problem caused Friends to act in contradictory ways for a long time to come." Drake, *Quakers and Slavery in America*, 8.

[72] [George Keith], *An Exhortation* . . . , 1.

careers to the cause of manumission when they repeatedly stressed the homely declaration that slavery involved traffic in "the Souls of men" and that it "contradicts Christ's command."[73]

The Golden Rule was at the vital center of the eighteenth-century anti-slavery movement. It affirmed that the Negro, though having black pigmentation and features, resembled a man, not an ape. He was black, it is true, and his features were different from those of white settlers; but he resembled a man, not an ape or a horse. Thus colonial clergymen, particularly Quakers and Anglicans, objecting to claims that the Negro had no soul to save, emphasized man's common humanity. In so doing they inevitably foreshadowed the secular equalitarians of the 1770's, the advocates of the natural rights of men. Declarations of natural rights, of course, antedated the Revolutionary era, indeed, anti-slavery writers had recourse to fundamental law almost from the outset. The early literature, however, was thoroughly religious in tone, generally joining divine and natural law. Witness, for instance, Samuel Sewall's statement: "all men, as they are the sons of Adam, are Coheirs, and have equal rights unto Liberty."[74] This dual assumption of the equality of the individual before God and before men was not separately considered until the approaching Revolution. Nor was it decisively and unequivocally splintered at any time in the eighteenth century: the basic meaning of the unity and equality of men remained essentially religious, and men traditionally linked the law of nature and the law of nature's God. The connection was inevitable for anti-slavery writers, since the colonial conception of natural rights had to share honors with the Christian doctrine of the spiritual unity of mankind in their common descent from Adam. No wonder, therefore, that Levi Lincoln asked, as late as 1781, "Is it not a law of nature that all men are equal and free? Is not the law of nature

---

[73] Anthony Benezet, *Some Historical Accounts of Guinea* . . . (Philadelphia, 1771), 78. See also: Woolman, *Considerations* . . . , 261; Benjamin Lay, *All Slave-Keepers that Keep the Innocent in Bondage* (Philadelphia, 1737), 43; Sandiford, *A Brief Examination* . . . , 15; Elihu Coleman, *A Testimony Against that Antichristian Practice of Making Slaves of Men* ([Boston], 1773), passim.

[74] Sewall, *The Selling of Joseph*, 2.

the law of God? Is not the law of God, then, against slavery?"[75]

Although the religious inflection was never entirely eliminated from equalitarianism, the colonial Enlightenment and the successive Revolutionary crises combined to shift the stress from the divine to the secular, with the accent eventually placed upon human equality. Men were equal precisely because they were men, because "nature has given them an equal right to liberty as to life."[76] They were "born in the same manner . . . , their bodies clothed in the same kind of flesh"; they were "under the same gospel dispensation, have one common Saviour, inhabit the same common globe of earth, die in the same manner; and though the white man may have his body wrapped in fine linen, and his attire may be a little decorated, there are all distinctions of man's making ends. We all sleep on the same level in the dust."[77] Thus the proliferating idea of natural rights not only stirred the Revolutionary cauldron, it caused a shift of emphasis among anti-slavery writers—from conversion to manumission, from heavenly equality to terres-

[75] Extracts from Levi Lincoln's brief, at a Massachusetts trial (of a white man who was found guilty of assaulting and imprisoning a Negro) in 1783, quoted in George Livermore, *An Historical Research Respecting the Opinions of the Founders of the Republic on Negroes as Slaves, as Citizens, and as Soldiers* (Boston, 1862), 30. Benjamin Coleman affirmed that Negroes were "as free by nature as we, or any people [and] have a natural right to liberty and freedom as much as we." He never lost sight of spiritual ends, warning that slavery was "a God-provoking and wrath procuring sin." *Essex Journal*, July 20, 1774, quoted in Joshua Coffin, *A Sketch of the History of Newbury, Newburyport, and West Newbury* (Boston, 1845), 339. Rush, too, made the connection: the slave trade was "a direct violation of the Lawes of Nature and religion." Rush, *An Address . . .* , 9. Others also saw the inextricable congruity of both factors. See Daniel Byrnes, *A Short Address to the English Colonies in North America* (Wilmington, 1775), 1; Levi Hart, *Liberty Described and Recommended* (Hartford, 1775), 16. Jacob Green stated: "I cannot but think that our practicing and patronizing negro slavery is the most crying sin. . . . The slaves have never forfeited their right to freedom: 'tis as the Congress say, a natural right, and an unalienable one." Jacob Green, *A [Fast] Sermon Delivered at Hanover . . .* (Chatham, 1779), 14.

[76] Hewatt, *An Historical Account . . .* , II, 121. See also Thomas Day, *Fragment of an Original Letter on the Slavery of the Negroes: Written in the Year 1776* (Philadelphia, 1784), passim; Hart, *Liberty Described . . .* , 16; and Cooper, *Mite Cast into the Treasury . . .* , 12, for statements of natural rights as applicable to Negroes.

[77] Livermore, *An Historical Research . . .* , 29.

trial inequality. It insisted that "liberty is the right of every human creature, as soon as he breathes the vital air. And no human law can deprive him of that right, which he derives from the law of nature."[78]

Hence the claim of colonial thinkers that all men were created equal was founded upon an essentially secular assumption of their common humanity. After all, it was only a short step from the Protestant tradition of the equality of men before God to the secular assertion of the equality of men before their fellow men. The Enlightenment had paved the way, since it had identified natural law with eternal law, integrated man within the general province of nature, and pushed God slowly outside the daily affairs of men. Equality was readily transferable from God's sphere to nature's. Men were by nature equal and, once admit that Negroes were men, it was axiomatic that they deserved *some* degree of acceptance. That many colonists accepted this logic is apparent from the outburst of anti-slavery literature in the pre-Revolutionary decade.

James Otis led the way, including Negro slaves in his assertion that "the colonists are by the law of nature free born."[79] David Cooper was representative: in 1772 he asserted, "with equal justification may negroes say, By the *immutable laws of nature*, we are equally entitled to life, liberty, and property with our lordly masters."[80] As the conception of man in a state of nature became increasingly important politically, therefore, it became such in anti-slavery thought, too. It was paralleled by another line of attack which vaulted into prominence. The inquiry of an anonymous writer suggests the approach: "I would ask those mighty Sticklers for *Slavery*, Whether the *Africans* were not born as free as *British* subjects? If so, are they not justly entitled to, and may they not expect, both by the Laws of God and man, to inherit and possess every Privilege which we enjoy?"[81] Slavery, the argument ran, was inconsistent

[78] Charles Crawford, *Observations Upon Negro Slavery* (Philadelphia, 1784), 21.

[79] James Otis, *The Rights of the British Colonies Asserted and Proved* (Boston, 1764), 29.

[80] David Cooper, *A Serious Address to the Rulers of America* (Trenton, 1773), 4.

[81] *The Appendix: or, Some Observations on the Expediency of the Petition of the Africans* (Boston, 1773), 4.

with the principles guiding Americans in their struggle against England: natural rights and the equality of all men. Understandable, therefore, were the sentiments of this unknown critic of the colonists: "Blush ye pretended votaries for freedom! ye trifling patriots! who make a vain parade of being the advocates for the liberties of mankind, who are making a mockery of your profession, by trampling on the sacred natural rights and privileges of the Africans, while you are fasting, praying, non-importing, non-exporting, remonstrating, resolving, and pleading for a restoration of your charter rights."[82]

Consonant with this appeal, natural rights theory was implemented in the legislative area. In June 1774, the Rhode Island legislators passed an emancipation measure, since it was in harmony with " 'the preservation of their own rights and liberties.' "[83] Three years later the Massachusetts assembly declared that slavery was a "disgrace to all good governments, more especially to such who are struggling . . . in favor of the natural and unalienable rights of human nature."[84]

[82] *The Watchman's Alarm to Lord N--h, or the British Parliamentary Boston Port Bill* . . . (Salem, 1774). See also Benjamin Rush to Nathaniel Greene, September 12, 1782, in *Letters of Benjamin Rush*, ed. L. H. Butterfield (Princeton, 1951), I, 286; Benezet, *Some Considerations on Several Important Subjects* (Philadelphia, 1778), 30; William Gordon to the printers of the *Independent Chronicle*, May 15, 1777; in Moore, *Notes on the History of Slavery*, 179–83; Green, *A Fast Sermon* . . . , 12, 13; Cooper, *A Serious Address* . . . , 12; Ambrose Serle, *The American Journal of Ambrose Serle, 1776–1778* (San Marino, The Huntington Library, 1940), 249; and *Extract from an Address in Virginia Gazette, of Mar. 19, 1767* (Philadelphia, 1780), 1. John Cooper, in still another analogous statement, affirmed: "Whilst we are spilling our blood and exhausting our treasure in defence of our own liberty, it would not perhaps be amiss to turn our eyes toward those of our fellow-men who are now groaning in bondage under us. We say, 'all men are equally entitled to liberty, the pursuit of happiness'; but are we willing to grant his liberty to all men? . . . If after we have made such a declaration to the world, we continue to hold our fellow-creatures in slavery, our words must rise up in judgment against us. And by the breath of our own mouths we must stand condemned." *New Jersey Gazette*, September 20, 1780.

[83] William D. Johnston, "Slavery in Rhode Island, 1755–1776," *Rhode Island Historical Society Publications*, n.s., II, 130.

[84] *Massachusetts Archives*, XCLII, 58, quoted in Moore, *Notes on the History of Slavery* . . . , 184. For other instances of the practical implementation of equalitarian sentiment in the Revolutionary era, see Mitchell and Flanders, *Statutes, Pennsylvania*, X, 67–73; Hening, *Statutes, Virginia*, XI, 39–40, 308–9; Bartlett, *Records, Colony of Rhode Island*, X, 7–8.

Thus equalitarianism became a popular theme, and sentiment for it derived from the Revolution. The Revolutionary mood resulted in less rigorous slave codes, legal abandonment of slavery in some northern states, an increasing number of personal manumissions, and a vigorous anti-slavery literature. Not only did pamphleteers point out the incompatibility of contending for liberty on one hand and denying it to black men on the other, they continued to stress Negro equality.[85] They were under great pressure to do so, owing to the nature of their political cause, the opposition to Negro soldiers in the army, the marked reluctance of the South to eradicate slavery and to admit the applicability of the appeal of natural rights to the peculiar institution.

Thus it appears that the foundation of pro-slavery and anti-slavery thought was laid in the colonial period. When colonists viewed the Negro as a political animal, they were forced to admit he was like themselves. But the movement for debasement also continued apace, immensely aided by the fact of an economic order which considered slavery essential to its survival. The equalitarian appeal to natural rights, therefore, was answered by those who sought to demonstrate an actual incapacity in nature. These opposing views, in embryonic form in the seventeenth and eighteenth centuries, forecast the future lines of controversy and the great debate which was to come.

[85] Hopkins, *A Dialogue* . . . , iii.

II

TREMAINE McDOWELL

The Negro in the Southern Novel
Prior to 1850

I

Although the English slave trade was well established by the middle of the seventeenth century, the Negro at that time had appeared infrequently on English soil and in English literature. By the end of the eighteenth century, he had been rather sketchily presented in British literature from, in the main, three standpoints: the naturalistic, the humanitarian, and the realistic. Goldsmith drew a typical naturalistic noble savage in his Negro of *The Traveller;* Mrs. Behn in *Oroonoko,* several Romantics (*e.g.:* Cowper, Blake, and Wordsworth), and certain Revolutionary novelists (such as Mackenzie in *Slavery* and Godwin in *St. Leon*) combined in varying proportions naturalism and humanitarianism; the latter element alone animated references to the Negro by Johnson, Southey, and Wilberforce; while Defoe in *Captain Singleton* and *Colonel Jack* and Grainger in *Sugar Cane* were practically unparalleled in their realistic approach. Yet despite this apparently rather considerable discussion of the Negro, it is difficult to find in the main channels of British literature previous to 1824 any black men portrayed in accurate detail or any account of Negro life written with fullness or realism. It was therefore unlikely, if not impossible, that American authors were extensively indebted to English models in dealing with the Negro.

The first Negro slaves were landed in the American colonies in 1619; when the Revolutionary War had demonstrated that all men are born free and equal, their number had increased to half a million. In American literature in the North, there was a

Reprinted from *Journal of English and Germanic Philology,* 25 (1926), 455–73, by permission of the *Journal of English and Germanic Philology* and Mrs. Costello J. Bishop.

continuous series of humanitarian references to the black man from Sewall to Woolman, Crèvecœur, Freneau, and Barlow. Humanitarianism was combined with a modified form of the doctrine of the noble savage by Mrs. Sarah Morton and by Bryant. Dwight is something of the realist in his account of the black man in *Greenfield Hill* in 1794, but in general these early references to the Negro are in the conventional English manner. With the appearance of satire in America, however, the sentimentalized noble Afric began to give way to a recognizable Negro. Examples are a brief incident in Brackenridge's *Modern Chivalry* (1792–1797) and again in Royall Tyler's *The Algerine Captive* (1797). More significant is *Salmagundi* (1807–8), for here the black man is, almost for the first time in America, the object, not the agent, of satire. Further, the theme is repeatedly the Haytian Negro, at a time when Toussaint L'Overture was yet a Romantic hero and symbol in England. The Negro is not always treated satirically in *Salmagundi*, however, for here appears one of the first sketches of a character soon to become most familiar—the loyal old black servant who seems invariably to consider himself "a personage of no small importance in the household."

When, in the 1820's, the American novel came into its own, with it came not only the American Indian, but the American Negro. Cooper, with his sense for the unusual in character, devoted unprecedented attention in *The Spy* (1821) to a Negro, Caesar Thompson, an example, as Cooper points out, of "the old family servant, who, born and reared in the dwelling of his master, identified himself with the welfare of those whom it was his lot to serve." Cooper did justice to Caesar's personality, revealing his loyalty, his humor, his shrewdness in judging character, his superstition, and a touch of racial self-consciousness. W. H. Gardner was therefore justified in stating in a contemporary review that Caesar is "a character which we have never before seen truly depicted."[1] Most significant of all, however, is Caesar's place in the plot, for he is allowed to assist substantially in the action, recognition not previously given a Negro in American fiction nor again granted before the work of Simms. Knowing the Negro and sympathizing with him,[2]

[1] *North American Review*, XV (October, 1822), 265.

[2] Cooper's daughter states that there were two slaves in her grandfather's home for twenty years during James Fenimore's youth and that

Cooper came surprisingly close to admitting the servant to literary equality with his master, for Caesar is, it seems, as carefully studied as any white man in *The Spy*.

To this achievement, contemporary novelists in the North added nothing, for they passed the Negro unnoticed save for brief mention in such inconsiderable things as John Neil's *Randolph* (1823). By 1824, therefore, the early misconceptions of the Negro as an ideal creature in the state of nature had almost entirely disappeared from the work of Northern authors. This had not been accomplished by the sentimentalists or the humanitarians, for they in America as in England had given little attention to a concrete presentation of the Negro, but by the satirists and the novelists, too familiar with the black man to transform him into a noble savage. And yet, even though Cooper made permanent the primary characteristics of the traditional black servant, Negro character and manners were as a whole untouched.

II

Before 1824, the South produced barely a half-dozen pieces of fiction which may be termed novels, and in none of them does the Negro appear. In the 1820's, however, there came something of a literary awakening, eventually producing a significant group of novelists in Virginia and a few scattered fictionists elsewhere in the Southern states. After the War of 1812, it had seemed that slavery would gradually disappear in the United States, but between 1820 and 1830, the introduction of the cotton gin and the power loom made cotton raising so profitable that the Negro became exceedingly significant from an economic standpoint. Many Americans now actively defended slavery where they had once merely excused it, and the Negroes themselves began to make conscious efforts toward freedom. It was during, and in part because of, this quickening of sectional feeling that the South began to write novels. Inevitably, the slave had a place in this new fiction, and it is here that a study of the Negro in the Southern novel becomes possible.

several Negroes were employed in her father's home (*Correspondence of James Fenimore Cooper* [New Haven, 1922], I, 13, 24). Cooper is sympathetic toward the Negro in *Notions of the Americans* (1828), *The Deerslayer* (1841), and *Wyandotte* (1843).

First of the Virginian group, George Tucker, lawyer, econo-
mist, historian, and university professor, was the earliest
Southern novelist of any literary distinction; likewise, he was
the first novelist to present the old system of Southern feudalism. His novel, *The Valley of the Shenandoah* (1824), is of
peculiar significance because of its dual attitude toward the
Negro. In one aspect Tucker is unusual, if not unique, among
ante-bellum novelists: he frankly admits that as a slave the
black man was frequently unfortunate and unhappy. Instead of
confining himself to the agreeable side of Negro life, he occasionally introduces its darker aspects, particularly in his realistic
account of a slave auction. Here he even goes as far as to admit
that "one not accustomed to this spectacle is extremely shocked
. . . . and even to those who have become accustomed to it, it is
disagreeable." It is true that the passages of unpleasant realism
are few and restrained, but they are sufficient to show that, unlike the fiction of the following decade, this novel was composed before the South became fully conscious of the acute controversial nature of the institution of slavery. In other aspects,
The Valley of the Shenandoah is the prototype of the plantation novel of the next twenty-five years, for in it appear two
conventions in the presentation of Negro characters which
control Southern authors for several generations. First, Tucker
to a high degree idealizes his slaves, emphasizing most of all their
undeviating loyalty. For example, his sketches of superannuated
Uncle Bristow, gallant young Peter, and old Granny Mott present those individuals in a most favorable light, and the faithful-
ness of his black men is so great that even the field hands "as
completely identify themselves with the family as if the crops
were their own." Secondly, despite his genuine if controlled
affection for the Negro, Tucker gives him no significant position in the plot of the novel. Slaves perform their customary
household and farm tasks, carry messages, and converse briefly
and respectfully with their masters, but they never directly influence the action. It would be difficult to determine whether
Tucker knew the English or early American naturalistic and
humanitarian treatments of the Negro. It is evident, however,
that such work did not influence him in *The Valley of the
Shenandoah:* his humanitarianism is obviously spontaneous,
arising from his own kindliness of heart, and his idealization of
the Negro is equally personal, due not to his devotion to the

concept of a noble savage but to Southern amiability of temper. In these respects, the book definitely indicates the place which the Negro was to occupy in Southern fiction before the Civil War.

It was the novelists of the next decade who firmly established the conventional Negro types in fiction. Writing after keen difference of opinion had developed over slavery, Kennedy, Nathaniel Beverley Tucker, and Caruthers naturally omitted almost without exception the unpleasant elements of plantation life. Nevertheless, each contributed his share of new details to the steadily developing portrait of the Negro and at the same time reënforced the general outlines drawn by Cooper and George Tucker.

Distinguished lawyer and public servant, John Pendleton Kennedy wrote in his leisure three novels. *Swallow Barn* (1832), a charming but inconsequential "book of episodes" written under the influence of Addison and Irving, contains considerable description of plantation life in Maryland. Particularly full is his account of the slave quarters, with their picturesque cabins, noisy poultry, and hordes of small Negroes. Yet, except for an old black hostler, Kennedy's slaves are not individualized. Abe and Lucy enter as realistic black folk, but as the story of Abe progresses, they are transformed, perhaps through the influence of sentimental romance, into the colorless conventions of polite fiction. By thus perfunctorily handling the incident, Kennedy destroys, possibly deliberately, its full tragic value as a revelation of the grief and misery of black life, and what might have been a moving portrayal of the tragedy of slavery becomes a formal episode. In the same novel, Kennedy amiably wrote: "To me Negroes have always appealed as a people of agreeable peculiarities and not without much of the picturesque," and yet he passes them over almost in silence in *Horse Shoe Robinson* (1835) and *Rob of the Bowl* (1838). It is true that Kennedy went far toward establishing in fiction the traditional details of aristocratic life on the Southern plantation, but he was too conventional and too well bred to go below the surface of Negro character or to present even surface conditions of slave life if they were offensive to a cultivated taste. His greatest significance in connection with the Negro therefore lies in his presentation of the black man as an urbane and cultured Southerner of ante-bellum days would have him appear, rather than as he actually existed.

It was to be expected that Nathaniel Beverley Tucker, as barrister and at length professor of law in William and Mary College, would continue the Virginian tradition in his dignified, even stately, novels. In *George Balcombe* (1836) appears a sentimental little spectacle which may be not unjustly viewed as an epitome of what a thoughtful and humane Southerner considered ideal relations between master and slave. The hero says of an old slave: "As he spoke thus in a tone of reverential affection, I held out my hand to him. He took it, and drawing it strongly downward to accommodate the lowness of his prostration, bowed himself upon it, and pressed it to his lips. I felt a tear upon it, and if an answering tear had not sprung to my eyes, I should not have deserved to be the object of such devotion, as ardent and devoted as it was hopeless." Beverley Tucker as a student of public affairs was more fully conscious of the slavery issue than were most novelists of the day, and his famous novel, *The Partisan Leader* (1836), is therefore well reasoned propaganda. In dealing with the probable conduct of Southern slaves in such a civil war as he imagines in the novel, he is convinced that their devotion would lead them to fight with unswerving loyalty for their masters. This, he explains, will be due to the fact that through the mammy, the black foster brother or sister, and even the mammy's other children, "the great black family . . . . in all its branches, is united by similar ligaments to the great white family." Old Tom is the only black in *The Partisan Leader* who possesses a personality of his own and, through Tucker's desire to illustrate the loyalty of the Negro in the coming war, he is even admitted to a minor position in the plot, a recognition without parallel in the minor fiction of the 1830's. Although George Tucker and Kennedy made little or no attempt to differentiate the speech of blacks from that of whites, Beverley Tucker repeatedly calls attention to the perfect enunciation of his educated Negroes, causes Old Tom to assume supposed Negro dialect to deceive Northern soldiers, and makes it evident that he finds no difference in the speech of the best informed Negroes and that of their masters.

William Alexander Caruthers has nothing important to say of the Negro in *Cavaliers of Virginia* (1832) or in *The Kentuckian in New York* (1834). Four rather well-drawn servants appear in *Knights of the Horseshoe* (1845), although Dr. Caruthers is too ardent a Virginian to place them in the main action of the novel. June's "small, terrapin-looking eye," "large mouth, kept constantly on the stretch," and particularly his "bandied legs set so much in the middle of the foot as to render it a difficult matter to tell which end went foremost," are almost verbatim confirmation of Cooper's portrait of Caesar, to which the reader suspects Caruthers may be indebted. The old Negro brings into the novel his banjo and songs, which last contain most of the ingredients of the later sentimental lyric. For example, June sings thus:

> Farewell, old Berginny,
> I leb you now, may be forebber;

then takes leave of nets and fish, swamps and woods, and his black friends.

> The chimney corner is all dark now
> No banjo dah to make him merry,
> A long farewell to my old missus,
> A long farewell to my old missus,
> Way down in old Berginny.

Sharply contrasted with June, representative of the field hands, is Essex, a member of the Negro aristocracy who served about the house, a class carefully distinguished from the field hands by Southern novelists of that day. Essex, "with his hair queued up behind and powdered all over," possesses to a remarkable degree the Negro's subtle skill in adapting the deference of his manner to the social rank of those he serves. Cato is a Negro gossip and Caesar is a runaway, whose unfaithfulness is duly and adequately explained, leaving the reader no cause to suspect that there may have been justified discontent among Southern slaves. Caruthers, last of the Virginians, was endowed with less genius than Kennedy or the Tuckers, but he is nevertheless more accurate in describing the black man and he lays a foundation for the later phonetic reproduction of his speech.

The single novel richest in detailed information concerning Negro life was written by an author wholly outside the Virginian group and, in fact, Northern born. The author, Mrs. Caroline Howard Gilman, married a New Englander, the Reverend Samuel Gilman, who for thirty years was a pastor in Charleston, South Carolina. Mrs. Gilman is therefore claimed by Southern literary historians as a Southern author. In her novel, *Recollections of a Southern Matron* (1836), the Negro portraits, while not always elaborate, outnumber those of her predecessors and contemporaries: old Jacque and Nanny of Revolutionary memories; Jim, good-humored general factotum; Chloe, lady's maid extraordinary; Kate, most atrocious of cooks; Binah, nurse who dies for her white charge; Dick, the runaway; Dinah, old-time dairy woman; widowed, heartbroken Anna; dumb, mad Bella; and a dozen more figures, old and young. Similarly, Negro characteristics are discussed with unprecedented fullness: loyalty, superstition, rabid religionism, humor, gaiety, a touch of cruelty, and considerable tenderness of heart. Negro customs had never before been as considerably detailed in fiction: a burial, two weddings, dances, Christmas festivities, a horse race, and a welcome for a white bride. It will be observed that tragedy and evil are by no means excluded from the picture. However, elaborate as is this background for the activities of master and mistress, it remains background; in accord with the unspoken but hardly unconscious Southern convention, blacks do not influence the plot. Yet, with the observing eye of the novelist and the curiosity of a Northerner, Mrs. Gilman caught much that passed unnoticed or unmentioned by those born in the South. Sympathetic with the Southern point of view but writing with Northern readers constantly in mind, this clergyman's wife produced the first novel before *Uncle Tom's Cabin* which to any degree approaches that book in fullness of detail concerning Negro life.

In his unregenerate youth, Joseph Holt Ingraham published a mad Gothic romance, *The Quadroone* (1841), which is oddly revelatory of the conventions of the period. A Northerner born, although counted a Southern author by Southern literary critics, Ingraham ventures to present in his romance of New Orleans in 1769 a titled Spanish gentleman (later revealed as the heir to the throne of Spain) as in love with Azelie, a beautiful octoroon, and her brother Renault as beloved by a noble Spanish gentlewoman. After emphasizing Azelie's innocently voluptuous charm due to her mixed blood and referring to the traces of similar ancestry in Renault's countenance, he carries the two love stories through two volumes, undoubtedly to the horror and wrath of his contemporaries. Eventually, however, Ingraham yields to the proprieties of his day and devises as conclusion a resolution and recognition scene so incredible that it becomes excellent, though unintentional, burlesque. Herein the two octoroons are shown to be free from Negro blood and are provided with unimpeachable Spanish pedigrees. During his generation, no novelist save this rash and prolific creator of paper-backed tales appears to have toyed even thus timidly with the forbidden theme of racial intermingling.

A few scattered novels supplement these authors but add little that is new concerning the Negro. Mrs. Anne Royall enumerates the duties of a black body-servant in *The Tennessean* (1827). In *Northwood* (1827), Mrs. Sarah J. Hale, one of the numerous authors who were later to devote entire volumes to the Negro once *Uncle Tom's Cabin* had furnished a precedent and a challenge, presents a Negro freeman serving as overseer. Certain serialized novels mentioning the Negro were apparently never republished in book form; examples are the anonymous *Lionel Granby* in the *Southern Literary Messenger* for 1835 and *Judith Bensaddi* by H. Ruffner, D.D., President of Washington College, Virginia, in the same magazine for 1839. Both authors make the Negro an exceedingly happy and contented person.

That realism in presenting the Negro is proportionate to each author's degree of freedom from polite convention is evident in several volumes of sketches produced during this period. Representative are A. J. Knott: *Novellettes of a Traveller* (1834); A. B. Longstreet: *Georgia Scenes* (1835); John S. Robb: *Streaks of Squatter Life* and *Odd Leaves from the Life of a Louisiana Swamp Doctor* (1843); William T. Tappan: *Major Jones' Chronicles of Pineville* (1843) and *Major Jones' Courtship* (1844); William Elliot: *Carolina Sports by Land and Water* (1848); and J. H. Hooper: *Adventures of Captain Simon Suggs* (1848). These productions, of small literary merit, are not included in the scope of this paper, but they deserve a word of comment as substantiating the conclusions suggested by contemporary novels. Longstreet shows an admirable understanding of Negro psychology in his treatment of black house-servants in *Georgia Scenes,* a book of such homely, jovial realism that its author in his later years regretted its existence and admitted its authorship most unwillingly. More farcical and not always in good taste are the sketches of John S. Robb of St. Louis, a primitive frontier humorist who elevated the Negro to unenviable prominence as the butt of vulgar practical jokers. As a country journalist, William T. Thompson wrote of

Georgia Crackers and Negro slaves with a hilarious honesty which some twenty-eight years later forced him to assume an apologetic tone in his preface to a reprint of the sketches (1872). His raciest scene is a runaway marriage between an absurd white man and a supposed gentlewoman, who proves to be one of the blackest Negresses in Georgia, with eyes like "peeled onions." This creature, throwing her arms about his neck, exclaims, "Shore did is my husband," whereupon the unfortunate man disappears from Pineville. Such works, on the fringe of literature and by their authors' own confession rather outside the pale of good breeding, contrast sharply with the cultured productions of Virginia.

III

William Gilmore Simms, the greatest of early Southern novelists, was distinctly not a member of the Southern aristocracy, nor was he ever completely recognized by its members. His mother was of respectable but undistinguished family; his father, Irish by birth, was an unsuccessful small merchant in Charleston, South Carolina. There in 1806 Simms was born and there he grew to manhood without coming into intimate contact with the great plantations or their proprietors. As a boy, he was fascinated by his grandmother's tales of the Revolution, and in his later years he became interested in the ruder side of Southern society by his father's wandering life on the frontier after bankruptcy in Charleston. As a druggist's apprentice, a law student, and a struggling young author, Simms rarely touched Carolinian culture or conventions, and not until his second marriage did he find himself master of a plantation with its feudalism and its slavery. Even then his wife's social standing could not make Simms acceptable to the exclusive South Carolinians, and in 1858 he wrote: "All that I have done has been poured to waste in Charleston, which has never smiled on any of my labours, which has steadily ignored my claims, which has disparaged me to the last."[3] Here obviously was a man likely to be free, at least in part, from the preconceptions of the old regime that are constantly evident in the novels of the Virginian group, and in his works the reader may justifiably expect a degree of realism in the presentation of the Negro.

Simms' only novel of pre-Revolutionary days which deals

[3] W. P. Trent, *William Gilmore Simms* (Boston, 1892), 239.

with the slave is *The Yemassee* (1835), a romance of Carolina
in the early eighteenth century, in which, as in the Leather-
stocking Tales, the Indian rather than the Negro takes the
stage. And yet Hector, a black body-servant, is thoroughly
individualized; he stands out as a skillful scout and Indian
fighter, resourceful, optimistic, and amusing. At the close of
the novel, Hector rejects offered liberty. This refusal of freedom, employed also by the earlier novelists, is repeatedly used
by Simms to exemplify the loyalty of the Negro.

In his minor melodramas,[4] Simms has no space for the Negro
or other realistic details; to study his treatment of the black
man one must turn therefore to the main body of Simms' work,
a series of novels laid in South Carolina during the Revolution.
According to the chronology of their events they stand thus:
The Partisan (1835); *Mellichampe* (1836); *Katherine Walton*
(1851); *The Kinsmen* (1841), renamed *The Scout; The Forayers* (1855); *Eutaw* (1856); and *The Sword and the Distaff*
(1853), later known as *Woodcraft*.[5] Simms was profoundly
interested in and thoroughly informed concerning the events
in Carolina during the Revolution, and he was more sympathetic with the people of that period than with his contemporaries. He was therefore successful in writing of "the dear,
black, dirty scamps of Negroes, big and little," as he terms
them, "on . . . . the old ante-Revolutionary plantations."

In these seven novels of the Revolution appear a motley
company of black folk. Perhaps the most novel types are the
responsible Negro overseer, as illustrated by Benny Bowlegs,
and the Negro scout, represented by Abram and Little Peter.
The type most often presented, however, is the faithful old
family servitor. Typical is Scipio in *Mellichampe*, notable for
"unvarying devotion" to his young mistress, her lover, and her
family, each of whom he is given an opportunity to aid. He
thus becomes one of the chief characters in the book. But it is
in the conclusion of the novel that he takes the center of the

---

[4] *Guy Rivers* (1834), *Richard Hurdis* (1838), *Border Beagles* (1840),
Beauchampe (1842), and *Charlemont* (1856).

[5] Although Simms took an active part in the slavery conflict, there is
no apparent change in the tone of his novels after the publication of
Uncle Tom's Cabin. It is therefore possible to include in this study all
his Revolutionary novels, even though several titles were published after
1850: the same attitude toward the Negro is maintained through the entire
series.

stage in unusual fashion. As young Mellichampe and Barsfield, an evil specimen of "white trash," come to a draw in their death grapple, Scipio is ordered to kill Barsfield. He naturally hesitates; "I mos' fraid—he dah buckrah—I dah nigger." At last he seizes a pine knot and scatters the villain's brains; "De head," afterward declares the old darkey, "mash flat like pancake." Thus the author's weakness for melodrama gives good Scipio ghastly distinction among his fictional prototypes and contemporaries.

An amusing variant of the customary personification of loyalty is Captain Porgy's cook, Tom. After minor activities in *The Partisan* and *Mellichampe*, he reaches his highest culinary triumph in *The Forayers*. In the post-war days of *The Sword and the Distaff*, he becomes also valet, barber, and keen but humorous general adviser to his master and heavy-handed tyrant to his subordinates. In the end, Tom refuses freedom, saying, "Free nigger no hab any body for fin' him bittle." "If *I* doesn't b'long to you," he tells the Captain, "*you* be'longs to me." "And thus," concludes Simms, "the matter was settled and Tom remained . . . . the cook and the proprietor of his master." This amiable domination of master by slave has now become a familiar situation, but in Simms' day novelists did not present such matters to the world at large.

Similar humorous realism places two white men in an unconventional position which a Tucker or a Caruthers would hardly have recorded in his pages. Coming one night on Porgy's sergeant wrapped in his blankets, old black Sappho seizes him firmly, hugs him to her bosom, and kisses him effusively, shouting: "My belubbed infant! I hab you in my arms again, 'fore I dead! De Lord be praise'!" Porgy, drawn by the uproar, appears; whereupon Sappho abandons her first victim and falls sobbing on the Captain's neck, crying: "Dis dah him! Dis dah my own chile!" Her affectionate demonstration finally subsides sufficiently to permit Porgy to discover that she is indeed his old nurse, and two hours of reminiscences follow.

Most unconventional of all is Mingo, Negro overseer in the novelette, *The Loves of the Driver* (1841). He is at first almost a heroic figure, "gallant, good-looking, and always well-dressed" and "brave as Julius Caesar in his angry mood." It soon develops, however, that Mingo is a servant of Venus, "pliant as Mark Anthony in the mood of indulgence." Slipping away from his duties and his wife, he attempts to win a young Indian matron, but as Caloya remains impervious, Mingo reveals a vast self-complacency and a beastly temper. Finally, when he deludedly believes that success is just before him, his termagant wife breaks in upon the maudlin scene, routs the Indians who are in reality about to murder Mingo, and drives him home in utter disgrace. The incidents of plantation life are made very real, and Negro conduct and mentality are presented with understanding. Inevitably, such realism offended Southern taste, and when the first installment appeared in *The Magnolia*, protest was at once made to the editor. In the next issue Simms replied, defending the work not for its truth, which no one appears to have challenged, but for its essential morality in that he makes evil unsuccessful. Sentiment in the North apparently agreed with that in the South, for a contemporary critic in the *North American Review* attacked "the coarseness which deforms this story" and concluded that not virtue but nausea led Caloya to refuse Mingo.[6]

Such are the more picturesque of the Negro characters in the novels of Simms. Other figures fill out the scene: Mira, affectionate mammy; faithful old Bacchus; Cato and Sam, stupid but well meaning coachmen; Pomp, gay little fiddler; intelligent John Sylvester; Congaree Polly, "mighty smart and scrumptious"; and many others—Bull-Head Dabney, Slick Sam, Tony, Bones, Caesar Fogle, Snub-Nose Martin.

Simms, although a whole-souled defender of slavery, clearly is not entirely orthodox in dealing with the Negro. Early interested in humble life, he had formed his conceptions of the black man before be became master of many slaves. His biographer, W. P. Trent, cautiously suggests that his inclinations and sympathies may have been somewhat plebeian and that he was perhaps never a thorough aristocrat. Only such an author could have found the courage to allow old Scipio to kill a white man as the climactic scene in a novel of Southern life, the cook Tom to browbeat his master or toothless Sappho to caress the luckless Captain, and Mingo to conduct in public his amorous pursuit of an Indian woman. Given a man who fails to appreciate the indecorum of recounting the sexual weaknesses of the black race and who is occasionally overcome by a desire to tell the truth in its entirety, and new aspects of the

[6] LXIII (October, 1848), 373.

Negro will inevitably appear. Simms is therefore to be credited with introducing or establishing in fiction the black man's pomposity, his overbearing nature, his untruthfulness, his insolence, his ungovernable temper, his liking for drink, and his lust. Although his later associations and aspirations were such that in many respects Simms could not but become a conventional idealizer of the Negro, the accidents of birth and early environment, perhaps reënforced by heredity, combined to make the chief Southern novelist the one outstanding realist among all ante-bellum Southern authors who ventured to describe the Negro. This realism may be estimated correctly only if one remembers that Simms defied not only the preconceptions of the Southern aristocracy but the good breeding of Northern critics as well; it was a New York magazine which rebuked him for the "spiritless vulgarity of the scenes in low life" in *The Partisan*.[7]

IV

As has long been recognized, the Southern colonies were settled by men who still retained much of the notion of feudalism, and the great slave plantations of Virginia and Maryland were therefore feudal in many respects, particularly during the first and the second century of American history. As a result, the Southern attitude toward the Negro was from the outset limited by taboos and restraints, many of them natural and necessary, all of them understandable. An aristocratic overlord could not publicly reveal concern in the personal activities of his serfs; well-bred gentlemen could not exhibit interest in the vulgar and often offensive doings of semi-barbarians. As has been indicated, these influences developed conventions in the early novel somewhat resembling those of the heroic drama in England, until the Negro was held to a subordinate position or eliminated altogether from fiction. On the other hand, the old regime developed in the typical master a very real love for the Negro, difficult for a Northerner to appreciate today and never paralleled in the North. It is possible that this affection led Southern authors to pass over in silence aspects of the Negro which were likely to be misunderstood by those not familiar with him. A kindly exponent of this old order was George Tucker, who produced in *The Valley of the Shenandoah* the

---

[7] *The American Monthly Magazine*, III (N.S.) (January, 1837), 86.

only novel dealing with the Negro in what may be called the older manner.

Then in the 1830's came a modification of this attitude. The conventions of feudalism and good breeding continued to be influential, but to them was added the requirement, more or less consciously realized, that slavery must be defended. It has been pointed out that Kennedy, Beverley Tucker, and Caruthers under these compulsions developed a Negro who often spoke excellent English and at times behaved like his master. As far as he was made a distinct racial figure, their Negro was idealized, his sentimental creators discreetly hinting at only a few vices. Such an extreme transformation of unruly material could not long be maintained, of course, and even while it was developing, realism began to intrude. The Southern conventions regarding the color line were so strong, however, that this realism came from Northern-born authors or from those somewhat outside the old Southern aristocracy. That Ingraham and Mrs. Gilman, Longstreet, Robb, Thompson, and, above all, Simms gave a larger proportion of space to the Negro than did the Virginian novelists reveals nothing regarding their relative literary ability, but it does indicate that the former were decidedly less handicapped by sectional inhibitions than were the Virginians. It may be concluded, therefore, that where Southern proprieties ruled, the Negro was a minor figure in fiction; only when the equalitarianism of primitive society or of non-slave holding groups intervened, or social inferiority broke the power of conventions, did the Negro rise to prominence.

By 1850, then, the personal appearance of most Negro types on the coastal plantations had been described; their speech was gradually being mastered, so that Simms was occasionally able to suggest their sonorous and musical expression; their habits and manners had in part been recorded; but Negro psychology was still in the main an unplumbed mystery into which no novelist particularly cared to intrude. If one may judge from the amount of attention devoted to each characteristic of the black man, the composite portrait of the Negro thus developed reveals a figure of perhaps six parts unadulterated loyalty, three parts minor virtues (mainly derived from that same devotion) and one part assorted vices. Although they mentioned such characteristics, the early novelists failed to present adequately his optimism, his native humor, his musical talent, his pietism, his indolence, his deceit, and his irresponsibility. Save in the work of Simms and an occasional veiled reference elsewhere, no one recognized his grumbling, his rebelliousness, and his extreme licentiousness, which some historians suggest almost destroyed the race. His insolence, his meanness and grossness, his essential barbarism were suppressed. No one adequately presented the Negro's amazing power of adaptation, fatalistic perhaps, which enabled him to find some happiness under the most adverse conditions. Inevitably many relations with the white man were never recounted, such as the actualities of field labor and the results of absentee landlordism. The phenomena of interbreeding between whites and blacks were dealt with by no one save Ingraham, and he eventually avoided the issue. Certainly, the portrait was greatly retouched.

When in 1852 *Uncle Tom's Cabin* appeared, it is not surprising that 3,000 copies sold on the day of publication and 300,000 in the first year. Mrs. Stowe was the first American novelist to center her attention on life among the lowly, and that alone, without the significance of the book as an abolition tract, was sufficient to make it sensational. In fact, aside from the unexampled emphasis on the horrors of slavery, *Uncle Tom's Cabin* was unusual chiefly in this very shift of emphasis and proportion, for most of the characteristics of her Negroes had already been suggested, at least in embryo, by Southern authors. That is, her Negroes were not novel in traits or manners, but in the detail and fullness with which she presented them and in the partisanly sympathetic point of view from which they are drawn. To be exact, Harriet Beecher Stowe, not Uncle Tom, was unique.[8]

Thus, controlled somewhat by eighteenth century good manners in literature but without restrictive literary models or even suggestive forerunners save Cooper, the Southern novelists idealized the Negro into a permanent convention. Ignoring and possibly ignorant of the British and early American noble Afric developed under the influence of Rousseau, these authors in their own fashion created a new Negro. Left free by the absence of substantial literary realism throughout the United States but moved by national worship of propriety and by

[8] Aspects of the treatment of the Negro in the following decade appear in Jeanette Reid Tandy, "Pro-Slavery Progapanda in American Fiction of the Fifties," *The South Atlantic Quarterly*, XXI (1922), 41–50, 170–78.

powerful regional inhibitions, they shaped his character not according to preconceived notions as to how primitive man should conduct himself, but in such a fashion as to provide an appropriate lay figure in the sympathetic staging of ideal plantation existence. Through the influence of forces beyond the control of any individual author involved, there was thus produced an appealing but falsified type which was to be accepted for fifty years as an actual portrait of the Negro, although it must be said that this sentimentalized Negro was an advance in realism over the slaves conceived by early humanitarians and is also nearer actuality than is the clogging, banjo-thumping "nigger" of twentieth century comedy. Not until the black race became partially articulate, some three hundred years after it reached America, did the pleasant old darkey of fiction begin to disappear and the real Negro to emerge in the serious work of recent novelists, white and black. In short, American literature, in one of its first encounters with native material, reacted in an entirely uncritical and sentimental fashion.

III

THEODORE L. GROSS

The Negro in the Literature
of the Reconstruction

Southern writers of Reconstruction did not create a literature of artistic merit—they produced propaganda. Their various political tracts were successful, for they promoted the lasting impression of the "tragic era" and succeeded in convincing the American reading public that carpetbaggers had misused the Southern people and had falsified the picture of the social and political difficulties that had attended Reconstruction.

Local-color writers did not pretend to have any real objectivity. They wrote lovingly of their areas and of their lives, and in all their work there was an implicit desire for reconciliation between North and South. None of these authors—no matter how desirous he might have been for a native Southern literature—was antagonistic toward the restored Union, and certainly none wished to relive the days of Reconstruction. No longer did Southern authors feel obliged to defend all institutions and customs of the South; the civil war of literature, as well as of history, was considered past, and popular writers did not compose polemical fiction. Indeed, Thomas Nelson Page was so sensitive to the problem that he was careful to remark in the introduction to the collected edition of his work [1908] that he had "never wittingly written a line which he did not hope might tend to bring about a better understanding between the North and South, and finally lead to a more perfect union."

Local colorists describing Reconstruction and the South recognized two alternatives available to them as writers. They could attempt the creation of political fiction and produce purely propagandist novels like Page's *Red Rock* (1898) or Albion W. Tourgée's *A Fool's Errand* (1879). This approach

Reprinted from *Phylon*, 22 (1961), 5–14, by permission of the editor of *Phylon*.

not only proved to be artistically fatal in many cases but eventually meant rejection at the literary market place as well. On the other hand, the authors could avoid as much as possible political considerations and concentrate on the description of their particular localities. This method, adopted by Constance Fenimore Woolson, Joel Chandler Harris, and others, was more practical, for in addition to using the South as a field for fiction, these authors urged reconciliation—they sought to cement bonds of good fellowship between the sections. Tourgée,[1] an ex-carpetbagger who revived the old hostilities that had existed during Reconstruction, affected only the most partisan readers in the 1880's and 1890's, whereas Harris wrote for an ever increasing number of people from the North as well as the South.

The differences between Tourgée and other Reconstruction authors are clearly illustrated by their presentation of the Negro character. The most common figure to appear in the fiction of Reconstruction, the Negro lent substance to time-worn sentimental fables. From the point of view of most Southern authors, he was villain or saint, depending on whether or not he actively asserted his rights as freedman. If he demanded

[1] Albion W. Tourgée was born in Ashtabula, Ohio, on May 2, 1838. He fought for the Union from July, 1861, to January 1, 1864, and moved to Greensboro, North Carolina, in July, 1865. A Radical Republican who established himself as one of the most controversial political figures ever to live in North Carolina, Tourgée was a humanitarian who urged reform measures for the Negro. He was a leader of the Union League in 1866, and made speeches in which he violently denounced Southern Conservatives, claiming that he was "against rebel hope, rebel ambition, and Confederate resurrection." His anti-Southern and pro-Negro attitudes were particularly evident in his denunciation of white supremacy at the Loyalist Convention, held at Philadelphia in September of 1866, in his repeated attempts to undermine the activities of the Ku Klux Klan, and in his voluminous newspaper writings. From 1868 to 1874 he was an exceptionally honest and well-respected judge. In 1879 he returned to the North, realizing that his career as a politician in the South would be unsuccessful after the Reconstruction period; at that time he began, in terms of fiction, a personal investigation of the reasons for the failure of Radical Republicanism in the South. His most readable and best known novels are *A Fool's Errand* (1879) and *Bricks Without Straw* (1880); other works concerned with Reconstruction are *A Royal Gentleman* (1874), *John Eax* (1882), *Hot Plowshares* (1883), and *Pactolus Prime* (1890). As a record of his own political failure, his Reconstruction novels form a political autobiography that was not attempted by any of his contemporaries.

equal opportunity as a newly enfranchised citizen, he was pictured as partner in the Republican conspiracy to undermine the congenial race relations that had existed in ante-bellum times; if, on the other hand, he desired to perpetuate his role as servant, he was drawn as a contented Negro who enjoyed status in Southern society, gained the admiration of his kindly masters, and in turn recognized the natural and proper supremacy of the white man. As Tourgée observed, there were two types of Negroes: "the devoted slave, happy if the scene was laid in days of slavery, the guardian of his white folks if the grimmer postwar South was the period of the story, and the confused freedman who usually was rescued from semi-ludicrous predicaments by the white people to whom he once had belonged."[2]

In the fiction of Thomas Nelson Page and Thomas Dixon this condescending attitude toward the Negro is most obvious, but it appears in the stories and novels of Joel Chandler Harris, Mary Murfree, Maurice Thompson, and innumerable minor writers. Harris seemed to be able to share the fears and laughter and anger of the Negro; and he contributed the most popular Negro characters to American fiction—Uncle Remus, Balaam, Ananias, and Mingo. But when he wrote his one Reconstruction novel, *Gabriel Tolliver*, in 1902, Harris could not completely sympathize with the Negro who had insisted on immediate reconstruction. The average Negroes—the illiterate colored men who blindly supported the Union League—he depicted as misguided children controlled by Republicans; for them Harris had only a feeling of compassion. "The niggers ain't no more to blame for all this trouble than a parcel of two-year-old children," a Southerner comments. "You mark my words: the niggers will suffer, and these white rascals will go scot free." But for the informed colored leader who supported the Union League Harris felt only hatred, certain that he was using his fellow Negroes for his own aggrandizement.

He [the Reverend Jeremiah, leader of the Negroes] was not a vicious Negro. In common with the great majority of his race—in common, perhaps, with the men of all races—he was eaten up by a desire to become prominent, to make himself conspicuous. Generations of civilization (as it is called) have gone far to control it to

2 "The South as a Field for Fiction," *The Forum*, VI (December, 1888), 409.

some extent, though now and then we see it crop out in individuals. But there had been no toning down of the Reverend Jeremiah's egotism; on the contrary, it had been fed by the flattery of his congregation until it was gross and rank.

Reconstruction, from Harris' viewpoint, was a tragedy for all participants. The final catastrophe of *Gabriel Tolliver* is a result of the immoral manipulation of Negroes: a colored man, who has been urged against his will to join the Radicals, murders the white Republican leader of the Union League because he believes erroneously that the carpetbagger is having an affair with his mulatto wife. The Republican is a pious, ascetic man, fanatically dedicated to a futile cause; the mulatto wife feels vaguely superior to her pure-bred Negro husband and attempts to seduce the carpetbagger; and the Negro, the most lamentable figure in the book, is an uncertain and confused man. Having forsaken the Southern white master whom he was able to trust, he is taught to desire luxuries that have never been a part of his culture. Harris does not censure the common Negro for his actions during Reconstruction; whatever anger is in his book—and there is comparatively little—is directed toward those Northerners who insisted on "Americanizing" the Southerner.

Harris primarily described the comic and local-color Negro, although, in writing of Reconstruction, he saw the colored man as wretched and bewildered. Thomas Nelson Page also saw the comic aspects of the Negro, but he, more than any other writer, fostered the image of the contented slave. His best stories—"Marse Chan," "Meh Lady," and "Ole 'Stracted"—recall the allegedly congenial race relations which existed "befoah the war," when, from the point of view of the Negro, "dyar warn' no trouble nor nuthin'." Thus Page expressed the legend of a past splendor through the ex-slaves themselves, "those upon whose labor the system was founded and for whose sake it was destroyed."[3]

In all of Page's writings there is an implicit racist note. This bias becomes particularly conspicuous whenever Page defends "The Old South" after the war:

In art, in mechanical development, in literature, in mental and moral science, in all the range of mental action, no notable work has up to this time come from a negro. . . . The leopard cannot change

[3] *The Nation*, XLV (September 22, 1881), 236.

his spots today nor the Ethiopian his skin, any more than they could in the days of Jeremiah, the son of Halkiah. . . . Where the negro has thriven it has invariably been under the influence and by the assistance of the stronger race.[4]

Although Page supported the restored Union, he felt that the only healthy solution to the race problem would stem from the master-slave relationship which existed before the Civil War. The Negro needed guidance, Page knew, but he asserted repeatedly that the guidance should be given by the Southerner —the Negro problem, after all, was a Southern problem. And the late nineteenth-century Northern legislators, as Rayford W. Logan has pointed out, tended to agree with him.[5]

In his two Reconstruction novels, *Red Rock* (1898) and *The Red Riders* (1924), Page was compelled because of his bias to picture the "Wretched" or "Brute Negro." The real villains, as in Harris' *Gabriel Tolliver*, are the carpetbaggers and scalawags, but Page could not be so sympathetic as Harris toward those Negroes who had deserted their masters and now misused their newly won rights. They idly hovered about railway stations, he noted; they were discourteous to the white gentry —to those who had been only benevolent and considerate in ante-bellum times; and they supported the most abhorrent Republican leaders. Page heightened his characterization by contrasting these "unfaithful" Negroes with the few loyal freedmen who refused to leave the plantation. "I was born 'pon dis plantation," remarks one devoted Negro in *The Red Riders*, "and I has lived here de length of man's allotted days, an' I seed three ginerations come and go right here, and I has always considered it my home and I still considers it so."

Page could not understand the freedman—he could not appreciate the difficulties which confronted the Negro because of emancipation. As one Negro critic, Sterling Brown, has pointed out, Page presents a distorted picture of what freedom meant to the Negro:

Slavery was to be shown as not slavery at all, but a happy state best suited for an inferior, childish but lovable race. In this normal condition, the Negro was to be shown thriving. Then came his emanci-

[4] *The Old South, Essays Social and Political* (New York, 1911), pp. 314–15.

[5] *The Negro in American Life and Thought. The Nadir, 1877–1901* (New York, 1954), p. 82.

pation, which the better class of Negroes did not want, and which few could understand or profit by. Freedom meant anarchy. Only by restoring control (euphemism for tenant farming, sharecropping, black codes, enforced labor, segregation and all the other ills of the new slavery) could equilibrium in the South, so important to the nation, be achieved.[6]

Because of Page's narrow point of view, *Red Rock* (1898) and *The Red Riders* (1924) fail as novels. All the characters are stereotypes as their names clearly suggest: Jonadab Leech, the carpetbagger; Joseph Grease, the scalawag; Captain Middleton, a respected Northern commander of Virginia. Characters are not defined as human beings; they are used as propaganda instruments. This statement is made in spite of the fact that Page struggled to avoid creating political tracts. In a letter to Arthur Hobson Quinn, he referred to his difficulties in writing *Red Rock:*

It may interest you to know that when I first undertook to write "Red Rock," after having written a third or more of the novel I discovered that I had drifted into the production of a political tract. I bodily discarded what I had written, and going back beyond the War, in order to secure a background and a point of departure which would enable me to take a more serene path, I rewrote it entirely. I had discovered that the real facts in the Reconstruction period were so terrible that I was unable to describe them fully. The story of this period of National madness will doubtless be written some time and if any man will steep himself as I did, myself, in such records as the "Ku Klux Reports" issued by the Government in 1872, and "A Voice from South Carolina" published in Charleston by Dr. Leland in 1879, "The Prostrate State," and the newspapers of the reconstruction period I think he will agree with me in feeling that we are too near the time to be able to present the facts with true art.[7]

Page did not witness the Reconstruction period as an adult; in 1867 he was only fourteen years of age. It seems clear, therefore, that his "sources," in addition to newspapers, were his memories of adult talk. *The Prostrate State*, the Ku Klux Reports, and John A. Leland's *A Voice from South Carolina*

[6] "The American Race Problem as Reflected in American Literature," *Journal of Negro Education*, VIII (July, 1929), 282.

[7] Thomas Nelson Page to Arthur Hobson Quinn, nd. Quoted in Arthur Hobson Quinn, *American Fiction, An Historical and Critical Survey* (New York, 1936), p. 360.

merely served to reinforce the bias he had acquired in his youth. And yet, despite the sensitive Southern pride which colors *Red Rock* and *The Red Riders*, despite the distortions which result from Page's bias, it should be noted that *Red Rock* was the first account of Reconstruction which was frankly rendered; Page felt no inhibitions in writing his novel.

The Southern authors' characterization of the Negro proved to be immensely popular. In the 1880's such Northern writers as Frank Stockton, Harriet Spofford, and Constance Fenimore Woolson accepted the Southern version of Reconstruction; the admirable freedman of Reconstruction was the devoted Negro who recalled his contented existence before the war and who voluntarily remained faithful to his past masters.[8] The favorite formula of Reconstruction authors—Northern and Southern— was one in which the Negro alleviated his ex-master's poverty. In Harris' "Aunt Fountain's Prisoner" he divided with the whites the rations he received from the Freedman's Bureau; in Jeanie Woodville's "Uncle Pompey's Christmas" he stole for his former owners; in Octave Thanet's *Half-a-Curse* (1887) he supported his previous master by fighting against a rapacious overseer. At times he maintained a pride in the disintegrating manor house, as in Virginia Boyle's *Brockenburne* (1897), Frances Baylor's *Claudia Hyde* (1894), and Paul Dunbar's "The Colonel's Awakening" (1898). Or, if he had been affected by the new radical ideas of the Republicans, he experimented with freedom—as in Harris' "Mom-Bi" (1887) and Mrs. Boyle's "A Kingdom for Micajah" (1900)—but he quickly returned to the contented existence of the slave. More often, however, the noble Negro—like Aunt Martha of William Baker's *Mose Evans* (1874)—refused to attempt freedom under any conditions. If one were to judge the pre-war status of the Negro from the fiction of these authors, one would be convinced that the colored man enjoyed rare security in ante-bellum times.[9]

[8] Northern authors imitated the Southern description of the Negro. See, as typical examples, Frank Stockton's *What Might Have Been Expected* (1874), *The Last Mrs. Null* (1886), and *The Christmas Wreck and Other Stories* (1886); Harriet Spofford's "A Thanksgiving Breakfast" in *Old Washington* (1906); and Constance Fenimore Woolson's "King David" in *Rodman the Keeper* (1886).

[9] The image of the contented slave and the beneficent master was reinforced in almost all the fiction of the period. In Richard Meade Bache's *Under Palmetto* (1880), for example, the slave quarters are de-

These Reconstruction novels and stories were a lament for a tradition authors felt was being undermined; the authors' condemnation of the freedman was largely reinforced by the reminder of better days before the war. Reconstruction writers were rarely bitter; indeed they can be considered only mild racists when their works are compared with those of the most reactionary apologist of slavery and the Ku Klux Klan, Thomas Dixon, Jr. Dixon employed many of the same characters, institutions, and situations as Page and other Southern authors; indeed Reconstruction writers had helped to prepare the reading public for Dixon's novels by recalling the healthy conditions before the war and endorsing, if only mildly, a caste system in the post-bellum South.

Dixon made no attempt to conceal his anti-Negro bias or staunch defense of an Aryan civilization in America. His novels were extremely popular, for they were published at a time when race relations had deteriorated in the South and

. . . the extremists of Southern racism [had] probably reached a wider audience, both within their own region and in the nation, than ever before. . . . It was a time when the hope born of Reconstruction had all but died for the Negro, when disfranchisement blocked his political advance and the caste system closed the door

---

scribed as attractively as those of *Swallow Barn;* in Elizabeth Meriwether's *Black and White* (1883) a young white master studies at a medical college so that he can provide for the health of his servants.

For a realistic picture of the Southerner's attitude toward the Negro before and after the war, see William Gilmore Simms, *The Letters of William Gilmore Simms,* coll. and ed. Mary C. Simms Oliphant, Alfred Taylor Odell, T. C. Eaves (Charleston, 1955), I, 343, 383, 502, 528. Before the war Simms could write to a friend, James Lawson, on March 17, 1861, that "I feed, physic, clothe, nurse & watch some 70 [Negroes], and have to live from hand to mouth myself—the mere steward of my negroes" (p. 353). Later in that same year, on November 18, he urged another friend, James Henry Hammond, to teach all Negroes "to feel that their owners are their best friends" (p. 383). But after the war, when the Negro was of little economic value to him, Simms discarded his paternal attitude; he knew now, as he wrote Evert A. Duyckinck on June 15, 1865, that he could "derive nothing from their labour, & what they shall make is yielded to them wholly" (p. 502). Soon he became openly bitter to the freedmen, and on December 19, 1865, wrote to Duyckinck that "the Negroes have been taught to believe that the lands of the country are to be divided among them, and they are no longer willing to work on any contract" (p. 528).

to integration in the white world, when the North had abandoned him to the South and the South was yielding to the clamor of her extremists.[10]

Dixon wrote what he described as "The Trilogy of Reconstruction," but in actuality his three novels, *The Leopard's Spots* (1902), *The Clansman* (1905), and *The Traitor* (1907), are a chronicle and a defense of the Ku Klux Klan. In *The Leopard's Spots*, the hero, a preacher, bemoans the fact that Negro dominion, deification, "equality and amalgamation" have been forced upon Southerners against their will. The Ku Klux Klan, he maintains, "was simply the old answer of organized manhood to organized crime. Its purpose was to bring order out of chaos, protect the weak and defenceless, the widows and orphans of brave men who had died for their country, to drive from power the thieves who were robbing the people, redeem the commonwealth from infamy, and reestablish civilisation."

Dixon describes the Reconstruction policies of the Republicans as an "attempt to establish with the bayonet an African barbarism on the ruins of Southern society," and he characterized such an attempt as "a conspiracy against human progress." The violent crimes of the Negro are delineated in detail; so antagonistic are the freedmen to their former masters, in fact, that the birth of the Ku Klux Klan is almost justified. The organization is led by a moderate Southerner and not a fanatic —Dixon models his hero after his own uncle, Colonel Leroy McAfee, who was actually Grand Titan of the Invisible Empire—and it is clearly indicated that the Klan is formed only as a defense of Southern rights. When the Republicans and Negroes have been completely overwhelmed by the Klan, its leader announces that he has been "a successful revolutionist— that Civilization has been saved, and the South redeemed from shame."[11]

Thomas Dixon was far more reactionary than most Southern writers. His novels appeared in the first decade of the twentieth century, and by that time Reconstruction, the Ku Klux Klan,

[10] C. Vann Woodward, *Origins of the New South, 1877–1913* (Baton Rouge, 1951), pp. 352, 356.

[11] *The Clansman, An Historical Romance of the Ku Klux Klan* (New York, 1905), p. 374. This novel was made into the film classic, *The Birth of a Nation*. *The Leopard's Spots* was converted into a successful play in 1903.

and the Union League were as dated and historical to Northerners as the subject matter of *Uncle Tom's Cabin* was to Southerners; the Ku Klux Klan of course was revived later in the century.[12] Few authors of the South shared Dixon's attitudes, and the lasting portrait of the Negro remained that of Joel Chandler Harris and Thomas Nelson Page. Nevertheless, Dixon's novels do recapture the feelings of many Southerners during Reconstruction, and they evoked an overwhelmingly favorable reaction when presented as dramas throughout the South.[13] From Albion W. Tourgée the novels evoked only violent protest. When asked by a reviewer to comment on Dixon's *The Leopard's Spots* (1902), Tourgée wrote a lengthy "personal and confidential" letter, denouncing Dixon's version of Reconstruction:

[12] In the 1920's when the Klan became active again, Dixon "repeatedly denounced the revived Ku Klux Klan as bigoted and in no way resembling its predecessor"; nevertheless, "he regarded whites as 'superior' to Negroes." Quoted in obituary of Dixon, *The New York Times,* April 4, 1946.

[13] See Dixon's report of the enormous success that a dramatization of *The Clansman* enjoyed in Charleston, South Carolina, on October 25, 1905. Thomas Dixon, Jr., "Why I Wrote 'The Clansman,'" *The Theatre,* VI (January, 1906), 20–22. Dixon quotes from *The New York Evening Post:*
"Already 'The Clansman' is almost the sole subject of conversation in every Southern house where the news of its presentation has come. In the city of Charleston, the day following the two performances, press reports and published criticisms were eagerly read. The Southern newspapers are flooded with letters from prominent men who could not be induced to so advertise a dramatic production which had not as its issue a question of tremendously vital importance. To those who have the future harmony of the races at heart, the presentation of 'The Clansman' must come as a crushing blow. . . . In 'The Clansman' the negro is shown at his worst. . . . When the cause of the carpetbaggers and the Black League seemed in the ascendant there was hissing. But it was not such hissing as one hears directed toward the eyebrows of the villain in the ordinary melodrama. The whole house, from pit to roof, seethed. At times the actors could not go on" (pp. 20–21).
Dixon defends himself in this same article: "The accusation that I wrote 'The Clansman' to appeal to prejudice or assault the negro race is, of course, the silliest nonsense. For the negro I have only the profoundest pity and the kindliest sympathy" (p. 22). Dixon goes on to say that the Negro cannot live with the white man as an equal and that he should be colonized.

The book is entirely worthless as a narration of events or an analysis of causes. It bears not the remotest similitude to anything that ever happened. As a picture of the times, it is not worth discussion, but as a delineation of the southern white man of yesterday and today, it is of inestimable value. I have known Dixon almost from his boyhood . . . know his type and the influences by which he and those like him have been shaped. There are many admirable things about these people. But their view of events is colored wholly by the prejudices of the class and section and their ideal of God is simply a being endowed with the impulses and sentiments of the southern white man. . . .

This is what Dixon's book teaches and luminously shows to be the animating and dominating impulse of the southern whites of the best class—of the perfect, inerrant, impeccable type. Annihilation [sic], deportation or eternal and unresisting subjection to the will and pleasure of the white people.—These are the only alternatives which a Christian minister offers to the colored people of the U.S.![14]

The Negroes in Tourgée's fiction are outcasts, independent people who refuse to resume their abject role of slave and are consequently denied full freedom by the whites. 'Toinette, the mulatto heroine of *A Royal Gentleman* (1874), has been educated by her white lover, but once the war is over she demands equal rights; Tourgée carefully informs us that 'Toinette has been emancipated intellectually as well as legally. Nimbus, the Negro protagonist of *Bricks Without Straw* (1880), insists on the opportunity to earn his own livelihood, to improve his economic status, but when he begins to prosper, the white community suppresses him, and he is forced to escape to the North.

Tourgée's portrait of the Negro is of course not wholly accurate. Since his knowledge of ante-bellum conditions was academic rather than personal, he knew little of the Negro as slave. In Tourgée's fiction the Negro is hero and is never

---

[14] Tourgée to E. H. Johnson, May 15, 1902. See also a scathing attack on Dixon by a Negro, Kelly Miller, *As to The Leopard's Spots, An Open Letter to Thomas Dixon, Jr.* (Washington, 1905).

Dixon, born in 1864, had been ordained as a Baptist minister in 1887 at Raleigh, North Carolina, and preached in Raleigh, Boston, and New York; "his sermons were sensational" in nature. After having lived in New York for ten years, he resigned his pastorate and began to lecture. In 1901 he began his literary career, writing *A Leopard's Spots*. He died on April 3, 1946. Mildred Lewis Rutherford, *The South in History and Literature* (Atlanta, 1906), pp. 604–11.

viewed as unruly or insurgent; and his former master becomes the villain. The portrait of the South during Reconstruction which Harris and Page drew is now reversed, and Tourgée, in attempting to explore the Negro character, errs in the opposite direction; whereas the independent freedman is described as a menace to a white Southern civilization in the literature of Southern authors, he is idealized by Tourgée.

Tourgée rebelled against the stereotyped portrait of the Negro that appeared in post-bellum fiction. Part of his rebellion was naturally caused by his political bias; all of these authors wrote with a conviction of Negro inferiority. But he was also convinced that even from the point of view of literature, the American writer was not appreciating the potentialities of the Negro as a fictional character.

About the Negro as a man [he wrote in 1888], with hopes, fears, and aspirations like any other man, our literature is very nearly silent. . . . The Negro is either the devoted slave, but such a man was a miracle—or he is the man to whom liberty has brought only misfortune. Much has been written of the slave and something of the freedman, but thus far no-one has been found able to weld the new life to the old. . . . The life of the Negro as a slave, freedman, and racial outcast offers undoubtedly the richest mine of romantic material that has opened to the English-speaking novelist since the Wizard of the North discovered and depicted the common life of Scotland. The Negro as a man has an immense advantage over the Negro as servant, being an altogether new character in fiction.[15]

Tourgée's literary theory was more accurate than his practice. The Negro as an outcast did offer vast possibilities to late nineteenth-century authors, though few of them—Mark Twain is a notable exception—took full advantage of the new fictional character. Tourgée himself saw the freedman too narrowly, and it was not until the twentieth century that authors were able to describe the Negro as essentially non-political, as someone not always being manipulated for political purposes.

As sentimental as the fiction of Thomas Nelson Page, Joel Chandler Harris, and lesser writers may have been, it succeeded in establishing the Southern conception of the Negro in the national mind. He was pictured as the bewildered victim of unscrupulous carpetbagger leaders; he, as well as the white man,

[15] Tourgée, "The South as a Field for Fiction," *The Forum*, VI (December, 1888), 408, 409, 410.

recalled a better time "befoah the war." In the hearts of all these Southerners there was no rebellion, no hatred, no desire for renewed strife; and their land became a welcome haven for Northerners who wished to live in an agrarian culture.

Tourgée portrayed a rather different South during Reconstruction—a South where immorality, lynchings, and rebelliousness still were rife—but his version was not that finally accepted by Northern readers of the 1880's. Tourgée recognized the unpopularity of his position; in 1888 he was finally compelled to admit the predominance—if not the historical truth—of Southern fiction and the Southern interpretation of Reconstruction:

> Our literature has become not only Southern in type, but distinctly Confederate in sympathy. . . .
> A foreigner studying our current literature, without knowledge of our history and judging our civilization by our fiction, would undoubtedly conclude that the South was the seat of intellectual empire in America, and the African the chief romantic element of our population.[16]

[16] *Ibid.*, p. 405.

IV

LESLIE A. FIEDLER

The Blackness of Darkness: The Negro and the Development of American Gothic

[In *The Narrative of Arthur Gordon Pym*] Poe presents us not with the standard resolution of the American's ambiguity toward the life of impulse: an opposition of good savage and evil savage, as in Cooper's confrontation of Pawnee and Sioux, or Mark Twain's contrast of benevolent Negro and malevolent Indian. Though the son of an Upsaroka mother preserves Pym from the menace of the black hordes of Too-Wit ("Seizing a club from one of the savages who has fallen, he dashed out the brains of the three who remained . . ."), Poe is not finally intent on playing the same symbolic game as Twain in reverse. He is rather portraying a world in which the primitive may save or destroy, but remains always brutal and amoral, from any Christian point of view—diabolic.

Poe espouses, that is to say, the view of instinctual life which is the common property of those writers whom he regards as "men of genius," the view of Brockden Brown and Hawthorne; and he quite consciously rejects the sentimentalizing of the savage which he finds in popularizers like Cooper. Poe is quite at home with that distinctively American strain of the gothic, in which the aristocratic villains of the European tale of terror are replaced by skulking primitives, and the natural rather than the sophisticated is felt as a primal threat. Indeed, Poe's aristocratic pretensions make it impossible for him to

From Leslie A. Fiedler, "The Blackness of Darkness: E. A. Poe and the Development of the Gothic," *Love and Death in the American Novel* (New York: Criterion Books, Inc., 1960), pp. 370–414. Copyright © 1960 by Criterion Books. Copyright © 1966 by Leslie A. Fiedler. Reprinted by permission of Stein and Day, Publishers, and Martin Secker & Warburg Limited.

adopt such an attitude without the equivocations and soul-searching demanded of such liberal gothicists as the young Brockden Brown. His fictional world needs no good Indians because he believes in none; and try as he will, he cannot keep quite distinct the mutinous black cook, whom he calls a "perfect demon," from the "dusky, fiendish" figure of Dirk Peters. Theoretically, the tale of *Gordon Pym* projects through its Negroes the fear of black rebellion and of the white man's perverse lust for the Negro, while symbolizing in the red man an innocent and admirable yearning for the manly violence of the frontier; but in the working out of the plot, the two are confused. Certainly, Pym has prepared himself for the encounter with Peters by reading the journals of Lewis and Clark in his coffin-refuge in the hold; but Peters refuses to become a harmless embodiment of the West, remaining to the end an ogre, his great, bare teeth displayed like fangs.

It is true that the half-breed line-manager offers protection against the shipboard mutineers and the vicious natives of Tsalal; but his sheltering embrace is identified with the mortal hug of the grizzly bear, whose skin he wears to cover his bald pate. The figure of the black man blends ambiguously with that of the slave, while that of the red man blurs into that of the wild beast! The West, at any rate, was always for Poe only half real, a literary experience rather than a part of his life; but the South moved him at the deepest personal level. Insofar as *Gordon Pym* is finally a social document as well as a fantasy, its subject is slavery; and its scene, however disguised, is the section of America which was to destroy itself defending that institution. Poe's novel is surely the first which uses gothicism to express a peculiarly American dilemma identifying the symbolic blackness of terror with the blackness of the Negro and the white guilts he embodies. It is, indeed, to be expected that our first eminent Southern author discover that the proper subject for American gothic is the black man, from whose shadow we have not yet emerged.

Though the movement of *Gordon Pym* seems to bear us away from America, once Nantucket and New Bedford have been left behind, and to carry us through remoter and remoter seas toward the exotic Antarctic, it ends in a region quite unlike the actual polar regions. Heading toward an expected world of ice and snow, Pym finds instead a place of tepid waters and luxuriant growth; seeking a white world, he discovers, beside and within it, a black one. What has gone wrong? It is necessary for Poe to believe, in that blessed ignorance which frees forbidden fancies, that Pym's fictional voyage is bearing him toward the polar region, just as it was necessary for him to believe the whole story a delicious hoax; but we, as latter-day readers, need not be the victims of either delusion. For all the carefully worked-up details about penguins, *bêche de mer*, galapagos tortoises (bait for the audience which was later to subscribe to the *National Geographic*), Poe follows the footsteps not of Captain Cook but of his own first voyage in the arms of his mother, undertaken before his memory began, from New England to the South. In his deepest imagination, any flight from the North bears the voyager not toward but away from the snow—not to the South Pole, but to the American South.

Certainly, it grows not colder, but warmer and warmer, as Pym aboard the last ship to rescue him, the *Jane Guy*, pushes closer and closer to the Pole. "We had now advanced to the southward more than eight degrees farther than any previous navigators. We found . . . that the temperature of the air, and latterly of the water, became milder." Whatever pseudo-scientific explanations Poe may have believed would sustain this improbable notion of a luke-warm Antarctica, certain *symbolic* necessities were of more importance; he is being, in fact, carried back to Ole Virginny—as the color of the natives he meets on the Island of Tsalal (latitude 83° 20′, longitude 43° 5′ W.) clearly indicates. They are brawny, muscular, and jet black, with "thick and woolen hair," "thick and clumsy lips," these "wretches," whom Pym describes, after they have destroyed all the white men but him and Peters, as "the most wicked, hypocritical, vindictive, blood thirsty, and altogether fiendish race of men upon the face of the globe." Poe very carefully does not ever call them Negroes, though he bestows on them those marks which, in a review of two books on abolition, he listed as the special stigmata by which God distinguished the race that were to become slaves. He "blackened the negro's skin and crisped his hair into wool." At any rate, where an informed reader might have expected some kind of Indian, Poe could only imagine plantation hands in masquerade; and he sets them in a world distinguished not only by blackness and warmth, but by a certain disturbing sexuality quite proper to Southern stereotypes of Negro life. That sexuality can only be expressed obliquely by Poe, who was so squeamish about matters of this kind that the much franker Baudelaire was driven to remark, "*Dans l'oeuvre d'Edgar Poe, il n'y a jamais d'amour.*" The phallicism of the island he, therefore, suggests not in human terms but by a reference to the islanders' chief crop, the *bêche de mer*—a kind of sea-cucumber of which, Poe informs us, the authorities say that it "renews the exhausted system of the immoderate voluptuary."

The inhabitants of Tsalal are not, of course, the burlesque Negroes, those black "rascals" or "scamps," named pompously "Jupiter" or "Pompey," who lend a minstrel-show note to Poe's lighter tales. Woolly-pated and bow-legged, these characters play the role of mischievous, cowardly, stupid and faithful dependents, good always for a laugh when they say "soldiers" for "shoulders" or "clause" for "cause." No more are the black savages of *Gordon Pym* like the ideal colored servants sketched by Poe in his review of *Slavery in the United States* by J. K. Paulding, the author whose suggestion led to Poe's writing his encoded Southern tale. The "degree of loyal devotion on the part of the slave to which the white man's heart is a stranger," Poe insists, is far "stronger than they would be under like circumstances between individuals of the white race"; and, indeed, such "loyal devotion" ranks high in "the class of feelings 'by which the heart is made better'. . . ." It is precisely such loyalty which the actions of the natives in Poe's novel belie, since it is his hidden doubts on this score which they embody. The dark hordes of Too-Wit project the image of what the Southerner privately fears the Negro may be; just as the idealized body-servant of Poe's review projects the image of what the anti-abolitionist publicly claims he is. But the two images are complementary halves of a single view based on wish and terror: the subdued dependent bent to the sick-bed in love and the resentful victim abiding in patience a day of vengeance. It is the darker half, however, which is true to Poe's memories of his boyhood and youth in the Allan household; while the lighter belongs only to certain patriarchal legends, to which he learned to subscribe during his days on *The Southern Literary Messenger*. In the single reference to the Negro in his correspondence, Poe complains to his step-father (the date is 1827): "You suffer me to be subjected to the whim & caprice, not only of your white family, but to the complete authority of the blacks."

At the climax of *Gordon Pym*, Poe dreams himself once more, though a grown man, subject to that nightmare authority; and the book projects his personal resentment and fear, as well as the guilty terror of a whole society in the face of those whom they can never quite believe they have the right to enslave. In Tsalal, blackness is no longer the livery of subjection but a sign of menace; so utterly black, that even the teeth concealed by their pendulous lips are black, the Antarctic savages inhabit a black land in which the vegetation and the animals, water itself are all subdued to the same dismal color. The voyage of Pym has transported him improbably into the black belt, a black belt transformed from the level of sociology to that of myth, in whose midst the reigning Caucasian is overwhelmed by a sense of isolation and peril. Not even the glimmer of white teeth bared in a heartening smile cuts the gloom of this exclusive and excluding dark world, whose ultimate darkness is revealed in that final chasm in which Pym and Peters are trapped after the treacherous destruction of their white shipmates. "We alone had escaped from the tempest of that overwhelming destruction. We were the sole living white men upon the island." At this point, the darkness of "Niggertown" merges at last into the darkness of the womb which is also a tomb, an intestinal chamber from which there is apparently no way of being born again into a realm of light.

How has Pym arrived here, in this place where whiteness itself is taboo, where even the flicker of a handkerchief, the flash of sunlight on taut sails, a little flour in the bottom of a pan stir terror, and doom the white man who feels at home in a world full of such pale symbols? Pym has sought a polar whiteness and has discovered instead a realm of the domination of black. It was (as Marie Bonaparte and other analytical critics have made clear) his mother whom Poe was pursuing in his disguise as Pym: that lost, pale mother, white with the whiteness of milk and the pallor of disease; and the imaginary voyage is a long regression to childhood. But hostilely guarding the last access to the White Goddess, stands the black killer, Too-Wit. In the ultimate reaches of his boyhood, where he had confidently looked for some image of maternal comfort and security, Poe-Pym finds *both* the white chasm and cascade and the black womb sealed off by black warriors. Surely, the latter fantasies represent memories of the black mammy and the black milk brother, who has sucked at the same black breast.

Writing from the conscious level of his mind and addressing a public largely Southern, Poe dealt with the effect of these quasi-maternal and fraternal bonds sanguinely enough. Those very feelings, he argued, " 'by which the heart is made better' . . . have their rise in the relation between the infant and his nurse. They are cultivated between him and his fostering brother. . . . They are fostered by the habit of affording protection and favors to the younger offspring of the same nurse. . . ." But the buried mind of Poe does not believe what the rationalizing intelligence propounds; in dreams (and in the fiction which is close to those dreams), the foster-brother arises to destroy and crush, to block the way to the lost, pale mother who preceded the Negro nurse. And even the good foster-brother, whom Poe split off from his dark image in Peters, he cannot finally feel as benign; for him the black man and the "blackness of darkness" are one. That they remain one in much distinguished American fiction after his time is probably not due to the direct influence of Poe. He rather prophetically anticipates than initiates a long line of American books, in which certain gothic writers exploit the fear and guilt which the comic Negro of popular art attempts to laugh out of existence.

II

Down through the history of the minstrel show, a black-faced Sambo (smeared with burnt cork, whether Negro or white, into the grotesque semblance of the archetypal nigger) tries to exorcise with high-jinks and ritual jokes the threat of the black rebellion and the sense of guilt which secretly demands it as penance and purge. But our more serious writers return again and again to the theme: Melville, for instance, in "Benito Cereno" treating quite explicitly the tragic encounter between certain sentimental and comic stereotypes of the Negro and a historic instance of a slave mutiny. In that story, Captain Amasa Delano fails to recognize the rebellion on a Spanish slave-ship which he encounters, precisely because he is a good American. He is endowed, that is to say, with an "undistrustful good nature" and will not credit "the imputation of malign evil in man." This means in fact that he is quite willing to believe almost any evil of a European aristocrat, like the Don Benito who gives the tale its title; and is prepared to accept the most incredible behavior as the kind of "sullen inefficiency" to be expected of a Latin crew. On the other hand, he is incapable of believing a Negro, particularly a body servant, anything but a "faithful fellow."

It is just this phrase which occurs to Captain Delano as he watches Babo, a black slave who is actually holding his master prisoner, threatening death with the razor he presumably wields to shave him. " 'Faithful fellow!' cried Captain Delano, 'Don Benito, I envy you such a friend, slave I cannot call him.' " But Melville will not let it go, adding on his own behalf —in a tone less ironical than one would expect:

Most negroes are natural valets and hairdressers. . . . There is . . . a smooth tact about them in this employment. . . . And above all is the great gift of good-humour. . . . a certain easy cheerfulness . . . as though God had set the whole negro to some pleasant tune. . . . to this is added the docility arising from the unaspiring contentment of a limited mind, and that susceptibility of bland attachment sometimes inhering in indisputable inferiors. . . . like most men of a good, blithe heart, Captain Delano took to negroes . . . just as other men to Newfoundland dogs.

But Babo is, in fact, the leader of a black uprising that has already murdered his master's closest friend and bound his corpse to the prow; and Captain Delano in his unwillingness to imperil his fondness for Negroes, almost kills Don Benito when he makes a last, desperate attempt to escape. Still convinced that the true source of moral infection is to be found only in the decaying institutions of Europe, Captain Delano cannot understand why, even after the exposure of Babo, Benito Cereno continues to pine away, seems to long only for death.

Though the fact of slavery, out of which all the violence and deceit aboard the Spanish ship has been bred, remains a part of his own democratic world as well as Don Benito's aristocratic one, Amasa Delano is undismayed. Though only an incident has been dealt with and its deep causes left untouched, he finds in this no cause for despair, but demands that the Spaniard join with him in recognizing a happy ending. "You are saved . . . ," he cries to Don Benito; "You are saved: what has cast such a shadow upon you?" And he will not understand when the Spanish captain answers, "The negro." Indeed, Melville seems to share the bafflement of his American protagonist; a Northerner like Captain Delano, Melville finds the problem of slavery and the Negro a little exotic, a gothic horror in an almost theatrical sense of the word. Before his story is done, at any rate, he lets it lapse back into the language of the written record where he had to look for it in the first instance—quite unlike Poe who found this particular theme at the very center of his own experience.

In this regard, Mark Twain is much more like Poe than Melville. Whatever his conflicting allegiances, he was a Southerner in his roots and origin, who all his life long carried on a family quarrel with the part of the country in which he had long ceased to live. He had enlisted briefly on the side of the Confederacy, though he became finally a convert to the abolitionist cause and wrote in his finest book an attack on slavery; and he could never really disavow the Southern notion of "honor," though he mocked all his life Sir Walter Scott and the mad chivalric codes which the South had derived from Scott's books. The town in which Twain was born and to which his imagination compulsively returned existed on a boundary between South and West; and, indeed, his two youthful careers led him to turn first in one direction then in the other. As a riverboat pilot before the Civil War, he followed the Mississippi down to New Orleans; as a journalist and fortune-hunter after Abolition, he headed across that same river toward Nevada and California. Both worlds lured him, turn and turn about; and in his two most profound books, he faces first one way then the other, but reverses the actual order of his life.

Huckleberry Finn ends with Huck pointed west, ready to light out for the territory in search of a freedom he had deludedly and vainly sought with Jim by going down the Mississippi. Why, critics have asked ever since the book appeared, did Huck not cross the river to the Illinois side, go east to where freedom really existed as a political fact? But the East, though it claimed Twain at last, had no symbolic meaning for him; the motion toward childhood is for him a motion toward the South, down the river. It was, therefore, down to Arkansas that Twain moved the Missouri farm of his mother's sister and her husband, the Great Good Place of his earliest years, which is celebrated in the most moving and lyrical section of the *Autobiography*, and which had appeared earlier as a mythical refuge in *Huckleberry Finn* (1885) and *Tom Sawyer Detective* (1896). Like Poe, Twain thought of the trip home as a voyage south; but like the earlier writer, too, he felt that trip a descent into hell. Though Twain was always consciously more attracted than repelled by the ambivalent Eden of his boyhood, and in his memoirs tends to idealize its terror almost out of existence, his fiction tells quite another story. Huck Finn is able to reject Aunt Sally's utopia out of hand—for all the redolence of its good home cooking; and in *Tom Sawyer Detective*, it takes all of Tom's ingenuity to exorcise murder and the threat of madness from the earthly paradise. In neither of these works, however, does Twain make it quite clear what has cast a shadow upon his idyllic world, what *particular* terror haunts his most nostalgic memories.

Only in *Pudd'nhead Wilson*, his most gothic book and an almost diagrammatic study in black and white, does he reveal that his specter is identical with Poe's and Don Benito's: "The negro." *Pudd'nhead Wilson* begins and ends in the village where *Huckleberry Finn* began and *Tom Sawyer* was played out, on the banks of the same symbolic river and in the same mythical pre-Civil War years. But between the "St. Petersburg" of the earlier books and the "Dawson's Landing" of the later one, there is a terrible difference. Pudd'nhead is represented as a mature and cynical stranger coming into the place at which Twain had never managed before to look from the outside. To his two boy heroes, it is so totally and entirely their world and they know it no more than their own faces. Only the outsider, the estranged adult Twain had become, rather than the unalienated child he remembered himself, offers an opportunity for perspective; and the opening of the novel pans slowly down on the village: its rose-clad houses, its cats, its sleepiness, and its fragrance—all preparing for the off-hand give-away of the sentence beginning, "Dawson's Landing was a slaveholding town. . . ."

Striving to return as a grownup to the limit of a boy's memory, Twain arrives at the fact of slavery, once as imperceptible to him as the town itself. The Civil War is the watershed, in Twain's life, between childhood and manhood, innocence and experience, joy and despair; and this very fact insures that in his time of experience and despair he come to know that his innocence and joy, as well as the life that sustained them, were based on the labor and indignities of slaves. Yet the lost happiness, however based, was real; and Twain, whose dogmatic anti-Christianity can conceive no other paradise, cannot leave off returning to it in reminiscence and in art. All the same, he cannot deny the shamefulness of his plight, the pity of being forced to dream a boy's dream of freedom acted out in the world of slavery.

In *Tom Sawyer*, the paradox at the heart of Twain's essential myth is hushed up for nostalgia's sake and in the interests of writing a child's book; in *Huckleberry Finn*, it is present as a constant tension, though camouflaged by the poetry and high spirits of the text; in *Pudd'nhead Wilson*, it falls apart into horror and horseplay. In that novel, Hannibal is rendered from the very start not as a Western but as a Southern town. The river is no longer presented as a just-passed frontier, a defining limit between the realms of civilization and nature, a boundary which America touches and crosses on its way west; it is felt as a passageway into the deep South. "Down the river" is the phrase that gives a kind of musical unity to the work: a guilt-ridden, terrible motif repeated with variations, from the jesting taunt of its heroine, the Negress Roxana, to a fellow slave, "If you b'longed to me I'd sell you down the river 'fo' you git too fur gone . . ." to the bleak irony of the novel's final sentence, "The Governor . . . pardoned Tom at once, and the creditors sold him down the river."

The contrast with *Huckleberry Finn* inevitably suggests itself; for here the direction of the river Twain loved is regarded as pointing *only* into the ultimate Southern horror, the unmitigated terror of conscienceless and brutal slavery. The movement of the plot, the very shape of *Pudd'nhead Wilson* is determined by this symbolic motion toward the Gulf of Mexico—the movement of the Father of Waters toward a confluence with the great maternal sea; though here that symbolic motion represents no longer a dream of the flight to freedom, but only a nightmare of the passage into captivity. And at the center of the motion and the plot, stands the figure of the slave-girl Roxana, precisely the black mammy of Poe's sentimental editorializing, who has held at her breast both her own child and her master's, black and white milk-brothers. Roxana, however, defies all clichés; she is no gross, comfortable, placid source of warmth, all bosom and grin, but a passionate, complex and beautiful mulatto, a truly living woman distinguished from the wooden images of virtue and bitchery that pass for females in most American novels. She is "black" only by definition, by social convention, though her actual appearance as described by Twain, "majestic . . . rosy . . . comely," so baffled the platitude-ridden illustrator of the official edition that he drew in her place a plump and comic Aunt Jemima!

Her own child, called Valet de Chambre, or Chambers, has been sired by Cecil Burleigh Essex, a white Virginia gentleman, and hence is even less the woolly-haired, swart, blubber-lipped caricature than she. Indeed he is scarcely distinguishable with his "blue eyes and flaxen curls" from his milk-brother, Thomas à Becket Driscoll, so that Roxana has no trouble switching the two in their cradles when Valet de Chambre is threatened with being sold down the river. Twain makes clear, that is to say, what Poe and Paulding have disingenuously concealed, that there is in the South no absolute distinction of black and white, merely an imaginary line—crossed and recrossed by the white man's lust—that makes one of two physically identical babies "by a fiction of law and custom a negro."

Once the "negro" Valet de Chambre has been dressed in a soft muslin robe and the "white" Thomas à Becket Driscoll in a tow-linen shirt, their roles are reversed and each plays the traditional role of his imagined race. The real Tom persists in protecting his "young master" despite the beatings he receives at his hands, and even saves him from drowning. But when, after his rescue, the white fellows of the false Tom tease him by calling his rescuer his "nigger pappy," the false Tom attempts to kill that rescuer. He cannot abide the suggestion that "he had a second birth into life, and that Chambers was the author of his new being," cannot assent to the American archetype embodied in Jim and Huck in *Huckleberry Finn*—and so drives a knife into his savior. No more can he abide being the son of a Negress, and ends by selling his mother down the river.

But it is not the only literally "false" Toms who betray their black mothers and play Cain to their Negro brothers; Twain's protagonists merely make melodramatically evident the fact that every mistreatment of a Negro, the simple continuance of slavery as an institution, is both a betrayal of the breast at which the Southerner who calls himself white has sucked, and of the brother he calls black, who has sucked at that breast beside him. In the mythical dénouement of Twain's book, it is suggested that all sons of the South, whether counted in the census as black or white, are symbolically the offspring of black mothers and white fathers, products of a spiritual miscegenation at the very least, which compounds the evil of slavery with an additional evil. The whitest aristocrat has nestled up to a black teat; the dullest slave may have been sired by some pure-blooded F. F. V. blade, discharging his blind lust upon a field wench or a house servant.

III

The family pattern of *Pudd'nhead Wilson* is opposite to that of *Huckleberry Finn;* for while the former is the portrait of a Southern, which is to say, a patriarchal society, the latter portrays a Western or matriarchal one. In the earlier book, the "sivilization" which Huck finally rejects is a world of mothers, that is, of what Christianity has become among the females who maintain it just behind the advancing frontier. It is a relatively simple-minded world, whose goal is virtue, which is defined as not cursing, stealing, smoking, or lying, but rather keeping clean, wearing shoes, and praying for spiritual gifts. In this world, the male principle is represented, if at all (Tom Sawyer has no father), by outcasts and scoundrels like Huck's unredeemable Pap—or some representative of nature and instinct like the runaway slave, Nigger Jim. In *Pudd'nhead Wilson*, on the other hand, it is the fathers who represent society, who are the defenders of a chivalric code which Twain elsewhere affects to despise, and the descendants of cavaliers. York Leicester Driscoll, Percy Northumberland Driscoll, Pembroke Howard, and Colonel Cecil Burleigh Essex: the names make the point perhaps too obviously. This is a world continuous with that of Renaissance England, a world in which "honor" is the sole code.

The patriarchal world of "honor" is also one of gallantry, of a kind of lustiness associated in Twain's mind with the court of Elizabeth, which for him represented a lost sexual Eden, contrasted (in his privately circulated *1601*) with a debilitated

America, where men "copulate not until they be five-and-thirty years of age . . . and doe it then but once in seven yeeres." Though the men of Dawson's Landing, being Virginians, are potent still, their white women, who languish and retreat and die, are latter-day Americans, almost asexually genteel, so that only the Negress can match the vigor of the fathers with a corresponding fertility and power. Roxy is just such a Negress, and her union with Cecil Burleigh Essex represents not only a sociological but a symbolic truth. If the fathers of the South are Virginia gentlemen, the mothers are Negro girls, casually or callously taken in the parody of love, which is all that is possible when one partner to a sexual union is not even given the status of a person.

Twain's own judgment of sexual relations between black and white, slave and free is not explicitly stated; but there seems no doubt that he regarded the union between Roxy and Essex with a certain degree of horror, regarded it as a kind of fall—evil in itself and a source of doom to all involved. Paired together, *Huckleberry Finn* and *Pudd'nhead Wilson* express both sides of a deep, half-conscious American conviction, which we have already noticed as it was reflected before Twain by Fenimore Cooper. There are two possible relations, two kinds of love between colored and white projected in our fiction, one of which is innocent, one guilty; one of which saves, one damns. The first provides a sentimental relation for the highbrow Western, the second a terrible one for the Southern gothic romance. The innocent relationship can exist only between men, or a man and a boy; the other, suspect and impure, tries to join the disjoined in heterosexual passion, and its end is a catastrophe: a catastrophe symbolized by the "blackness" of the Negro, outward sign of an inward exclusion from grace. For Poe, who accepted slavery as God-given, a divine mystery, this catastrophic fact remains merely a fact not a riddle; but for Melville and Twain, committed to the abolitionist cause, it poses a terrible problem. Why should the Negro be condemned to wear the livery of the guilt which is really the white man's? It is a question which is asked everywhere in the strain of American gothic we have begun to examine; and the answers only compound the ambiguity which prompts them.

At one level, Twain seems willing to accept the tragic position of the Negro as an inexplicable curse, crying out through the mouth of the pseudo-Tom in his moment of bafflement and despair, "What crime did the uncreated first nigger commit that the curse of birth was decreed for him. . . ." And certainly Roxy seems to share her master's assumption that blackness of the skin, the invisible taint of the blood carries with it an inevitable moral weakness. Her son's malice and cowardice, she is disconcertingly willing to attribute to the quantum of Negro blood which she has bequeathed him. "It's de nigger in you, dat's what it is," she screams at her son when he has refused to fight a duel; "Thirty-one parts o' you is white en on'y one part nigger, en dat po' little one part is yo' soul." Conversely, she has assured him at an earlier moment, after revealing to him the secret of his birth ("You's a *nigger—bawn* a nigger en a *slave!*"), that his white father at least had been a great man, who had been honored with "de bigges' funeral dis town ever seed." "Dey ain't another nigger in dis town dat's as high-bawn as you is . . . jes you hold yo' head up as high as you want to—you has de right. . . ."

This is, of course, a conventional kind of humor; and Twain is after the laughs which are easy enough to get by portraying one Negro calling another "nigger" in the proper dialect. But certain ironies proliferate disturbingly beneath the burlesque; and we are left baffled before the spectacle of slaves and outcasts accepting, as they insult each other, not only the offensive epithet "nigger," but all the assumptions implicit in that epithet. Insofar as Twain asks us to accept certain vaudeville gags as social history, we find his book and its meanings distasteful, an uncomfortable reminder of his own human failings; but we cannot help suspecting that behind the horseplay and grotesque melodrama of his plot, he may be attempting to translate an account of local prejudice into a fable revealing man's more universal implication in guilt and doom. If the false Tom is meant to represent not merely a Negro vainly pretending to be white, but the fruit of the betrayal and terror and profaned love which join all men, white and black, in our society—he must be made to embody the seeds of self-destruction which that relationship contains within it. He must therefore lie, steal, kill, and boast of his crimes, until he reveals himself out of hybris as a secret slave.

Though it is Pudd'nhead Wilson, local character, fingerprint expert and amateur detective, who presumably unmasks the impostor and wins the town's applause, it is really the false Tom himself who brings on his own downfall. Twain cannot resist a courtroom dénouement, a revelation and reversal sprung by some self-appointed sleuth at the darkest moment of a plot. Tom Sawyer, indeed, exists precisely to make such exposures not only in the books called by his name, but even in the one written in Huckleberry Finn's. Most readers will remember (and the reader of *Pudd'nhead Wilson* must to fully savor that book) how at the climax of *Huckleberry Finn,* Tom Sawyer, "his eyes hot, and his nostrils opening and shutting like gills," cries out of Jim: "They hain't no *right* to shut him up. . . . Turn him loose! He ain't no slave; he's as free as any cretur that walks this earth!" "As free as any cretur," the boy hero declares, blithely convinced that freedom is real, realer than the illusion of slavery; and we believe him, putting down that sanguine book.

But a wry joke is already implicit in the phrase, which Twain no more sees than does Tom; and we as readers are not permitted to see it, as long as we remain within the spell of the happy ending. In *Pudd'nhead Wilson,* however, the protagonist, who is obviously Tom himself permitted at long last to grow up, rises to answer his own earlier courtroom cry, in just such a situation as he has always loved: " 'Valet de Chambre, Negro and slave . . . make upon the window the finger prints that will hang you!' " The double truth is in that instant complete: the seeming slave is free, but the free man is really a slave. It is an odd dénouement to a detective story enlivened by touches of farce: this relevation which condemns a hitherto free man to a life of servitude down the river, and leaves his mother sobbing on her knees, "De Lord have mercy on me, po' miserable sinner dat I is!" There is a happy ending this time for no one really except David Wilson (no longer called contemptuously "Pudd'nhead"), if one considers his acceptance by the philistine community really a blessing. To be sure, the same fingerprints which prove the presumed Tom a slave, establish the presumed Chambers as free; but his "curious fate" is equivocal if not actually tragic. Neither black nor white in his self-consciousness, he is excluded by long conditioning from the world of upper-class society, and barred from the "solacing refuge" of the slave kitchens by the fact of his legal whiteness. Had he turned on his foster-brother at the moment of revelation, he

could only have yelled what he earlier cried out to his presumed mother, "Yah-yah-yah! . . . Bofe of us is imitation *white*
—dat's what we is. . . ." And what would he have made of
Twain's afterthought, one of the final jottings in his journal,
"The skin of every human being contains a slave"?

Certainly, Pudd'nhead Wilson, in his exhibitionist courtroom
speech, when he rises to announce once more the old scandal
that the son has killed his father (Twain somewhat timidly
makes them only step-father and step-son), does not succeed in
restoring to the community a sense of its own innocence by
establishing the guilt of a single culprit. Yet this, as W. H.
Auden convincingly argues, is the archetypal function of the
detective story, to which genre *Pudd'nhead Wilson* seems to
belong. It is, in fact, an *anti*-detective story, more like *The
Brothers Karamazov* than *The Innocence of Father Brown*, its
function to expose communal guilt: our moral bankruptcy,
horror and shame, the stupidity of our definition of a Negro,
and the hopeless trap of our relations with him. Wilson's disclosure of Roxy's hoax coalesces with Mark Twain's exposure
to America of its own secret self. Each of Twain's chapters is
headed by a quotation from "Pudd'nhead Wilson's Calendar,"
a collection of small-town dangerous thoughts; and at the head
of the final chapter, under the rubric "Conclusion," he inscribes
the following text: "*October 12, The Discovery*. It was wonderful to find America, but it would have been more wonderful
to miss it." It is the most improbable of endings for a detective
story, which depends precisely upon its readers' faith in discovery; but it is one appropriate enough for the anti-Western
novel at the moment that it becomes anti-American in its revul-
sion from all clichés of innocent, new frontiers.

IV

The assault upon the Western and its image of America did
not, of course, die with Twain. In our time, it is most notably
carried forward by Robert Penn Warren, a poet, critic, and
pedagogue as well as a novelist, who has attempted the risky
game of presenting to our largest audience the anti-Western in
the guise of the Western, the anti-historical romance in the
guise of that form itself. In this enterprise, he has followed the
example of Twain himself, who pretended to be writing in
Pudd'nhead Wilson a popular detective story even as he mocked

the form; and who in "A Double-Barrelled Detective Story" carried the process even further, specifically parodying the methods of Conan Doyle. It is with historical fiction that Warren prefers to deal, seeing himself perhaps as the researcher (his first book dealt with the life of John Brown) just as Twain sees himself as the sleuth. In *World Enough and Time* (1952), at any rate, Warren attacks directly the myth of the West, using for his purposes the famous Beauchamp case, which had been treated earlier by Simms and Edgar Allan Poe. Warren, however, is not primarily interested in the fable of seduction and revenge, on which we have commented earlier; by shifting the point of interest from the Persecuted Maiden to her avenging lover, whom he calls Jeremiah Beaumont, he converts the tale from a study of the encounter of innocence and lust to a study of the encounter of romanticism and reality. Through all his attempts to substitute for life, or impose on life itself a sentimental dream of life, Beaumont has assumed the existence of a paradisal West, an unfallen Eden to which he can flee when all else fails him. In the end, Warren permits him to escape hanging (changing the facts of the original story for this purpose) and to seek out the wilderness of which he has so long dreamed. But that wilderness he finds to be no more than a festering swamp, in which he is ultimately murdered and his beloved, withered and haggard, commits suicide; and presiding over the travesty of the Great Good Place, no noble and immaculate Natty Bumppo, but a hump-backed monster dying in sensuality and filth: *la grande Bosse*, river pirate and nightmare made flesh, the visible shape of original sin which Beaumont's sentimental version of the West had denied.

In *Brother to Dragons* (1953), a long verse narrative, Warren continues his assault on the theory of original innocence, drafting Thomas Jefferson as a ghostly witness to a particularly brutal and meaningless crime committed by two of his nephews, who slaughter in a meat-house, for trivial reasons, a Negro—acting out ritually the guilt of the white man toward those he has enslaved.

It is not until *Band of Angels* (1955), however, that Warren, a Southerner himself and once involved in the Agrarian movement, turns to a full-scale treatment of the subject Twain had broached in *Pudd'nhead Wilson*, the plight of the white Negro. By turning the false Tom into a girl, however, Warren transforms the novel of miscegenation from the masculine murder mystery to the feminine bosom book, the erotic historical romance, creating a hybrid form whose strange pedigree would read: out of Margaret Mitchell by Mark Twain! Its fable deals with Amantha Starr, a young woman who discovers on her father's death that she is legally a slave and a Negro—and of her difficulty in deciding what, beneath "the fiction of law and custom," she really is.

The problem of identity is not for her as simple as it was for the exposed Valet de Chambre; what his mother confides in him and Pudd'nhead declares in open court, he himself believes. But Amantha does not know what to believe, for she has been sent as a child to an enlightened and pious college, where she has acquired a set of abolitionist clichés as useless to her in understanding the realities of slavery and being a Negro as are the opposite clichés of the Southern slaveholders. Nonetheless, an aura of miscegenation hangs over the series of love affairs which make up the history of Amantha, threatening to dissolve each embrace into a spasm of nausea or to convert it into a rape; yet she will not, she cannot bring herself to say, "I am a Negro!" No more capable of declaring herself white, she chooses to be nothing: an abstract victim without a particular identity. Like the hero of Ralph Ellison's *Invisible Man*, she fades from sight because she becomes nothing except her role; but in her case, the invisibility is willed. Her decision justifies her lovers in approaching her with disgust or condescension or pity—anything, that is to say, but love; and it is for that reason, that they are destroyed. Only when her white husband comes to realize that he, too, is a victim, she, too, a human ("The skin of every human being contains a slave" and its obverse), is he able to live with her not as a master or a benefactor, but as one weak and suffering being with another; and Amantha is at last free. It is a finally sentimental resolution, a retreat from the tragic blackness toward which Mark Twain had, however falteringly, moved.

To find a writer capable of accepting the darker implications of Twain's gothicism and pressing on to even more terrible resolutions, we must turn back to Warren's immediate master, William Faulkner. Faulkner instinctively begins with the realization, which we have discovered in Twain, that not murder only but miscegenation, too, must preside over the relations of

black and white to produce the full gothic shiver. More shocking to the imagination of the South than the fantasy of a white
man overwhelmed by a hostile black world is the fear that finally all distinctions will be blurred and black and white no longer
exist. On what can the assurance of a God-given right to enslave Negroes or deprive them of rights be based, when no man
can say with security who is the real Thomas à Becket Driscoll,
who some black pretender? Precisely this prevision of total
assimilation and chaos is entrusted to the young Canadian
Shreve at the end of Faulkner's *Absalom, Absalom!* (1935):

I think that in time the Jim Bonds are going to conquer the western
hemisphere. Of course it won't be quite in our time and of course
as they spread toward the poles they will bleach out again like the
rabbits and birds do, so they won't show up so sharp against the
snow. But it will still be Jim Bond; and so in a few thousand years,
I who regard you will also have sprung from the loins of African
kings.

But Jim Bond in the novel is an idiot, elusive as a ghost, a specter haunting the ravaged white family whose blood he shares.

In Faulkner's work, the threat of miscegenation is posed not
only in terms of future racial contamination, but also in those
of a present sexual threat. Out of the semi-obscene sub-litera-
ture of Southern racists, he captures and redeems the hysterical
vision of the black rapist, the Negro who, by stealth or force
(in Faulkner it is typically by stealth, which is to say, under the
cover of a pseudo-white skin), possesses a white woman. The
archetype answers precisely the abolitionist myth of the helpless Negro servant girl assaulted by her master. Against Roxana,
pitifully proud of her relationship with the gentleman who
leaves her pregnant with a flaxen-haired slave, is set the mother
of Joe Christmas in *Light in August* (1932), trying to convince
the doctor who attends her that the man who had fathered her
bastard "was a Mexican. When old Doc Hines could see in his
face the black curse of God Almighty." And against Simon
Legree in *Uncle Tom's Cabin*, pursuing the terrified and vir-
ginal Emmeline, is balanced (in *Absalom, Absalom!*) the figure
of Charles Bon, who has persuaded a white woman to marry
him. A charming and handsome Negro, who has "passed" without difficulty, he turns to the somewhat younger white man,
who has adulated him and to whose sister he is engaged, de-
liberating evoking the vulgar taunt of the crudest Negro-bait-

ers, "I'm the nigger that's going to sleep with your sister. Unless you stop me, Henry." And Henry, as he must, though only after long delay, shoots him!

Yet just before Bon speaks the words that doom him, Henry has cried to him, "You are my brother." Such brotherhood is more than a metaphor in *Absalom, Absalom!*, more even than the bond of having shared a single breast that links Twain's Tom to Chambers. In Faulkner's plot, the white man and the Negro who love and destroy each other are quite literally the sons of the same father, of Thomas Sutpen, the passionate, damned hero of the action. The younger, white son was born of a timid, genteel, rustic, puritanical creature, married for the sake of the status and respectability she could bestow; the older, black one was the offspring of a Haitian breed, foisted on an ignorant and ambitious young man by her unscrupulous parents. Of that first wife, Sutpen says somewhat cryptically, "I found that she was not and could never be through no fault of her own, adjunctive and incremental to the design which I had in mind, so I provided for her and put her aside." He cannot, however, avoid the miasma of miscegenation by so simple a device as flight; and Sutpen's children, white and black, find themselves locked finally in a terrible triangle, the two brothers more in love with each other than either with the sister (perhaps Bon loves no one, only wants to provoke his proud father into admitting the relationship from which he has fled), and the threat of incest over them all.

This is the final turn of the screw, the ultimate gothic horror which serves both to produce one more shock and to add one more level of symbolic relevance to the action. Not only in Faulkner's plot but in the general life of the South, the man who screams in panic that some black buck is about to rape his sister is speaking of one who is, indeed, his brother, and whom secretly he loves. But the event of such love is only guilt and death and a retreat into a dark house, already sacked and gutted in a war fought to maintain the order which had bred the relationship itself. Sutpen and his Negro bride had already mated, already produced a child neither white nor black; and the frustration of a second incestuous match saves nothing. It serves only to prevent the grafting onto the narrow, Protestant provincialism of the rural South of a Catholic and urban grace, nurtured in Creole New Orleans. The adulterated Sutpen line eventuates not in the sensuous, elegant hybrid that might have been produced out of a mating of Charles Bon and Sutpen's white daughter, but in Jim Bond, mindless child of the offspring of Bon's self-punishing marriage to an ignorant, ugly Negress: "... there was nothing left now, nothing out there now but that idiot boy to lurk around those ashes and those four gutted chimneys and howl until someone came and drove him away. They couldn't catch him and nobody ever seemed to make him go very far away, he just stopped howling for a little while."

Jim Bond (the name which meant "good" corrupted to one which means "slave") is not so much living flesh and blood as the terrible ghost that haunts the mind of such Southerners as Quentin Compson, who has been driven to uncover step by step the mystery of the Sutpens, and who represents the conscience of Faulkner himself. No wonder he grows frantic under his roommate's questioning: " 'Now I want you to tell me just one thing more. Why do you hate the South?' 'I don't hate it,' Quentin said, quickly, at once, immediately; 'I don't hate it,' he said. *I dont hate it* he thought, panting in the cold air, the iron New England dark; *I dont. I dont! I dont hate it! I dont hate it!*" These are the final words of the book; but they are followed by a genealogy, in which we read of Quentin Compson that he died in the very year in which he uncovered the secret of the death of Charles Bon, not yet twenty years old: a suicide, we learn in another place. It is the only possible ending to a novel in which the "Southern" as a genre reaches its final form. At the same time that *Absalom, Absalom!* solves the detective-story problem of who killed Charles Bon, it is answering another, profounder question, satisfying the Southerner's need to "know at last why God let us lose the war." The query is as desperate as that posed by Captain Delano: "What has cast such a shadow upon you?" And the answer is the same: "The Negro."

Yet the theme we have been examining does not exhaust the meanings of Faulkner's book. It represents only a single strand in an intricately constructed and immensely complex work, a showpiece of sustained rhetoric, whose total effect makes it at first bewildering, but which, in the long run, proves the most deeply moving of all American gothic fictions. In the history of that genre, *Absalom, Absalom!* is remarkable for having first joined to the theme of slavery and black revenge, which is the essential sociological theme of the American tale of terror, that of incest, which is its essential erotic theme. Poe had already treated the latter subject in his shorter fictions, though in his work it is kept quite separate from the subject of the encounter of Negro and white. In Faulkner's early book, *The Sound and the Fury* (1929), it is thus isolated, too, functioning as fantasy rather than fact, the private horror of a family drama only incidentally connected with larger social problems. So also Faulkner deals by itself with the theme of miscegenation in *Light in August*, throughout which Joe Christmas revenges himself upon the world of women by informing each new girl as he lies beside her in bed, that he is a Negro! Not until *Absalom, Absalom!*, however, does he find a story in which he can project the dual theme of incest and miscegenation, which was the concern of Cooper and Twain and that of Edgar Allan Poe.

V

EUGENE ARDEN

The Early Harlem Novel

Three fine novels published within the past few years give eloquent testimony to the continued vigor of "the Harlem novel," as compared, for example, to the disappearing "immigrant novel." The variety alone impresses us: Eugene Brown's *Trespass* delicately probes the implications of a Negro-white love affair; William Krasner's *North of Welfare* surveys the violence of the "dark ghetto's" slums and gangs; and Evan Hunter's *Blackboard Jungle* brings to dramatic focus all the vague stories we hear about teachers' problems in a "bad" neighborhood.

The Harlem novel has, in short, come of age. The setting now lends itself to good and bad fiction, to delicate psychological exploration or to social propaganda, and addresses itself both to special readership and to the general public.

I propose to look back, however, and describe something of the beginning of Harlem fiction, and to remind the reader of a nearly forgotten but nearly great novel which was the forerunner of the whole school. The novel I speak of is Paul Laurence Dunbar's *The Sport of the Gods* (1902), the first novel to treat Negro life in New York seriously and at length.

A naturalistic novel, *The Sport of the Gods* embodies something of the "plantation-school concept,"[1] which implies that the Negro becomes homesick and demoralized in the urban North. The inexperienced youths in this novel, Joe and Kitty Hamilton, migrate from the South to a treacherous New York environment which deterministically produces their degeneration and disaster. When Joe Hamilton finally strangles his mis-

Reprinted from *Phylon*, 20 (1959), 25–31, by permission of the editor of *Phylon*.

[1] Hugh M. Gloster, *Negro Voices in American Fiction* (Chapel Hill, 1948), p. 46.

tress after many sordid scenes, a character in the novel exclaims:

Here is another example of the pernicious influences of the city on untrained negroes. Oh, is there no way to keep these people from rushing away from the small villages and country districts of the South up to cities, where they cannot battle with the terrible force of a strange and unusual environment?

The answer is that

the stream of young negro life would continue to flow up from the South, dashing itself against the hard necessities of the city and breaking like waves against the rock,—that until the gods grew tired of their cruel sport.[2]

The attitude of the Hamiltons toward New York and their experiences in the city follow a familiar pattern, reminiscent of all "evil city" folklore. In *The Sport of the Gods*, New York at first represents a promised land of freedom, where the protagonists expect to shed their troubles and start a fresh happy life.

They had heard of New York as a place vague and far away, a city that, like Heaven, to them had existed by faith alone. All the days of their lives they had heard about it, and it seemed to them like the centre of all the glory, all the wealth, and all the freedom in the world. New York. It had an alluring sound.[3]

But fate in this naturalistic novel is inexorable, and the forces of the city, so alluring and yet so disastrous to the inexperienced, quickly demoralize Joe and then his sister Kitty. A visit to the Banner Club—"a social cesspool"—starts Joe's decline, and a place in the chorus starts Kitty on a life which includes "experiences" obviously leading to no good end for her.

At the time Dunbar wrote this novel, there was not yet a Harlem as we know it today. Just after the turn of the century, most of New York's Negroes lived in cramped quarters near the Pennsylvania Railroad Station (the region to which the Hamilton family went on arrival), or else wedged in amongst the Irish on San Juan Hill. Another colony existed on West 53rd Street, but the Negroes there were mainly stage folk, mu-

[2] Paul Laurence Dunbar, *The Sport of the Gods* (New York, 1902), pp. 212, 213–14.

[3] *Ibid.*, pp. 77–78.

sicians, and journalists—and even there the over-crowding was notorious.

By the turn of the century, more room somewhere on the island of Manhattan had to be made for the Negro. The needed space was found in Harlem, a district which had been by-passed by many of the white people expanding north into new sections. In 1905 an apartment in one nearly empty building on 134th Street near Fifth Avenue was rented to a Negro family, and soon the rest of the building was filled up by Negroes who followed. Other apartment buildings were then opened to Negro tenancy, the area spreading westward to Seventh Avenue by 1910. In the two decades that followed, the Negro population in New York grew from less than sixty thousand to more than two hundred thousand, most of the arrivals settling in Harlem. The greatest increase took place during the First World War, when many Southern Negroes flocked to Northern industrial centers and swelled the established Negro communities.

For a time, the white residents did everything possible to stem the tide. They attempted to buy up houses occupied by colored tenants and have them vacated; they strove to prevent white realtors from selling or renting to Negroes.[4] But it was all to no avail. One great factor, that of money, worked in the Negroes' favor. Needing the apartments so desperately, they paid two or three times as much rental as the whites. Downtown they were badly cramped for space, and repeated incidents of interracial strife were breaking out in Hell's Kitchen, the Tenderloin, and San Juan Hill. The Negroes arriving from the South served further to increase the pressure to expand the Harlem beachhead. By the end of the first Great War, the battle for Harlem was settled decisively in the Negroes' favor.

Their victory, however, was to prove a bitter one. Forced to pay exorbitant rents, families had to double up in apartments to meet the rentals, and even then extra boarders had to be taken in. Every space was utilized—sometimes even bathrooms were improvised to serve as extra bedrooms.[5] Thus did Harlem become the most densely settled Negro community in the world, extending from 125th Street to 147th Street between Fifth and

[4] Claude McKay, *Harlem: Negro Metropolis* (New York, 1940), pp. 16–20.

[5] *Ibid.*

Eighth Avenues, and soon to press downtown to meet the Puerto Ricans surging up from 110th Street.

In the 1920's Harlem and its celebrities began to attract wide attention, white folk swarming into the "black ghetto" in the search of "exuberant escape in the so-called exotic primitivism of Negro cabaret life."[6] In fiction, Carl Van Vechten was the first to capitalize successfully on the new, swarming Harlem, though he and his imitators were really following the lead of Dunbar in treating the comparatively unworked scenes of Harlem low-life. Indeed, Van Vechten expressed the indebtedness of his *Nigger Heaven* (1926) to Dunbar's *The Sport of the Gods* by writing that Dunbar

described the plight of a young outsider who comes to the larger New York Negro world to make his fortune, but who falls a victim to the sordid snares of that world, a theme I elaborated in 1926 to fit a newer and much more intricate social system.[7]

That "intricate social system," however, gets lost in the sensationalism of *Nigger Heaven*, which paints Harlem with too obvious a gusto. Van Vechten must have been fascinated by the barbaric rhythms of Negro jazz, the intoxicating dances, and the wild abandon of cabaret life after midnight; or at any rate, he must have known that his readers would be. His book enjoyed immediate popularity and became, according to Hugh M. Gloster, "a sort of guide book for visitors who went uptown seeking a re-creation of the primitive African jungle in the heart of New York City." The songs and snatches of the "blues" by Langston Hughes incorporated into the text of *Nigger Heaven* also helped to enhance the reputation of the book. Roi Ottley, in another study of Harlem, joined in crediting the Van Vechten novel with doing much to establish Harlem as a great vogue; Ottley also points out, however, that the loose money and the jazziness of the 'Twenties were basically responsible for Harlem's short happy career as the Mecca of the thrill-seeker.[8]

But the sensational qualities of *Nigger Heaven* do not obscure

[6] Gloster, *op. cit.*, p. 113.

[7] Carl Van Vechten, "Introduction," in James W. Johnson, *Autobiography of an Ex-Coloured Man* (New York, 1928), p. vii.

[8] Gloster, *op. cit.*, p. 158; and Roi Ottley, *New World A-Coming* (Boston, 1943), p. 66.

the fact that Van Vechten had much of serious interest to say about the urban Negro. The major problem he discusses is the rejection of the Negro by a predominantly white society. There are no sermons pleading "tolerance," but the injustice of segregation is expressed by one character who bitterly remarks, "A white prostitute can go places where a coloured preacher would be refused admission."[9]

Much more subtle, however, is the whole conflict between the growing race consciousness of the Negro and the opposite pressure of the white society, a conflict which turned Negro against Negro. Reflecting the "Africa for Africans" movement led by Marcus Aurelius Garvey in the years just following the First World War, the Negro intelligentsia demonstrated a rousing enthusiasm for primitive African art pieces and Negro folk spirituals, matters which figure predominantly in the characterization of Mary Love in this novel. But in spite of all the outward signs of chauvinism, the Negro world of Harlem made frantic attempts to emulate white cultural values. Mary speaks heatedly, for example, of advertising statistics which showed that "her race spent more money on hair-straighteners and skin-lightening preparations than they did on food and clothing."[10] The way to success for a Negro, to put it as plainly as possible, was to be as much a white as possible, to be something, in short, which he was not.

This pressure to conform and imitate was bound to produce all sorts of disruptive tensions, both personal and communal. The Negroes' problem, like the immigrants' problem, was that of the outsider. The "ghetto," both for immigrants and Negroes, was not only geographical but cultural. To leave one's own "kind" in favor of the great, white, "American" world was possible only after an intense conflict of loyalties. Van Vechten cleverly organized these tensions around one central and provocative consideration: that the Negroes have succumbed to white values to such a degree that amongst the Negroes themselves there is a pervasive system of color prejudice. The very dark, kinky-haired, negroid-featured of them were at the bottom of the social ladder, which was a situation not peculiar to New York alone or to the Jazz Age. Charles W. Chesnutt had earlier described a Cleveland "Blue Vein Club" among Negroes

9 Carl Van Vechten, *Nigger Heaven* (New York, 1926), p. 46.
10 *Ibid.*, p. 11.

in *The Wife of His Youth and Other Stories of the Color Line* (1899). The protagonist of the title story in this collection must choose between the faithful black wife of his youth and a refined "light" woman of his own caste. The problem in each case is rooted in a compulsive urge to imitate white values and the attacks of conscience which inevitably follow.

At the top of the ladder were those Negroes for whom it was possible to pass as white, a decision often made on the basis of disillusionment. Dick Sill, a cynic who "passes," hotly defends his position to Byron, the young hero of Van Vechten's novel, who has just returned to Harlem from the University of Pennsylvania. Dick is a lawyer, but, he says, "the race doesn't want colored lawyers. If they're in trouble they go to white lawyers, and they go to white banks and white insurance companies. . . . Most of 'em . . . pray to a white God. You won't get much help from the race."[11]

Byron, living amongst such tensions, is himself a sorry figure of confusion. Outwardly, he is a model hero of fiction: he is handsome, well-educated, comes to Harlem with letters of introduction to influential leaders, and is loved by women both good and bad. Actually, his way of living becomes more and more dissolute, and he spends much time whining that the whole world is against him. He wants to be a writer and he is living in a Negro metropolis which is practically unknown in any real sense to the outside world; but he insists upon writing wild melodramatic tales of miscegenation completely outside the realm of his experience. We are not surprised that his stay in Harlem ends abruptly with an act of sordid, pointless violence.

Claude McKay's *Home to Harlem* (1928) bears many similarities to *Nigger Heaven*, though McKay has insisted that he is in no way indebted to Van Vechten. The germ of *Home to Harlem* was supposed to be a 1925 short story of McKay's which had been entered without success in a contest conducted by *Opportunity* magazine. Although *Nigger Heaven* was published in 1926, McKay explains that he did not read it until 1927, by which time he had almost completed the expansion of his two-year-old short story into a novel.[12] To the reader in 1928,

---

[11] *Ibid.*, p. 119.

[12] Claude McKay, *A Long Way from Home* (New York, 1937), pp. 282–83.

however, McKay's novel must have seemed very much a part of the Van Vechten vogue, in its descriptive tours through Harlem's cabarets, pool rooms, gambling dives, dance halls, and houses of prostitution.

As in *Nigger Heaven*, the more sensational elements of the novel are balanced by the treatment of serious racial questions. The two main characters are Jake, who deserts the United States Army in Brest because he is put to work in a labor battalion rather than allowed to fight, and his friend Ray, a sensitive, well-educated Negro who has an aversion for Harlem low-life. Confused by a social order under white domination, Ray can see no meaning to his existence, and can find none in his wide reading. Dimly he begins to feel that his education has shackled rather than freed him and that his greatest content-ment would be to lose himself "in some savage culture in the jungles of Africa."[13]

Another novel of the Van Vechten type is Wallace Thur-man's *The Blacker the Berry* (1929) about Emma Lou Morgan, whose black skin alienates her from a light-skinned family in Idaho, from her classmates at the University of Southern Cali-fornia, and finally from her Harlem lover, a mulatto-Filipino. There is the familar exploitation of Harlem local color in scenes of midnight vaudeville shows, ballroom dances, and frenzied drinking in speakeasies. The very material, in other words, which had once been regarded as destructive in the "evil city" novel, was now manipulated to suggest a romantic view of the big city. Gaiety in New York came to mean living in a state just this side of hysteria; and the Harlem tour began to loom as large as the Rockies in the imagination of the tourists.

It is clear that by the end of the 1920's a stereotyped Negro of Harlem had been created, acknowledged, and assumed; his existence seemed confined to drink, sex, gambling, and brooding about racial matters, with an edge of violence always in view. In attempting to distinguish the new Negro from what had been the "typical Negro" in earlier fiction—"no minstrel coon off the stage, no Thomas Nelson Page's nigger, no Octavus Roy Cohen's porter, no lineal descendant of Uncle Tom"[14]—the Van Vechten-McKay-Thurman school created another type as damaging and unrepresentative as that which was replaced.

---

[13] Claude McKay, *Home to Harlem* (New York, 1928), p. 274.

[14] *Ibid.*, pp. 63–64.

Amongst the Harlem writers themselves, a counter-movement of realism in Negro fiction grew and was given impetus by Rudolf Fisher and the influential Countee Cullen. Less interested in the exotic and animalistic aspects of Negro life, Fisher and Cullen attempted to provide a more representative picture which would show that in Harlem, too, there was some regard for quiet living, hard work, serious thinking, and mature standards of morality.

The Walls of Jericho (1928) by Fisher realistically describes the general social life of Harlem, including glimpses of church life, the Sunday promenade on Seventh Avenue, and the annual costume ball of the General Improvement Association (an organization probably suggested by the National Association for the Advancement of Colored People). The Harlem scene is treated with considerable detachment, and Fisher masters the Harlem slang so skillfully that he has been called the peer of Ring Lardner in idiomatic writing.[15]

Countee Cullen's personal background fitted him admirably to write *One Way to Heaven* (1932), a novel which deals intimately with the place of church and religion in the lives of Negroes in Harlem. The son of Reverend Frederick A. Cullen, founder of the Salem Methodist Episcopal Church, Countee Cullen is able to include descriptions of watch-night meetings, conversions of sinners, and other services of the African Methodist Episcopal Church, all of which bear the mark of authenticity. The job of the Negro writer, Cullen once said, is to "create types that are truly representative of us as a people,"[16] thus explaining both the strength and the weakness of his novel. *One Way to Heaven* offers a sane, realistic picture of typical Negro urban life; but it also suffers by the creation of types rather than individuals, and by a looseness of construction which strings the events together in such a way as to make their sequence seem almost accidental. Cullen, for all his good intentions, thus emerges as a less compelling novelist than Van Vechten or even Claude McKay, though when taken together, the exotics and the realists were already suggesting that Harlem offered the materials for extraordinary fiction.

Perhaps the most important thing to say about the Harlem novel is the most obvious: a new character in American fiction

15 Gloster, *op. cit.*, p. 177.
16 "The Negro in Art," *The Crisis*, XXXII (August, 1926), 193.

was created. Just as the plantation Negro was typical of nineteenth-century fiction, so in our own day the prototype was the Negro in an urban, industrial environment. There he was confronted with new pressures evolving from a new *mise en scène* and a set of social imperatives different from those which had once dominated his tradition. The process of choice sometimes proved ennobling and sometimes corrosive. The novels which sought to represent him found a need for newer and larger dimensions, for this urban Negro was more pliable, less likely to fit into stock categories than any of the earlier Negro characters. The Harlem novel, in short, has made possible the development of such variety in characterization that a third dimension has at last been added to the Negro in fiction.

VI

RALPH ELLISON

Twentieth-Century Fiction and the Black Mask of Humanity

Perhaps the most insidious and least understood form of segregation is that of the word. And by this I mean the word in all its complex formulations, from the proverb to the novel and stage play, the word with all its subtle power to suggest and foreshadow overt action while magically disguising the moral consequences of that action and providing it with symbolic and psychological justification. For if the word has the potency to revive and make us free, it has also the power to blind, imprison, and destroy.

The essence of the word is its ambivalence, and in fiction it is never so effective and revealing as when both potentials are operating simultaneously, as when it mirrors both good and bad, as when it blows both hot and cold in the same breath. Thus it is unfortunate for Negroes that the most powerful formulations of modern American fictional words have been so slanted against him that when he approaches for a glimpse of himself he discovers an image drained of humanity.

Obviously the experiences of Negroes—slavery, the grueling and continuing fight for full citizenship since Emancipation, the

With the publication of this essay in *Confluence*, Mr. Ellison requested the editor to print the following note: "When I started rewriting this essay it occurred to me that its value might be somewhat increased if it remained very much as I wrote it during 1946. For in that form it is what a young member of a minority felt about much of our writing. Thus I've left in much of the bias and shortsightedness, for it says perhaps as much about me as a member of a minority as it does about literature. I hope you still find the essay useful, and I'd like to see an editorial note stating that this is an unpublished piece written not long after the 2nd World War."

stigma of color, the enforced alienation which constantly knifes into our natural identification with our country—have not been that of white Americans. And though as passionate believers in democracy Negroes identify themselves with the broader American ideals, their sense of reality springs, in part, from an American experience which most white men not only have not had, but one with which they are reluctant to identify themselves even when presented in forms of the imagination. Thus when the white American, holding up most twentieth-century fiction, says, "This is American reality," the Negro tends to answer (not at all concerned that Americans tend generally to fight against any but the most flattering imaginative depictions of their lives), "Perhaps, but you've left out this, and this, and this. And most of all, what you'd have the world accept as *me* isn't even human."

Nor does he refer only to second-rate works but to those of our most representative authors. Either like Hemingway and Steinbeck (in whose joint works I recall not more than five American Negroes) they tend to ignore them, or like the early Faulkner, who distorted Negro humanity to fit his personal versions of Southern myth, they seldom conceive Negro characters possessing the full, complex ambiguity of the human. Too often what is presented as the American Negro (a most complex example of Western man) emerges an oversimplified clown, a beast, or an angel. Seldom is he drawn as that sensitively focused process of opposites, of good and evil, of instinct and intellect, of passion and spirituality, which great literary art has projected as the image of man. Naturally the attitude of Negroes toward this writing is one of great reservation. Which, indeed, bears out Richard Wright's remark that there is in progress between black and white Americans a struggle over the nature of reality.

Historically this is but a part of that larger conflict between older, dominant groups of white Americans, especially the Anglo-Saxons, on the one hand, and the newer white and non-white groups on the other, over the major group's attempt to impose its ideals upon the rest, insisting that its exclusive image be accepted as *the* image of the American. This conflict should not, however, be misunderstood. For despite the impact of the American idea upon the world, the "American" himself has not (fortunately for the United States, its minorities, and perhaps for the world) been finally defined. So that far from being socially undesirable this struggle between Americans as to what the American is to be is part of that democratic process through which the nation works to achieve itself. Out of this conflict the ideal American character—a type truly great enough to possess the greatness of the land, a delicately poised unity of divergencies—is slowly being born.

I

But we are concerned here with fiction, not history. How is it then that our naturalistic prose—one of the most vital bodies of twentieth-century fiction, perhaps the brightest instrument for recording sociological fact, physical action, the nuance of speech, yet achieved—becomes suddenly dull when confronting the Negro?

Obviously there is more in this than the mere verbal counterpart of lynching or segregation. Indeed, it represents a projection of processes lying at the very root of American culture and certainly at the central core of its twentieth-century literary forms, a matter having less to do with the mere "reflection" of white racial theories than with processes molding the attitudes, the habits of mind, the cultural atmosphere, and the artistic and intellectual traditions that condition men dedicated to democracy to practice, accept, and, most crucial of all, often blind themselves to the essentially undemocratic treatment of their fellow citizens.

It should be noted here that the moment criticism approaches Negro-white relationships it is plunged into problems of psychology and symbolic ritual. Psychology because the distance between Americans, Negroes and whites, is not so much spatial as psychological; while they might dress and often look alike, seldom on deeper levels do they think alike. Ritual because the Negroes of fiction are so consistently false to human life that we must question just what they truly represent, both in the literary work and in the inner world of the White American.[1]

---

[1] Perhaps the ideal approach to the work of literature would be one allowing for insight into the deepest psychological motives of the writer at the same time that it examined all external sociological factors operating within a given milieu. For while objectively a social reality, the work of art is, in its genesis, a projection of a deeply personal process, and any approach that ignores the personal at the expense of the social is neces-

Despite their billings as images of reality, these Negroes of fiction are counterfeits. They are projected aspects of an internal symbolic process through which, like a primitive tribesman dancing himself into the group frenzy necessary for battle, the white American prepares himself emotionally to perform a social role. These fictive Negroes are not, as sometimes interpreted, simple racial clichés introduced into society by a ruling class to control political and economic realities. For although they are manipulated to that end, such an externally one-sided interpretation relieves the individual of personal responsibility for the health of democracy. Not only does it forget that a democracy is a collectivity of *individuals*, but it never suspects that the tenacity of the stereotype springs exactly from the fact that its function is no less personal than political. Color prejudice springs not from the stereotype alone, but from an internal psychological state; not from misinformation alone, but from an inner need to believe. It thrives not only on the obscene witch-doctoring of men like Jimmy Byrnes and Malan, but upon an inner craving for symbolic magic. The prejudiced individual creates his own stereotypes very often unconsciously by reading into situations involving Negroes those stock meanings which justify his emotional and economic needs.

Hence whatever else the Negro stereotype might be as a social instrumentality it is also a key figure in a magic rite by which the white American seeks to resolve the dilemma arising between his democratic beliefs and certain antidemocratic practices, between his acceptance of the sacred democratic belief that all men are created equal and his treatment of every tenth man as though he were not.

Thus on the moral level I propose that we view the whole of American life as a drama acted out upon the body of a Negro giant, who, lying trussed up like Gulliver, forms the stage and the scene upon which and within which the action unfolds. If

---

sarily incomplete. Thus when we approach contemporary writing from the perspective of segregation, as is commonly done by sociology-minded thinkers, we automatically limit ourselves to one external aspect of a complex whole, which leaves us little to say concerning its personal, internal elements. On the other hand, American writing has been one of the most important twentieth-century literatures, and though negative as a social force it is technically brilliant and emotionally powerful. Hence were we to examine it for its embodiment of these positive values there would be other more admiring things to be said.

we examine the beginning of the Colonies, the application of this view is not, in its economic connotations at least, too far-fetched nor too difficult to see. For then the Negro's body was exploited as amorally as the soil and climate. It was later, when white men drew up a plan for a democratic way of life, that the Negro began slowly to exert an influence upon America's moral consciousness. Gradually he was recognized as the human factor placed outside the democratic master plan, a human "natural" resource who, so that white men could become more human, was elected to undergo a process of institutionalized dehumanization.

Until the Korean War this moral role had become obscured within the staggering growth of contemporary science and industry, but during the nineteenth-century it flared nakedly in the American consciousness, only to be repressed after the Reconstruction. During periods of national crisis when the United States rounds a sudden curve on the pitch-black road of history, this moral awareness surges in the white American's conscience like a raging river revealed at his feet by a lightning flash. Only then is the veil of anti-Negro myths, symbols, stereotypes, and taboos drawn somewhat aside. And when we look closely at our literature it is to be seen operating even when the Negro seems most patently the little man who isn't there.

II

I see no value either in presenting a catalogue of Negro characters appearing in twentieth-century fiction or in charting the racial attitudes of white writers. We are interested not in quantities but in qualities. And since it is impossible here to discuss the entire body of this writing, the next best thing is to select a framework in which the relationships with which we are concerned may be clearly seen. For brevity let us take three representative writers: Mark Twain, Hemingway, and Faulkner. Twain for historical perspective and as an example of how a great nineteenth-century writer handled the Negro, Hemingway as the prime example of the artist who ignored the dramatic and symbolic possibilities presented by this theme, and Faulkner as an example of a writer who has confronted Negroes with such mixed motives that he has presented them in terms of both the "good nigger" and the "bad nigger"

stereotypes, and who yet has explored perhaps more successfully than anyone else, either white or black, certain forms of
Negro humanity.

For perspective let us begin with Mark Twain's great classic,
Huckleberry Finn. Recall that Huckleberry has run away from
his father, Miss Watson, and the Widow Douglas (indeed the
whole community, in relation to which he is a young outcast)
and has with him as companion on the raft upon which they are
sailing down the Mississippi the Widow Watson's runaway
Negro slave, Jim. Recall too that Jim, during the critical moment of the novel, is stolen by two scoundrels and sold to
another master, presenting Huck with the problem of freeing
Jim once more. Two ways are open: he can rely upon his own
ingenuity and "steal" Jim into freedom or he might write the
Widow Watson and request reward money to have Jim returned to her. But there is a danger in this course, remember,
since the angry widow might sell the slave down the river into
a harsher slavery. It is this course which Huck starts to take, but
as he composes the letter he wavers.

"It was a close place," he tells us, "I took [the letter] up, and held
it in my hand. I was trembling, because I'd got to decide, forever,
'twixt two things, and I knowed it. I studied a minute, sort of holding my breath, and then says to myself:

" 'Alright, then, I'll *go* to hell'—and tore it up, . . . It was awful
thoughts and awful words, but they was said . . . And I let them
stay said, and never thought no more about reforming. I shoved the
whole thing out of my head and said I would take up wickedness
again, which was in my line, being brung up to it, and the others
warn't. And for a starter I would . . . steal Jim out of slavery
again. . . ."

And a little later, in defending his decision to Tom Sawyer,
Huck comments, "I know you'll say it's dirty, low-down business but *I'm* low-down. And I'm going to steal him . . ."

We have arrived at a key point of the novel and, by an ironic
reversal, of American fiction, a pivotal moment announcing a
change of direction in the plot, a reversal as well as a recognition scene (like that in which Oedipus discovers his true identity) wherein a new definition of necessity is being formulated.
Huck Finn has struggled with the problem poised by the clash
between property rights and human rights, between what the
community considered to be the proper attitude toward an

escaped slave and his knowledge of Jim's humanity, gained through their adventures as fugitives together. He has made his decision on the side of humanity. In this passage Twain has stated the basic moral issue centering around Negroes and the white American's democratic ethics. It dramatizes as well the highest point of tension generated by the clash between the direct, human relationships of the frontier and the abstract, in-human, market-dominated relationships fostered by the rising middle-class—which in Twain's day was already compromising dangerously with the most inhuman aspects of the dispersed slave system. And just as politically these forces reached their sharpest tension in the outbreak of the Civil War, in *Huckle-berry Finn* (both the boy and the novel) their human implica-tions come to sharpest focus around the figure of the Negro.

Huckleberry Finn knew, as did Mark Twain, that Jim was not only a slave but a human being, a man who in some ways was to be envied, and who expressed his essential humanity in his desire for freedom, his will to possess his own labor, in his loyalty and capacity for friendship, and in his love for his wife and child. Yet Twain, though guilty of the sentimentality com-mon to humorists, does not idealize the slave. Jim is drawn in all his ignorance and superstition, with his good traits and his bad. He, like all men, is ambiguous, limited in circumstance but not in possibility. And it will be noted that when Huck makes his decision he identifies himself with Jim and accepts the judg-ment of his superego—that internalized representative of the community—that his action is evil. Like Prometheus, who for mankind stole fire from the gods, he embraces the evil implicit in his act in order to affirm his belief in humanity. Jim, there-fore, is not simply a slave, he is a symbol of humanity, and in freeing Jim Huck makes a bid to free himself of the conven-tionalized evil taken for civilization by the town.

III

This conception of the Negro as a symbol of Man—the reversal of what he represents in most contemporary thought—was organic to nineteenth-century literature. It occurs not only in Twain but in Emerson, Thoreau, Whitman, and Melville (whose symbol of evil, incidentally, was white), all of whom were men publicly involved in various forms of deeply personal rebellion. And while the Negro and the color black were associated with the concept of evil and ugliness far back in the Christian era, the Negro's emergence as a symbol of value came, I believe, with Rationalism and the rise of the romantic individual of the eighteenth century. This, perhaps, because the romantic was in revolt against the old moral authority, and if he suffered a sense of guilt, his passion for personal freedom was such that he was willing to accept evil (a tragic attitude) even to identifying himself with the "noble slave"—who symbolized the darker, unknown potential side of his personality, that underground side, turgid with possibility, which might, if given a chance, toss a fistful of mud into the sky and create a "shining star."

Even that prototype of the bourgeois, Robinson Crusoe, stopped to speculate as to his slave's humanity. And the rising American industrialists of the late nineteenth century were to rediscover what their European counterparts had learned a century before: that the good man Friday was as sound an investment for Crusoe morally as he was economically, for not only did Friday allow Crusoe to achieve himself by working for him, but by functioning as a living scapegoat to contain Crusoe's guilt over breaking with the institutions and authority of the past he made it possible to exploit even his guilt economically. The man was one of the first missionaries.

Mark Twain was alive to this irony and refused such an easy (and dangerous) way out. Huck Finn's acceptance of the evil implicit in his "emancipation" of Jim represents Twain's acceptance of his personal responsibility in the condition of society. This was the tragic face behind his comic mask.

But by the twentieth century this attitude of tragic responsibility had disappeared from our literature along with that broad conception of democracy which vitalized the work of our greatest writers. After Twain's compelling image of black and white fraternity the Negro generally disappears from fiction as a rounded human being. And if already in Twain's time a novel which was optimistic concerning a democracy which would include all men could not escape being banned from public libraries, by our day his great drama of interracial fraternity had become, for most Americans at least, an amusing boy's story and nothing more. But, while a boy, Huck Finn has become by the somersault motion of what William Empson terms "pastoral" an embodiment of the heroic, and an exponent of humanism. Indeed, the historical and artistic justification for his adolescence lies in the fact that Twain was depicting a transitional period of American life; its artistic justification is that adolescence is the time of the "great confusion" during which both individuals and nations flounder between accepting and rejecting the responsibilities of adulthood. Accordingly, Huck's relationship to Jim, the river, and all they symbolize, is that of a humanist; in his relation to the community he is an individualist. He embodies the two major conflicting drives operating in nineteenth-century America. And if humanism is man's basic attitude toward a social order which he accepts, and individualism his basic attitude toward one he rejects, one might say that Twain, by allowing these two attitudes to argue dialectically in his work of art, was as highly moral an artist as he was a believer in democracy, and vice versa.

IV

History, however, was to bring an ironic reversal to the direction which Huckleberry Finn chose, and by our day the divided ethic of the community had won out. In contrast with Twain's humanism, individualism was thought to be the only tenable attitude for the artist.

Thus we come to Ernest Hemingway, one of the two writers whose art is based most solidly upon Mark Twain's language, and one who perhaps has done most to extend Twain's technical influence upon our fiction. It was Hemingway who pointed out that all modern American writing springs from *Huckleberry Finn*. (One might add here that equally as much of it derives from Hemingway himself.) But by the twenties the element of rejection implicit in Twain had become so dominant an attitude of the American writer that Hemingway goes on to warn us to "stop where the Nigger Jim is stolen from the boys. That is the real end. The rest is just cheating."

So thoroughly had the Negro, both as man and as a symbol of man, been pushed into the underground of the American conscience that Hemingway missed completely the structural, symbolic and moral necessity for that part of the plot in which the boys rescue Jim. Yet it is precisely this part which gives the novel its significance. Without it, except as a boy's tale, the novel is meaningless. Yet Hemingway, a great artist in his own right, speaks as a victim of that culture of which he is himself so critical, for by his time that growing rift in the ethical fabric pointed out by Twain had become completely sundered—snagged upon the irrepressible moral reality of the Negro. Instead of the single democratic ethic for every man, there now existed two: one, the idealized ethic of the Constitution and the Declaration of Independence, reserved for white men, and the other, the pragmatic ethic designed for Negroes and other minorities, which took the form of discrimination. Twain had dramatized the conflict leading to this division in its earlier historical form, but what was new here was that such a moral division, always a threat to the sensitive man, was ignored by the artist except in the most general terms, as when Hemingway rails against the rhetoric of the First World War.

Hemingway's blindness to the moral values of *Huckleberry Finn* despite his sensitivity to its technical aspects duplicated the one-sided vision of the twenties. Where Twain, seeking for what Melville called "the common continent of man," drew upon the rich folklore of the frontier (not omitting the Negro's) in order to "Americanize" his idiom, thus broadening his stylistic appeal, Hemingway was alert only to Twain's technical discoveries—the flexible colloquial language, the sharp naturalism, the thematic potentialities of adolescence. Thus what for Twain was a means to a moral end became for Hemingway an end in itself. And just as the trend toward technique for the sake of technique, and production for the sake of the market, lead to the neglect of the human need out of which they spring, so does it lead in literature to a marvelous technical virtuosity won at the expense of a gross insensitivity to fraternal values.

It is not accidental that the disappearance of the human Negro from our fiction coincides with the disappearance of deep-probing doubt and a sense of evil. Not that doubt in some form was not always present, as the works of the lost generation, the muckrakers, and the proletarian writers make very clear. But it is a shallow doubt, which seldom turns inward upon the writer's own values; almost always it focuses outward, upon some scapegoat with which he is seldom able to identify himself as Huck Finn identified himself with the scoundrels who stole Jim and with Jim himself. This particular naturalism explored everything except the nature of man.

And when the artist would no longer conjure with the chief

moral problem in American life, he was defeated as a manipulator of profound social passions. In the United States, as in Europe, the triumph of industrialism had repelled the artist with the blatant hypocrisy between its ideals and its acts. But while in Europe the writer became the most profound critic of these matters, in our country he either turned away or was at best half-hearted in his opposition—perhaps because any profound probing of human values, both within himself and within society, would have brought him face to face with the rigidly tabooed subject of the Negro. And now the tradition of avoiding the moral struggle had led not only to the artistic segregation of the Negro but to the segregation of real fraternal, i.e., democratic, values.

The hard-boiled school represented by Hemingway, for instance, is usually spoken of as a product of World War I disillusionment, yet it was as much the product of a tradition which arose even before the Civil War—that tradition of intellectual evasion for which Thoreau criticized Emerson in regard to the Fugitive Slave Law, and which had been growing swiftly since the failure of the ideals in whose name the Civil War was fought. The failure to resolve the problem symbolized by the Negro has contributed indirectly to the dispossession of the artist in several ways. By excluding its largest minority from the democratic process it made for the weakening of all national symbols by rendering sweeping public rituals dramatizing the American dream impossible; it robbed the artist of a body of unassailable public beliefs upon which he could base his art; it deprived him of a personal faith in the ideals upon which society supposedly rested; and it provided him with no tragic mood indigenous to his society upon which he could erect a tragic art. The result was that he responded with an attitude of rejection, which he expressed as artistic individualism. But too often both his rejection and individualism were narrow; seldom was he able to transcend the limitations of pragmatic reality, and the quality of moral imagination—the fountainhead of great art—was atrophied within him.

Malraux has observed that contemporary American writing is the only important literature not created by intellectuals, and that the creators possess "neither the relative historical culture, nor the love of ideas (a prerogative of professors in the United States)" of comparable Europeans. And is there not a connection between the non-intellectual aspects of this writing (though many of the writers are far more intellectual than they admit or than Malraux would suspect) and its creators' rejection of broad social responsibility, between its non-concern with ideas and its failure to project characters who grasp the broad sweep of American life, or who even attempt to state its fundamental problems? And has not this affected the types of heroes of this fiction, is it not a partial explanation of why it has created no characters possessing broad insight into their situations or the emotional, psychological, and intellectual complexity which would allow them to possess and articulate a truly democratic world view?

V

It is instructive that Hemingway, born into a civilization characterized by violence, should seize upon the ritualized violence of the culturally distant Spanish bullfight as a laboratory for developing his style. For it was, for Americans, an amoral violence (though not for the Spaniards) which he was seeking. Otherwise he might have studied that ritual of violence closer to home, that ritual in which the sacrifice is that of a human scapegoat, the lynching bee. Certainly this rite is not confined to the rope as agency, nor to the South as scene, nor even to the Negro as victim.

But let us not confuse the conscious goals of twentieth-century fiction with those of the nineteenth century, let us take it on its own terms. Artists such as Hemingway were seeking a technical perfection rather than moral insight. (Or should we say that theirs was a morality of technique?) They desired a style stripped of unessentials, one that would appeal without resorting to what was considered worn-out rhetoric, or best of all without any rhetoric whatsoever. It was felt that through the default of the powers that ruled society the artist had as his major task the "pictorial presentation of the evolution of a personal problem." Instead of recreating and extending the national myth as he did this, the writer now restricted himself to elaborating his personal myth. And although naturalist in his general style, he was not interested, like Balzac, in depicting a society, or even, like Mark Twain, in portraying the moral situation of a nation. Rather he was engaged in working out a personal problem through the evocative, emotion-charged images and ritual-therapy available through the manipulation of art forms. And while art was still an instrument of freedom, it was now mainly the instrument of a questionable personal freedom for the artist, which too often served to enforce the "unfreedom" of the reader.

This because it is not within the province of the artist to determine whether his work is social or not. Art by its nature *is* social. And while the artist can determine within a certain narrow scope the type of social effect he wishes his art to create, here his will is definitely limited. Once introduced into society, the work of art begins to pulsate with those meanings, emotions, ideas, brought to it by its audience and over which the artist has no control. The irony of the "lost generation" writers is that while disavowing a social role it was the fate of their works to perform a social function which reenforced those very social values which they most violently opposed. How could this be? Because in its genesis the work of art, like the stereotype, is personal; psychologically it represents the socialization of some profoundly personal problem involving guilt (often symbolic murder—parricide, fratricide—incest, homosexuality, all problems at the base of personality) from which by expressing them along with other elements (images, memories, emotions, ideas) he seeks transcendence. To be effective as personal fulfillment, if it is to be more than dream, the work of art must simultaneously evoke images of reality and give them formal organization. And it must, since the individual's emotions are formed in society, shape them into socially meaningful patterns (even Surrealism and Dadaism depended upon their initiates). Nor, as we can see by comparing literature with reportage, is this all. The work of literature differs basically from reportage not merely in its presentation of a pattern of events, nor in its concern with emotion (for a report might well be an account of highly emotional events), but in the deep personal necessity which cries full-throated in the work of art and which seeks transcendence in the form of ritual.

Malcolm Cowley, on the basis of the rites which he believes to be the secret dynamic of Hemingway's work, has identified him with Poe, Hawthorne, and Melville, "the haunted and nocturnal writers," he calls them, "the men who dealt with images that were symbols of an inner world." In Hemingway's work, he writes, "we can recognize rites of animal sacrifice . . . of sexual union . . . of conversion . . . and of symbolic death and rebirth." I do not believe, however, that the presence of these rites in writers like Hemingway is as important as the fact that here, beneath the dead-pan prose, the cadences of understatement, the anti-intellectualism, the concern with every "fundamental" of man except that which distinguishes him from the animal—that here is the twentieth-century form of that magical rite which during periods of great art has been to a large extent public and explicit. Here is the literary form by which the personal guilt of the pulverized individual of our rugged era is expiated: not through his identification with the guilty acts of an Oedipus, a Macbeth, or a Medea, by suffering their agony and loading his sins upon their "strong and passionate shoulders," but by being gored with a bull, hooked with a fish, impaled with a grasshopper on a fish hook; not by identifying himself with human heroes, but with those who are indeed defeated.

On the social level this writing performs a function similar to that of the stereotype: it conditions the reader to accept the less worthy values of society, and it serves to justify and absolve our sins of social irresponsibility. With unconscious irony it advises stoic acceptance of those conditions of life which it so accurately describes and which it pretends to reject. And when I read the early Hemingway I seem to be in the presence of a Huckleberry Finn who, instead of identifying himself with humanity and attempting to steal Jim free, chose to write the letter which sent him back into slavery. So that now he is a Huck full of regret and nostalgia, suffering a sense of guilt that fills even his noondays with nightmares, and against which, like a terrified child avoiding the cracks in the sidewalk, he seeks protection through the compulsive minor rituals of his prose.

The major difference between nineteenth- and twentieth-century writers is not in the latter's lack of personal rituals—a property of all fiction worthy of being termed literature—but in the social effect aroused within their respective readers. Melville's ritual (and his rhetoric) was based upon materials that were more easily available, say, than Hemingway's. They represented a blending of his personal myth with universal myths as traditional as any used by Shakespeare or the Bible, while until *For Whom the Bell Tolls* Hemingway's was weighted on the personal side. The difference in terms of perspective of belief is that Melville's belief could still find a public object. Whatever else his works were "about" they also managed to be about democracy. While by our day the democratic dream had become too shaky a structure to support the furious pressures of the artist's doubt. And, as always when the belief which nurtures a great social myth declines, large sections of society become prey to superstition. For man without myth is Othello with Desdemona gone; chaos descends. faith vanishes and superstitions prowl in the mind.

Hardboiled writing is said to appeal through its presentation of sheer fact, rather than through rhetoric. The writer puts nothing down but what he pragmatically "knows." But actually one "fact" itself—which in literature must be presented simultaneously as image and as event—became a rhetorical unit. And the symbolic ritual which has set off the "fact"—that is, the fact unorganized by vital social myths (which might incorporate the findings of science and still contain elements of mystery)—is the rite of superstition. The superstitious individual responds to the capricious event, the fact that seems to explode in his face through blind fatality. For it is the creative function of myth to protect the individual from the irrational, and since it is here in the realm of the irrational that, impervious to science, the stereotype grows, we see that the Negro stereotype is really an image of the unorganized, irrational forces of American life, forces through which, by projecting them in forms of images of an easily dominated minority, the white individual seeks to be at home in the vast unknown world of America. Perhaps the object of the stereotype is not so much to crush the Negro as to console the white man.

VI

Certainly there is justification for this view when we consider the work of William Faulkner. In Faulkner most of the relationships which we have pointed out between the Negro and contemporary writing come to focus: the social and the personal, the moral and the technical, the nineteenth-century emphasis upon morality and the modern accent upon the personal myth. And on the strictly literary level he is prolific and complex enough to speak for those Southern writers who are aggressively anti-Negro and for those younger writers who appear most sincerely interested in depicting the Negro as a rounded human being. What is more, he is the greatest artist the South has produced. While too complex to be given more than a glance in these notes, even a glance is more revealing of what lies back of the distortion of the Negro in modern writing than any attempt at a group survey might be.

Faulkner's attitude is mixed. Taking his cue from the Southern mentality in which the Negro is often dissociated into a malignant stereotype (the bad nigger) on the one hand and a benign stereotype (the good nigger) on the other, most often Faulkner presents characters embodying both. The dual function of this dissociation seems to be that of avoiding moral pain and thus to justify the South's racial code. But since such a social order harms whites no less than blacks, the sensitive Southerner, the artist, is apt to feel its effects acutely—and within the deepest levels of his personality. For not only is the social division forced upon the Negro by the ritualized ethic of discrimination, but upon the white man by the strictly enforced set of anti-Negro taboos. The conflict is always with him. Indeed, so rigidly has the recognition of Negro humanity been tabooed that the white Southerner is apt to associate any form of personal rebellion with the Negro. So that for the Southern artist the Negro becomes a symbol of his personal rebellion, his guilt, and his repression of it. The Negro is thus a compelling object of fascination, and this we see very clearly in Faulkner.

Sometimes in Faulkner the Negro is simply a villain, but by an unconsciously ironic transvaluation his villainy consists, as with Losh in *The Unvanquished*, of desiring his freedom. Or again the Negro appears benign, as with Ringo, of the same novel, who uses his talent not to seek personal freedom but to remain the loyal and resourceful retainer. Not that I criticize loyalty in itself, but that loyalty given where one's humanity is unrecognized seems a bit obscene. And yet in Faulkner's story, *The Bear*, he brings us as close to the moral implication of the Negro as Twain or Melville. In the famous "difficult" fourth section, which Malcolm Cowley advises us to skip very much as Hemingway would have us skip the end of *Huckleberry Finn*, we find an argument in progress in which one voice (that of a Southern abolitionist) seeks to define Negro humanity against the other's enumeration of those stereotypes which many Southerners believe to be the Negro's basic traits. Significantly, the mentor of the young hero of this story, a man of great moral stature, is socially a Negro.

Indeed, through his many novels and short stories, Faulkner fights out the moral problem which was repressed after the nineteenth century, and it was shocking for some to discover that for all his concern with the South Faulkner was actually seeking out the nature of man. Thus we must turn to him for that continuity of moral purpose which made for the greatness of our classics. As for the Negro minority, he has been more willing perhaps than any other artist to start with the stereotype, accept it as true, and then seek out the human truth which it hides. Perhaps his is the example for our writers to follow, for in his work technique has been put once more to the task of creating value.

Which leaves these final things to be said. First, that this is meant as no plea for white writers to define Negro humanity, but to recognize the broader aspects of their own. Secondly, Negro writers and those of the other minorities have their own task of contributing to the total image of the American by depicting the experience of their own groups. Certainly theirs is the task of defining Negro humanity, as this can no more be accomplished by others than freedom, which must be won again and again each day, can be conferred upon another. A people must define itself, and minorities have the responsibility of having their ideals and images recognized as part of the composite image which is that of the still forming American people.

The other thing to be said is that while it is unlikely that American writing will ever retrace the way to the nineteenth century it might be worth while to point out that for all its technical experimentation it is nevertheless an ethical instrument, and as such it might well exercise some choice in the kind of ethic it prefers to support. The artist is no freer than the society in which he lives, and in the United States the writers who stereotype or ignore the Negro and other minorities in the final analysis stereotype and distort their own humanity. Mark Twain knew that in *his* America humanity masked its face with blackness.

Individual Talents

VII

SIDNEY KAPLAN

Herman Melville and the American National Sin

. . . . Why is there evil in this God-created world? Whence comes the depravity innate in some men? Wherefore, in the words of Paul, the mystery of iniquity? With these problems Herman Melville wrestled hard during his whole life. The struggle was waged not so much in the cloudy terms of theologic tract as in the earth-bound images of a great artist of brain and heart. For the most part it was a ceaseless inner dispute, made public in characters of fiction from Taji to Captain Vere—characters who confronted the specific problems of Melville's own time. It was with fiction as with religion, he would once observe of his own work, "it should present another world, and yet one to which we feel the tie."

What was the world to which Melville felt a tie? In his most creative years it was the world of mid-nineteenth century America during the twenty tense years that stretched from the Mexican to the Civil War. Since the most dramatic and shameless evil of that world was the peculiar institution of Negro slavery—the American national sin, as it were—it is not surprising that from *Typee* in 1846 to the *Battle-Pieces* of 1866 there is scarcely an important item in the Melville canon that does not contain Negro characters or touch in some way on the question of bondage and revolt. Somewhere in the center of this company of black men stands the most elaborately described and controversial figure of them all—that of Babo the slave, monster for some readers, hero for others, to understand whom it will perhaps be helpful to survey the men of color who precede him on Melville's pages.

Reprinted from *Journal of Negro History*, 41 (1956), 311–38; 42 (1957), 11–37, by permission of the Association for the Study of Negro Life and History, Inc., and the author.

Typee, Melville's first book, although it makes only brief mention of one Mungo, a "black cook" aboard the whaler *Dolly*, has many human things to say about people whose skins are dark. True enough, Melville speaks crudely of the "dark-skinned Hawaiians and the wooly-headed Feejees" as "immeasurably inferior" to the "voluptuous Tahitians," and of the Sandwich Islanders, whose monarch is a "negro-looking block head," as "depraved and vicious"—yet this book should not be passed over without noting its clean atmosphere of physical democracy. "He writes of what he has seen *con amore*," commented a reviewer in *Graham's Magazine*, "and at times almost loses his loyalty to civilization and the Anglo-Saxon race." Does not the affair of Fayaway prefigure the "bridegroom clasp" of her countryman, Queequeg?

In *Omoo*, which followed, two Negroes appear: Billy Loon, pounder of the tambourine, one of "a low rabble of foreigners" at the Hawaiian court, and "the poor old black cook" Baltimore, a runaway Maryland slave. Both are stereotypes of the time. Billy Loon, "a jolly little negro," who faintly foreshadows Pip sane in his music and Pip mad in his name, is first of a series of stage-Negro types that Melville will portray, while Baltimore, a stock-character familiar in the sea narratives of the period, as well as in the novels of Cooper, Kennedy, Bird and Simms, will shuffle through Melville's pages from time to time—the old shambling Negro sea-cook, butt of practical jokes by his white mates, the "doctor" of the voyage, whose trials are "indeed sore," but whom Melville will too often display as another minstrel figure. Yet in the treatment of Baltimore there is deep sympathy without the nasty chauvinism so frequently present in other writers.[1] When a deck-climbing wave almost drowns the old cook, the white whalemen roar with laughter.

[1] As for example, in Cooper's *Ned Myers* and Bird's *Nick of the Woods*. Dana's *Two Years Before the Mast* is an honorable exception. A passage from Francis A. Olmsted's *Incidents of a Whaling Voyage* (1841) displays a model that Melville was often to lean on: the cook, Mr. Freeman, "of the ebony race," receives a "serio-comic punishment from the captain and officers every day . . . with his various appelations of 'Spot,' 'Jumb,' 'Congo,' 'Skillet,' 'Kidney foot,' etc. . . . is extremely polite and bids me 'good morning,' with a very graceful bow . . . predicts that 'we are going to have some very plausible weather, so far as the *aspection* of the sky would seem to *elucidate*. . . . The cook with his 'fiddle,' and the steward with his tambourine, hold musical *soirees* on the forecastle every evening in pleasant weather."

"Poor fellow!" comments Melville, "he was altogether too good-natured. Say what they will about easy-tempered people, it is far better, on some accounts, to have the temper of a wolf."

While *Typee* and *Omoo* were being put on paper, the fledgling author, feeling his mental oats, was taking part in the lively, even violent, literary-political life of "Young America" in New York under the tutelage of Evert A. Duyckinck, lion of Gotham's literary circles. It was the era of the Mexican War; free soil and slavery were everywhere the inevitable topics of discussion; and Duyckinck, close friend of Simms, who in 1853 would join Dew and Harper in their *Pro-Slavery Argument*, had definite opinions on the subject. Although he had opposed the Mexican War and the election of Zachary Taylor, he now looked forward eagerly to the annexation of the whole of Mexico and to the profit that would thereby accrue to the merchants of New York—a view in which Herman's brothers, Gansevoort, a Wall Street lawyer, and Allan, both Democratic stalwarts, probably concurred. All sorts of ideas seethed around the popular young author. At literary soirees in the home of Anne Charlotte Lynch or at Duyckinck Saturday nights, Melville could chat with Horace Greeley, William Cullen Bryant, Edgar Allan Poe, James Russell Lowell and Margaret Fuller.

Nor was the air of New York, where the American great, both pro-slavery and anti-slavery, lived or visited, the only tonic that stimulated young Melville at this time. There were trips to Boston, too, where Judge Lemuel Shaw, his father's old friend and father of his bride-to-be, was a central, stiff-necked figure of the raging slavery polemic. In Boston and its environs, as in New York, polite letters were often embroiled with impolite politics, and Judge Shaw, who, a few years later would uphold the legality of the Fugitive Slave Law, was to become the target of the anti-slavery wrath of such writers as Emerson, Thoreau, Longfellow and the younger Dana. With Dana, who was especially active in the defense of the slave, there must have been political discussion as well as good sea-talk when the two dined together at the Parker House. And then, of course, there was the voracious reading of this period—the tapeworm hunger to bolt down all the books and all the ideas he had missed during the whaling years and before.

This, then, was the milieu in which Melville worked out the

political and social ideas shortly to be bandied about by the talkative philosophers of Mardi. Did Melville pass through the Duyckinck stage of thinking before he reached the positions of *Mardi?* It would seem so from a series of articles that he penned at this time for the weekly *Yankee Doodle*, a short-lived venture—its editorial office was sometimes the Duyckinck library —conceived partly to discredit Polk's imperialist ambitions and to lampoon the presidential destiny of General Zachary Taylor, the hero of Palo Alto. With the struggle against the war as an attempt to expand the slave power and fasten the chains of bondage more firmly on the Negro, or with the political character of Taylor as a big slaveholder, the *Yankee Doodle* campaign had little to do, and Melville's series on Old Zack, neither wise nor funny, repeats one more facet of the stage-Negro of his day in the person of a black servant, Sambo. "I 'spect you go now, Massa, lick the Mexicans," clowns Sambo, when a Mexican shell tosses a pie on old Zack's head; "you armed *cap a pie*—cause aint you got the hot pie for a cap ha ha!"

But to see in Billy Loon, Baltimore and Sambo Melville's total thinking about the Negro at this time would be to ignore other utterances of a different sort. While *Mardi* and *Redburn* were being completed and *White-Jacket* turned over in mind, Melville wrote a number of book reviews, most interesting of which was that of Francis Parkman's *The California and Oregon Trail*. Rebutting Parkman's defamation of the Indian as brute, he declared that we are "all of us—Anglo-Saxons, Dyaks, and Indians—sprung from one head, and made in one image," and that "if we regret this brotherhood now, we shall be forced to join hands hereafter; for misfortune is not a fault; and good luck is not meritorious."[2]

It was with *Mardi*, however, that Melville set down his first considered ideas on the plight of the black man in America.

---

[2] How tough Melville's thinking on the problem was in this review may be seen in two revisions in a sentence of its first draft. In the original version he had written: "It is too often the case, that civilized human beings sojourning among savages soon come to regard them with disdain and contempt. But though in many cases this feeling is natural, it is not defensible; and it is visibly wrong." In the revised version, in the second sentence, the word "almost" is inserted before "natural," and the word "wholly" replaces "visibly." Two years later, however, reviewing J. Ross Browne's *Etchings of a Whaling Cruise*, he did not see fit to remark the Negrophobic comments scattered throughout it.

Herman Melville

F. O. Matthiessen's opinion that one "can hardly construct a coherent view of man and society from the many counter-statements" made in this book does not apply to its chapters on the tribe of Hamo and the sins of Vivenza. Indeed, *Mardi* clearly reveals a crucial dichotomy in Melville's thinking about Negro slavery. In their bitter estimate of the Negro's lot in American society all the chief talkers of Mardi agree, and their analysis, grimly factual, is close to that of Frederick Douglass and Wendell Phillips; but on the possibility of the Negro's gaining his freedom there is only mystical moaning. Whereas the abolitionists are optimistic actionists of one kind or another, for Melville the slave's plight is completely hopeless. What is offered as solution to the problem of Hamo is little more than a defeatist twist of the doctrine of innate depravity: "from the inbred servility of mortal to mortal; from all the organic causes, which inevitably divide mankind into brigades and battalions, with captains at their head," there is no escape; and "though all evils may be assuaged; all evils cannot be done away. For evil is the chronic malady of the universe; and checked in one place, breaks forth in another." Thus Taji's comfortless application of the law of conservation of wicked matter, to abolitionist evangel and beaten slave. The problem, in short, cannot be solved, and though "great reforms, of a verity be needed; nowhere are bloody revolutions required...." What the outcome will be "must be left to the commentators on Mardi some four or five centuries hence."[3]

Round and round the talk goes. "What art thou?" asks Babbalanja of a slave, "... say whether thou beliest thy Maker." In Blakeian accents the slave replies: "Speak not of my Maker to me. Under the lash, I believe my masters, and account myself a brute; but in my dreams, bethink myself an angel." "Just One!" exclaims Yoomy, the poet, "do no thunders roll—no lightnings flash in this accursed land?" "Incendiaries!" screams Nulli (Calhoun); the serfs, incited to liberty, will wreak dreadful vengeance. Yoomy will not listen: "Pray,

[3] Even before Taji reaches Mardi this fatalistic view is adumbrated in the opening un-allegorical pages of the book: "Thus all generations are blended; and heaven and earth of one kin ... one and all, brothers in essence.... All things form but one whole; the Universe a Judea, and God Jehovah its head.... No custom is strange; no creed is absurd; no foe, but who will in the end prove a friend. In heaven, at last, our sociality forever prevail."

heaven, they may yet find a way to loose their bonds without one drop of blood," he cries. "But hear me, Oro! were there no other way, and should their masters not relent, all honest hearts must cheer this tribe of Hamo on though the blood run; 'tis right to fight for freedom whoever be the thrall." But Babbalanja, the philosopher, demurs. Oro does not always champion the right; his sympathy is as hot as Yoomy's, but for these serfs he would not cross spears: "Better present woes for some, than future woes for all. . . ." Yoomy readily—too readily—assents; it is perhaps not necessary to risk a fight for the immediate liberation of Hamo; a way may be found without violence and unavoidable evil. But neither Taji, nor Yoomy, nor Babbalanja—nor Melville—knows what that way may be.

Babbalanja is honest enough to confess where his reasoning has led him; the weeping voices of the seekers now in fact "all but echo hard-hearted Nulli." But what can they do? Humanity is tossed on the horns of a dilemma; it damns slavery, yet "not one man knows a prudent remedy." A rationalization begins: the slave-masters must be wisely judged, for before Vivenza became "responsible as a nation, slavery, was planted root-deep in their midst." Moreover, not all slaves are as wretched as Nulli's; some even seem happy, although, Babbalanja is quick to add, "not as men." Nulli stands alone in his "insensate creed."

What then is the outcome? Although slavery is "a blot, foul as the crater-pool of hell," and although the slave-master, no matter how penitent, shall "die forever damned," the final judgment is abandonment of the slave to his bondage: "methinks the great laggard time must now march up apace," muses Babbalanja, "and somehow befriend these thralls. . . . Yes: Time—all-healing Time—Time, great Philanthropist!—Time must befriend these thralls!" "Oro grant it!" prays Yoomy, convinced, "and let Mardi say, Amen!"[4] It was an argument not unfamiliar to Northern Democrats. Slavery was "one of those evils which divine Providence does not leave to be remedied by human contrivances, but which, in its own

[4] When Henry Ward Beecher, arguing the slavery question a few years after *Mardi*, declared that "Time is her [slavery's] enemy. Liberty will, if let alone, always be a match for oppression," Frederick Douglass replied "With a good cow-hide, I could take all that out of Mr. Beecher in five minutes."

good time, by some means impossible to be anticipated . . . it causes to vanish like a dream"—so Hawthorne put it in the campaign biography of his friend, Franklin Pierce.

But Melville, restless in his own counsel, cannot as yet say amen. He has little in aid to offer, but the sin of slavery haunts him. "Oh tribe of Hamo!" cries Yoomy, "thy cup of woe so brims, that soon it must overflow upon the land which holds ye thrall. . . . No misery born of crime, but spreads and poisons wide." What would happen, Babbalanja speculates, if Alma (Christ) returned to Mardi?—"as an intruder he came; and as an intruder would he be this day. On all sides would he jar our social systems." Yet it is this jar that Melville fears—that persuades him to counsel patience to the scourged bondsman and to preach the doctrine that the fears of masters measure the rights of slaves.

Mardi contained Melville's first explicit statement on the subject of Negro revolt. In *Redburn,* published the next year, the question does not arise, but in its pages the sympathetic equalitarian of the Parkman review has much to say. "There is something in the contemplation of the mode in which America has been settled," he exclaims in *Redburn,*

that, in a noble breast, should forever extinguish the prejudices of national dislikes. . . . You can not spill a drop of American blood without spilling the blood of the whole world. . . . No! our blood is as the flood of the Amazon, made up of a thousand noble currents all pouring into one federated whole . . . . there is a future which shall see the estranged children of Adam restored as to the hearthstone in Eden. . . . The seed is sown. . . . Frenchmen and Danes and Scots; and the dwellers on the shore of the Mediterranean, and in the regions round about; Italians, and Indians, and Moors: there shall appear unto them cloven tongues as of fire.

Aboard young Redburn's ship, the *Highlander,* the cook, Thompson, who washed so rarely that it was only his color that "kept us from seeing his dirty face," is in great part once more the serio-comic minstrel type, patronizingly if tenderly treated. Yet there is something new in Melville's attitude towards him—respect and even admiration for our "woolly Doctor of Divinity," this serious "old fellow much given to metaphysics, and used to talk about original sin," who pores over the Book of Chronicles seeking explanations of mysterious passages. Church member Thompson points forward, indeed, to the brief but powerful figure of the unchurchly cook Fleece of the *Pequod*. Thompson is a crony of Lavender the steward, "a handsome, dandy mulatto that had once been a barber in West-Broadway . . . a sentimental kind of darky," fond of novels like *The Three Spaniards* and *Charlotte Temple*. The tone leads us to expect a performance of Tambo and Bones, and, regrettably, we are not wholly disappointed, but again something different emerges. Three or four times, in Liverpool, Redburn encounters Lavender "walking arm in arm with a good-looking English woman." Redburn's initial reaction is shock: "so young and inexperienced, and unconsciously swayed in some degree by local and social prejudices . . . at first I was surprised that a colored man should be treated as he is in this town, but a little reflection showed that, after all, it was but recognizing his claims to humanity and normal equality." In England, he continues, "the negro steps with a prouder pace, and lifts his head like a man; for here, no such exaggerated feeling exists in respect to him, as in America." With pride he recalls the friendship of his father with "the good and great Roscoe," the "intrepid enemy" of the slave-trade.[5] In New York, "such a couple would have been mobbed in three minutes; and the steward would have been lucky to escape with whole limbs." Such hatred, he observes, is "the marring of most men," yet from it—the tone is that of Mardian fatalism—"there seems no possible escape." Too often is civilization a coach of which the lower classes are the wheels. In some things, he concludes, "we Americans leave to other countries the carrying out of the principle that stands at the head of our Declaration of Independence."

White-Jacket appeared close on the heels of *Redburn*. "In writing these two books," Melville confided to Judge Shaw, "I have not repressed myself much . . . but have spoken pretty much as I feel." *White-Jacket,* indeed, adds a rich store of

[5] In Liverpool, surveying the statue of Nelson, at the base of which are four figures in chains, Redburn cannot look on "their swarthy limbs and manacles without being involuntarily reminded of four African slaves in the market-place." Never could he pass that statue without recalling that the wealth of Liverpool had once been "indissolubly linked" to the slave trade. It is noteworthy also that Melville's first extended description of the monster, Jackson, is an account of the "diabolical relish" with which he used to tell of his service on Portuguese slavers and of the horrors of the middle-passage.

insights into Melville's feelings about the Negro. In its long muster of characters, seven Negroes—a cook and his three helpers, the captain of a carronade, an old sheet-anchor man, and the purser's slave—not only repeat the old minstrel stereotypes, but a new figure, the Negro as human being, even heroic American, neither endman nor interlocutor nor Old Jim Crow, makes his entrance on the deck of an American warship.

What has been said about the stock-character aspect of Melville's sea-cooks can be more accurately pinpointed in the persons of the *Neversink's* Old Coffee, "high and mighty functionary" of the galley, and his three assistants, Sunshine, Rose-Water and May-day. As later in *Moby-Dick*, Melville drew here on the literature of his subject to supplement his own first-hand knowledge, and from a popular narrative printed eight years before, entitled *Life in a Man-of-War*, he constructed the galley-hands of the *Neversink*. Yet again with a difference. Whereas the authors of his source, in their treatment of Quashee, the cook, and of Caleb Chuffy, Sam Grubbings and Swampseed, the ward-room boys of the old *Constitution*, are not only condescending and facetious, but coarse and brutal as well, Melville, while retaining a good deal of current Joe Miller idiom, adds an egalitarian sympathy which transmutes his galley-hands into living men. True, most Negroes are for him still Billy Loons—"jolly Africans . . . making gleeful their toil by their cheering songs"—but when Rose-Water becomes the special victim of Captain Claret's brutality, Melville does not laugh and jeer: "Poor mulatto; thought I, one of an oppressed race, they degrade you like a hound. Thank God! I am a white. Yet I had seen whites also scourged; for black or white, all my shipmates were liable to that." And then follows comment in the trenchant analytical spirit of *Mardi* and *Redburn:* "Still, there is something in us, somehow, that in the most degraded condition, we snatch at a chance to deceive ourselves into a fancied superiority to others, whom we suppose lower in the scale than ourselves"—followed again by the vague defeatism of those same books: "Poor Rose-water! thought I; Heaven send you a release from your humiliation!"

If in his sketches of the *Neversink's* galley-hands Melville adulterated sympathy with condescension, there are two Negro seamen aboard the warship who evoke in him complete and unambiguous admiration. The first, Melville's superior at battle-stations, is the captain of Gun No. 5—"a fine negro"—in honor of whose sweetheart, "a coloured lady of Philadelphia," the gun's crew had christened the carronade Black Bet. "Of Black Bet," says Melville, "I was rammer-and-sponger; and ram and sponge I did, like a good fellow." The second was "an old negro, who went by the name of Tawney, a sheet-anchor man, whom we often invited into our top of tranquil nights, to hear him discourse. He was a staid and sober seaman, very intelligent, with a fine, frank bearing, one of the best men in the ship, and held in high estimation by everyone." From Tawney —"and he was a truth-telling man"—Melville got the "inside narrative" of the capture of the *Macedonian* by the *United States* during the War of 1812, for the Negro gunner had been an American sailor impressed by the British warship out of a New England merchantman.[6] Later, when the *Macedonian* had come to close quarters with the *United States*, he had been one of those who had protested to the captain of the British vessel "that it was a most bitter thing to lift their hands against the flag of that country which harboured the mothers that bore them." The answer had been a pistol at their heads. Tawney had many "stories to tell of this fight and frequently he would escort me along our main-deck batteries—still mounting the same guns used in the battle—pointing out their ineffaceable indentations and scars." When, further on in *White Jacket*, Melville describes the hatred shown by naval officers towards the morally sensitive and dignified tar, the image that he employs— "He is as unendurable, as an erect, lofty-minded African would be to some slave-driving planter"—recalls Tawney and the captain of Gun No. 5, and points forward to lordly Daggoo of *Moby-Dick*.

White-Jacket's seventh Negro character—Guinea, the purser's slave—is not so important for himself as for Melville's attitude towards his owner. Although Congress had prohibited the use of slaves in the navy, Guinea was shipped regularly as a

[6] The young Tawney reminds one that Billy Budd—whose prototype as "Handsome Sailor" is a Negro seaman whom Melville remembered seeing half a century before in Liverpool—was impressed out of the English merchantman *Rights-of-Man* into the warship *Indomitable*. The Negro seaman of *Billy Budd*, "so intensely black that he must needs have been a native African of the unadulterated blood of Ham," moved among his white fellow-tars "like Aldebaran among the lesser lights of his constellation."

seaman, while the purser, a "Southern gentleman," using him solely as a body servant, nevertheless collected his pay. When the *United States* reached Boston, Guinea, whose real name was Robert Lucas, at the instigation of the abolitionists, and by means of a decision handed down by Melville's father-in-law, Judge Lemuel Shaw, was given his freedom. It is the description of Guinea's master that reveals a facet of Melville's feeling about "good" Southern slaveholders, who, as he noted in *Mardi,* were not "insensate" Nullis. Although the purser "never in any way individualized me while I served on board the frigate," he remarks, "and never did me a good office of any kind . . . yet from his pleasant, kind, indulgent manner toward his slave, I always imputed to him a generous heart, and cherished an involuntary friendliness toward him. Upon our arrival home, his treatment of Guinea, under circumstances particularly calculated to stir up the resentment of a slaveowner, still more augmented my estimation of the purser's good heart."[7]

When Melville came to the last page of *White-Jacket*, it is probable that the total indictment he had levelled against naval brutality and corruption frightened even himself. That the book had been intended as an allegory of man's plight could be seen in its subtitle, *The World in a Man-of-War*. What then must his shipmates and the world do to lessen their misery? As with the tribe of Hamo, the analysis seemed to point inescapably to action of some sort. But, as with Hamo, once more the counsel is patience. "Oh, shipmates and worldmates, all round!" begins the peroration, "we the people suffer many abuses. Our gundeck is full of complaints. In vain from Lieutenants do we appeal to the Captain; in vain—while on board our world-frigate—to the indefinite Navy Commissioners, so far out of sight aloft. Yet it must be remembered that man's worst evils are self-inflicted; from the last ills each man must save himself." Can nothing be done to right the world's wrongs? Perhaps, but

whatever befall us, let us never train our murderous guns inboard; let us not mutiny with bloody pikes in our hands. Our Lord High

---

[7] In other parts of *White-Jacket*, Melville speaks of the "chivalric Virginian," John Randolph of Roanoke, "as a good master of his five-hundred slaves," and of the fact that "American men-of-war's men have often observed, that the Lieutenants from the Southern States, the descendants of the old Virginians, are much less severe, and much more gentle and gentlemanly in command, than the Northern officers, as a class."

Admiral will yet interpose; and though long ages should elapse, and leave our wrongs unredressed, yet, shipmates and world-mates! let us never forget, that,

> Who ever affect us, whatever surround,
> Life is a voyage that's homeward-bound!

The answer is, of course, Babbalanja's: Old Coffee and his galley-helpers, the Captain of Black Bet and Tawney, as well as their white shipmates—all must wait on their Lord High Admiral, Oro, and Time. In the chapter "Flogging Not Lawful," Melville had speculated that a "sailor's resistance to scourge . . . would be religiously justified in what would be judiciously styled 'the act of mutiny' itself."[8] But the end of *White-Jacket*, so fiery and Garrisonian in its deadly earnest catalogue of grievance, turns out to be something else.

And so we come to the White Whale. To F. O. Matthiessen, re-reading *Moby-Dick* half-a-dozen years after he had so ably dealt with it in his *American Renaissance*, Melville's essay on Hawthorne's *Mosses*, which he wrote in the heat of conceiving Ahab's fiery hunt, gave a new clue to his "creative intention" in his declaration that "American literature ought to be most characterized by writers who breathe the unshackled, democratic spirit of Christianity in all things." Melville's sense of Christianity, thought Matthiessen, was "most living" at the point where Christianity and democracy fused in his belief in the equality of man with man. More than ever before was Matthiessen moved by Melville's "reflections on the lack of superiority owing to a race's whiteness" that cropped up in *Moby-Dick* oftener than he had remembered. Was it irony that made Melville put his demand that American writers must "carry republican progressiveness into literature as well as into life" into the mouth of "A Virginian Spending July in Vermont" on holiday from "quiet plantation life"? Is it an accident that *Moby-Dick* does not turn out to be the story of a mutiny, or that, as Matthiessen points

---

[8] Melville's attitude towards resistance to injustice might be clarified, if we had space, by his attitude towards man-of-war discipline in general. How different seems his earlier outlook (although not essentially so) in *Omoo:* "I do not wish to be understood as applauding the flogging system practiced in men-of-war. As long, however, as navies are needed, there is no substitute for it. War being the greatest of evils, all its accessories necessarily partake of the same character; and this is about all that can be said in defence of flogging." Billy Budd is in part an elaboration of this problem.

out, it "does not go on to a fulfillment of the 'divine equality' among men," while even the friendship between Queequeg (whose idol is a "little negro") and Ishmael is "dwarfed and finally lost sight of in the portrayal of Captain Ahab's indomitable will"?

Whatever the answer, there is no doubt that among those meanest renegades and castaways on whom Melville meant to bestow high qualities, tragic graces and ethereal light, the *Pequod's* people of color—children also of that Just Spirit of Equality, the great democratic God—have their equal place.

There is "Black Little Pip," who "'loved life, and all life's peaceable securities," hailed as hero in heaven, in whom can be seen all the deep, painful longing for escape to peace from the world's Stubbs—the Stubbs who can say seriously: "We can't afford to lose whales by the likes of you; a whale would sell for thirty times what you would Pip, in Alabama. . . ." Is it white Christianity that is indicted when Pip, symbol of the humanities in Ahab, shrinking under the windlass as the squall comes up, cries, "Oh, thou big white God aloft there somewhere in your darkness, have mercy on this small black boy down here"? As Charles Olson points out, Pip is the first fellow-being whom Ahab offers to help, and it is Pip who almost turns the monomaniac captain from his course: "Oh! spite of million villains," cries the old man, "this makes me a bigot in the fadeless fidelity of man!—and a black! and crazy! . . ." Pip is neither a Billy Loon (though he has fiddled on a Connecticut village green) nor an idiot-child who sees visions and hears voices—at least not at first. "In outer aspect," notes Ishmael, "Pip and Dough-Boy made a match, like a black pony and a white one. . . . But while hapless Dough-Boy was by nature dull and torpid in his intellects, Pip, though over tender-hearted, was at bottom very bright with that pleasant, genial, jolly brightness peculiar to his tribe"; and, as if conscious of the cliché of jollity that mars the contrast, Ishmael hastens to add: "Nor smile so, while I write that this little black was brilliant, for even blackness has its brilliancy; behold yon lustrous ebony, panelled in king's cabinets."[9]

---

[9] In other parts of *Moby-Dick* Melville uses the cliché of the Jolly Negro without qualification, as in his earlier books. Thus he speaks of Africans as "a tribe which ever enjoy all holidays and festivities with finer, freer relish than any other race. For blacks, the year's calendar

If, transfigured by terror and inhumanity, Pip becomes a coward of the waters, against any misreading of his fear as uniquely racial rise the heroic forms of proud Daggoo and his colleagues of color, the fearless harpooneers of the *Pequod*. Daggoo, in one view, is Tawney and the Captain of the Black Bet, poetically transformed: "a gigantic, coal-black, negro-savage, with a lion-like tread—an Ahasuerus to behold," a white man "standing before him seemed a white flag come to beg truce of a fortress." The word "savage" may be unfortunate, but it is a label of appearance, not an assessment of character; indeed, the kingly gait of Daggoo, who risks his life to save Tashtego, drowning in milky spermaceti, is the mark of a noble nature. As the whale-boats rush to the kill, there's little Flask mounted upon gigantic Daggoo, who, "sustaining himself with a cool, indifferent, easy, unthought of, barbaric majesty," rolls his Herculean form harmoniously with the sea.

The effort here is consciously to redeem the color black from its historic, symbolic servitude to evil. "The bearer looked nobler than the rider. Though truly vivacious, tumultuous, ostentatious little Flask would now and then stamp with impatience . . . not one added heave did he thereby give to the negro's lordly chest." Observes Ishmael: "So have I seen Passion and Vanity stamping the living magnanimous earth, but the earth did not alter her tides and her seasons for that." The symbolism embodied in the ebony skins of Pip and Daggoo is but part of Melville's drive throughout *Moby-Dick* to shatter two traditional images in the iconography of white Western art, both deeply rooted in myth and language—the images of blackness as evil and whiteness as good.[10] Had Melville perhaps run

---

should show naught but three hundred and sixty Fourth of Julys and New Year's Days." Compare also his stereotypical description of the "three Long Island negroes, with glittering fiddle-bows of whale ivory . . . presiding over the hilarious jig" on the whaler, *Bachelor.*

[10] There are honorable exceptions, among them Homer, Herodotus, Shakespeare in *Othello,* Quevedo in *La Hora de Todos,* Swift in the fourth book of *Gulliver's Travels,* Lorca in *The House of Bernarda Alba.* The image was an early part of American culture; in Puritan ideology the "Black Man" was the bugaboo principle of evil, and the phrase "moral negro" is to be met with in the works of Puritan divines. Hawthorne employed the "Black Man" as a symbolic device within the Puritan meaning, and in general exploited the conventional black-white symbolism, as, for instance, in the "dark complexioned personage" of "Earth's Holocaust." Poe's practice was the same and is especially vicious at the

across Hazlitt's brief polemic in his *Life of Napoleon* against the use of black and white as tokens of right and wrong? Old Fuller's "quaint rhetoric," observed Hazlitt, contained a better moral, for the author of *The Holy State* had praised the "good sea-captain" as one who would treat his Negro captives as God's images "cut in ebony as if done in ivory," and who would see in "the blackest Moors . . . the representation of the King of Heaven." Was there perhaps an echo of this passage from Fuller's book, which Melville had read carefully a few years before, in the description of Pip's brilliant blackness as "lustrous ebony, panelled in King's cabinets"? The "preeminence" of whiteness, he would point out in his famous chapter on "The Whiteness of the Whale," applied "to the human race itself, giving the white man ideal mastership over every dusky tribe." It was an ideal that Melville tried to discredit throughout his epic.

Thus, Daggoo is no meek and servile Baltimore or Old Coffee. When the Spanish sailor, recalling the "old grudge" between Spaniard and Moor, mocks his flashing teeth, Daggoo springs up, crying "Swallow thine, mannikin, white skin, white liver!" and rushes forward to meet the dagger-armed Spaniard, while Melville's choric comment is made quite appropriately by an old sailor from the Isle of Man, who asks the basic skeptical question—but this time with a tone of challenge quite different from the maudlin peroration of *White-Jacket:* "Ready formed, There! the ringed horizon. In that ring Cain struck Abel. Sweet work, right work, No? Why then, God, mad'st thou the ring?"

Daggoo and Pip are heroic symbolic figures, which is perhaps why Melville endowed them with the same Shakespearian speech that he put in the mouths of Ahab and his officers. It is the first time that his Negro characters have been stripped of comic dialect, for Tawney and the Captain of Gun No. 5 never speak out directly. With the *Pequod's* cook, Fleece, who says that he is ninety years old and was born on a Roanoke ferryboat, the pattern seems at first to be that of the comic-grave cooks of the previous novels; there is still a touch of condescension in the portrait of "this old Ebony," who shambles along from his galley, because, "like many old blacks, there was some-

---

close of his *Narrative of Arthur Gordon Pym,* where the social philosophy that he shared with Simms receives allegorical treatment. [See Kaplan's Introduction to the Hill and Wang edition of *The Narrative of Arthur Gordon Pym* (New York, 1960), pp. vii–xxv.—EDITOR's NOTE] thing the matter with his kneepans, which he did not keep well-scoured like his other pans. . . ." Yet this Fleece is a transfigured cook. Unlike his predecessors, he is no devout Uncle Tom. "Cook," plagues Stubb, "do you belong to the Church?" "Passed one once in Cape-Down," replies the old man sullenly. Fleece, too, has been touched with "tragic grace," and he is given his philosophical piece to say along with the rest. Goaded by Stubb, he delivers a sermon to the sharks, briefer but perhaps more profound than Father Mapple's: "You is sharks, sartin; but if you govern de shark in you, why den you be angel; for all angel is not'ing more dan de shark well governed. . . . Don't be tearin' de blubber out of your neighbour's mout, I say." Exasperated finally by Stubb's heckling, Fleece passes what amounts to judgment on Stubb-kind and prophecy for Ahab: "Wish, by gor! whale eat him, 'stead of him eat whale. I'm bressed if he ain't more of shark den Massa Shark hisself."

Thus does Melville delineate the Negro in three greatly conceived characters of *Moby-Dick,* the first to be meted full justice in American literature, not equalled even by the panting runaway or the statuesque drayman of *Leaves of Grass;* each of the three teaching a lesson to the "boobies and bumpkins," who, in their intense greenness, jeered and marvelled at those "two fellow beings," white Ishmael and brown Queequeg, for being so companionable—"as though a white man were anything more than a white washed negro." "It's a mutual joint-stock world in all meridians," Queequeg seems to say to himself after he snatches the booby from the drink; "We cannibals must help these Christians." All men are members of the same church, points out Ishmael to old Bildad, "the great and ever-lasting First Congregation of this whole worshipping world; we all belong to that; only some of us cherish crotchets noways touching the grand belief; in that we all join hands."[11]

How, then, shall we sum up our impressions of Melville's art as it took for its subjects the Negro and his problems during his first five years of authorship from *Typee* to *Moby-Dick?* Al-

[11] These notes on *Moby-Dick* do not, of course, exhaust all its references, direct and indirect, to the Negro and his problems. It should be noted that on many of its pages the conventional black-white symbolism is employed, especially in the pre-*Pequod* chapters that cover Ishmael's experiences in New Bedford and Nantucket, and in the treatment of yellow Fedallah. On slavery and the slave trade there are some notable lines in the critical spirit of the more incisive passages of *Mardi.*

though in one view it may be seen as an ascending development, beginning conventionally enough with old Baltimore and Billy Loon and reaching a peak in the memorable figures of Daggoo and Pip, from another standpoint, looked at as a composite, it is variously tinted with the "corresponding coloring" of its times. It would be a mistake to search in Melville for the intransigent humanitarianism of a Garrison or a Weld, or even for the milder yet consistent anti-slaveryism of lesser figures. Melville was never an abolitionist, neither then nor later, nor was his writing, for the most part, ever directly applied to influencing immediate events in the manner of an Emerson, a Lowell, a Thoreau or a Whittier. Indeed, if he was anything at all in the active political sense, he was a liberal Democrat in a period when the official Democracy was moving into stronger and stronger alliance with the Southern slavocracy.

Yet it must nonetheless be gladly admitted that in forms of fiction he uttered from time to time the most powerfully democratic words of his age on the dignity of the Negro as a part of American life. Where else in American literature, prior to *Leaves of Grass,* can one meet up with a Negro who is truthfully portrayed in his work and in his character? Yet scattered through Melville's writings of these first years there is a goodly company of such men—imperishable images of the democratic tradition of our native art.

But to speak in praise and remain silent on other matters—the minstrel stereotypes, the comic patronization, the chauvinist lapses, the mystic defeatism—would be to do Melville less than justice and to deny ourselves a tool of insight into that part of his creative life, which extending from *Pierre* in 1852 to *The Confidence Man* five years later, includes *Benito Cereno.* . . .

It was in the atmosphere of the slave insurrection panic of the middle fifties, of the mounting tension of the slavery controversy (in which Melville's relatives and friends took varying positions), of the *Amistad* and *Creole* mutinies, that *Benito Cereno* was conceived and written.

Is it credible, then, that Melville meant *Benito Cereno* to have little or nothing to do with slavery and rebellion, or with the character of the Negro as slave and rebel? Given the Melville we have described and his times, such an opinion seems hardly tenable. . . .

The most central and completely described character of

Benito Cereno is Amasa Delano, through whose temperament filters most, although not all, of the action of the tale. On Delano both schools of interpretation concur in at least one respect: in the Yankee captain Melville meant to paint a satiric portrait. An important question, however, still remains to be answered: What is satirized? What in Delano is the target of Melville's irony? That the duped Delano was meant to be simple, even stupid, both schools agree. It is at the point where agreement stops and divergence begins that we find the crux of the problem of *Benito Cereno*, for whereas one school holds that Delano was naive because he could not discern the motiveless malignity in Babo and his fellows, it is the contention of the other that his stupidity lay in his blindness to the innate and heroic desire of the Negroes for freedom, to their dignity as human beings.

Which side is right? What did Melville mean?

The major premise for the development of Delano's character is given quite clearly in Melville's first assessment of it: Delano was "a person of a singularly undistrustful good-nature, not liable, except on extraordinary and repeated incentives, and hardly then, to indulge in personal alarms, any way involving the imputation of malign evil in man." Thus Melville declares that Delano is blind—not to goodness or courage or the love of freedom in anybody—but to the "malign evil in man." Delano is trusting. Is he intelligent? Not at all. That he is a good-natured fool Melville points up in the ironic sentence that follows: "Whether, in view of what humanity is capable, such a trait implies, along with a benevolent heart, more than ordinary quickness and accuracy of intellectual perception, may be left to the wise to determine." Now, the tale that follows is precisely the parable by which the wise may so determine; by it readers are to be educated; in it Captain Delano is to be educated. Yet, as we shall see, the final truth that Delano will learn is that Babo is the embodiment of "malign evil," Cereno of goodness maligned. For Delano to learn this new truth, he must unlearn the old errors of his period of delusion.

What are these old errors about Negroes in general and about those of the *San Dominick* in particular that Delano must unlearn? He thinks that they are all jolly, debonair, "sight-loving Africans," who invariably love bright colors and fine shows; that their gentleness peculiarly fits them to be good body servants and that they possess the "strange vanity" of faithful slaves; that they sing as they work because they are uniquely musical; that they are generally stupid, the white being the shrewder race; that mulattoes are not made devilish by their white blood and that the hostility between mulattoes and blacks will not allow them to conspire against whites; that yellow pirates could not have committed the cruel acts rumored of them. And of all these beliefs he is disabused. He is a man who has had "an old weakness for negroes"; who has always been "not only benign, but familiarly and humorously so" to them; who has been fond of watching "some free man of color at work or play," and if on a voyage he chanced to have a black sailor, had inevitably been on "chatty and half-gamesome terms with him." He is a man who, "like most men of good, blithe heart . . . took to negroes, not philanthropically, but genially, just as other men to Newfoundland dogs," and who on the *San Dominick* speaks a "blithe word" to them; who admires the "royal spirit" of Atufal and pities his chains; who suspects that Don Benito is a hard master and that slavery breeds ugly passions in men—and in every item he will be proven blind.

To Delano, in short, Negroes are jolly primitives, uncontaminated nature, simple hearts, people to be patronized. The "uncivilized" Negro women aboard the *San Dominick* are "tender of heart"; as the "slumbering negress" is awakened by her sprawling infant, she catches the child up "with maternal transports," covering it with kisses. "There's naked nature, now; pure tenderness and love," thinks Captain Delano, "well pleased." Gazing at the kindly sea and sky, he is sorry for betraying an atheist doubt about the goodness of Providence.

All these things Delano has believed—and they are all to be proven false in fact, masquerades behind which lurk "ferocious pirates," barbarous sadists, both male and female, shrewd wolves, devilish mulattoes. In the course of events he must learn what Cereno already knows, and Cereno it is who rams the lesson home, generalizing what the obtuse Yankee has been constitutionally unable to comprehend. His last words are, "The negro." Delano has no answer; it is the silence of agreement. "You were undeceived," Cereno had said to him, "would it were so with all men." Delano has been stripped of his delusions; he is wiser. But wiser in what respect? In that he now knows that Negroes are courageous lovers of freedom? Not at all; rather wiser in that he has at last discerned the blacks to be wolves in the wool of gentle sheep.

The shock of recognition makes brothers of Delano and Cereno; they now can speak with "fraternal unreserve"; indeed, there was never any real basic opposition between them. Delano was no philanthropic abolitionist; he was not even anti-slavery— he offered to buy Babo; for him the *San Dominick* carries "negro slaves, amongst other valuable freight"; he intends his sugar, bread and cider for the whites alone, the wilted pumpkins for the slaves; he orders his men to kill as few Negroes as possible in the attack, for they are to divide the cargo as a prize; he stops a Spanish sailor from stabbing a chained slave, but for him the slaves are "ferocious pirates" and he says no word against their torture and execution, far more cruel than the machinations of Babo. Like Cereno he too has been "a white noddy, a strange bird, so called from its lethargic, somnambulistic character, being frequently caught by hand at sea." No more will he be a somnambulist in the presence of evil. Meeting another *San Dominick* he will not again be duped.

And Cereno? He is the good man, the religious man, whose nobility may be seen in his hidalgo profile, in health, perhaps, something like the graceful Spanish gentry who listened to Ishmael tell his Town-Ho story, the real aristocrat that the superficial democrat, Delano, had wrongly suspected. Everywhere Melville pruned the Cereno of Delano's *Narrative* to vein and flesh him with altruism and goodness. In life, he was a swindler, a liar, the scorn of his friends, the stabber of a helpless Negro slave; as Lewis Mumford justly declares, in the original narrative Cereno is "far more cruel, barbarous, and unprincipled than the forces he contends against." All this is gone in the tale. Pathetic and beaten he is, done to death by his experience, but only because he has been an altruist and trusted the slaves as tractable; the good man's illusions of goodness have been fatally overthrown. At the last Cereno reminds one of Bartleby the scrivener, who has rejected life as a blank and monstrous wall he cannot pierce. Wheeras in "Bartleby the Scrivener" the wall is the enigma of life, in *Cereno* it is Babo. . . .

True it is, of course, that Melville, even in his failures, is almost always an adroit artist, and as many have noted, there are moments of undeniable power in *Benito Cereno*. But looked at objectively, the tale seems a plummet-like drop from the unconditionally democratic peaks of *White-Jacket* and *Moby-Dick*—an "artistic sublimation" not, as Joseph Schiffman maintains, of anti-slaveryism, but rather of notions of black primitivism dear to the hearts of slavery's apologists, a sublimation in fact of all that was sleazy, patronizing, backward and fearful in the works that preceded it. It is to put the matter too mildly perhaps to say, as Charles Neider does, that "Melville glosses over extenuating circumstances in his effort to blacken the blacks and whiten the whites, to create poetic images of pure evil and pure virtue," so that the result is "sometimes unfortunate in the feelings it arouses against the Negro," or to say, as Matthiessen does, that "the embodiment of good in the pale Spanish captain and of evil in the mutinied African crew, though pictorially and theatrically effective, was unfortunate in raising unanswered questions." When Melville, at a certain point in his development, repudiated his superficial, old notions (which were Delano's too) about the innately jolly, minstrel, religious nature of Negroes, it was, sadly enough, not to perceive the free spirit of the Tawneys and the Daggoos as the reality behind the masks. Instead, in *Benito Cereno*, the fear and doubt of slave-revolt proclaimed in *Mardi* and implied in *White-Jacket* were to be transmuted into hatred of the "ferocious pirates" of the *San Dominick*—as were demoniac Bembo into demoniac Babo; lordly Daggoo into Atufal, prince of hell; the "poor mulatto," Rose-Water, into the sinister mulatto, Francesco; the good slavemaster—Randolph of Roanoke, the purser of the *Neversink*, the slaveholder of Vivenza who was not an insensate Nulli—into Don Benito Cereno. . . .

Is there anything in Melville's thinking and writing from *Pierre* to *The Confidence Man* that might yield data on his attitude towards the Negro during these second five years of his authorship?[12]

[12] Melville's political views around this time are difficult to pin down. Although a detailed examination is beyond our scope here, it may be said that on the whole he seems to have been a rather unpolitical person during the fifties and thereafter. In 1853 he vainly solicited a consular post at Honolulu through both his abolitionist friend, Dana, and one H. W. Bishop, apparently a Democratic wheel-horse, who wrote to the Democratic Secretary of State: "He belongs to one of the oldest and most distinguished democratic families of this state. With us the name of Melville is associated with early republicanism & Jeffersonian doctrines. What his political views now are, I hardly know. His literary tastes & habits have withdrawn him from party controversies." Contemporary descriptions by Phineas Allen and Augusta Melville substantiate Bishop, although Peter Gansevoort, in a letter of recommendation, went so far as to state that "Herman has always been a firm Democrat." Later, the Democrat, Caleb Cushing, at the behest of Justice Shaw and Hawthorne, tried to

Pierre deals neither with the Negro nor slavery as character or event, yet in its hero's nostalgic remembrance of things past there is the tone of the Delano who loved Negroes as he might his Newfoundland dogs and spoke blithely to them. It is Melville's memory of the family tradition of his grandfather, General Gansevoort, the hero of Fort Stanwix. The gigantic General, a Hudson River patroon, had kept slaves and he lived in family history as "the kindest of masters" to his chattels—to Moyar, "an incorruptible and most punctual old black," to Cranz, Kit, Douw and the other stable-slaves. Never would the General flog them; such cruelty was something "unknown in that patriarchal time and country—but he would refuse to say his wonted pleasant word to them." Yes, "all of them loved grand old Pierre, as his shepherd loved old Abraham." Three years later, these loyal stable-slaves would become the mutineers of *Benito Cereno*. If there is any color symbolism at all in *Pierre*, it is the conventional type present in *Mardi*—albino Yillah becomes blonde Lucy (lux), while dark Hautia is transformed into the brunette Isabel, the "Nubian power" of whose eyes will be interpreted as one does or does not subscribe to the alleged allegorical Zoroastrianism of the novel.

Throughout the sixteen short stories and sketches that Melville wrote during the fifties,[13] conventional black-white imagery is the unbroken rule, as in the second sketch of *The Encantadas*, where the whiteness and blackness of the two sides of the tortoise are equated to good and evil. In *The Tartarus of Maids*, with its detailed sexual imagery, the devil who condemns women to the twin slaveries of the factory and childbirth is the "dark-complexioned man," feared by the pale girls, whose Dantean hell is filled with darkness. Through a "dusky pass"—the Mad Maid's Bellows' Pipe of the Black Notch in Woedolor Mountain, whose "cloven walls of haggard rock" with their

---

get Melville a post at Rome. Up to Jan. 7, 1854, he subscribed to the *New-York Herald*, a rabid anti-Abolitionist paper, although he perhaps read it mainly for its complete shipping news. In 1857, when the *Atlantic Monthly* was founded, partly as an anti-slavery journal, Melville was invited to be a listed contributor. He was happy to accept, but apparently never contributed.

[13] Close adherence to his source in *Israel Potter* did not permit Melville to deal with Negroes, although John Paul Jones, the romantic hero of the novel, tells Israel that he is not "notional" about his bedfellows—he has even slept in a hammock alternately occupied by a Negro.

"strangely ebon hue" are once more reminiscent of the black ravine of *Pym*—Melville drives his horse, Black, away from "bright farms and sunny meadows." The Black Notch opens into "a great, purple" hollow in which may be seen the "black-mossed bulk" of an old saw-mill on the cataract's "gloomy brink." At the bottom of this Devil's Dungeon stands "a large whitewashed building, relieved, like some great whited sepulchre, against the sullen background of mountain-side firs." One thinks of the whitewashed monastery of the *San Dominick*, and, as in *Benito Cereno*, the atmosphere throughout is an ambiguous gray. It is on a "gray Friday noon" that Melville starts on his journey. The horse, Black, shies at "an old distorted hemlock" in his path, "darkly undulatory as an anaconda." Snow covers the blackness of the papermill—which at first reminds Melville of "dark and grimy Temple Bar"—painting it like a sepulchre. Inside the mill, "a dark colossal waterwheel, grim with its own immutable purpose," appalls.

The Bell Tower of 1855, closely linked with *The Tartarus of Maids* in its allegorical attack on the enslaving machine, is the parable of Talus, the metal monster constructed by the Frankenstein, Bannadonna. The story seems surely to have been implicated in Melville's mind with the slave-revolt of *Benito Cereno*. "Like negroes," proclaims its epigraph, "these powers own man sullenly; mindful of their higher master; while serving, plot revenge," and its closing paragraph repeats the note: "so the blind slave obeyed its blinder lord; but, in obedience, slew him."[14] The fallen tower, a "black-mossed stump of some immeasurable pine," has its flawed bell like that of the *San Dominick*, and the penultimate image, strangely like that of the dark, masked satyr trampling its master on the bow of the *San Dominick*, is the masked slave Talus with manacled hands standing over his murdered creator.[15]

Is there anything here to indicate the predilection of a mind that would conceive Babo or blackness as hero? Is this the same

[14] Melville deleted the epigraph from the *Piazza Tales* printing of *The Bell Tower*.

[15] Other plausible implications occur throughout *The Bell Tower* which perhaps link it with *Benito Cereno*: the name, Bannadonna, seems a play on Don Benito; Bannadonna calls his mechanical slave Haman, which may refer also to Ham, the Negro. *Bartleby* contains an obscure hint of whiteness as connoting an indifferent universe, but does not touch on the Negro.

mind that by a radical reordering of aesthetic values fashioned the egalitarian color symbolism and the great Negro figures of *Moby-Dick?*

Nor do two items of the collection in which Negroes appear as characters change the picture. About *The Happy Failure*, with its "grizzled old black man," one Yorpy—the familiar serio-comic type, who speaks this time in a queer "Dutch-African" dialect—there is little that need be said.[16] *The 'Gees*, a sketch written for *Harper's* just after *Benito Cereno* was completed, is something of a different sort. This sketch, the ugliest, most tasteless thing Melville ever wrote, concerns the Portuguese-African islanders of Fogo, one of the Cape de Verdes, whose nickname was given them "in pure contumely." Of all men, notes Melville, "seamen have strong prejudices, particularly in the matter of race. They are bigots here." Then, in paradoxically bigoted fashion, he continues: "But when a creature of inferior race lives among them, an inferior tar, there seems no bound to their disdain. . . ." With forced and backward humor he describes the 'Gees: "As the name is a curtailment, so the race is a residuum. Some three centuries ago certain Portuguese convicts were sent as a colony to Fogo—an island previously stocked with an aboriginal race of negroes, ranking pretty high in incivility, but rather low in stature and morals. In course of time, from the amalgamated generation all the likelier sort were drafted off as food for powder, and the ancestors of the since-called 'Gees were left as the caput mortuum, or melancholy remainder." The auction block facetiousness of this sketch may be sampled in the following sentence: "Like the negro, the 'Gee has a peculiar savor, as in the seabird called haglet. Like venison, his flesh is firm but lean."[17]

Although *The 'Gees* furnishes some insight into the mind

---

[16] Yorpy's dialect was probably based on the speech of Negroes brought up in Dutch-speaking households of the Hudson River valley. Melville seems to have known at least one such Negro. Sojourner Truth was brought up in such a family and spoke for a time with a Dutch accent.

[17] In American sea-literature of the nineteenth century there are many references to the Portuguese-Negro sailor and whaleman. They are usually described as expert seamen in all departments; many captained their own craft. In *Omoo*, one of the sailors of the *Dolly* is "Antone, a Portuguese, from the Cape-de-Verd Islands"; Melville does not refer to him as a 'Gee or in any way derogate him.

that conceived the malign slave Babo, in the morality play of *The Confidence Man* there are more positive answers to our questions. It is in this book that Melville reaches his nadir of Timonism; the rainbow itself becomes an arch over hell; all colors—white, gray, black, violet, ruby, yellow—become the symbols of fraud and folly. To the confidence man, "that good dish, man" is a poisonous one, whether "served up a la Pole, a la Moor, a la Ladrone, or a la Yankee." If the first masquerade of the confidence man is the mute in cream-colors—the fleece-like lamb of Christ with placards of charity, the second is poor black Guinea, and the third the gold-brick salesman of the Black Rapids Coal Company, a corporation located on the Styx. The "piebald parliament" of Anacharsis Clootz, federated along one keel of brotherhood in the opening pages of *Moby-Dick*, reappears once more on the *Fidèle;* but now it is a parcel of knaves and fools of all colors: "Japanese-looking Mississippi cotton-planters . . . slaves, black, mulatto, quadroon; modish young Spanish creoles . . . Dives and Lazarus . . . grinning Negroes and Sioux chiefs solemn as high priests." Gone is the exuberant democratic faith of the Melville who penned *Hawthorne and his Mosses*, gone the vision of the new America rising out of the West, now given in the image of a multi-colored Maldive shark followed by smiling pilot-fish. Guinea is Lazarus as swindler. A "daedal boat" Melville calls the *Fidèle*, that starts its voyage on April Fool's Day—but no one on the *Fidèle*, not even the most cunning, ever escapes from its labyrinth of fraud.

Once more the type-image of *Benito Cereno* and *The Tartarus of Maids* emerges: the *Fidèle* "might at distance have been taken for some whitewashed fort . . ."; indeed it is the black man-of-war world whitewashed by Bible texts about charity. And once more Babo is exposed. It is Guinea now who is the deck-crowd's "Newfoundland dog"—"a grotesque negro cripple," his "bushy wool . . . the curled forehead of a black steer," a "half-frozen black sheep," "a free dog," product of the charitable heavenly baker who "bakes such in his oven, alongside of his nice white rolls, too." There are Delanos in the crowd, but they become suspicious far more rapidly than had the Yankee captain. There is sympathy first for poor Guinea "upon whom nature has placarded the evidence" of hurt, but it quickly turns to distrust of the "black Jeremy Diddler."

More importantly, *The Confidence Man* is an indictment of all friends of the Negro, a fatalistic assessment of all anti-slavery efforts. The merchant, a dupe of the confidence man, points out the misery of the Negro in American society. The confidence man counters by asking "whether the alleged hardships of that alleged unfortunate might not exist more in the pity of the observer than in the experience of the observed."

Could one but get at the real state of his heart, he would be found about as happy as most men, if not, in fact, full as happy as the speaker himself [for] negroes were by nature a singularly cheerful race; no one ever heard of a native-born African Zimmerman or Torquemada; that even from religion they dismissed all gloom; in their hilarious rituals they danced, so to speak, and, as it were, cut pigeon wings. It was improbable, therefore, that a negro, however reduced to his stumps by fortune, could be ever thrown off the legs of a laughing philosophy.

The irony is obvious. We have seen it before in *Benito Cereno*. Both the confidence man and Don Benito "understand" the shrewd malignity behind the jolly black masquerade. It is the Mississippi plantation-owner, Pitch, the last of Melville's many Ishmaels, and, after the confidence man himself, Melville's spokesman more than anyone else in the novel, who believes that nature is disease ("What's deadly nightshade")—who, although he is against slavery, not only flays moderate understrappers who would offend nobody, but also abolitionists, brother-slaves of black slaves at heart. His is the "general law of distrust systematically applied" to the human race, that makes him distrust all boys, black and white; it is Melville's way of saying that although he would not have slavery, he has no confidence in either slave or philanthropist.

Yet, if throughout *The Confidence Man* Melville is careful to decolorize all colors to a hueless evil, it is on the more familiar note of the traditional black-white symbolism that the volume ends: "The next moment, the waning light expired, and with it the waning flames of the horned altar, and the waning halo around the robed man's brow; while in the darkness which ensued, the cosmopolitan led the old man away."

If the epic of the white whale marked the culmination of one phase of Melville's life and art, *Pierre* ushered in another, which in turn came to a close six years later with *The Confidence Man*. At the center of this period he composed *Benito Cereno*. From the unnamed war canoe of *Mardi* to the whaler *Pequod* of *Moby-Dick*, the mariners and passengers of Melville's metaphysical fleet had conducted a running debate on God and Satan, on society and man. Yet the anchor, so to say, had always been up, the quest unceasing. As they fade out of sight, the mystery of iniquity haunting Taji and Ishmael still remains a series of open questions. There is anger, frustration, querulousness, doubt—but underneath all the God-challenging optimism of one whose highest dignity is to reject all easy answers to his questions, who sees the evil in the world but who still has faith in humanity and joys to see the sticky little leaves in the spring.

The *San Dominick* and the *Fidèle* are craft of quite another line. From *Pierre* through *The Confidence Man* all this feeling of restless quest seems gone; for the most part the tone of these works is one of patly answered questions. Nor are the answers doubtful: rotten is the core of the universe; goodness is a sport, an abnormality; nature and society are essentially disease; Jackson and Bland are archetypal realities. The quarrel that Melville surely did wage with God was, of course, never to be settled completely, even during these misanthropic years, nor would it be right to forget the ultimate testaments to man's worth in *Clarel* and *Billy Budd*. Although it closes without hint of catharsis, not even the pessimistic answers of *The Confidence Man* are wholly nihilist, for that masquerade gets its critical leverage by basing itself on an unattainable ethic rather than an anarchic moral relativism. Yet, if even in this period of near-Timonism Melville did not reach the absolute zero of complete disillusion with God and man, he came very near to it. "Something further may follow of this Masquerade," is Melville's tentative promise in the last line of *The Confidence Man*. As a matter of fact, nothing of the sort ever followed. From his visit to the Middle East, which began even before the book was published, a chastened Melville returned. Indeed, it is a rejuvenated Redburn who, in a lecture on "Travelling," at the end of 1859, proclaimed from the platform that the traveller "prejudiced against color," finding "several millions of people of all shades of color, and all degrees of intellect, rank, and social work scattered through the world," is persuaded "to give up his foolish prejudice," thus enlarging his "sphere of comprehensive benevolence till it includes the whole human race."

But this is not to say that Herman Melville ever wholly

returned to the unconditionally democratic platform he once outlined for himself to his friend Hawthorne during the writing of *Moby-Dick*. The *Battle-Pieces* that emerged from the Civil War were to be flawed with the old doubts, and in the prose supplement that followed the poems Melville would plead for lenity to the defeated South, stating as one of his reasons that after all, as whites, the rebels were "nearer to us in nature" than to the freed blacks. (One recalls Captain Amasa Delano thinking to himself: "Besides, who ever heard of a white so far a renegade as to apostasize from his very species almost, by leaguing against it with negroes.")

Precisely why Melville, in the period of *Benito Cereno*, retreated from the advanced positions of his earlier works while so many of his contemporaries grew more resolute to battle the sin of slavery, it is difficult to say. To hold, with John Howard Lawson, that he was "only seeking to taste a little of the wine of literary success" in the "ready commercial market for proslavery material," that "the ignoble motive must be weighed in the scales of political reality," and that "the story made its contribution to the southern campaign in the crucial election of 1856" is to underestimate the integrity of an artist who may have been wrong at times but who was never a hypocrite. The roots of *Benito Cereno* are more gnarled than that. "The greatest man," Goethe, who knew, once remarked, "is always linked to his own century through some weakness." Suffice it to repeat at this point that there were conflicting elements in Melville's early art and that in *Benito Cereno* it was the least original and least humanitarian of those elements that received fullest development. Horace Trauble, baiting Whitman for his views on the Negro, received the candid reply from the old man that, after all, he "may have been tainted a bit, just a little bit, with the New York feeling with regard to anti-slavery." The observation is not inapplicable to Melville. Unlike an abolitionist artist like Whittier, Melville was in a sense the complex embodiment of the warring attitudes of the most troubled years in the history of the nation, and in his heart there was almost always a kind of fighting that would not let him rest. At various times, various strains in his environment forged to the front in his art. With *Benito Cereno* it can scarcely be said that Melville was in the humanitarian van. Babo and his fellow mutineers of the *San Dominick* he touched with neither tragic grace nor ethereal light.

VIII

SEVERN DUVALL

"Uncle Tom's Cabin": The Sinister Side of the Patriarchy

Mrs. Harriet Beecher Stowe, warned the *Southern Literary Messenger* late in 1852, speaks for a large and dangerous faction which must be put down with the pen, else "we may be compelled one day (God grant that day may never come!) to repel [them] with the bayonet."[1] Many pens got busy but *Uncle Tom's Cabin* was not to be washed away even in Southern blood, much less in Southern ink. A decade later, so runs the legend, Lincoln himself was to greet Mrs. Stowe as the little woman who "made this great war."

The critical reexaminations of *Uncle Tom's Cabin* in recent years have not so far probed very deeply the Southern response to Mrs. Stowe's most famous work.[2] Yet *Uncle Tom's Cabin* created its meaning out of experience so peculiarly Southern that this response needs to be considered as a measure of the novel's contemporary significance. Mrs. Stowe showed an uncanny talent (as Southern readers often revealed) for dramatizing the essential torture of Southern life; in 1852 she faced her readers squarely with issues which in their modern form are still unsettled.

Reprinted from the *New England Quarterly*, 36 (1963), 3–22, by permission of the *New England Quarterly*.

[1] *Southern Literary Messenger*, XVIII (October, 1852), 638. This magazine will hereafter be abbreviated as *SLM*.

[2] The most impressive of these have been C. H. Foster, *The Rungless Ladder* (Durham, 1954), 12–64; Edmund Wilson, *Patriotic Gore* (New York, 1962), 3–58; W. R. Taylor, *Cavalier and Yankee* (New York, 1961), 307–13; and, most recently, Kenneth Lynn, "Introduction," *Uncle Tom's Cabin* (Cambridge, 1962), vii–xxiv.

The only extended effort to survey the Southern response is an unpublished M.A. dissertation by Margaret A. Browne, "Southern Reactions to *Uncle Tom's Cabin*" (Duke University, 1941), but our work does not overlap.

I

In her letter to Gamaliel Bailey in 1851, offering her "series of sketches" to the *National Era,* Mrs. Stowe explained that she would give "the lights and shadows of the 'patriarchal institution,' . . . [showing] the *best side* of the thing, and something *faintly approaching the worst.*" In announcing the forthcoming story a short time later, the *National Era* printed the subtitle of *Uncle Tom's Cabin* (subsequently changed) as "The Man That Was a Thing."[3] These two themes are drawn together in the first chapter:

Whoever visits some estates . . . , and witnesses, the good-humored indulgence of some masters and mistresses, and the affectionate loyalty of some slaves, might be tempted to dream the oft-fabled poetic legend of a patriarchal institution, and all that; but over and above the scene there broods a portentous shadow—the shadow of *law*. So long as the law considers all these human beings, with beating hearts and living affections, only as so many *things* belonging to a master,—so long as the failure, or misfortune, or imprudence, or death of the kindest owner, may cause them any day to exchange a life of kind protection and indulgence for one of hopeless misery and toil,—so long it is impossible to make anything beautiful or desirable in the best regulated administration of slavery.[4]

Mrs. Stowe thus at the outset questioned not only the legal definition of slavery but also the crucial "domestic" metaphor by which so many Southerners had sought for so many years to defend the fabric of their society. Contradictory as these two defenses were, Mrs. Stowe drew out of them the tensions through which the novel gains much of its coherence.

She reminds us again and again, for example, that the slave has no substantial identity under the Southern laws (ironically, in a society which boasted of its domestic institutions there was not even legal validity to slave marriages). If the slaves may witness for Christ, they may not witness for the murder of Tom; in a legal world they are simply "things." Yet though the law may ignore their human identity, society cannot; the

[3] Quoted in Forrest Wilson, *Crusader in Crinoline* (New York, 1941), 259, 262.

[4] *Uncle Tom's Cabin* (New York, 1938), 12. All subsequent references will be to this Modern Library Edition; the title will be hereafter abbreviated in the notes as *UTC.*

legal paradox is palpable for more than one of the white characters. Senator Bird of Ohio, sworn to uphold the Fugitive Slave Law, is caught between abstract legal duty and sympathy for Eliza; on the Southern side Mr. Wilson, former employer of George Harris, is equally confused and torn when he meets George on the run. Each man capitulates to humanity, the Southerner in a manner anticipating the dilemma of Huck Finn: "I s'pose, perhaps, I an't following my judgment,—hang it, I *won't* follow my judgment!" (*UTC*, 141). Others, less sensitive, demonstrate the inadequacy of legal definition to restrain the coarser human passions. George's owner, Mr. Harris, who had hired his slave out to Mr. Wilson (at good wages and thus at a profit to himself), in a fit of unbridled spite at George's bearing and talents takes his chattel back to degraded labor on the plantation. And the supreme example is Simon Legree, who destroys Uncle Tom in brutal anger when unable to break his will.

The narrative, after all, follows essentially the wanderings of the lowly; as readers we must stand in with the slave, seeing things largely from his perspective if not directly through his perception. In other words, our reading is controlled chiefly by the slave's frame of reference—not the patriarch's—and Mrs. Stowe's insistent focus assures us in general and in detail of the slave's equivalent humanity. Establishing the slave as a unique and human personality, reinforcing concrete characterization by angle of vision, she then goes on to trap the white man into admitting it in word and deed. Inescapably the Thing turns out to be a Man.

The most formidable feature of Mrs. Stowe's work, however, was her attack on the domestic metaphor of proslavery thought. These same legal codes so restricting the slave were for the slaveholder notoriously elastic and permissive. The slaveholder, in fact, was released freely into the custody of his own character, and that character, according to the "oft-fabled poetic legend," was patriarchal. Even as *Uncle Tom's Cabin* was running in the *National Era*, this thesis was given classic expression by a Georgian:

The Slave Institution at the South increases the tendency to dignify the family. Each planter in fact is a Patriarch—his position compels him to be a ruler in his household. From early youth, his children and servants look up to him as the head, and obedience and subordination become important elements of education. Where so many depend upon one will, society assumes the Hebrew form. Domestic relations become those which are most prized—each family recognizes its duty—and its members feel a responsibility for its discharge. The fifth commandment becomes the foundation of Society. The state is looked to only as the ultimate head in external relations while all internal duties, such as support, education, and the relative duties of individuals, are left to domestic regulation.[5]

Paternalistic in image and argument, this gambit was closely allied in its Old Testament origins to the Scriptural defense of slavery. Perhaps Biblical imagery eased the slaveholder's conscience; at any rate, the patriarchal thesis provided the mitigating "poetry" which, acknowledging the *man* in the *thing*, flatly contradicted the legal formulation of slavery.

Flowering after 1830, the patriarchal legend had roots deep in the past. As American slavery slowly and systematically evolved during the seventeenth century, one of the issues disturbing the colonists was the legal effect of baptism for the exotic African stranger. In the beginning the sacrament seems to have freed him—or at least to have given him equal status with the European laborer. This in turn led many planters to oppose his baptism. Yet as the color line or "racial" line became more and more important in distinguishing the African, legal codes arose to reinforce it and the religious issue faded.[6] By the early eighteenth century, a Virginia planter like William Byrd II could find his own image in the Pentateuch:

Like one of the Patriarchs, I have my Flocks and my Herds, my Bond-men and Bond-women, and every Soart of Trade amongst my own Servants, so that I live in a kind of Independence on every one but Providence. However tho' this Soart of Life is without expence, yet it is attended with a great deal of trouble. I must take care to keep all my People to their Duty, to set all the Springs in motion and to make every one draw his equal Share to carry the Machine forward.[7]

[5] C. G. Memminger, Lecture before the Young Men's Library Association of Augusta, Georgia, . . . (Augusta, 1851); quoted in W. S. Jenkins, *Pro-Slavery Thought in the Old South* (Chapel Hill, 1935), 210.

[6] Jenkins, pp. 14–22; Oscar Handlin, *Race and Nationality in American Life* (Garden City, New York, 1957), Ch. I.

[7] Letter to Charles, Earl of Orkney, July 5, 1726; *Virginia Magazine of History and Biography*, XXXII (January, 1924), 27.

To make the master responsible for his religious education, colonial clergymen taught that the slave was engrafted into the master's family; even a Harvard debater, on the eve of the Revolution when the Northern colonies were well on their way to full emancipation, defended slavery with the domestic metaphor.[8]

For the next fifty years the familial image (not, be it noted, without considerable foundation in the existing social order) became more and more central in the defences of "our peculiar institution." And after the Nat Turner rebellion, the Virginia debates on slavery, and the founding of Garrison's *The Liberator,* after Northern antislavery agitation entered the halls of Congress, the patriarchal theme grew more insistent. Classic defenders of slavery like T. R. Dew, J. H. Hammond, and W. G. Simms continued to sweeten the harsh facts with the poetic legend. And at the war's edge a Southern clergyman was still explaining that

> our institution of slavery is now domestic and patriarchal; the slave has all the family associations, and family pride, and sympathies of the master. He is born in the house, and bred with the children. The sentiments which spring from this circumstance, in the master and the slave, soften all the asperities of the relation, and secure obedience as a sort of filial respect.[9]

But Mrs. Stowe was fully prepared to expose the legend. At the opening of *Uncle Tom's Cabin* the Shelbys' Kentucky plantation seems generally an affectionate enclave, as does, later, the New Orleans town mansion of the St. Clares. Yet there is a notable ambiguity in the black-white relationships; the white masters play both filial and patriarchal roles. That is, Uncle Tom's fatherly solicitude for young George Shelby, and later for Eva St. Clare, is no more apparent than his concern for their respective male parents. Slave and boy he may be on one level, on another he seems more the avuncular figure his name suggests. In Eva St. Clare's world, the maternal figures—Mamma (white) and Mammy (black)—are ironically if obviously juxtaposed to emphasize the greater parental affection of the slave.

[8] Jenkins, pp. 14–15; 44–46. Jenkins concludes that the debate "probably reflected the prevailing pro-slavery thought of the period."

[9] Quoted in B. M. Palmer, *The Life and Letters of James Henley Thornwell* (Richmond, 1875), 422.

Kinship titles of *Mammy, Uncle,* and *Aunt* applied to slaves throughout the novel reinforce the familial metaphor no less forcefully in *Uncle Tom's Cabin* than in Southern life and legend. Especially in the scenes of St. Clare's household Mrs. Stowe represents the easy domestic intermingling of black and white, and a parental privilege appropriated with equal familiarity in both groups.

But *"so long as the law considers all these human beings, with beating hearts and living affections, only as so many* things *belonging to a master,—so long as the failure, or misfortune, or imprudence* [Shelby], *or death* [St. Clare] *of the kindest owner, may cause them any day to exchange a life of kind protection and indulgence for one of hopeless misery and toil* [Legree],— *so long it is impossible to make anything beautiful or desirable in the best regulated administration of slavery."* This exposes the crushing paradox of the patriarchal legend; for the principle of "exchange" could never be eliminated within the institution of slavery as legally defined, and without legal definition the institution would founder. "This trade is a sore subject with the defenders of slavery," observed an English traveler. "It is difficult to weave it handsomely in among the amenities of the patriarchal institution."[10]

To exchange one life for another is a form of separation from familiar surroundings, and separation is the leitmotif of *Uncle Tom's Cabin.*[11] Separations occur throughout *Uncle Tom's Cabin* within white families as well as black (death and sale become equivalent images)—separations of husband and wife, brother and sister, parent and child. At first glance they merely seem natural vicissitudes, inherent in slave-trading of course but in many cases equally common to life in general. In a patriarchal society, however, there are additional relationships; as the English traveler had intimated, the separation of slave and master is also destructive of the "institutional" family, a flagrant violation of the patriarchal enclave. Familial harmony is ruptured by the sale of slave "kinfolk"; deprivation and anguish touch even the master group. Witness Mrs. Shelby: she had "mothered" her slaves, had "cared for them, instructed them,

10 Quoted in K. M. Stampp, *The Peculiar Institution* (New York, 1956), 265–66.

11 Professor Foster has elaborated this insight most helpfully; see *The Rungless Ladder,* 35–40.

watched over them, and known all their little cares and joys, for years" (*UTC*, 42). Eliza's husband, George Harris, recognized her parental care for Eliza; and when Eliza comes to her tearfully, fearing the sale of little Harry, Mrs. Shelby tells her, "I would as soon have one of my own children sold" (*UTC*, 22, 14). Later, faced with the accomplished sale of Uncle Tom and Harry, she remarks helplessly that it contradicts all she had endeavored to teach her slaves of "the duties of the family, of parent and child, and husband and wife" (*UTC*, 42). With every sale, then, the unity of the plantation family and the integrity of the patriarchal vision are shattered.

But the tragic complication lay in the darkest tangle of relations within the patriarchy—when the two "families" blended. For the separation of master and slave was, often enough, a separation of husband and wife, brother and sister, parent and child. How literally related to the master's family some "aunts," "uncles," and "mammies" were, after all. Miscegenation compounded by separation was the ultimate irony in the face of the patriarchal legend and its familial, domestic imagery. What could be a sharper contradiction of the legal definition of the slave—"the man that is a thing"—than the fact of miscegenation? What a more obvious admission of the Negro's humanity? Miscegenation should have reinforced the patriarch's boast; but this was a contradiction few patriarchs were willing to embrace. Through its visible results it actually signified for society only another fracture—that of the white family which the patriarch headed.

Of course in *Uncle Tom's Cabin* the complex issue of miscegenation is peripheral to Uncle Tom's trials. The compound of miscegenation and separation asserts itself most forcefully in the backgrounds of Eliza and George Harris, and their escape North is overshadowed (in the popular imagination, at least) by the story of Tom's journey downriver. But the story of Cassy, Legree's mistress and (as it turns out) Eliza's mother, is a paradigm of slavery's Negro-white relations founded on an unstable and extra-legal "domestic" emotion which constantly dissolves in the face of outside pressures. And if Cassy's white father had at least loved her, and had intended to free her, George Harris was not even that fortunate. Son of a proud white man, his mother "was one of those unfortunates of her race, marked out by personal beauty to be the slave of the passions of her possessor, and the mother of children who may never know a father" (*UTC*, 135). George tells Mr. Wilson, as he plots escape, that his father didn't "think enough of me to keep me from being sold with his dogs and horses, to satisfy the estate, when he died. I saw my mother put up at sheriff's sale, with her seven children. They were sold before her eyes, one by one, all to different masters" (*UTC*, 138).

Although only these histories of miscegenation are retold in the novel, the tragic situation of the "mixed-bloods" is hinted at often enough. Usually unremembered by readers, Mrs. Stowe faced not merely the brute fact of color; she examined the subtle and refining detail of its gradations. In brief vignette a mulatto mother and a quadroon daughter are separated on the auction block, their destinies seamlessly woven from their heritage (*UTC*, ch. xxx). In St. Clare's household, 'Dolphe, Jane, and Rosa, the "white niggers," are posed in perilous imbalance. As Dinah the cook remarks to Rosa, "You seem to tink yourself white folks. You an't nerry one, black *nor* white. I'd like to be one or turrer" (*UTC*, 297). Even these lesser figures are products of a shadowy broken family—like the Joe Christmases of future fiction, they "don't know who [they] are."

The thrust of Mrs. Stowe's imagination was firmly established in her second novel; the social and psychological complications of miscegenation in a patriarchal society were to hold her attention in *Dred* (1856), which we might glance at here. For if black Uncle Tom receives more of our consideration in Mrs. Stowe's first novel than George and Eliza Harris, "mixed-bloods," the dramatic emphasis is reversed in *Dred*. Several lines of narrative are interwoven in this novel, but much of the time we follow the fortunes of the Gordon family, *dexter* and *sinister*. Harry Gordon, a quadroon, managing his deceased father's estate for his white sister, Nina, suffers the harsh abuse of his younger white brother, Tom (Harry is the only child aware of the kinship), until at Nina's death, unprotected by law, he is forced to flee into the swamp with his quadroon wife (the object of Tom's vengeful lust). We learn also, by report, that Harry's quadroon sister, Cora, had become the mistress and then the wife of a white cousin who moved North freeing both Cora and their children; but after his death Cora murders their children when, trying to claim family property in Mississippi, they are all sold back into slavery.

Lurid complications these, but Mrs. Stowe never loses sight of the primary issues. A crucial scene returns us to that paradox with which she had begun *Uncle Tom's Cabin*. In a suit of criminal battery brought against a slaveholder on behalf of a slave, the patriarchal thesis and its familial analogy, advanced as a corollary argument, fall before the law. Mrs. Stowe puts into the mouth of a fictitious judge the actual decree of a North Carolina decision: the court will not recognize the application of the familial analogy in the relation of master and slave since slavery is for the master's profit and security, not for the slave's happiness. "There is no likeness between the cases. They are in opposition to each other, and there is an impassable gulf between them. . . ." The master's power must be absolute.[12]

Here again is a sharp reminder of the basic inconsistencies of proslavery argument, lurching back and forth between legal and patriarchal defenses. Slavery remained paradoxical viewed from legend or from fact. However much any given slaveholder governed his chattels by the one, he could not escape correlative conditions of the other; he was himself a victim of the institution. To return finally to *Uncle Tom's Cabin:* Shelby, St. Clare, and Legree reveal, each in his characteristic behavior, the vices and contradictions inherent in the system. Simply refusing to articulate the dilemma, Shelby rides away from home after the sale of Uncle Tom to avoid the sight of his departure; a man made essentially hypocritical and evasive, what he does not see does not exist. St. Clare, deeply and sensitively aware of the human issues and striving to practise the patriarchal ideal, is hemmed into indolence and cynicism by legal definition and social pressure. The brutal Legree, finally, stands arrogantly on his rights of absolute possession in law but is defeated ultimately by the human will whose existence both he and the law have denied. In three different slaveholders, men supposedly "elevated" by the system, Mrs. Stowe discovers the poisonous effects of slavery on the master.

As Mrs. Stowe portrays it, the actual effects of slavery (that "bar sinister" as one character calls it) directly contradict the patriarchal rhetoric of the slaveholder. Degradation visits black and white alike; the one is humiliated and physically violated, the other morally and spiritually brutalized. The center could not hold. Instead of an axial domestic society, stable and con-

[12] *Dred; a Tale of the Great Dismal Swamp* (Boston, 1856) II, 102–3.

servative, patriarchal slavery promoted a confusion of moral values and an endless succession of fractures, covering the land with the homeless, the lonely, and the unidentified.

II

"Truly it would seem that the labour of Sisyphus is laid upon us, the slaveholders of these southern United States," wrote Louisa S. C. McCord as she began her review of *Uncle Tom's Cabin* late in 1852.[13] It was a penetrating allusion which confessed more than she probably intended. Long trained in proslavery dialectic, the South mobilized its reviews, but this must have seemed a hatefully repetitious and tiresome task to many Southerners. From periodical to periodical the overlapping criticism indicates that the same stale arguments at least a generation old had been woven together again. Although the astonishing sales of the novel forced some to admit that Mrs. Stowe was "possessed of a happy faculty of description, an easy and natural style, an uncommon command of pathos and considerable dramatic skill,"[14] not many reviewers offered specifically literary criticism. They seemed constrained to analyse the "arguments" of the book, to challenge the propositional logic of thesis—unwilling, if not unable, to examine its organic and imaginative sufficiency. Even the language of the more temperate reviews reveals the legalistic and logical framework within which they were conceived.[15] Reviewing *Uncle Tom's Cabin* seemed almost literally another round in the vast regional debate which had begun with the Missouri Compromise, if not earlier.

Nothing new was added to old arguments. Critics attacked the improbability of character and story, of course, but most of their effort was directed at other "errors": if the novel was not a deliberate travesty on the South, it improperly generalized from isolated particulars; Mrs. Stowe in her ignorance of the South misinterpreted Southern law and Southern justice, and failed to see that emancipation would be fatal to the welfare of the slave; Northern traders had in their characteristic money-greed developed the slave trade, and Mrs. Stowe should

[13] *Southern Quarterly Review*, XXIII (January, 1853), 81. The title of the magazine will be abbreviated hereafter as *SQR*.

[14] *SLM*, XVIII (October, 1852), 630.

[15] Cf. *SLM*, XVIII (December, 1852), 721–31.

now look to the evils closer home and compare the Southern slave with the hireling poor of the Northern manufacturer. So familiar were the arguments that one finds Mrs. Stowe had anticipated most of them in the novel itself.

For example, both the *Southern Literary Messenger* and the *Southern Quarterly Review* insisted that no slaveholder would treat his slave as Legree had treated Tom; "property interest" alone was sufficient to insure for the slave the kindness and attention of his master:

No man will, in cold blood, burn down his house, because he has got out of temper with its manner of construction; no man will torment to death, or uselessness, whether his beast or his slave, simply because he has taken a prejudice against the structure of body, or turn of mind, of the article. In either case, however much as he may dislike the concern, he will very much prefer handing it over to the first purchaser for a reasonable equivalent in dollars and cents. The malignity of jealous spite can only arise in cases where rivalry has existed. The deadly venom of smothered hatred may rise in the bosom of rival against rival; of friend against friend; of brother against brother; but not—of master against slave.[16]

To write this was not only to ignore the novel but to ignore human nature as well. With momentary effectiveness Cassy, in defending Uncle Tom, had argued the "property interest" with Legree. But in such a personality as Legree both brutality and anger are dramatically credible, and his vicious outrage at the end is the ultimate acceptance of Uncle Tom's humanity. Sharply focused in this instance, the master's economic interest in the slave as chattel was no protection to the slave as man.

Nevertheless, this quotation is significant, for it pivots on an axiomatic Southern belief: the racial inferiority of the Negro, an inferiority ordained by God. It was the keystone of the institution from any point of view. Simms, among others, admitted that without such basis in nature slavery was inexcusable on moral grounds alone. It was likewise the excuse by which abolitionist argument from the natural rights philosophy was parried, since only among "natural" equals would "natural" rights obtain. So with inferiority a basic presupposition, the reviewers of *Uncle Tom's Cabin* claimed that Mrs. Stowe, ignoring the natural disparity of race, misrepresented the slaves as equal in sentiment and feeling to their white masters. They

16 *SQR*, XXIII (January, 1853), 112.

were, in effect, echoing Marie St. Clare: "as to putting down on any sort of equality with us, you know, as if we could be compared, why it's impossible! . . . just as if Mammy could love her little dirty babies as I love Eva!" (*UTC*, 216). Yet the repeated effort was to establish the slippery and paradoxical principle that the Negro slave was *both* man and thing.

Thus the slave occupies a unique status "just at the point we touch upon humanity," as one review expressed it. This was not a denial of sympathy—quite the reverse. Human relationships as well as social organization follow an hierarchical design: "the affections which pass from the child to the slave, descend still by gradation to the brute."[17] And this unique status was a justification for the patriarchal analogy which, as extenuating or descriptive allusion, had larded nearly all proslavery argument. "By nature a grown-up child, [the Negro] requires the authority and indulgence" accorded the child; "such he enjoys under our system."[18] The relationship of master and slave in this system, the defense maintained, is a personal, even a familial one.

Usually at this point the reviewers in one way or another acknowledged *Uncle Tom's Cabin*'s complex image of separation. Few of them ignored the dramatic power of its appeal. But they sought to turn it against the novel. Thus they continued: occasional abuses occurring within the vertical structure of the traditional family (such as separation) are hardly sufficient cause for dis-establishing *that* institution; the unequal status of husband and wife or of parent and child create the natural authority of the one over the other. Should these relationships be destroyed? The agitation for equality of status in either case is equally dangerous. Under such judgment, accepting the argument "from the abuse against the use," no institution in society will escape condemnation. Abolitionist agitation for the slave, then, not only is destructive of the "peculiar institution" but prefigures the overthrow of all institutions of society; ultimately even the order of Nature—and of God—is threatened.[19]

So went one general line of argument. It was a note of warning, a recognition of the revolutionary element involved, which sounded over and over again in the reviews and in all pro-

[17] *DeBow's Review*, XIV (March, 1853), 279.

[18] *Ibid.*, 274. [19] E.g., *SQR*, XXIII (January, 1853), 106–9.

slavery dialectic. "The proposition [of natural equality], then, which may be regarded as embodying the peculiar essence of *Uncle Tom's Cabin*, is a palpable fallacy, and inconsistent with all social organization."[20] The slave, like the wife and the child, is in his proper place on the scale of Nature, and the flow of affection and responsibility can only be maintained along the vertical line. So with a curious obtuseness the critics of *Uncle Tom's Cabin*, even in answering the charge of separation, continued to use the domestic metaphor, apparently blind to the fact that Mrs. Stowe had exposed the South in the glare of its contradiction.

Perhaps at the last, however, an indistinct sense of the weight of his rock and the height of the hill goaded the Southern Sisyphus to anger, for he inevitably descended to the retort personal. The editor of the *Southern Literary Messenger*, for example, in requesting G. F. Holmes to review Mrs. Stowe's novel, had written, "I would have the review as hot as hell fire, blasting and searing the reputation of the vile wretch in petticoats who could write such a volume."[21] Holmes did his best to oblige though his best was rather mild compared to some. Yet he was neither the first nor the last to censure the little woman for having "stepped beyond the hallowed precincts" of her sex.[22]

Here was the domestic issue from another angle, for Southerners were much concerned about the status of woman in antebellum society. The liberating flow of ideas in the nineteenth century had generated innumerable reform movements in the North ("-isms" the South called them, disparagingly)—abolitionism, prohibitionism, Fourierism, Mormonism, . . . and feminism. Increasing Southern suspicion were the obvious links between the abolitionists and the feminists; many of the same agitators divided their time and effort between the two movements. Feminism had been given its impulse by female abolitionists, and Wendell Phillips, spokesman for the abolitionists, had promised "first the Negro then the woman."[23]

[20] *SLM*, XVIII (December, 1852), 729.

[21] Quoted in Clement Eaton, *Freedom of Thought in the Old South* (Durham, 1940), 36–37.

[22] *SLM*, XVIII (December, 1852), 721–22.

[23] Quoted in Helen Papashvily, *All the Happy Endings* (New York, 1956), 74.

That a woman would enter into such masculine affairs as the discussion of the slavery question horrified the Southerner and to his mind offered prima facie evidence that she had "unsexed herself." If Mrs. Stowe would abandon the sanctuary of true womanhood, she left herself open to personal vilification. To Southern sensibilities her novel was diseased, the "loathsome rakings of a foul fancy," and the collection of evidence against slavery which she presented in 1853 as *A Key to Uncle Tom's Cabin* was further confirmation, if any were needed, of her desire to dabble in putrescence.[24] The *ad hominem* was the South's oblique response to the novel's treatment of miscegenation and its broad hints of the sexual gains available in the peculiar institution. Simms himself, a defender of the chivalric faith, sneered at her fondness for the voluptuous portrait of George Harris "whose personal beauty so possesses her imagination," and he would have her condemned to a "perpetual bed-fellowship" with the favorite creature of her own imagination.[25]

Could it be that the connection of the Negro and the female made in the reform movements was to the Southerners some kind of symbol, a shadow thrown by some greater lurking danger? Did they remember, for example, the Nashoba colony where that prodigious female reformer, Frances Wright, had even advocated an amalgamation of the races?[26] It might have been with a sense of relief, as well as of appropriateness, that Southerners saw in print reviews or responses to *Uncle Tom's Cabin* from such women as Louisa McCord and Julia Tyler, wife of the ex-President.[27] These Southern ladies, speaking for their sisters, could put that yankee woman in her place; they could assert and declare the peculiar domestic harmony which was the Southern social order.

They did reinforce the general Southern response to *Uncle Tom's Cabin*, but their claim to represent the Southern female mind is at least open to question. After all, the "hallowed precinct" of the feminine sex was the domestic circle; and if

[24] *SQR*, XXIII (January, 1853), 82; XXIV (July, 1853), 217.

[25] *SQR*, XXIV (July, 1853), 223, 229.

[26] A. Y. Lloyd, *The Slavery Controversy, 1831–1860* (Chapel Hill, 1939), 57.

[27] *SQR*, XXIII (January, 1853), 81–120; *DeBow's Review*, XIV (March, 1853), 258–80; *SLM*, XIX (February, 1853), 120–26.

Uncle Tom's Cabin was anything, it was "essentially domestic and of the family," as George Sand put it.[28] In 1850 the Swedish novelist, Fredrika Bremer, had called for an American mother to write the novel of slavery since "it is the privilege of the woman and the mother which suffers most severely through slavery."[29] Her comment is somewhat ambiguous, but taken simply, she spoke for an unknown number of Southern white women in the midst of slavery.

Simms was certainly aware of the opposition to slavery among many Southern women. In his review of Mrs. Stowe's *A Key to Uncle Tom's Cabin* he remarked that "every old woman's story of private griefs, fancied wrongs and foolish fancies, is greedily seized upon, and held up with exultation [by Mrs. Stowe], if it speaks for her bias." She had built her case, in part, "with here and there a speech complimentary, or letter, from some silly white woman of the South, who has doubts of her husband's good behaviour when he goes abroad o' nights."[30] This was not the only time a hint of Simms's antifeminism entered his proslavery comment. One wonders what his reaction might have been had he been able to peek into the diary of his Charleston acquaintance, Mary Boykin Chesnut, wife of a contributor to his own quarterly, who read *Uncle Tom's Cabin* at least twice. Do her comments reveal, in Simms's phrase, the "jealous apprehensions of a jaundiced wife?"[31]

A respected overseer told Mrs. Chesnut in 1861, " 'in all my life I have only met one or two womenfolk who were not abolitionists in their hearts, and hot ones too.' "[32] Loyal to husband, family, and region they surely were, especially in the public eye. But among them were many Mrs. Shelbys. And other sore doubts were expressed about certain corollaries of patriarchal slavery. In the summer of 1861, Mrs. Chesnut recorded the conversation of a gathering of Confederate ladies which raised the fascinating but forbidden issue: " 'Are our men worse than the others? Does Mrs. Stowe know? You

[28] Quoted in *Life and Letters of Harriet Beecher Stowe,* ed. Annie Fields (Boston, 1897), 153.

[29] Quoted in Foster, p. 57.

[30] *SQR,* XXIV (July, 1853), 216, 233.

[31] "The Morals of Slavery," *The Pro-Slavery Argument* (Charleston, 1852), 231.

[32] *A Diary from Dixie,* ed. Ben Ames Williams (Boston, 1961), 169.

know what I mean?' " The specific reply is " 'No, no worse,' "
but the dialogue continues to ebb and flow about the topic of
the white man's black harem within his white family. "You
see," comments Mrs. Chesnut, "Mrs. Stowe did not hit the
sorest spot. She makes Legree a bachelor."[33]

Other entries in this famous diary indicate that Mrs. Chesnut
never lost sight of the fundamental challenge to the slaveholder's wife posed by the institution. Over a month before
the attack on Sumter she wrote, "like a spider spinning my own
entrails,"

I wonder if it be a sin to think slavery a curse to any land. Men
and women are punished when their masters and mistresses are
brutes, not when they do wrong. Under slavery, we live surrounded
by prostitutes, yet an abandoned woman is sent out of any decent
house. Who thinks any worse of a Negro or mulatto woman for
being a thing we can't name? God forgive us, but ours is a monstrous system, a wrong and an iniquity! Like the patriarchs of old,
our men live all in one house with their wives and their concu-
bines; and the mulattoes one sees in every family partly resemble
the white children. Any lady is ready to tell you who is the father
of all the mulatto children in everybody's household but her own.
Those, she seems to think, drop from the clouds. My disgust sometimes is boiling over. Thank God for my country women, but alas
for the men! They are probably no worse than men everywhere,
but the lower their mistresses, the more degraded they must be."[34]

Perhaps it was not merely fortuitous that a woman wrote
the most successful antislavery work. Simms had complained
that Mrs. Stowe, reasoning "sensuously, from the woman nature," misused the mode of romance for the purposes of sociological criticism: the novel's argument was not logical but
emotional and analogical.[35] In a narrow critical sense he may
have been right. *Uncle Tom's Cabin* is hardly a perfect novel,
even for its own day; the decade of the fifties produced far
richer work. But as Henry James said many years later, *Uncle
Tom's Cabin* was a "wonderful 'leaping' fish" which had
"simply flown through the air."[36] Logic, even the logic of
literary criticism, was too coarse a net to arrest it; perhaps only

[33] *Ibid.*, 121–23.

[34] *Ibid.*, 21–22.   [35] *SQR*, XXIV (July, 1853), 215, 218.

[36] Henry James, *Autobiography*, ed. F. W. Dupee (London, 1956), 92.

a sensuous argument "from the woman nature" could have so illuminated the contradictions of a patriarchal thesis and the extensions of miscegenation.

The implications of Simms's critical complaint suggest that the assertive masculine tenor of Southern society created by the self-willed patriarchy at its apex had really for the first time been challenged—and by powers it had long delegated to women. An apparently logical and self-sufficient rhetoric had crippled the imagination, drying up the springs of sensibility. As a representative defender of the patriarchal faith himself, Simms had only the institutional vision and rhetorical feelings peculiar to his caste and sex; how could he comprehend life among the lowly? Without a wider sympathy for the human condition, the patriarchy was now being undermined by the pressing flood of a sensuous argument it could hardly comprehend, let alone acknowledge. *Uncle Tom's Cabin* challenged the Southerner to grope too deeply below the surface logic of his stance, to confront his own hidden motives and desires. The only real alternatives were evasion or confession, the choice of Shelby or of St. Clare (there were never many Legrees in the antebellum South though Legree stood as the ultimate desperation of both the others). One is not surprised that most chose the former.

III

There were many attempts before the war to answer Mrs. Stowe in fiction. But the proslavery novelists got no more critical support than they deserved. Written usually, G. F. Holmes had declared, "by weak and incompetent persons,"[37] the proslavery novels simply lifted traditional proslavery argument directly into narrative.[38] Simms himself had boasted of answering *Uncle Tom's Cabin* in his novel, *Woodcraft*.[39] But even

[37] *SLM*, XVIII (December, 1852), 727.

[38] See J. R. Tandy, "Pro-Slavery Propaganda in American Fiction of the Fifties," *South Atlantic Quarterly*, XXI (January–April, 1922), 41–50; 170–78.

[39] *The Letters of William Gilmore Simms*, ed. M. C. S. Oliphant, A. T. Odell, and T. C. D. Eaves (Columbia, S.C., 1952–56), III, 222–23. The boast seems petulant and something of an afterthought. But J. V. Ridgely has examined the claim in detail. See "*Woodcraft*: Simms's First Answer to *Uncle Tom's Cabin*," *American Literature*, XXXI (January, 1960), 421–33.

though avoiding the issue of miscegenation, Simms was caught in an old dilemma. If *Woodcraft* espouses the patriarchal ideal, it does not do so without considerable opposition. When the hero protects or "spoils" his slaves, he defeats his overseer's plans for plantation efficiency. Self-assured in his knowledge of what he calls "nigger-nature," the overseer, for his part, constantly resists the hero's excursions into patriarchal generosity. Only the economical use of slave labor can establish domestic security, for patriarchal prodigality endangers the enclave, risking bankruptcy and the sale of slaves. Creating perpetual tension, economic necessity constantly opposes the "domestic sentiments."

The constant repetition of threadbare arguments in the "anti-Tom" literature suggests that any effort to break out of the patriarchal vision of society in the antebellum South had been thwarted by a determined conspiracy of the will which, if it could not create, could at least hobble or destroy.

Response from the South has not yet exhausted Mrs. Stowe's literary challenge. The legendary solace of paternalism and the fearful bogy of miscegenation still flourish, the old litanies are still intoned, below the Mason-Dixon line. Over the years, however, have come Southern writers like Cable and Faulkner willing to face imaginatively the contradictions of their peculiar heritage. Certainly no modern reader of *The Grandissimes* and *Madame Delphine*, of *Light in August*, *Absalom, Absalom!*, and *Go Down, Moses* can escape the conclusion that miscegenation is still a crucial theme, or that the patriarchal legend still establishes its ironic patterns through the collateral genealogy of black and white. Simply juxtaposing Faulkner and Mrs. Stowe, we can see the evasive lineaments of Shelby more subtly drawn in both Ike McCaslin and Sutpen, the protective verbal façade of St. Clare in Gavin Stevens, and established by the weaknesses of these, the "untraditional" bushwhacker's descendant, Flem Snopes, who refines the coarser, cruder depredations of Simon Legree. Other writers, far more talented and much closer to the scene, have taken up the themes of Mrs. Stowe. But however lurid and glaring it may seem to the sophisticate of today, however crude its appeal, *Uncle Tom's Cabin* still knifes to the heart of the matter.

IX

JAMES M. COX

"Pudd'nhead Wilson": The End of Mark Twain's American Dream

The recent revival of interest in *Pudd'nhead Wilson* should not surprise us, trapped as we are in the ancient American racial dilemma. Indeed, our troubled awareness of the approaching crisis may have provided the insight with which to see the book through the obscurity which had surrounded it for sixty years. Reading it today, we recognize that it had the kind of finality for Twain that our recent experience of Little Rock has had for us. For *Pudd'nhead* was his last American novel, the final volume in what we may justly call his Mississippi trilogy, and deserves the central position he assigned it in the Author's National Edition—immediately following *Tom Sawyer* and *Huckleberry Finn*. The bleak irony with which Twain, from the saddened vantage point of manhood, surveyed his boyhood Eden is a prevision of the corrosive disillusion so apparent in his late work. After *Pudd'nhead*, his fiction tended to divide into the bald sentimentality of *Joan of Arc* on the one side and into the puerile cynicism of *The Mysterious Stranger* on the other. Although the fissures of such a disintegration are clearly visible in *Pudd'nhead Wilson*, the novel precariously holds together, containing the coming separation in a vision which is neither cynical nor sentimental; it thus possesses a wholeness which Twain was never again to achieve.

Pudd'nhead Wilson is thus Twain's last *long* look at America and his last major work. This is not to say that it approaches the greatness of *Huckleberry Finn*. Cast in the cramped mold of the sentimental Victorian closet drama, *The Prince and the Pauper*, the plot of *Pudd'nhead* lacks the range and organic movement of Huck Finn's narrative. Any unforewarned reader,

Reprinted from the *South Atlantic Quarterly*, 58 (1959), 351–63, by permission of the Duke University Press and the author.

seeing Twain turn the plot on the arbitrary changeling device, will no doubt expect the novel to demonstrate how the Negro, given the advantages of white status, can prove himself worthy in the manner of Tom Canty. Yet having seen the ultimate direction of the action, one can hardly imagine Olivia Langdon Clemens adapting *Pudd'nhead Wilson*, as she adapted *The Prince and the Pauper*, and presenting it—with the Clemens girls in the major roles—as a Christmas surprise for her husband.

No, *Pudd'nhead Wilson* is of a different order. Hemmed in though it is by its mechanical plot, its depth of reach gives a redeeming substance to the flimsy superstructure which first obtrudes upon us. For Twain, in moving from class lines to racial barriers, had once more come upon his own great animating theme. If we cannot extricate ourselves from the racial dilemma, neither could he; and in this novel he came again to powerful grips with it in a struggle which, challenging him more deeply as he moved, called into action the deepest resources of his imagination. He even bequeathed us a humorous account of the compulsive engagement in his prefatory note to *Those Extraordinary Twins*, the slight farce from which *Pudd'nhead* evolved. Beginning with a frothy tale about Siamese twins, one virtuous and fair and the other vicious and swarthy, Twain found himself suddenly confronted by strange intruders who seized control of the farce:

Among them came a stranger named Pudd'nhead Wilson, and a woman named Roxana; and presently the doings of these pushed up into prominence a young fellow named Tom Driscoll, whose proper place was way in the obscure background. Before the book was half finished those three were taking things almost entirely into their own hands and working the whole tale as a private venture of their own—a tale which they had nothing at all to do with by rights.

Seeing the evolving story of the strangers as a tragedy, Twain solved the problem of his hybrid form by extracting the farce, an act which he called a "literary Caesarean operation."

But the novel which remained and which bears the vestigial scars of that operation is hardly a tragedy. It begins with a seemingly pointless joke, chronicles the history of a crime, and ends as Pudd'nhead Wilson, an amateur detective, brings to justice the false Tom Driscoll, who has harassed the peace of Dawson's Landing. What we have is a detective story assuming the proportions of an American problem comedy. The arbitrary neatness of the ending serves only to remind us that the problem has not been finally settled; the triumph of justice, the defeat of the criminal, the success of the long-suffering hero are thin masks which seem deliberately to reveal the larger doom, the deeper crime, and the final failure to which we have been exposed. Coward, thief, and murderer though Tom Driscoll is, his indictment is as disturbing as it is gratifying, and his presence remains to haunt us long after he has been conveniently sold down the river in the closing moment of the novel. His career, which seemed poised at launching to lead us toward a raceless utopia, but which veered instead through a series of atrocities culminating in selling his mother down the river and murdering his white foster father, is marked more with plight than anything else. We sense, as we review that career, that Tom is the instrument of an avenging destiny which has overtaken Dawson's Landing.

And he is indeed a marked man—a Negro, but how different from Nigger Jim, whom Huck ultimately saw as "white inside." Tom Driscoll is white *outside*, his white face and white talk hiding the mark within. If Jim was the figure responsible for Huck's moral awakening, Tom Driscoll is the nightmare terrorizing the moral sleep of Dawson's Landing. Only one thirty-second black, he is invisible to his victims, for the six generations of white patrimony contributing to his creation have physically equipped him to assume the role of changeling which Twain assigns him. He thus stands always in the foreground as the avatar of the long history of miscegenation in the background, and, although Twain never elaborated that background, his book is nevertheless the history of a time, a place, and a crime. He had good reason for insistently referring to his narrative as a chronicle. Because miscegenation could culminate in the problem of mistaken identity, his arbitrary fictional device was justified and became the organic means of dramatizing the last phase of a society trapped by its secret history. For although the slaveholding society of Dawson's Landing is built around an aristocracy of Virginia gentlemen who worship honor, we discover as the novel unfolds that across their coats of arms runs a dark bar sinister, an indelible stain disfiguring not only the Driscoll heraldic pattern but that of every white man who upholds the social structure. The First Families cannot, of course, see the stain, simply because they have conditioned themselves not to see it, but from our coign of vantage outside the novel we see it in the person of Thomas à Becket Driscoll.

Spawned at the very center of their legalized institution of slavery, he crosses the color line in a white disguise they themselves have given him, and their inability to recognize him constitutes the moral blindness pervading the white world of Dawson's Landing. For he is, after all, the son of white men's casual lust gratified by a series of aggressive sexual acts at the expense of their slaves. Although the masters may have assumed economic responsibility for these actions, their repeated willingness to cross the color line—the legal fiction they have created to define the unbridgeable gulf separating the races—merely underlines their refusal of any moral responsibility in the matter. The miscegenation which they tacitly permit within the framework of slavery is in fact their own covert affirmation of the inexorable bond between the races. This submerged ligature carrying white blood steadily down into the area of human life separated and suppressed by slavery makes possible the emergence of the false Tom Driscoll into the white world, and the dark force he possesses upon his return represents the loss of power sustained by the ruling classes.

Pudd'nhead Wilson thus portrays a world in which the power of those who rule has been transferred to those who serve, for if the origin of Tom's power is the lust out of which he was created, the immediate source is embodied in the personality of his mother, Roxana, who shifts him into the cradle of the white heir. One of Twain's greatest creations, she possesses the strength, the passion, and the fertility so strikingly absent in the white women she serves; indeed, her darker beauty merely emphasizes their fragility. Twain remarks that on the same day she bore her son she was "up and around," while Mrs. Percy Driscoll "died within the week" of her ordeal of childbirth. The long logic underlying this chronicle explains why she claims such power, for the secret channel which the white men have established as an outlet for their lust has transferred into her orbit the passion they have denied their wives. If the transfer has bestowed an innocence upon the white women, it has also left them impotent. Small wonder that in the slave South of Mark Twain's memory the Negro women became the Mammies who were the real mothers in a society so obsessed with innocence that it divested, figuratively if not literally, its ordained mothers of their vitality. The white women of the privileged classes could not be real mothers at all—at least in the Southern gentleman's idealized vision of existence—and were relieved of the odious obligation as soon after the travails of childbirth as possible.

In rearing the white man's legitimate children and giving birth to his illegitimate ones, Roxana bears what their honor cannot bear; the innocence in which they pride themselves is maintained by thrusting all guilt upon her. Even her release of Tom into the white world grows appropriately out of her arraignment before Percy Driscoll on the false charge of petty larceny; moreover, she acts not in vengeance but out of desperation to save him from the fate of slaves sold down the river. That her defensive action has such aggressive consequences indicates the unconscious power she commands. And when Tom Driscoll is finally unmasked, she is naturally the sole person in the courtroom who can assume any responsibility for the crime. Her cry, "De Lord have mercy upon me, po' misable sinner dat I is!" is an agonized wail of self-awareness in a world of moral blindness and confirms the real nobility she has possessed throughout the novel. She is the dark queen, but the real queen nevertheless, in the social order which Twain envisions. Although the "nobles" of the society bear the names of the court lovers of the Elizabethan world, the white queens in this new world imitation of the old remain as remotely in the background of the novel as the real Tom Driscoll who shambles about the slave quarters. Roxana alone has the magic power to create drama and to become a primary force in the world she serves.

The moral responsibilities thrust upon her become her moral force, enabling her to vitalize with primitive insight the empty illusions which she inherits from the world above her. Reprimanding Tom for his failure to meet the terms of the code duello, she affirms her honor and origins with a summary of the family pedigree:

Whatever has become o' yo' Essex blood? Dat's what I can't understan'. En it ain't ony jist Essex blood dat's in you, not by a long sight —deed it ain't! My great-great-great-granfather en yo' great-great-great-great-granfather was Ole Cap'n John Smith, de highest blood dat Ole Virginny ever turned out, en *his* great-great-granmother or somers along back dah, was Pocahontas de Injun Queen, en her husban' was a nigger King outen Africa—en yit here you is, a-slinkin' outen a duel en disgracin' our whole line like a ornery low-down hound! Yes, it's de nigger in you!

Even as she unintentionally parodies the genealogical obsessions of the First Families, she confronts our distinctive national heritage, the strange and remarkable history which defines and sets us apart from the Old World. Can we not say that the outrageous truth of her vision of history is largely responsible for the high humor of her parody? Her sketch of the American family tree is surely far more accurate than the tenuous tracings educed by the First Families of Virginia, at least insofar as the terms of this novel describe that history. The self-styled aristocrats of Dawson's Landing, in refusing the crucial burdens of their real past, cut themselves off from the power which responsibility conveys. Since their denial of their secret history is a denial of themselves, their blood which flows in that covert tradition becomes their nemesis in the form of Tom Driscoll.

As long as Tom is ignorant of his identity, he does not direct his inborn hostility upon his fathers but gratifies his uncontrollable temper with cruel jokes perpetrated upon the slaves who serve him. His brutal treatment of Roxy, however, eventually angers her into humiliating him with the facts of his lineage. His discovery of his true mother, paralyzing though it is in its impact, is nevertheless a discovery of himself and a half-conscious realization of his destiny; the malevolence of his will, which has for so long been indiscriminately aggressive, begins to find its fated target. Thus, when Roxy tauntingly asks him what his father would think of his refusal to accept the dueler's challenge, Tom "said to himself that if his father were only alive and in reach of assassination his mother would soon find that he had a very clear notion of the size of his indebtedness to that man, and was willing to pay it up in full, and would do it too, even at risk of his life. . . ." At such a moment, when even Twain's rhetoric points forward to Faulkner, outward and inward action of the narrative coalesce to give us both social and psychological reality. We see—how can we keep from seeing?—that Thomas à Becket Driscoll is the secret agent who carries back across the color line the repressed guilt which has gathered at the heart of slavery.

Although he withholds his terrible intention from Roxy,

Tom has willingly seized upon his fated mission, and the narrative moves with compelling logic toward the catastrophe: the murder of Judge Driscoll. For the Judge, who harbors within his walls the invisible assailant, is not only Tom's foster father and inevitable target of his malice; he is also the living symbol of law and order in the community, and his murder suggests the anarchy which the white men have, by their own actions, released upon themselves. There is a final justice in Tom's being disguised as a Negro when he plunges the Indian knife into the Judge's heart, for in this disguise he becomes at last what his fathers have made him at the moment of his fated act.

This then is the crime which strikes at the heart of Dawson's Landing. The man who finally "sees" Tom Driscoll and restores a semblance of honor to the community is quite appropriately the rank outsider, Pudd'nhead Wilson. Having wandered west from his native New York to seek his fortune, Wilson comes into the community a free agent. His "freedom" places him at opposite poles from the fate in which Driscoll is caught. So far apart are they—Wilson on the periphery of the society, Tom at the center—that Twain resorts to arbitrary devices to draw them together. Thus we have a series of accidents by which a sense of relationship is established: Pudd'nhead arrives in Dawson's Landing during the month in which Tom is born; Wilson is rejected by the society at almost the same time Tom enters it; his rise to fame begins the moment Tom's honor is questioned; he even shares character traits with his opposite—both are notorious idlers, both are collegiately sophisticated, and both are given to droll and cutting irony. Finally, both share a desire for the limelight, and when Wilson exploits the drama of the final courtroom scene, he has merely usurped the role of showman which Tom has played in the society. At opposite points on the wheel of fortune, the destinies of these two figures are inexorably related through the axis of their polarity, and the ascending fortune of Pudd'nhead comes necessarily at the expense of Tom's fall. The novel appropriately ends with Wilson standing above his cowering antagonist to pronounce his doom.

This plot machinery often fails to rise above mere mechanical contrivance, and yet Twain's insistence on these surface similarities points to a deeper relationship which becomes manifest as Wilson maneuvers through the novel. His first act upon entering Dawson's Landing is to mutter the joke which launches the novel. Hearing an "invisible" dog barking behind the scenes, he expresses to a group of idle citizens the wish that he owned half the dog. Upon being asked why, Wilson rejoins, "Because I would kill my half." The only response the literal minded inhabitants can make to this sally is summed up by one of the gullible bystanders, who inquires of his comrades, "What did he reckon would become of the other half if he killed his half? Do you reckon he thought it would live?" Although we may be inclined to agree with Jay B. Hubbell's contention that the joke is typically small town and that "the village yokels would have yelled with delight at it," the wise-crack, coming as it does from a total stranger, reveals a discomforting familiarity at the same time that it betrays a brazen threat, and they instinctively withdraw, rejecting the newcomer as a "pudd'nhead."

Wilson's subsequent behavior lends a measure of justification to their puzzled distrust, for although he ultimately discloses the invisible assassin in their midst, he is also the one who plants in Roxy's mind the possibility that her son is indistinguishable from the legitimate Driscoll heir. "How do you tell them apart, Roxy, when they haven't any clothes on?" he asks with idle innocence, and in the light of the ensuing action his casual remark assumes the significance it does by providing the excuse for that action. Remembering it and assuming that if the shrewd Wilson cannot distinguish the children neither can the dull-witted villagers, Roxy determines to shift her son into the cradle of the real Tom Driscoll. And if Wilson is capable of suggesting the possibility of mistaken identity in the village, he is also busily engaged in erecting a system of detection which will counteract such a possibility. Just as his casual observation to Roxy reveals his assumption that personal identity in Dawson's Landing is a matter of mere appearance, his reliance upon the use of fingerprints as a means of criminal detection undercuts the whole structure of familial identity which characterizes the community. His determination to establish a complete fingerprint file of every member of the society is a stratagem for checking personal identity against the one unchanging characteristic of human physiology. Trusting only these "natal autographs," as he calls them, Wilson refuses to rely on names and faces, the conventional hallmarks of identity. His arduous "hobby" is in fact based on an essential distrust of the identity of the entire community.

Having helped precipitate the problem which only his system can solve, Wilson's final apprehension of the criminal should surprise us much less than it seems to surprise him. But the detached curiosity with which he surveys the village renders him peculiarly blind to the series of incidents set in motion by his own idle remark to Roxy, and, although he holds Tom Driscoll's true signature within arm's reach, he is almost as bewildered by the murder case as the dullest citizen in Dawson's Landing. The fatal attraction between detective and criminal is the only thing that finally saves him from failure, despite his foolproof system. For Tom compulsively seeks Wilson out to taunt him for failing to solve the murder of the Judge, only to leave his tell-tale print on one of Wilson's glass slides. Seeing Wilson's shocked countenance and unaware of his fatal error, Tom grants his host's request to be left in peace, but he cannot resist a parting gibe. "Don't take it so hard," he says; "a body can't win every time; you'll hang somebody yet." Wilson's reply is a mutter to himself: "It is no lie to say I am sorry I have to begin with you, miserable dog though you are."

More than being a silent retort to Driscoll's taunt, Wilson's remark is an oblique answer to the joke which initiated his career, for, in addition to finding the "invisible dog" which disturbed the peace of the community, he has assumed the role of killer which he first proposed for himself. The terms of the joke thus become the terms of the novel, and Wilson's casual wish to own half of the unseen dog is realized at the dramatic moment in which he establishes Tom's identity and guilt. As a result of Wilson's discovery, Tom reverts from his role of secret agent to the status of property "owned" by the society at the same instant that Wilson's twenty-three year period of rejection is ended and he is embraced into the community of owners as a reward for his achievement. As the two figures merge into the social order at the conclusion of the narrative, we see at last that they are the real twins in this novel which grew around a farce about Siamese twins. Having come upon their invisible ligature, Twain instinctively embraced the pair, choosing to pursue their careers even at the embarrassing cost of ignoring the true Tom Driscoll, who humbly keeps his place in the slave quarters outside the action of the drama.

As the curtain falls on the problem comedy, Pudd'nhead has convinced the townspeople that honor is restored and the blot removed from the community escutcheon. By exposing the flaw of Tom Driscoll's identity, however, he has actually disclosed the flaw in the entire society, for Tom is, under the terms of slavery and by virtue of the final court decision, irrevocably the property of the community. Knowing this, we must also know that the honor of Dawson's Landing is merely respectability. This is not to say that Twain hated the Virginia gentlemen who bestrode the society of Dawson's Landing. Wilson, the stranger, sides with them and struggles to protect them from the criminal they have fathered. But to say, as F. R. Leavis has said, that "Mark Twain unmistakably admires Judge Driscoll and Pembroke Howard" is to forget that the irony of this chronicle takes the measure of the honor they uphold. If York Leicester Driscoll's only religion was "to be a gentleman—a gentleman without stain or blemish," we are forced to see that such a religion is as false a front as the shabby whitewash on the houses of the sleeping village. Although Twain sympathizes with the white patriarchs and although he never portrays them as vicious, he does judge them; they are the ones who are indicted before the bar when the false Thomas à Becket Driscoll is brought to justice.

Both Twain's and Wilson's awareness of this larger indictment is reflected in Pudd'nhead's calendar maxims which provide epigraphs for each chapter and which constitute an extra dimension of the novel. Standing above and beyond the narrative in a timeless moral realm outside, yet against, the temporal history of the chronicle, the aphorisms of this latter-day Poor Richard are his final comments on the time of man. They form the brief of his case against the society which has enthralled Tom Driscoll at the same time that they disclose the disenchantment at the core of Wilson's vision. Reading these grim last words, we realize how far this novel, cast in a sentimental mold, has thrust toward cynicism. And yet the bleak disillusion of these last words—three times Wilson cries for the deliverance of death through the compact grammar of his apothegms—suggests that, despite the moral rigor with which his knowledge of the larger crime has endowed him, he cannot quite bring himself to bear the burden of his discovery. His price of admission into the society has been to co-operate in pushing Tom Driscoll down the dark river of the social mind into the harsher areas of repression, and as the hero of Dawson's Landing he owns as much of Tom Driscoll as any of the Virginia gentlemen. The redeeming pathos pervading his cynical wit is a mode of expressing his own awareness of his refusal to face the guilt surrounding the crime he has laid bare.

Thus, this Yankee stranger's participation in the crime of the slaveholding community on the banks of the Mississippi extends the import of the novel beyond the South to the nation at large, and his disclosure of the criminal becomes a disillusioning rediscovery of America. When Pudd'nhead, in his final maxim, remarks of October 12, the date of Columbus' discovery, "It was wonderful to find America, but it would have been more wonderful to miss it," we can, with our knowledge of the novel, see beyond his droll observation that it would have been remarkable for the old explorer to miss a continental land mass the size of America. For Pudd'nhead and Mark Twain have made a newer discovery. Columbus had sailed forward to a new world, but Twain, although he dreamed backward through Tom Sawyer's mind toward a boyhood vision of such an Eden, was ceaselessly confronted by an Injun Joe or a Jim—dark figures suggesting the guilt at the center of the garden. Pudd'nhead's discovery of Tom Driscoll is a final unmasking of the heart of darkness beneath the American dream. Columbus' new world has become an old one.

Knowing the nature of Wilson's discovery, we can understand why Twain turned from his native land to search for Eden in the white innocence of Joan of Arc and why, in *The Mysterious Stranger*, he transferred his warm, remembered Mississippi paradise into a remote and frozen European past. Like Hawthorne and Melville before him, he had glimpsed a dark reality behind the American dream of innocence. For him that reality wore the face with which it has so persistently confronted us in America—the face of racial guilt. Remembering Twain's deep abhorrence of slavery, William Dean Howells wrote that "he held himself responsible for the wrong which the white race had done the black race in slavery, and he explained, in paying the way of a Negro student through Yale, that he was doing it as his part of the reparation due from every white man to every black man." And Howells went on to record an incident which strikingly bears upon *Pudd'nhead Wilson:* "About that time a colored cadet was expelled from West Point for some conduct 'unbecoming an officer and gentleman' . . . The man was fifteen parts white, but 'Oh yes,' Clemens said with bitter irony, 'It was the one part black that undid him. It made him a 'nigger' and incapable of being a gentleman. It was to blame for the whole thing.' "

Pudd'nhead Wilson is a penetrating imaginative vision of the attitude Twain expressed to Howells. Although the logic of that vision drove him to undermine the image of his personal past and to retreat in disillusion from it, he at least realized the consequences at which he had arrived. Thus, in a comic foreword to *Pudd'nhead*, aptly entitled "A Whisper to the Reader," Twain vouched for the authenticity of the legal chapters in his book and "sealed" the novel with these words:

Given under my hand this second day of January, 1893, at the Villa Viviani, village of Settignano, three miles back of Florence, on the hills—the same certainly affording the most charming view to be found on this planet, and with it the most dreamlike and enchanting sunsets to be found in any planet or even in any solar system—and given, too, in the swell room of the house, with the busts of Cerretani senators and other grandees of this line looking approvingly down upon me as they used to look down upon Dante, and mutely asking me to adopt them into my family, which I do with pleasure, for my remotest ancestors are but spring chickens compared with these robed and stately antiques, and it will be a great and satisfying lift for me, that six hundred years will.

To take this humor seriously is to take Twain as he wished to be taken. Moreover, viewed in the light of the literary course he ultimately pursued, his seal assumes the finality of the legal form in which it is cast.

Having tracked his sense of guilt to the bitter end, Twain evidently felt in the Italian hills, despite whatever terrors that enchanting old world vision might conceal, a measure of the assured innocence with which Pudd'nhead Wilson had first faced Dawson's Landing. In such a residence he could regain a certain comic poise and irony. He also knew that from that climate and environment Dante had emerged with a vision which could contain Hell and yet culminate in a vision of the radiantly white Beatrice. In the world of Dawson's Landing, however, there was only the dark queen, Roxy, whose final plea for mercy rang past the "happy" ending of his novel to emphasize the guilt from which there was no escape, not even for Pudd'n-head. Perhaps it was with Dante's Inferno in mind that Twain, at the outset of his novel, described the Mississippi as flowing "from the frosty Falls of St. Anthony down through nine climates to torrid New Orleans." Certainly Twain knew, after completing his chronicle, that the "mulatto" waters of the Mississippi, as he referred to them in *Life on the Mississippi,* afforded no beatific vision. After our exposure to the subversive family history of the Driscoll genealogy we can understand why Twain wished to adopt the Cerretani senators as his ancestors. The six hundred year "lift" made possible by such an adoption took him back beyond Columbus' discovery and all the history he felt impinging on his personal memories.

For the world of Twain's personal past, which he kept coming back and back to, lay irrevocably on the west bank of the Mississippi in the slave state of Missouri. Although he followed Tom Sawyer's imaginative forays outside that world, foreshadowing the Hemingway hero's later journeys, he also charted the geography within its borders, following the great river through all its nine climates and discovering along the way a heart of darkness beneath the mask of innocence. His discovery, although he fled from it, remained—a bequest to the many writers who have succeeded him. Thus, if literary influence extends beyond the confines of library walls to act as a force within a cultural continuum, *Pudd'nhead Wilson* stands as a prevision of the world of William Faulkner, Robert Penn Warren, and Ralph Ellison, to name but three writers who have explored the territory which Twain, more than any of the great writers of the nineteenth century, surveyed; for the fates of Joe Christmas, Amantha Starr, and Ellison's invisible man are inextricably bound up with the careers of Thomas à Becket Driscoll and Pudd'nhead Wilson. Indeed, it is hardly surprising that Faulkner, who has explored and developed both the tragic and comic aspects of Twain's province further than any contemporary writer, should trace his literary genealogy to its true source. During his recent tour of Japan, he told Japanese students at Nagano that "Mark Twain was the first truly American writer, and all of us since are his heirs; we descended from him."

X

ARTHUR P. DAVIS

The Harlem of Langston Hughes' Poetry

In a very real sense, Langston Hughes is the poet-laureate of
Harlem. From his first publication down to his latest, Mr.
Hughes has been concerned with the black metropolis. Returning to the theme again and again, he has written about Harlem
oftener and more fully than any other poet. As Hughes has
written about himself:

I live in the heart of Harlem. I have also lived in the heart of Paris,
Madrid, Shanghai, and Mexico City. The people of Harlem seem not
very different from others, except in language. I love the color of
their language: and, being a Harlemite myself, their problems and
interests are my problems and interests.

Knowing how deeply Langston Hughes loves Harlem and
how intimately he understands the citizens of that community,
I have long felt that a study of the Harlem theme in Hughes'
poetry would serve a twofold purpose: it would give us insight into the growth and maturing of Mr. Hughes as a social
poet; it would also serve as an index to the changing attitude
of the Negro during the last quarter of a century.

When Mr. Hughes' first publication, *The Weary Blues*
(1926), appeared, the New Negro Movement was in full
swing; and Harlem, as the intellectual center of the movement,
had become the Mecca of all aspiring young Negro writers
and artists. This so-called Renaissance not only encouraged and
inspired the black creative artist, but it served also to focus as
never before the attention of America upon the Negro artist
and scholar. As a result of this new interest, Harlem became
a gathering place for downtown intellectuals and Bohemians
—many of them honestly seeking a knowledge of Negro art
and culture, others merely looking for exotic thrills in the black

Reprinted from *Phylon*, 13 (1952), 276–83, by permission of the editor of
Phylon.

community. Naturally, the latter group was much the larger of the two; and Harlem, capitalizing on this new demand for "primitive" thrills, opened a series of spectacular cabarets. For a period of about ten years, the most obvious and the most sensational aspect of the New Negro Movement for downtown New York was the night life of Harlem. The 1925 Renaissance, of course, was not just a cabaret boom, and it would be decidedly unfair to give that impression. But the Harlem cabaret life of the period was definitely an important by-product of the new interest in the Negro created by the movement, and this life strongly influenced the early poetry of Langston Hughes.

Coming to Harlem, as he did, a twenty-two-year-old adventurer who had knocked around the world as sailor and beachcomber, it was only natural that Hughes should be attracted to the most exotic part of that city—its night life. The Harlem of *The Weary Blues* became therefore for him "Jazzonia," a new world of escape and release, an exciting never-never land in which "sleek black boys" blew their hearts out on silver trumpets in a "whirling cabaret." It was a place where the bold eyes of white girls called to black men, and "dark brown girls" were found "in blond men's arms." It was a city where "shameless gals" strutted and wiggled, and the "night dark girl of the swaying hips" danced beneath a papier-mâché jungle moon. The most important inhabitants of this magic city are a "Nude Young Dancer," "Midnight Nan at Leroy's," a "Young Singer" of *chansons vulgaires*, and a "Black Dancer in the Little Savoy."

This cabaret Harlem, this Jazzonia is a joyous city, but the joyousness is not unmixed; it has a certain strident and hectic quality, and there are overtones of weariness and despair. "The long-headed jazzers" and whirling dancing girls are desperately trying to find some new delight, and some new escape. They seem obsessed with the idea of seizing the present moment as though afraid of the future: "Tomorrow . . . is darkness / Joy today!" "The rhythm of life / Is a jazz rhythm" for them, but it brings only "The broken heart of love / The weary, weary heart of pain." It is this weariness and this intensity that one hears above the laughter and even above the blare of the jazz bands.

There is no daytime in Jazzonia, no getting up and going to work. It is wholly a sundown city, illuminated by soft lights, spotlights, jewel-eyed sparklers, and synthetic stars in the scenery. Daylight is the one great enemy here, and when "the new dawn / Wan and pale / Descends like a white mist," it brings only an "aching emptiness," and out of this emptiness there often comes in the clear cool light of morning the disturbing thought that the jazz band may not be an escape, it may not be gay after all:

> Does a jazz-band ever sob?
> They say a jazz-band's gay . . .
> One said she heard the jazz-band sob
> When the little dawn was gray.

In this respect, the figure of the black piano player in the title poem is highly symbolic. Trying beneath "the pale dull pallor of an old gas light" to rid his soul of the blues that bedeviled it, he played all night, but when the dawn approached:

> The singer stopped playing and went to bed
> While the Weary Blues echoed through his head.
> He slept like a rock or a man that's dead.

It is hard to fool oneself in the honest light of dawn, but sleep, like dancing and singing and wild hilarity, is another means of escape. Unfortunately, it too is only a temporary evasion. One has to wake up sometime and face the harsh reality of daylight and everyday living.

And in the final pages of *The Weary Blues*, the poet begins to sense this fact; he realizes that a "jazz-tuned" way of life is not the answer to the Negro's search for escape. The last poem on the Harlem theme in this work has the suggestive title "Disillusionment" and the even more suggestive lines:

> I would be simple again,
> Simple and clean . . .
> Nor ever know,
> Dark Harlem,
> The wild laughter
> Of your mirth . . .
> Be kind to me,
> Oh, great dark city.
> Let me forget.
> I will not come
> To you again.

Evidently Hughes did want to forget, at least temporarily, the dark city, for there is no mention of Harlem in his next work, *Fine Clothes to the Jew*, published the following year. Although several of the other themes treated in the first volume are continued in this the second, it is the only major production[1] in which the name Harlem does not appear.

But returning to *The Weary Blues*—it is the eternal emptiness of the Harlem depicted in this work which depresses. In this volume, the poet has been influenced too strongly by certain superficial elements of the New Negro Movement. Like too many of his contemporaries, he followed the current vogue, and looking at Harlem through the "arty" spectacles of New Negro exoticism, he failed to see the everyday life about him. As charming and as fascinating as many of these poems undoubtedly are, they give a picture which is essentially false because it is one-dimensional and incomplete. In the works to follow, we shall see Mr. Hughes filling out that picture, giving it three-dimensional life and being.

The picture of Harlem presented in *Shakespeare in Harlem* (1942) has very little in common with that found in *The Weary Blues*. By 1942 the black metropolis was a disillusioned city. The Depression of 1929, having struck the ghetto harder than any other section of New York, showed Harlem just how basically "marginal" and precarious its economic foundations were. Embittered by this knowledge, the black community had struck back blindly at things in general in the 1935 riot. The riot brought an end to the New Negro era; the Cotton Club, the most lavish of the uptown cabarets, closed its doors and moved to Broadway; and the black city settled down to the drab existence of WPA and relief living.

In the two groups of poems labeled "Death in Harlem" and "Lenox Avenue," Hughes has given us a few glimpses of this new Harlem. There are no bright colors in the scene, only the sombre and realistic shades appropriate to the depiction of a community that has somehow lost its grip on things. The inhabitants of this new Harlem impress one as a beaten people. A man loses his job because, "awake all night with loving," he cannot get to work on time. When he is discharged, his only

---

[1] *The Dream Keeper* (1932) is not considered a major publication and will not be examined here. It is a collection of Mr. Hughes' poems edited by Miss Effie L. Powers and designed for young readers.

comment is "So I went on back to bed . . ." and to the "sweet-est dreams" ("Fired"). In another poem, a man and his wife wrangle over the family's last dime which he had thrown away gambling ("Early Evening Quarrel"). Harlem love has lost its former joyous abandon, and the playboy of the cabaret era has become a calculating pimp who wants to "share your bed / And your money too" ("50-50"). In fact all of the lovers in this section—men and women alike—are an aggrieved lot, whining perpetually about being "done wrong." Even the night spots have lost their jungle magic, and like Dixie's joint have become earthy and sordid places: "Dixie makes his money on two-bit gin;" he also "rents rooms at a buck a break." White folks still come to Dixie's seeking a thrill, but they find it unexpectedly in the cold-blooded shooting of Bessie by Arabella Johnson, in a fight over Texas Kid. As Arabella goes to jail and Bessie is taken to the morgue, Texas Kid, the cause of this tragedy, cal-lously "picked up another woman and / Went to bed" ("Death in Harlem"). All of the fun, all of the illusion have gone from this new and brutal night life world; and as a fitting symbol of the change which has come about, we find a little cabaret girl dying forlornly as a ward of the city ("Cabaret Girl Dies on Welfare Island").

There is seemingly only one bright spot in this new Harlem— the spectrum-colored beauty of the girls on Sugar Hill ("Har-lem Sweeties"); but this is only a momentary lightening of the mood. The prevailing tone is one of depression and futility:

> Down on the Harlem River
> Two A.M.
> Midnight
> By yourself!
> Lawd, I wish I could die—
> But who would miss me if I left?

We see here the spectacle of a city feeling sorry for itself, the most dismal and depressing of all spectacles. Hughes has given us a whining Harlem. It is not yet the belligerent Harlem of the 1943 riot, but it is a city acquiring the mood from which this riot will inevitably spring.

The Harlem poems in *Fields of Wonder* (1947) are grouped under the title "Stars Over Harlem," but they do not speak out as clearly and as definitely as former pieces on the theme have done. The mood, however, continues in the sombre vein of *Shakespeare in Harlem*, and the idea of escape is stated or implied in each of the poems. In the first of the group, "Trumpet Player: 52nd Street," we find a curious shift in the African imagery used. Practically all former pieces having an African background tended to stress either the white-mooned loveliness of jungle nights or the pulse-stirring rhythm of the tom-tom. But from the weary eyes of the 52nd Street musician there blazes forth only "the smoldering memory of slave ships." In this new Harlem even the jazz players are infected with the sectional melancholy, and this performer finds only a vague release and escape in the golden tones he creates.

In "Harlem Dance Hall" there is again an interesting use of the escape motif. The poet describes the hall as having no dignity at all until the band began to play and then: "Suddenly the earth was there, / And flowers, / Trees, / And air." In short, this new dignity was achieved by an imaginative escape from the close and unnatural life of the dance hall (and of Harlem) into the freedom and wholesomeness of nature and normal living.

Although it is rather crytic, there is also the suggestion of escape in "Stars," the last of these poems to be considered here:

> O, sweep of stars over Harlem streets . . .
> Reach up your hand, dark boy, and take a star.

One Way Ticket (1949) and *Montage of a Dream Deferred* (1951), especially the latter work, bring to a full cycle the turning away from the Harlem of *The Weary Blues*. The Harlem depicted in these two works has come through World War II, but has discovered that a global victory for democracy does not necessarily have too much pertinence at home. Although the Harlem of the 1949–51 period has far more opportunity than the 1926 Harlem ever dreamed of, it is still not free; and the modern city having caught the vision of total freedom and total integration will not be satisfied with anything less than the ideal. It is therefore a critical, a demanding, a sensitive, and utterly cynical city.

In *One Way Ticket*, for example, Harlem remembers "the old lies," "the old kicks in the back," the jobs it never could have and still cannot get because of color:

> So we stand here
> On the edge of hell
> In Harlem
> And look out on the world
> And wonder
> What we're gonna do
> In the face of
> What we remember.

But even though Harlem is the "edge of hell," it still can be a refuge for the black servant who works downtown all day bowing and scraping to white folks ("Negro Servant"). Dark Harlem becomes for him a "sweet relief from faces that are white." The earlier Harlem was a place to be shared with fun-seeking whites from below 125th Street; the new city is a sanctuary from them.

So deep is the unrest in this 1949–51 Harlem it may experience strangely conflicting emotions. Like aliens longing sentimentally for the "old country," it may feel momentarily a nostalgia for the South, even though it has bought a one way ticket from that region. In "Juice-Joint: Northern City," we find sad-faced boys who have forgotten how to laugh:

> But suddenly a guitar playing lad
> Whose languid lean brings back the sunny South
> Strikes up a tune all gay and bright and glad
> To keep the gall from biting in his mouth,
> > Then drowsy as the rain
> > Soft sad black feet
> > Dance in this juice joint
> > On the city street.

The deepest tragedy of a disillusioned city is the cruelty it inflicts on its own unfortunates, and this bitter Harlem wastes no pity on a poor lost brother who was not "hep":

> Harlem
> Sent him home
> In a long box—
> Too dead
> To know why:
> The licker
> Was lye.

The longest and most revealing Harlem poem in *One Way Ticket* is the thumping "Ballad of Margie Polite," the Negro girl who "cussed" a cop in the lobby of the Braddock Hotel and caused a riot when a Negro soldier taking her part was shot in the back by a white cop. In these thirteen short stanzas, Langston Hughes has distilled, as it were, all of the trigger-sensitiveness to injustice—real or imagined; all of the pent-up anti-white bitterness; and all of the sick-and-tired-of-being-kicked-around feelings which characterize the masses of present-day Harlem. It is indeed a provocative analysis of the frictions and the tensions in the black ghetto, this narrative of Margie Polite, who

> Kept the Mayor
> And Walter White
> And everybody
> Up all night!

In *Montage of a Dream Deferred*, Mr. Hughes' latest volume of poems, the Harlem theme receives its fullest and most comprehensive statement. Devoting the whole volume to the subject, he has touched on many aspects of the city unnoticed before. His understanding is now deep and sure, his handling of the theme defter and more mature than in any of the previous works. In this volume, the poet makes effective use of a technique with which he has been experimenting since 1926—a technique he explains in a brief prefatory note:

In terms of current Afro-American popular music . . . this poem on contemporary Harlem, like be-bop, is marked by conflicting changes, sudden nuances, sharp and impudent interjections, broken rhythms, and passages sometimes in the manner of the jam session, sometimes the popular song, punctuated by the riffs, runs, breaks, and distortions of the music of a community in transition.

According to this scheme, we are to consider the whole book of ninety-odd pieces as really one long poem, marked by the conflicting changes, broken rhythms, and sudden interjections characteristic of a jam session. This "jam session" technique is highly effective because, tying together as it does fragmentary and otherwise unrelated segments in the work, it allows the poet, without being monotonous, to return again and again to his over-all theme, that of Harlem's frustration. Like the deep and persistent rolling of a boogie bass—now loud and raucous, now soft and pathetic—this theme of Harlem's dream deferred marches relentlessly throughout the poem. Hughes knows that

Harlem is neither a gay nor healthy but basically a tragic and frustrated city, and he beats that message home. Because of the fugue-like structure of the poem, it is impossible for the reader to miss the theme or to forget it.

This 1951 Harlem is a full and many-sided community. Here one finds the pathos of night funerals and fraternal parades: "A chance to let / the whole world see / old black me!"; or the grim realism of slum-dwellers who like war because it means prosperity; or the humor of a wife playing via a dream book the numbers suggested by her husband's dying words. This is the Harlem of black celebrities and their white girl admirers, the Harlem of vice squad detectives "spotting fairies" in night spots, the Harlem of bitter anti-Semitism, and the Harlem of churches and street corner orators, of college formals at the Renaissance Casino and of Negro students writing themes at CCNY. It is now definitely a class-conscious Harlem, a community of dicties and nobodies; and the Cadillac-riding professional dicties feel that they are let down by the nobodies who "talk too loud / cuss too loud / and look too black." It is a Harlem of some gaiety and of much sardonic laughter; but above all else, it is Harlem of a dream long deferred; and a people's deferred dream can "fester like a sore" or "sag like a heavy load."

Whatever else it may or may not believe, this Harlem has no illusion about the all-inclusiveness of American democracy. Even the children know that there is still a Jim Crow coach on the Freedom Train.

> What don't bug
> them white kids
> sure bugs me;
> We knows everybody
> ain't free.

Perhaps the dominant over-all impression that one gets from *Montage of a Dream Deferred* is that of a vague unrest. Tense and moody, the inhabitants of this 1951 Harlem seem to be seeking feverishly and forlornly for some simple yet apparently unattainable satisfaction in life: "one more bottle of gin"; "my furniture paid for"; "I always did want to study French"; "that white enamel stove"; "a wife who will work with me and not against me." The book begins and ends on this note of dissatisfaction and unrest. There is "a certain amount of nothing in a dream deferred."

These then are the scenes that make up the Harlem of Langston Hughes' poetry. The picture, one must remember, is that of a poet and not a sociologist; it naturally lacks the logic and the statistical accuracy of a scientific study, but in its way the picture is just as revealing and truthful as an academic study. As one looks at this series of Harlems he is impressed by the growing sense of frustration which characterizes each of them. Whether it is in the dream fantasy world of *The Weary Blues* or in the realistic city of *Montage of a Dream Deferred*, one sees a people searching—and searching in vain—for a way to make Harlem a part of the American dream. And one must bear in mind that with Langston Hughes Harlem is both place and symbol. When he depicts the hopes, the aspirations, the frustrations, and the deep-seated discontent of the New York ghetto, he is expressing the feelings of Negroes in black ghettos throughout America.

XI

IRVING HOWE

Faulkner and the Negroes

All of the tensions in Faulkner's work reach an extreme in his presentment of Negro life and character. Problems of value which in his novels emerge as problems of perception, become magnified and exacerbated when he writes about Negroes. In saying this, I would stress that my concern is not with Faulkner's explicit views about the "racial question," or at least that my concern with those views extends no further than the way they condition the novels. In their own right, Faulkner's opinions are usually the least interesting aspect of his work: they matter only when absorbed into his art, there to undergo transformations of a kind that justify our speaking of literature as a mode of creation.

Complex and ambiguous responses to the Negroes are predictable, almost conventional among sensitive Southern writers; they stem partly from an inheritance of guilt and uncertainty, partly from a ripening of heart. But in Faulkner's fiction, beneath its worried surface of attitude and idea, there is also a remarkable steadiness of feeling toward the Negro. His opinions change, his early assurance melts away, his sympathies visibly enlarge; but always there is a return to one central image, an image of memory and longing.

In *The Unvanquished* the boy, Bayard Sartoris, and his Negro friend, Ringo, eat, play, and live together. When the two boys and Granny Rosa Millard begin a long journey, Bayard and Ringo, to whom Miss Rosa is also "Granny," take turns, in simple equality, holding a parasol over her head. "That's how Ringo and I were," Bayard nostalgically recalls. "We were almost the same age, and Father always said that Ringo was a little smarter than I was, but that didn't count with us, anymore

Reprinted from *William Faulkner: A Critical Study*, Second Edition, by Irving Howe. Copyright 1952 by Irving Howe, by permission of Random House, Inc.

than the difference in the color of our skins counted. What counted was what one of us had done or seen that the other had not, and ever since that Christmas I had been ahead of Ringo because I had seen a railroad." Bayard is here expressing an ideal of boyhood friendship, unaffected by social grade and resting on that intuitive sense of scruple, that belief in "fairness," common to boys.

The same vision, or a similar one, appears in other Faulkner novels. In *The Sound and the Fury* the only happy memories the Compsons retain are memories of scenes in which white and Negro children play together. In *Absalom, Absalom!* there are no glimpses of friendship between boys of the two races, but the pioneer innocence of young Sutpen is defined as a freedom from both racial feeling and economic acquisitiveness. In "The Bear" the boy, Isaac McCaslin, unconsciously—and then with considered assent—claims as his spiritual parent the old Negro, Sam Fathers; and a similar claim determines the relationship between Chick Mallison and Lucas Beauchamp in *Intruder in the Dust*. In the story "Go Down, Moses" an old white woman, Miss Worsham, explains her wish to help an old Negro woman, Mollie Beauchamp, by invoking a childhood friendship of decades ago: "Mollie and I were born in the same month. We grew up together as sisters would." By contrast, Joe Christmas in *Light in August* seems the most deprived of Faulkner's characters precisely because he has no childhood memories to fall back on.

The most dramatic rendering of this theme occurs in the story, "The Fire and the Hearth." For the white man Roth Edmonds, Mollie Beauchamp is "the only mother he ever knew, who had not only delivered him on that night of rain and flood . . . but moved into the very house, bringing her own child, the white child and the black one sleeping in the same room with her so that she could suckle them both." As a boy, Roth feels that his home and the home of his Negro friend Henry Beauchamp have "become interchangeable: himself and his foster-brother sleeping on the same pallet in the white man's house or in the same bed in the negro's and eating of the same food at the table in either, actually preferring the negro house. . . ." And then the moment of pride: Roth refuses to share his bed with Henry and lies alone "in a rigid fury of the grief he could not explain, the shame he would not admit." Later he knew "it was grief and was ready to admit it was shame also, wanted to admit it only it was too late then, forever and forever." Forever and forever—the terribleness of this estrangement recurs in Faulkner's work, not simply as a theme, but as a cry of loss and bafflement.

Beneath the white man's racial uneasiness there often beats an impatience with the devices by which men keep themselves apart. Ultimately the whole apparatus of separation must seem too wearisome in its constant call to alertness, too costly in its tax on the emotions, and simply tedious as a brake on spontaneous life. The white man is repeatedly tempted by a memory playing on the rim of his consciousness: a memory of boyhood, when he could live as a brother with his Ringo or Henry Beauchamp—his Nigger Jim or Queequeg—and not yet wince under the needle of self-consciousness. The memory—or a longing in the guise of memory—can be downed by the will and blunted by convention, but it is too lovely and in some final sense too real to be discarded entirely. Beneath the pretense to superiority, the white man reaches for what is true: the time when he could compare bits of knowledge about locomotives with Ringo, share food with Henry Beauchamp, not in equality or out of it—for the mere knowledge of either is a poison—but in a chaste companionship. This is what the white man has lost, forever and forever; and the Negro need not remind him of it, he need only walk past him on the street.

It is a memory fed by guilt. As a confession of failure within society, it shows that status has brought not satisfaction but grief and shame. By questioning the entirety of adult relations, it reveals a hidden weight of despair. Because it glances at the possibilities of life beyond society, the writer can imagine it only in a setting of pastoral simplicity or childhood affection. It is a plea to be forgiven for what is and perhaps—but here Faulkner is uncertain—must be. And it is a yearning to find release, to fall away from the burden of one's whiteness.

Touching as this vision of lost fraternity is, it also involves an outrageous naïveté. As Leslie Fiedler has remarked, the white man "dreams of his acceptance at the breast he has most utterly offended. It is a dream so sentimental, so outrageous, so desperate that it redeems our concept of boyhood from nostalgia to tragedy." Miss Worsham says of Mollie Beauchamp, "We grew up together as sisters would"—but how many decades of distance have intervened she does not add. It is as though she and Roth Edmonds and all the other whites unconsciously hoped they need but turn again to their childhood companions to find in undiminished purity the love destroyed by caste. How the Negroes themselves might look upon this violated dream they do not think—perhaps they do not dare—to ask.

This image of the white man's longing is not, of course, unique to Faulkner; it appears with astonishing frequency in American writing, and often together with that pastoral impulse so strong among our novelists and poets. Faulkner has rendered it with a particular urgency and sadness, in a setting where at best the races live in quiet rancor. That he has repeatedly turned to this image may be considered a triumph of instinct, but the shape and weight he has given it are a triumph of art.

No such singleness or steadiness can be found in Faulkner's more conscious depiction of the Negro. One finds, instead, a progression from Southern stereotype to personal vision, interrupted by occasional retreats to inherited phobias and to an ideology that is morally inadequate to the vision. These shifting attitudes may be broken into three stages, each symbolized by a major Negro character: Dilsey, Joe Christmas and Lucas Beauchamp.

In *Soldiers' Pay*, Faulkner's first novel, a Negro (George the train porter) briefly appears as a conventional accessory. In *Sartoris* the Negro servants are regarded with truculent condescension, Joby and Simon, the old family retainers who are mere comic stereotypes. When Joby lights a fire on Christmas Day, Faulkner assures us that he feels "the grave and simple pleasures of his race." And when Simon visits some Negro ladies, there follows an uncomfortable moment of low comedy:

"Ef it ain't Brother Strother," they said in unison. "Come in, Brother Strother. How is you?"

"Po'ly, ladies; po'ly," Simon replied. He doffed his hat and unclamped his cigar stub and stowed it away in the hat. "I'se had a right smart mis'ry in de back."

". . . . Whut you gwine eat, Brother Strother?" the cook demanded hospitably. "Dey's party fixin's, en day's some col' greens en a little sof' ice cream lef fum dinner."

"I reckon I'll have a little ice cream en some of dem greens, Sis Rachel," Simon replied. "My teef ain't so much on party doin's no mo'. . . ."

Faulkner does this sort of thing skilfully enough, and since the speech of some Negroes may well verge on self-burlesque, the passage cannot simply be dismissed as "unreal." But its reality is of a superficial order, displaying a gift for condescending mimicry rather than the moral sympathy and perception we may expect from a novelist of the first rank.

In *The Unvanquished* a similar stereotyped response to the Negro soon gives way to an awareness that his psychology is not quite so accessible to the white man as the latter would like to believe. Faulkner stresses the free-and-easy relations between white master and Negro slave in the Old South, the peculiar intimacy between a man sure of his command and another who sees no possibility or feels no desire to challenge it; and we know from historical record that, together with brutality, such relationships did once exist. But new voices appear now, particularly the voice of Loosh, a discontented Negro who deserts the Sartoris manor for the Northern lines. "I done been freed," says Loosh, "God's own angel proclamated me free and gonter general me to Jordan. I don't belong to John Sartoris now; I belong to me and God." When asked why he has spirited the Sartoris silver to the Yankees, Loosh replies with vehemence and point: "You ax me that? ... Where John Sartoris? Whyn't he come and ax me that? Let God ax John Sartoris who the man name that give me to him. Let the man that buried me in the black dark ax that of the man what dug me free."

Loosh's pregnant questions are repeated, in *Sartoris*, by a Negro of a later era. Caspey, home from the First World War, announces: "I don't take nothin' fum no white folks no mo' ... War done changed all dat. If us cullud folks is good enough ter save France fum de Germans, den us is good enough ter have de same rights de Germans is. French folks think so, anyhow, and ef America don't, dey's ways of learnin' 'um." For such "sullen insolence" Caspey is knocked down by Bayard Sartoris with a stick of stove wood and told by Simon, his father, to "save dat nigger freedom talk fer town-folks."

Neither Loosh nor Caspey is conceived in warmth or developed in depth. Both are singled out for an uneasy kind of ridicule, and their rebelliousness is hardly taken seriously. What is damaging here is not so much Faulkner's laziness of statement as the assumption, throughout his early treatment of Negroes, that they are easily "knowable," particularly by disenchanted

Southerners with experience in handling them. Since Faulkner at his weakest, however, remains a writer of some consequence, overtones of doubt and uneasiness shade his portraiture of Negroes even in the minor novels. The discontented ones are seen as loutish or absurd, but this impression is undercut by the power with which their discontent is now and again rendered. One of Faulkner's most admirable qualities as a writer is that even when he wishes to settle into some conventional or trite assumption, a whole side of himself—committed forever to restless inquiry—keeps resisting this desire.

In *Sartoris* there is also a glimpse of another kind of feeling toward the Negro. Visiting the MacCallums, young Bayard instinctively—out of a natural courtesy in abiding by the manners of his hosts—treats their Negro cook with the same rough easiness that the hillsmen do. Bayard does not stop to reflect upon the meaning of this companionship, nor does Faulkner stop to give it any special emphasis: it comes through in a brief ceremony of shaking hands. But in an unfinished way, it points toward a strong motif in Faulkner's work: his conviction that fraternity is morally finer than equality, a fraternity which in his early novels makes the demand for equality seem irrelevant but which in his later ones can come only after equality has been so long secured as to be forgotten.

A gifted artist can salvage significant images of life from the most familiar notions: witness Dilsey in *The Sound and the Fury*. Dilsey is a figure remarkable for her poise, her hard realism, her ability to maintain her selfhood under humiliating conditions. Yet the conception behind Dilsey does not seriously clash with the view of the Negro that could be held by a white man vaguely committed to a benevolent racial superiority. Accepting her inferior status and surviving as a human being despite that acceptance, Dilsey is the last of Faulkner's major Negro characters who can still feel that the South is a "natural" community to which they entirely belong. No sensitive reader would care to deny her strength and moral beauty, but I should like to register a dissent from the effort of certain critics to apotheosize her as the embodiment of Christian resignation and endurance. The terms in which Dilsey is conceived are thoroughly historical, and by their nature become increasingly unavailable to us: a fact which if it does not lessen our admiration for her as a figure in a novel, does limit our capacity to regard her as a moral archetype or model.[1]

In *The Sound and the Fury* there is an important modulation of attitude toward the Negro. While Dilsey's strength and goodness may be acceptable to traditional paternalism, she gradually assumes a role not quite traditional for the Southern Negro; she becomes, toward the end of the book, an articulate moral critic, the observer with whom the action of the novel is registered and through whom its meanings are amplified. She is not merely the old darky in the kitchen champing at the absurd and evil ways of the folks up front; at the climax of the novel she rises beyond that role, to a concern with universal problems of justice. This is not to suggest that Dilsey is in any way a rebel against the old order of Southern life. She regards most of the Compsons with contempt not because they are white or representative of the ruling social group but because they do not fulfill the obligations that have accrued to their status. Judging the whites in terms of their own proclaimed values, she criticizes not their exploitation of Negroes but their moral mistreatment of each other. This judgment, held with force and purity, leads Dilsey to a principled respect for the human person as such. When the name of the idiot Compson child is changed from Maury to Benjy, she snaps: "He *aint wore out the name he was born with yet, is he.*" When her daughter whines that "people talk" because Dilsey brings Benjy to the Negro church, the old woman replies: "Tell um the good Lawd don't keer whether he smart or not. Dont nobody but poor white trash keer dat." This sense of honor toward every person in her orbit, this absolute security in her own judgment, is Dilsey's most admirable trait, and a sign, as well, of the more complex treatment of Negroes that is to appear in Faulkner's books.

From traditional paternalism to an awareness of the injustice suffered by the Negro in Southern society—this, one could say, is the change that now occurs in the Yoknapatawpha novels.

[1] But is not Don Quixote, surely a moral archetype, also conceived in historical terms unavailable to us? Yes, he is. Don Quixote, however, survives as a figure "beyond" history, we no longer care about his historical genesis or purpose; while Dilsey, we cannot but remember, is a woman caught up in the recent historical condition of the Southern Negro. Whether time will do for Dilsey what it has done for Don Quixote, no one can say.

But the change is more complicated still, for the growing concern with injustice as a problem flows from an expansion of paternalism to its widest human limits. Dilsey and Joe Christmas are very different kinds of people, but Christmas is possible only because Dilsey already exists.

With *Light in August* the Negro assumes a new role in Faulkner's work. If Dilsey is characterized by an unbreakable sense of "belonging" in a world she knows to be falling apart, Joe Christmas feels that he has no home, that he always has been and must always remain homeless. If in the earlier work the focus of attention is on the white man's feelings toward the Negro, now there is a shock of discovery, a discovery of the Negro "as Negro."

The Faulkner to whom the Looshes and Caspeys and even Dilseys had seemed so accessible now emphasizes that for the whites the Negro often exists not as a distinct person but as a specter or phantasm. He writes brilliantly of what might be called the fetishism of false perception, the kind of false perception that has become systematic and has acquired both a pseudo-religious sanction and an intense emotional stake. Joanna Burden, daughter of abolitionists raised in the South, confesses that "I had seen and known Negroes since I could remember. I just looked at them as I did at rain, or furniture, or food or sleep. But after that I seemed to see them for the first time not as people, but as a thing, a shadow in which I lived, we lived, all white people, all other people. I thought of all the children coming forever and ever into the world, white, with the black shadow falling already upon them before they drew breath. And I seemed to see the black shadow in the shape of a cross." What is so remarkable about this passage—and it seems to me one of the most remarkable in all of Faulkner—is that here the false perception comes from a mixture of humaneness and fright, the two no longer separable but bound together in an apocalyptic image of violation and martyrdom.

In *Light in August* a lynch mob "believed aloud that it was an anonymous negro crime committed not by a negro but by Negro . . . and some of them with pistols already in pockets began to canvass about for someone to crucify." The phrase "not by a negro but by Negro" reflects a deepened understanding; the reference to men canvassing "for someone to crucify" suggests that Faulkner has been thinking hard about the role of frustration in shaping white behavior. In Percy Grimm, the small-town boy who has absorbed sadism from the very air, Faulkner gives form to his pained awareness that a society of inequality can lead only to abuse of status and arbitrary violence. This idea is expressed more abstractly in *The Wild Palms* when Faukner describes the "indelible mark of ten thousand Southern deputy sheriffs, urban and suburban—the snapped hatbrim, the sadist's eyes, the slightly and unmistakably bulged coat, the air not swaggering exactly but of a formally preabsolved brutality." Precise in each detail, this description opens to brilliance in the final phrase, "a formally pre-absolved brutality"—a phrase that epitomizes a vision of society.

That the white man has been calloused by status and the fear and guilt inevitable to status is not a novel insight; but to a writer wrestling with the pieties of the Southern tradition the price of such knowledge can hardly come low. For it is not, after all, the "South," that convenient abstraction of geography or history, about which Faulkner sees this; it is his own immediate cut of land, the place where he will spend his remaining time and die. Consider, then, the significance of the scene in *Light in August* where a sheriff, preparing to sweat some information out of a Negro, tells his deputy, "Get me a nigger"—get me a nigger, no matter which, they are indistinguishable.

We witness in Faulkner's novels a quick and steep ascent: from benevolence to recognition of injustice, from amusement over idiosyncrasies to a principled concern with status, from cozy familiarity to a discovery of the estrangement of the races. Realizing that despite their physical nearness Negroes must coil large parts of themselves beyond the vision of white society, Faulkner remarks in the story "The Old People" upon "that impenetrable wall of ready and easy mirth which negroes sustain between themselves and white men." Instead of being easily reached, the Negro is now locked behind suspicion; and while he may be, as Quentin Compson has said, "a form of behavior ... [an] obverse reflection of the white people he lives among," he is also and more importantly something else: a human being whom the whites can seldom know. (One of Faulkner's later stories, "Pantaloon in Black," dramatizes this idea: after the death of his wife, a Negro runs berserk with grief while the whites, blind to the way he expresses it, sneer at his apparent insensitivity.) As Faulkner discovers the difficulty of approaching

Negroes, he also develops an admirable sense of reserve, a blend of shyness and respect; trusting few of his preconceptions he must look at everything afresh.

A curious result of this growth in perception is, occasionally, a loss of concreteness in the presentation of character. Faulkner's discovery of the power of abstraction as it corrupts the dealings men have with one another, can lead him to portray Negroes in abstract terms. If the mob in *Light in August* looks upon black men as "Negro" in order to brutalize them, Faulkner sometimes looks upon them as "Negro" in order to release his sympathy. Joe Christmas and Charles Bon are sharply individualized figures, but there also hangs over them a racial aura, a halo of cursed blackness. In an early story, "Dry September," this tendency toward the abstraction of character is still clearer; like a paradigm of all lynching stories, it is populated not with men but with Murderer and Victim.

Nor is it accidental that those Negroes whom Faulkner most readily imagines in the posture of the victim should be mulattoes. Trapped between the demarcated races, the mulatto is an unavoidable candidate for the role of victim. Velery Bon in *Absalom, Absalom!* is a man adrift. The Negroes "thought he was a white man and believed it only the more strongly when he denied it," while the whites, "when he said he was a negro, believed that he lied in order to save his skin." Joe Christmas is cursed by "that stain on his white blood or his black blood, whichever you will." Whether he actually has Negro blood is never clear, and this uncertainty points a finger of irony at the whole racial scheme.

Such symbolic uses of the mulatto do not exhaust the reasons for his prominence in Faulkner's novels. Mulattoes are living agents of the "threat" of miscegenation, a "threat" which seems most to disturb Faulkner whenever he is most sympathetic to the Negro. All rationalizations for prejudice having crumbled, there remains only an inherited fear of blood-mixture. The more Faulkner abandons the "ideas" of the folk mind in relation to Negroes, the more does he find himself struggling with the deeper phobias of the folk mind. In two of the novels where miscegenation is a major theme, *Light in August* and *Absalom, Absalom!*, it arouses a painfully twisted response. Miscegenation releases the fears of the white unconscious but also suggests, as Faulkner will hint in a later book, an ultimate solution to the racial problem. Even as it excites a last defense for the dogma of superiority, the thought of miscegenation opens a vision of a distant time when distinctions of blood and barriers of caste will be removed. In *Absalom, Absalom!* there is a whole range of responses to miscegenation, from the strongly-articulated sympathy for its victims to the conventional phophecy that it will lead to a corruption of the races; and it is quite impossible to say with any assurance where Faulkner's final sympathy, or the final stress of the novel itself, lies. Because of this ambivalent response, the mulatto occasions some of Faulkner's most intense, involuted and hysterical writing. As a victim the mulatto must be shown in all his suffering, and as a reminder of the ancestral phobia, must be made once or twice to suffer extravagantly. But since Faulkner is trying to free himself from both phobia and the injustice it sustains, the mulatto also excites in him his greatest pity, a pity so extreme as often to break past the limits of speech. On the mulatto's frail being descends the whole crushing weight of Faulkner's world.

With the appearance of Lucas Beauchamp, most of Faulkner's previous attitudes toward the Negro are transcended. Lucas is neither at home in the South, like Dilsey, nor homeless, like Joe Christmas; he exists in himself. He is well enough aware of white society and he knows exactly what it is; in "The Fire and the Hearth" he does not hesitate to express his bitterness. But as he strides into sight in *Intruder in the Dust*, powerful and complete, he is entirely on his own: he has put society behind him. Too proud to acquiesce in submission, too self-contained to be either outcast or rebel, Lucas has transformed the stigma of alienation into a mark of dignity and assurance. He is truly a character who has "made" himself, who has worked through to his own kind of authenticity. The gain is high, so too the price; for Lucas is friendless, and his grandeur is a crotchety grandeur. Apparently meant by Faulkner as a tribute to the strength and endurance of the Negroes, Lucas is something better still: a member of an oppressed group who appears not as a catalogue of disabilities or even virtues, but as a human being in his own right. He is not a form of behavior but a person, not "Negro" but a Negro.

Occasionally Faulkner lets him slip into the stubborn old nigger who grumbles and bumbles his way to domination over the delightfully helpless whites. This may be justifiable, for, to an extent difficult to specify, the "stubborn old nigger" is Lucas' social mask—and Faulkner realizes now that in white society Negroes must often use a social mask. Because he is so aware that they can seldom risk spontaneity in the company of whites, Faulkner, like the boy Chick Mallison, circles about Lucas with humor and a shy respect, never daring to come too close lest the old Negro growl at him. He feels about Lucas somewhat as Chick and Stevens do, sharing the boy's irritated awe and the man's uneasy admiration. Toward no other character in any of his books does Faulkner show quite the same uncomfortable deference; of none other can it be said that Faulkner looks up to him with so boyish and pleading an air, as if he wishes to gain from the old man a measure of forgiveness or acceptance, perhaps finally even love.

By indirection, Lucas challenges a good many of the notions Faulkner has previously expressed about the Negroes. In the final scene of *Intruder in the Dust* Lucas shows himself unyielding and unforgiving; he insists upon taking the white man's gesture of equality as if it came from condescension—and who will dare bluntly to contradict him? In an earlier scene Lucas stares up at Stevens from his jail cell, refusing to speak to him openly because he senses that the white lawyer believes him guilty. Completely dramatized and without any intruding comment, this scene suggests the insight that even the best whites are full of ambiguous feelings toward the Negroes and hence not to be trusted by them.

This insight acknowledged, one is tempted to speculate about certain of Faulkner's attitudes toward the Negroes. Throughout his work there is an admiring emphasis on their patience and "endurance." Negroes are "better than we" because "they will endure." In the Appendix to *The Sound and the Fury* Faulkner honors Dilsey and her kin with a bare sentence, "They endured." Such sentiments, fondly quoted by traditionalist critics, have their obvious bearing when advanced as statements about the past; but if, as Faulkner intimates, they are also meant as prescription and prediction, they invite a measure of doubt.

How Negroes "really" feel about Southern, or American, society is terribly hard for any white man to say. Serious whites, as they learn more about the hidden, the true life of Negroes, grow hesitant to generalize: they discover how little they know. Yet one may wonder whether Negroes are quite as ready to "endure" as Faulkner suggests—a question that has a decided relevance to his work, since a fixed idea about Negro "endurance" can limit his capacity to see Negro life freshly.

Faulkner wishes to dramatize his admiration for their ability to survive injustice, and he is right to do so. Nor is his respect for the power and virtues of passivity confined to his treatment of Negro figures; it comes through with great assurance in his portraits of Lena Grove and Ike McCaslin; and indeed, it forms one of his deepest personal feelings toward human existence. But it may still be suggested that Faulkner, like any other man of his color, has less "right" to admire the posture of passivity in the Negroes than he does in the whites. And we must also suppose that those human beings, like the Negroes, who have long been subjected to humiliation will probably resent it, no matter how much they may be required to veil their more intimate responses. Is this not exactly what Faulkner begins so brilliantly to show in his treatment of Lucas Beauchamp, a man whose irascible desire for justice—he demands nothing else from white society—is quite distant from the style of "endurance"? May it not be that the patient willingness to "endure," far from being a root attitude among Negroes, is another of the masks they assume in order to find their way through a hostile world? Again I add that this is not merely a question concerning the social order of the South: it arises repeatedly and with growing urgency in some of Faulkner's later novels.

Though he has given us a wider range and taken a deeper sounding of Negro character than any other American writer, Faulkner has not yet presented in his novels an articulate Negro who speaks for his people. No one has the right to demand that he do so, but it is a legitimate problem in literary criticism to ask why he has not. That such a Negro may not be within Faulkner's range of personal experience is unimportant, unless one accepts the naïve assumption that fictional characters must always be drawn from a writer's immediate knowledge. Faulkner's honesty, his continuous moral growth, but above all, the inner logic of his own work—all these would seem to require that he confront the kind of Negro who is in serious, if covert, rebellion against the structure of the South.

To present such a character, Faulkner would have to take the risk of examining Negro consciousness from within, rather than as it is seen or surmised by white characters. It may be said that precisely Faulkner's awareness of the distance between the races and of the ultimate inaccessibility of the Negroes makes him hesitate to use a Negro as his center of consciousness. Such scruples deserve to be honored, yet the fact is that great writers, including Faulkner himself, are always coming up with characters "they do not know"—surely this must be part of what is meant when we say they are using their imagination. To portray Negro consciousness from the inside would be a hazard for Faulkner, as it must be for any white novelist, but the possibility, perhaps the need, for such an attempt arises from his own achievement. And he has never been a writer to avoid risks.

Such speculations apart, Faulkner's most recent books testify to the almost obsessive role the Negro continues to play in his imaginative life. *Requiem for a Nun* casts a Negro prostitute and dope addict, Nancy, as scourge and saviour of white society. Nancy's murder of a white child is traced back to the earlier guilt of the child's parents; and even as she prepares to die in her repentance and piety, she becomes a nemesis calling them back to their moral obligations. In assigning this role to Nancy, Faulkner is perhaps placing too heavy a weight of responsibility on the Negroes, and in a way opposite to the harangues of *Intruder in the Dust* he may even be doing them a certain injustice. For it is a little unreasonable—though surely also desperate—to burden the Negroes with the salvation of the whites. Whatever the whites will be able to manage in this latter department, they will have to do for themselves.

One suspects that the difficulties behind the creation of Nancy reflect a charge of emotion, a surging mixture of guilt and impatience, which Faulkner cannot objectify in conduct or character and which, therefore, forces him toward a kind of Dostoevskian apocalypse. Because of this ideological weight, Nancy figures in the novel more as an abstract intention than as a blooded human being. Lacking the rich particularity of a Lucas Beauchamp, she is "Negro" rather than a Negro, and "Negro" put to very special and unclarified uses. Still, the novel shows that Faulkner continues to brood over the Negroes, passionately and erratically; and as long as these questions remain alive for him, there is reason to hope they will take on fresh embodiment in future novels.

The shift of response toward the Negro forms a moral history, a record of growth from early work to last. But it would be a grave distortion to suppose that this history is entirely reckoned once attitudes and underlying themes have been traced—these are only the raw materials from which literature is made or, perhaps more accurately, the abstractions critics like to draw from or impose upon literature. Despite the ideological passages in *Intruder in the Dust*, Faulkner is not, and should not be considered, a systematic thinker; he has no strictly formulated views on the "Negro question," and as a novelist he is under no obligation to have them. In the more than two decades of his literary career he has taken a painful journey of self-education, beginning with an almost uncritical acceptance of the more benevolent Southern notions and ending with a brooding sympathy and humane respect for the Negroes. His recent books indicate that no other social problem troubles him so greatly, and that his mind is constantly driven to confront it. What counts in his work is not the occasional splinter of program that can be scratched out of it—whoever wants a precise platform or a coherent sociology for the Negroes had better look elsewhere. Faulkner's triumph is of another kind, the novelist's triumph: a body of dramatic actions, a group of realized characters. No other American novelist has watched the Negroes so carefully and patiently; none other has listened with such fidelity to the nuances of their speech and recorded them with such skill; none other has exposed his imagination so freely, to discover, at whatever pain or discomfort, their meaning for American life.

In the end, Faulkner's great homage to the Negroes is that one need only hear and see. There is the sermon ("I got de ricklickshun en de blood of de Lamb!") delivered by the visiting St. Louis preacher in the Negro church at the close of *The Sound and the Fury*, as magnificent in its way as the sermons of Father Mapple in *Moby Dick*, Dinah Morris in *Adam Bede* and the Jesuit father in *Portrait of the Artist as a Young Man*. Since the St. Louis preacher speaks at length, listen instead to the shorter movement of Negro dialogue, the ripples of accent and meaning, at the beginning of *The Sound and the Fury*:

"Is you all seen anything of a quarter down here." Luster said.

"What quarter."

"The one I had here this morning." Luster said. "I lost it somewhere.

It fell through this here hole in my pocket. If I dont find it, I cant go to the show tonight."

"Where'd you get a quarter, boy. Find it in white folks' pocket while they aint looking."

"Got it at the getting place." Luster said. "Plenty more where that one comes from. Only I got to find that one. Is you all found it yet."

"I aint studying no quarter. I got my own business to tend to."

"Come on here." Luster said. "Help me look for it."

"He wouldn't know a quarter if he was to see it, would he."

"He can help look just the same." Luster said. "You all going to the show tonight."

"Dont talk to me about no show. Time I get done over this here tub I be too tired to lift my hand to do nothing."

"I bet you be there." Luster said, "I bet you was there last night. I bet you all be right there when that tent open."

"Be enough niggers there without me. Was last night."

"Niggers money good as white folks, I reckon."

"White folks give niggers money because know first white man comes along with a band going to get it all back, so nigger can go to work for some more."

Or listen to Jason Compson as he reports an exchange with a Negro:

And then a Yankee will talk your head off about niggers getting ahead. Get them ahead, what I say. Get them so far ahead you cant find one south of Louisville with a blood hound. Because when I told him about how they'd pick up Saturday night, and carry off at least a thousand dollars out of the country, he says,

"I don't begrudge um. I kin sho afford my two bits."

"Two bits hell," I says. "That dont begin it. How about the dime or fifteen cents you'll spend for a damn two cent box of candy or something. How about the time you're wasting right now, listening to that band."

"Dat's de troof," he says. "Well, ef I lives twell night hit's gwine to be two bits mo dey takin out of town, dat's sho."

"Then you're a fool," I says.

"Well," he says, "I dont spute dat neither. Ef dat uz a crime, all chain-gangs wouldn't be black."

And finally to the cadences of the passage in "Red Leaves" where an escaped Negro slave is captured by his Indian masters, a passage which forms an elegy for all human effort, all defeat:

Two Indians entered the swamp, their movements noisy. Before they reached the Negro they stopped, because he began to sing. They could see him, naked and mud-caked, sitting on a log, singing. They squatted silently a short distance away, until he finished. He was chanting something in his own language, his face lifted to the rising sun. His voice was clear, full, with a quality wild and sad. "Let him have time," the Indians said, squatting, patient, waiting. He ceased and they approached. He looked back and up at them through the cracked mud mask. His eyes were bloodshot, his lips cracked upon his square short teeth. The mask of mud appeared to be loose on his face, as if he might have lost flesh since he put it there: he held his left arm close to his breast. From the elbow down it was caked and shapeless with black mud. They could smell him, a rank smell. He watched them quietly until one touched him on the arm. "Come," the Indian said. "You ran well. Do not be ashamed."

XII

JOHN EDWARD HARDY

Eudora Welty's Negroes

Eudora Welty is not notably concerned with problems of "race relations," if we take that phrase in the socioeconomic and political sense. Stories in which Negroes figure prominently make up a relatively small portion of her total fiction. And her treatment of Negroes defies almost any definable stock response.

Her constant themes, regardless of whether she is dealing with white or Negro characters, are the themes of human loneliness and alienation, of recognition, of the rarity and brevity of the moments of real awareness in which we awaken from the troubled dream that is the usual state of our existence. But precisely what is remarkable about her treatment of Negroes—especially considering her upper-middle class, Mississippi origins—is this unforced recognition of their essential humanity. As clearly as any other white American author, including among the others Twain and Faulkner, she has penetrated the clichés of social stereotype in the creation of her Negro characters. She is intensely aware of the clichés, and often deliberately sets them up as a foil to the final, intuitive recognition of the human person. And she has a finally discriminating eye and ear for the characteristics of speech and manner that set the Negro apart from the white—an at least entirely *plausible* sense of what constitutes Negroness even in thought processes. (When I say plausible, I suppose I mean to the white reader; I haven't made a point of finding out, but perhaps Negro readers would disagree.) But, once more, the ultimate fineness goes beyond this without negating it. The final authenticity of the characters is in their carefully delineated, human individuality, not in their however complex typicality, while at the same time they remain distinctly Negro.

The title character of "Keela, the Outcast Indian Maiden"—in his "real life" male identity known as Little Lee Roy—is hardly a good example of the art of individuation of which I have spoken. But the story provides a convenient paradigm of attitudes and values implicit in the structure of the other two pieces to which I shall give detailed attention.

The story is done, with regard to the Negro, from outside, that is, from the point of view of the whites. One can hardly say even that it is basically Lee Roy's (or Keela's) story. The center of psychological interest, rather, is in the white man called Steve. Lee Roy is important only as the object of Steve's concern, as the allegorical "it" about whose fate he is so disturbed. But we are aware of the basic, human importance of individuality in the very intensity of Steve's frustration, his essential inability, through the haze of his guilty self-preoccupation, to "recognize" the little Negro man.

The story is a very short one. The little, clubfooted old Negro man, Lee Roy, is sitting alone on the porch of his cabin one day—while all his sons and daughters are out plum-picking—when two white men arrive. Through the conversation of the white men—Steve, and the one called Max, who operates a roadhouse somewhere in the vicinity—we piece together the terrifying story of Lee Roy's "other life" as Keela. But the sordid horrors of that tale, of Lee Roy's kidnapping by the carnival sideshow owners and his involuntary servitude in the guise of the wild woman "geek," chained in a pen to eat live chickens and make threatening animal sounds and shake an iron rod at the customers, are finally of less interest than Steve's attitude in telling it.

During Steve's disjointed narrative, Max interrupts from time to time to ask him whether the little man sitting on the steps, Lee Roy, is in fact "him," that is, Keela, the "it" of Steve's account. And we begin to get to the heart of the whole story's significance when we realize that Steve never gives Max a direct answer to this question.

It appears that Steve has searched a long time for the little man, has finally arrived in Cane Springs, Mississippi, that day, has made inquiries, and has been brought out to the Negro's farm by Max, to see whether Lee Roy is the person for whom he is looking. And yet, from the first, and throughout, Steve is curiously indifferent to the actual presence of Lee Roy—or not indifferent, but as if oblivious. "They came nearer and nearer to Little Lee Roy and then stopped and stood there in the middle of the yard. But the young man was so excited he did not seem to realize they had arrived anywhere." And again, "Little Lee Roy sat huddled and blinking, a smile on his face. . . . But the young man did not look his way."

Steve talks obsessively in circles, repeating over and over again details of his story. He is especially preoccupied with the recollection of the gravely frowning white man who had come to the show while it was playing in Little Oil, Texas, and, seeing through the disguise after several visits, had called in the sheriff to free Lee Roy and arrest the show owners.

Just as he never answers the question of whether the present Little Lee Roy is "the party" for whom he has been searching, so Steve also fails ever to answer directly Max's question of whether, during the time he was a barker at the show, he had suspected Keela was a fake before the arrival of the frowning stranger. Several times, in passing, he denies that he had: "I didn't know. I can't look at nothin' an' be sure what it is." The phrasing of the denial is ambiguous. He does say that he knew they had to "whup it some" to make "it" eat the chickens, that the clubfoot was visible when "it" walked, and so on. And the violence of his response to Max's complacent assertion—" 'But I could tell a man from a woman and an Indian from a nigger' . . . then Steve sighed, and as if he did not know what else he could do, he reached out and hit Max in the jaw with his fist"—is sufficient evidence of his uneasy conscience on the point. Regardless of the relative validity or invalidity of his arguments to himself that he "didn't know" beforehand, his knowledge after the stranger's intervention is irrevocable and overwhelming. Whether he knew or didn't know, or suspected or didn't suspect, once having known he feels an inescapable complicity in the crime, and a need to make reparation. He ought to have known; and that is sufficient for his self-conviction.

But the ultimate irony is in the impossibility of reparation. Steve's disquietude is rooted in something deeper than the question of specific knowledge, of complicity in a specific crime. To repeat, his very self-preoccupation in his guilt, his obscure sense of his own deficient humanity, prevents his clearly "seeing" Lee Roy—the real, other human being (not simply the embodiment of his haunted conscience) when he has finally found him. He cannot "see" him; and he is uncertain what he had had in mind to do for him when he did find him. In the end:

"I got to be going," said Max. . . . "What you want to transact with Keela? You come a long way to see him."

"Well, I was goin' to give him some money or somethin', I guess, if I ever found him, only now I ain't got any," said Steve defiantly.

Max supplies the money, a handful of change from his pocket, which Keela-Lee Roy accepts with alacrity. But it is obvious that for Steve the money, any amount of money, was not quite the "or somethin' " he meant to give in the first place. And when we learn at the very end that Lee Roy has, in fact, received from the visit something that he values, beyond the money—that, at least in retrospect, "de old times when I used to be wid de circus," about which he tells his children the two white men had come to talk to him, are for him glamorous times, an experience that more than anything else in his life made him a person of importance—then, the irony of Steve's empty-handedness is doubled and redoubled.

The story, I take it, is an allegory of emancipation. Not, necessarily, of *the* Emancipation—with the frowning stranger as the Lincoln of the piece, but of all our little, would-be emancipations, wherever and whenever. The animalistic growlings and rod-shakings of live-chicken-eating Keela, her inability to "talk like a man, like you or me," of which "they" had convinced Steve by simple dint of having "tole" him it was so, embody the familiar, white man's legend of the Negro's essential bestiality. The "pair of little bitty crutches" on which, back home in Mississippi, he "got around just fine" are the vestigial gratifications, spiritual and material, the truncated dignities, that the Negro is permitted in our society—with which we persuade ourselves he is content, or ought to be, and to which we complacently send him back if and whenever we are forced by sheer disgust to liberate him from grosser and more obvious forms of enslavement. If, and to some extent I think we must, we take Lee Roy as "the Negro," then Lee Roy in most horrid fact *is* Keela, is "the party in question." Or, with reference again to the ending of the story, and the children's response of "Hush, pappy" when he starts to tell them of the white men's visit, perhaps a more accurate way of putting it would be to say that Lee Roy, as "the Negro," would rather be Keela than what he is. To be an Indian, a redskin, even in captivity, even growling and eating live chickens, even a redskin woman (his very manhood denied), is preferable to black "freedom" on the crutches. At least, *Keela* scared hell out of them.

Steve, of course, is you. The ordinary, decent white man, who sees always too little and too late, who is never quite big enough to accommodate the truth of his own experience.

Miss Welty offers little readily definable hope for repairing the situation she allegorizes. The gratification Lee Roy takes from the visit has, to put it mildly, small human dignity. And the partial insight into evil that Steve has gained can issue in no effective action for good. He is, rather, morally paralyzed by his vision—not led on to a better life, but only deprived of the common satisfactions and responsibilities. "Been feelin' bad ever since," he explains to Max. "Can't hold onto a job or stay in one place for nothin' in the world." Nor, obviously, is Steve's knocking him down very likely to enlighten the likes of Max. Max leaves the scene determined only to "be more careful" in the future, when the next "dope" comes into his place ready to "give him the lowdown on something"—determined to keep his juke box turned up good and loud, so that he can't hear the next visionary. (I imagine that the function of Max and his juke box, in the allegory, will be clear enough without detailed commentary.)

But beyond the redemptive effect of the story's humor, however macabre, I would emphasize once more the kind of negative comfort Miss Welty offers in the uncompromising clarity of her vision of evil. In some way, we see the more clearly what human relationships ought to be, by having our noses pressed so firmly, if good-humoredly, into the mess that they are.

The story "A Worn Path," unlike "Keela," is done entirely from the point of view of the central Negro character, the old woman called Phoenix, whose name is clearly symbolic of the self-regenerative power of the human spirit. This story embodies several of the patterns of association that are more or less constantly characteristic of Miss Welty's treatment of country Negroes.

Somewhat like Faulkner, she sees the Negro in very close physical and spiritual intimacy with the land, with the nature of fields and woods and streams, and the lower animals. There is something of this even in "Keela"—as when, while Lee Roy sits quietly listening to the two white men talking, a sparrow comes and lights on his foot. In my essay, in *Man in the Modern*

Novel,[1] on Welty's *Delta Wedding,* I have noted the complex development of this association in the novel—how the lower-class white overseer Troy Flavin, who is to marry into the aristocratic planter family, has something of the character of a god of rejuvenation, a field god, and how his intimate acquaintance with the lives of the Negroes qualifies him in this role. The motif appears also in the much-anthologized story "Livvie," where the young Negro man, Cash, who appears at the end in his Easter clothes, ready to take the young wife of Solomon away as soon as the old man dies, is an altogether allegorical figure of regeneration in nature, a god of the Spring. In "A Worn Path," old Phoenix is on intimate speaking terms with the trees, the earth, the sky, the birds and beasts of the forest. The story takes on the tone of myth. But the habit of mythologizing the lives of Negroes, as Miss Welty is keenly aware, is one of the best established and most effective methods that the white man has devised for denying them full status in his cultural community. It is I think deliberately, therefore, that she risks here and there letting the "mythiness" degenerate into mere quaintness, tempting us to a view of the old Negress as one of a race apart, about whom we are obliged to feel no more than a certain condescending curiosity—and then, at the very end of the story, suddenly puts matters in quite a different light.

The plot is much simpler than that of "Keela, The Outcast Indian Maiden." The old woman, who lives far back over the ridge, "out by the Old Natchez Trace," from the city of Natchez, is walking slowly into town on a day shortly before Christmas. She talks to herself and to the things around her, checking her progress by the sun, warning herself of the difficult places on the journey—a creek to cross on a narrow log-bridge, a barbed-wire fence to get through; at one point, when she has sat down feeling faint, suffers an hallucination of a little boy offering her a piece of marblecake; dances with a scarecrow, which she has at first mistaken for a ghost; loses her balance after being frightened by a dog and falls into a grassy ditch, from which she is lifted out by a young white hunter; distracts the man's attention while she picks up a nickel she has seen fall out of his pocket; and resumes her journey, with silent self-reproaches for the theft of the nickel. But it is not until very

[1] John Edward Hardy, *Man in the Modern Novel* (Seattle: University of Washington Press, 1964).

late in the narrative, after she has already reached the city and made her way to an office building, that we get the slightest hint of the purpose of the trip. Then it is revealed with an overpowering directness and matter-of-fact simplicity. Her little grandson is suffering from an apparently incurable throat ailment, the result of having swallowed lye two or three years before, that has left him dumb and in constant pain and danger of suffocation. She has come into town, having to leave the child alone in the house in the back-country, to get a bottle of the medicine that a white Natchez doctor allows her for the boy as a "charity" patient.

She enters the office, standing with "a fixed and ceremonial stiffness over her body," and for a few minutes, in the final weariness of her arrival, forgets what she has come for. Then, after some prompting, she remembers, is given the bottle of medicine, and a nickel for Christmas—which, together with the one she has taken from the hunter, she proposes to spend on a present for the child, a little paper windmill—and leaves.

The story has built to its climax so quietly that it is over almost before one knows it. One is immediately aware that something has happened, and something of breath-taking impact. But precisely what it is can be defined only upon re-reading.

The key word, perhaps, is "charity." When old Phoenix first reaches the doctor's office, a new receptionist, who is unacquainted with the case history and assumes that she has come for herself, says "a charity case, I suppose." But even when the older office nurse has explained the situation to the new girl, meanwhile offering Phoenix a seat—"We won't keep you standing after your long trip"—it is obvious that neither of the two white women has any comprehension of what they are witnessing, that they are all but totally incapable of the human recognition that is essential to true charity. To Phoenix, assuring not so much them as herself, after her momentary lapse of memory, that she is "not going to forget him again, no, the whole enduring time," the child whom she loves is unique; she "could tell him from all the others in creation." To the white women, he is merely "a stubborn case." (Obviously, from the tone of her first inquiries, the nurse has almost hoped that this time Phoenix will tell them he is dead.) They are impatient with the old woman, with an air indeed of self-complacent moral reproach in the impatience, for having forgotten what she came for. They have no conception of just how long, and how difficult for her, the "trip" is that she has made—nor of how truly profound is her remorse for having, in the infirmity of her age, even for a moment forgotten the child and his need and suffering. Nor, yet again, do they sense how entirely indifferent she is, in her remorse, to them, and to their impatience with having her "take up their time."

But the devastating irony of this final scene is subtly prepared for in two previous episodes. The first is the encounter with the white hunter, who helps her out of the ditch, where she has been lying on her back, in her own words "like a June-bug waiting to be turned over." The hunter is very pleased with himself, in the superior strength of his youth and whiteness, and, again like the women in the doctor's office, if a little more good-humoredly, is impatient with Phoenix's old-nigger foolishness in having undertaken the trip. "I know you old colored people!" he says self-assuredly. "Wouldn't miss going to town to see Santa Claus!" In retrospect, the irony is plain. He does not, of course, know the "old colored people" at all. Or not, at any rate, *this* old colored person; has not the faintest idea of how she is celebrating Christmas, with the gift of her love to the child. He does not know, precisely because, of course, it would never occur to him to think of her in the singular, as a person rather than as "people."

Another episode shares with this one a certain quality of folk humor that might at first seem merely playful. Phoenix is wearing an old pair of men's shoes. Arriving in Natchez, she encounters on the sidewalk a perfumed white woman, notably a "lady," bearing Christmas packages, and stops her to ask that she lace up and tie the old shoes, explaining that she cannot bend over to do it for herself. The lady puts down her packages and complies. Phoenix has at first glance spotted the young hunter for a fool, and easily tricks him into running off after the dogs for a few minutes, so that she can more easily pick up and pocket the nickel she has seen him drop. Her instinct in the later encounter is just as sure; precisely *because* the woman with the packages is so much a lady, so high-and-mighty and sweet-smelling, she won't refuse the outrageous request that she stop and lace up the shoes. Miss Welty has a very keen eye for this sort of thing—the ways in which southern Negroes have learned to take subtle revenge on the "superior" race, to exploit, for their own material or psychological advantage, the weaknesses of white pride.

But in the total context of the story, when we learn what Phoenix proposes to do with the nickel she has taken from the hunter and the second one she extracts from the women in the office, what the occasion is that demands the dignity of tied shoes, when in brief we finally see why the action occurs at Christmas time, then both episodes take on a significance beyond humor. The "theft" (with Phoenix's private remorse: "God watching me the whole time. I come to stealing") and the shoelacing are acts, signs, of sanctification. Phoenix is finally accorded something even greater than ordinary human dignity. She is a saint, one of those who walks always in the eye of God, on whom He has set His sign, whether ordinary men are prepared to see it or not. For we realize finally that she has done nothing for herself, for her own advantage, either psychological or material. Just because sanctity is never self-regarding, she must see herself as a sinner. But in the ultimate perspective she is, by virtue of her sanctity, exempt from the usual requirements of economic and social morality, and, witness again her talking to the animals of the forest and to the bushes and trees, is mysteriously intimate with external nature.

But, lest this seem to fix things up a trifle too smoothly, and relieve the human community of any further responsibility in the matter, we should observe again how consistently, in the story, the ordinary men who do not see happen to be white men—or, the point is worth noting, white women. There is nowhere in modern literature a more scathing indictment of the fool's pride of the white man in the superiority of his civilization, of his fool's confidence in the virtue of the "soothing medicine" he offers to heal the hurts of that "stubborn case," black mankind.

In the last of the three stories I have chosen, "Powerhouse," Miss Welty presents a kind of Negro very different from either Keela-Lee Roy or old Phoenix. The title character, the Negro musician, is in no immediately obvious way either saintly or pitiable. He is, perhaps, even Satanic (" 'Nigger man'?—he looks more Asiatic, monkey, Jewish, Babylonian, Peruvian, fanatic, devil"). Certainly, he is superior, all mysterious grandeur and self-possession in his seat up on the stage behind his piano, master of all he surveys—including both his band and the all-white audience for which they are playing the dance in Alligator, Mississippi. In the first place he is big, and a city Negro, and a northerner, at least by residence if not by birth. All of that is important. But the final and decisive thing is that he is a jazz man, a prominent member of perhaps the one and only profession in which the American Negro has unquestioned and original supremacy. Here, if anywhere, black man calls the tune, and white man dances, or is too entranced to do anything but listen.

Technically, the story itself is a jazz composition. A complete stylistic analysis is out of place in this essay. But suffice it to say that "style" and "story" are inseparable, more completely in this instance even than in most of Miss Welty's fiction, and that with this achieved fusion she brilliantly suggests how Powerhouse's art is inseparable from his life—and how in this way he is, perhaps, the essential Negro.

One of the fundamental ironies is that the realest jazz is played, so to speak, at intermission, when there is no white audience, and, for a time, no audience at all. The band members go out for beer, into a pouring-down rain to which they are not indifferent, not impervious; it enters their mood, but, precisely, they make it work for them; and their conversation all the way to the beer joint, while there, and all the way back, is a verbal jam session. Already talking, just to the band, while they play the last number before intermission—"the only waltz they will ever consent to play, 'Pagan Love Song'"—Powerhouse has given them the theme for improvisation with reference to a telegram he says he has received, announcing that his wife is dead.

"Telegram say—here the words: Your wife is dead." He puts 4/4 over 3/4.

....

"Uranus Knockwood is the name signed." Powerhouse lifts his eyes open. "Ever heard of him?"

....

"Say it agin."
"Uranus Knockwood."
"That ain't Lenox Avenue."
"It ain't Broadway."

....

"Hell, that's on a star, boy, ain't it?" Crash of the cymbals.

And later, in the café:

"You know him."

"Uranus Knockwood!"

"Yeahhh!"

"He come in when we goes out!"

"Uh-huh!"

"He go out when we comes in!"

"Yeahhh!"

....

"Middle-size man."

"Wears a hat."

"That's him."

We never know for sure—maybe they don't either, even Powerhouse—whether the telegram is wholly imaginary. But they have to, under Powerhouse's domination, "play" it. One of them ("that is one crazy drummer that's going to get his neck broken some day") is skeptical, others frightened, others obscurely depressed, all delighted, all toward the end, on the way back to the dance hall, a little tired of it; but Powerhouse won't let it go, until he has got the resolution he wants, until he has, with their jaded collaboration, "answered" the telegram.

"Here's the answer. I got it right here. "What in the hell you talking about? Don't make any difference: I gotcha." Name signed: Powerhouse."

"That going to reach him, Powerhouse?" Valentine speaks in a maternal voice.

....

"Reach him and come out the other side."

And it is this mastered theme, of death and betrayal, of the inscrutability of shabby fate, the something "on a star" that inexplicably and pitilessly intrudes upon the patterns of mundane prudence and solicitude, that informs the rest of the "official" performance after they return to the hall. The white audience naïvely suppose that it is the beer that they are "full of" when they come back that accounts for the new freedom and power of their playing.

But we, perhaps unfortunately for us, haven't, through the offices of Miss Welty, stayed in the dance hall during intermission. We've been along to World Café, and seen what was served there, besides beer. So that we are, or ought to be, in a position to interpret more accurately, to make some fuller and more meaningful response than the white citizens of Alligator can to the final music.

And yet again, it is not easy. Was there a telegram? Who is Uranus Knockwood? Where? Maybe the "middle-size man, wears a hat" is "the man." Maybe we sent the telegram, thinking we're on a star.

Miss Welty sees through, feels through, the racist clichés. But she also sees through the easy sentimentalities of white liberalism, the white man's wishful thought that a man like Powerhouse, *in* his power, is only and essentially a man like himself.

Powerhouse is "humanized," somewhat. We learn that he is in the habit of calling his wife long distance, to see how she is while he is on the road. But that information is from the crazy drummer, "that's going to get his neck broken some day." (Powerhouse steadfastly refuses to call this time, to check on the telegram.) It is dangerous to presume. Mostly, he is associated, or identified, with vast and elemental forces. "Mississippi River," the waitress at the café calls him. As they start out at intermission, he has pulled open the back door for the others, "and with a wild, gathered-up face is smelling the terrible night." At the very end, singing, on the chorus of "Somebody Loves Me!" his mouth "gets to be nothing but a volcano." It is out of that terrifying aperture, orifice of chaos and old night, that the final, powerfully mocking suggestion comes, thrown down to the white dancers: "Maybe . . . Maybe . . . Maybe it's you." And only the fool or the saint among us would be quick to answer that call, either to affirm or to deny.

XIII

JAMES BALDWIN

Many Thousands Gone: Richard Wright's "Native Son"

It is only in his music, which Americans are able to admire because a protective sentimentality limits their understanding of
it, that the Negro in America has been able to tell his story. It is
a story which otherwise has yet to be told and which no American is prepared to hear. As is the inevitable result of things un-
said, we find ourselves until today oppressed with a dangerous
and reverberating silence; and the story is told, compulsively, in
symbols and signs, in hieroglyphics; it is revealed in Negro
speech and in that of the white majority and in their different
frames of reference. The ways in which the Negro has affected
the American psychology are betrayed in our popular culture
and in our morality; in our estrangement from him is the depth
of our estrangement from ourselves. We cannot ask: what do
we *really* feel about him—such a question merely opens the
gates on chaos. What we really feel about him is involved with
all that we feel about everything, about everyone, about ourselves.

The story of the Negro in America is the story of America—
or, more precisely, it is the story of Americans. It is not a very
pretty story: the story of a people is never very pretty. The
Negro in America, gloomily referred to as that shadow which
lies athwart our national life, is far more than that. He is a series
of shadows, self-created, intertwining, which now we helplessly
battle. One may say that the Negro in America does not really
exist except in the darkness of our minds.

This is why his history and his progress, his relationship to all
other Americans, has been kept in the social arena. He is a social

and not a personal or a human problem; to think of him is to think of statistics, slums, rapes, injustices, remote violence; it is to be confronted with an endless cataloguing of losses, gains, skirmishes; it is to feel virtuous, outraged, helpless, as though his continuing status among us were somehow analogous to disease —cancer, perhaps, or tuberculosis—which must be checked, even though it cannot be cured. In this arena the black man acquires quite another aspect from that which he has in life. We do not know what to do with him in life; if he breaks our sociological and sentimental image of him we are panic-stricken and we feel ourselves betrayed. When he violates this image, therefore, he stands in the greatest danger (sensing which, we uneasily suspect that he is very often playing a part for our benefit); and, what is not always so apparent but is equally true, we are then in some danger ourselves—hence our retreat or our blind and immediate retaliation.

Our dehumanization of the Negro then is indivisible from our dehumanization of ourselves: the loss of our own identity is the price we pay for our annulment of his. Time and our own force act as our allies, creating an impossible, a fruitless tension between the traditional master and slave. Impossible and fruitless because, literal and visible as this tension has become, it has nothing to do with reality.

Time has made some changes in the Negro face. Nothing has succeeded in making it exactly like our own, though the general desire seems to be to make it blank if one cannot make it white. When it has become blank, the past as thoroughly washed from the black face as it has been from ours, our guilt will be finished—at least it will have ceased to be visible, which we imagine to be much the same thing. But, paradoxically, it is we who prevent this from happening; since it is we, who, every hour that we live, reinvest the black face with our guilt; and we do this—by a further paradox, no less ferocious—helplessly, passionately, out of an unrealized need to suffer absolution.

Today, to be sure, we know that the Negro is not biologically or mentally inferior; there is no truth in those rumors of his body odor or his incorrigible sexuality; or no more truth than can be easily explained or even defended by the social sciences. Yet, in our most recent war, his blood was segregated as was, for the most part, his person. Up to today we are set at a division, so that he may not marry our daughters or our sisters, nor may he—for the most part—eat at our tables or live in our houses. Moreover, those who do, do so at the grave expense of a double alienation: from their own people, whose fabled attributes they must either deny or, worse, cheapen and bring to market; from us, for we require of them, when we accept them, that they at once cease to be Negroes and yet not fail to remember what being a Negro means—to remember, that is, what it means to us. The threshold of insult is higher or lower, according to the people involved, from the bootblack in Atlanta to the celebrity in New York. One must travel very far, among saints with nothing to gain or outcasts with nothing to lose, to find a place where it does not matter—and perhaps a word or a gesture or simply a silence will testify that it matters even there.

For it means something to be a Negro, after all, as it means something to have been born in Ireland or in China, to live where one sees space and sky or to live where one sees nothing but rubble or nothing but high buildings. We cannot escape our origins, however hard we try, those origins which contain the key—could we but find it—to all that we later become. What it means to be a Negro is a good deal more than this essay can discover; what it means to be a Negro in America can perhaps be suggested by an examination of the myths we perpetuate about him.

Aunt Jemima and Uncle Tom are dead, their places taken by a group of amazingly well-adjusted young men and women, almost as dark, but ferociously literate, well-dressed and scrubbed, who are never laughed at, who are not likely ever to set foot in a cotton or tobacco field or in any but the most modern of kitchens. There are others who remain, in our odd idiom, "underprivileged"; some are bitter and these come to grief; some are unhappy, but, continually presented with the evidence of a better day soon to come, are speedily becoming less so. Most of them care nothing whatever about race. They want only their proper place in the sun and the right to be left alone, like any other citizen of the republic. We may all breathe more easily. Before, however, our joy at the demise of Aunt Jemima and Uncle Tom approaches the indecent, we had better ask whence they sprang, how they lived? Into what limbo have they vanished?

However inaccurate our portraits of them were, these portraits do suggest, not only the conditions, but the quality of their lives and the impact of this spectacle on our consciences. There was no one more forbearing than Aunt Jemima, no one stronger or more pious or more loyal or more wise; there was, at the same time, no one weaker or more faithless or more vicious and certainly no one more immoral. Uncle Tom, trustworthy and sexless, needed only to drop the title "Uncle" to become violent, crafty, and sullen, a menace to any white woman who passed by. They prepared our feast tables and our burial clothes; and, if we could boast that we understood them, it was far more to the point and far more true that they understood us. They were, moreover, the only people in the world who did; and not only did they know us better than we knew ourselves, but they knew us better than we knew them. This was the piquant flavoring to the national joke, it lay behind our uneasiness as it lay behind our benevolence: Aunt Jemima and Uncle Tom, our creations, at the last evaded us; they had a life—their own, perhaps a better life than ours—and they would never tell us what it was. At the point where we were driven most privately and painfully to conjecture what depths of contempt, what heights of indifference, what prodigies of resilience, what untamable superiority allowed them so vividly to endure, neither perishing nor rising up in a body to wipe us from the earth, the image perpetually shattered and the word failed. The black man in our midst carried murder in his heart, he wanted vengeance. We carried murder too, we wanted peace.

In our image of the Negro breathes the past we deny, not dead but living yet and powerful, the beast in our jungle of statistics. It is this which defeats us, which continues to defeat us, which lends to interracial cocktail parties their rattling, genteel, nervously smiling air: in any drawing room at such a gathering the beast may spring, filling the air with flying things and an unenlightened wailing. Wherever the problem touches there is confusion, there is danger. Wherever the Negro face appears a tension is created, the tension of a silence filled with things unutterable. It is a sentimental error, therefore, to believe that the past is dead; it means nothing to say that it is all forgotten, that the Negro himself has forgotten it. It is not a question of memory. Oedipus did not remember the thongs that bound his feet; nevertheless the marks they left testified to that doom toward which his feet were leading him. The man does not remember the hand that struck him, the darkness that frightened him, as a child; nevertheless, the hand and the darkness remain with him, indivisible from himself forever, part of the passion that drives him wherever he thinks to take flight.

The making of an American begins at that point where he himself rejects all other ties, any other history, and himself adopts the vesture of his adopted land. This problem has been faced by all Americans throughout our history—in a way it *is* our history—and it baffles the immigrant and sets on edge the second generation until today. In the case of the Negro the past was taken from him whether he would or no; yet to forswear it was meaningless and availed him nothing, since his shameful history was carried, quite literally, on his brow. Shameful; for he was heathen as well as black and would never have discovered the healing blood of Christ had not we braved the jungles to bring him these glad tidings. Shameful; for, since our role as missionary had not been wholly disinterested, it was necessary to recall the shame from which we had delivered him in order more easily to escape our own. As he accepted the alabaster Christ and the bloody cross—in the bearing of which he would find his redemption, as, indeed, to our outraged astonishment, he sometimes did—he must, henceforth, accept that image we then gave him of himself: having no other and standing, moreover, in danger of death should he fail to accept the dazzling light thus brought into such darkness. It is this quite simple dilemma that must be borne in mind if we wish to comprehend his psychology.

However we shift the light which beats so fiercely on his head, or *prove*, by victorious social analysis, how his lot has changed, how we have both improved, our uneasiness refuses to be exorcized. And nowhere is this more apparent than in our literature on the subject—"problem" literature when written by whites, "protest" literature when written by Negroes—and nothing is more striking than the tremendous disparity of tone between the two creations. *Kingsblood Royal* bears, for example, almost no kinship to *If He Hollers Let Him Go*, though the same reviewers praised them both for what were, at bottom, very much the same reasons. These reasons may be suggested, far too briefly but not at all unjustly, by observing that the presupposition is in both novels exactly the same: black is a terrible color with which to be born into the world.

Now the most powerful and celebrated statement we have

yet had of what it means to be a Negro in America is unquestionably Richard Wright's *Native Son*. The feeling which prevailed at the time of its publication was that such a novel, bitter, uncompromising, shocking, gave proof, by its very existence, of what strides might be taken in a free democracy; and its indisputable success, proof that Americans were now able to look full in the face without flinching the dreadful facts. Americans, unhappily, have the most remarkable ability to alchemize all bitter truths into an innocuous but piquant confection and to transform their moral contradictions, or public discussion of such contradictions, into a proud decoration, such as are given for heroism on the field of battle. Such a book, we felt with pride, could never have been written before—which was true. Nor could it be written today. It bears already the aspect of a landmark; for Bigger and his brothers have undergone yet another metamorphosis; they have been accepted in baseball leagues and by colleges hitherto exclusive; and they have made a most favorable appearance on the national screen. We have yet to encounter, nevertheless, a report so indisputably authentic, or one that can begin to challenge this most significant novel.

It is, in a certain American tradition, the story of an unremarkable youth in battle with the force of circumstance; that force of circumstance which plays and which has played so important a part in the national fables of success or failure. In this case the force of circumstance is not poverty merely but color, a circumstance which cannot be overcome, against which the protagonist battles for his life and loses. It is, on the surface, remarkable that this book should have enjoyed among Americans the favor it did enjoy; no more remarkable, however, than that it should have been compared, exuberantly, to Dostoevsky, though placed a shade below Dos Passos, Dreiser, and Steinbeck; and when the book is examined, its impact does not seem remarkable at all, but becomes, on the contrary, perfectly logical and inevitable.

We cannot, to begin with, divorce this book from the specific social climate of that time: it was one of the last of those angry productions, encountered in the late twenties and all through the thirties, dealing with the inequities of the social structure of America. It was published one year before our entry into the last world war—which is to say, very few years after the dissolution of the WPA and the end of the New Deal and at a time when bread lines and soup kitchens and bloody industrial battles were bright in everyone's memory. The rigors of that unexpected time filled us not only with a genuinely bewildered and despairing idealism—so that, because there at least was *something* to fight for, young men went off to die in Spain—but also with a genuinely bewildered self-consciousness. The Negro, who had been during the magnificent twenties a passionate and delightful primitive, now became, as one of the things we were most self-conscious about, our most oppressed minority. In the thirties, swallowing Marx whole, we discovered the Worker and realized—I should think with some relief—that the aims of the Worker and the aims of the Negro were one. This theorem—to which we shall return—seems now to leave rather too much out of account; it became, nevertheless, one of the slogans of the "class struggle" and the gospel of the New Negro.

As for this New Negro, it was Wright who became his most eloquent spokesman; and his work, from its beginning, is most clearly committed to the social struggle. Leaving aside the considerable question of what relationship precisely the artist bears to the revolutionary, the reality of man as a social being is not his only reality and that artist is strangled who is forced to deal with human beings solely in social terms; and who has, moreover, as Wright had, the necessity thrust on him of being the representative of some thirteen million people. It is a false responsibility (since writers are not congressmen) and impossible, by its nature, of fulfillment. The unlucky shepherd soon finds that, so far from being able to feed the hungry sheep, he has lost the wherewithal for his own nourishment: having not been allowed—so fearful was his burden, so present his audience!—to re-create his own experience. Further, the militant men and women of the thirties were not, upon examination, significantly emancipated from their antecedents, however bitterly they might consider themselves estranged or however gallantly they struggled to build a better world. However they might extol Russia, their concept of a better world was quite helplessly American and betrayed a certain thinness of imagination, a suspect reliance on suspect and badly digested formulae, and a positively fretful romantic haste. Finally, the relationship of the Negro to the Worker cannot be summed up, nor even greatly illuminated, by saying that their aims are one. It is true only insofar as they both desire better working conditions and useful only insofar as they unite their strength as workers to achieve these ends. Further than this we cannot in honesty go.

In this climate Wright's voice first was heard and the struggle which promised for a time to shape his work and give it purpose also fixed it in an ever more unrewarding rage. Recording his days of anger he has also nevertheless recorded, as no Negro before him had ever done, that fantasy Americans hold in their minds when they speak of the Negro: that fantastic and fearful image which we have lived with since the first slave fell beneath the lash. This is the significance of *Native Son* and also, unhappily, its overwhelming limitation.

Native Son begins with the *Brring!* of an alarm clock in the squalid Chicago tenement where Bigger and his family live. Rats live there too, feeding off the garbage, and we first encounter Bigger in the act of killing one. One may consider that the entire book, from that harsh *Brring!* to Bigger's weak "Good-by" as the lawyer, Max, leaves him in the death cell, is an extension, with the roles inverted, of this chilling metaphor. Bigger's situation and Bigger himself exert on the mind the same sort of fascination. The premise of the book is, as I take it, clearly conveyed in these first pages: we are confronting a monster created by the American republic and we are, through being made to share his experience, to receive illumination as regards the manner of his life and to feel both pity and horror at his awful and inevitable doom. This is an arresting and potentially rich idea and we would be discussing a very different novel if Wright's execution had been more perceptive and if he had not attempted to redeem a symbolical monster in social terms.

One may object that it was precisely Wright's intention to create in Bigger a social symbol, revelatory of social disease and prophetic of disaster. I think, however, that it is this assumption which we ought to examine more carefully. Bigger has no discernible relationship to himself, to his own life, to his own people, nor to any other people—in this respect, perhaps, he is most American—and his force comes, not from his significance as a social (or anti-social) unit, but from his significance as the incarnation of a myth. It is remarkable that, though we follow him step by step from the tenement room to the death cell, we know as little about him when this journey is ended as we did when it began; and, what is even more remarkable, we know almost as little about the social dynamic which we are to believe created him. Despite the details of slum life which we are given, I doubt that anyone who has thought about it, disengaging himself from sentimentality, can accept this most essential premise of the novel for a moment. Those Negroes who surround him, on the other hand, his hard-working mother, his ambitious sister, his poolroom cronies, Bessie, might be considered as far richer and far more subtle and accurate illustrations of the ways in which Negroes are controlled in our society and the complex techniques they have evolved for their survival. We are limited, however, to Bigger's view of them, part of a deliberate plan which might not have been disastrous if we were not also limited to Bigger's perceptions. What this means for the novel is that a necessary dimension has been cut away; this dimension being the relationship that Negroes bear to one another, that depth of involvement and unspoken recognition of shared experience which creates a way of life. What the novel reflects—and at no point interprets—is the isolation of the Negro within his own group and the resulting fury of impatient scorn. It is this which creates its climate of anarchy and unmotivated and unapprehended disaster; and it is this climate, common to most Negro protest novels, which has led us all to believe that in Negro life there exists no tradition, no field of manners, no possibility of ritual or intercourse, such as may, for example, sustain the Jew even after he has left his father's house. But the fact is not that the Negro has no tradition but that there has as yet arrived no sensibility sufficiently profound and tough to make this tradition articulate. For a tradition expresses, after all, nothing more than the long and painful experience of a people; it comes out of the battle waged to maintain their integrity or, to put it more simply, out of their struggle to survive. When we speak of the Jewish tradition we are speaking of centuries of exile and persecution, of the strength which endured and the sensibility which discovered in it the high possibility of the moral victory.

This sense of how Negroes live and how they have so long endured is hidden from us in part by the very speed of the Negro's public progress, a progress so heavy with complexity, so bewildering and kaleidoscopic, that he dare not pause to conjecture on the darkness which lies behind him; and by the nature of the American psychology which, in order to apprehend or be made able to accept it, must undergo a metamorphosis so profound as to be literally unthinkable and which there is no doubt we will resist until we are compelled to achieve our own identity by the rigors of a time that has yet to come. Bigger, in the meanwhile, and all his furious kin, serve only to whet the notorious national taste for the sensational and to reinforce all that we now find it necessary to believe. It is not Bigger whom we fear, since his appearance among us makes our victory certain. It is the others, who smile, who go to church, who give no cause for complaint, whom we sometimes consider with amusement, with pity, even with affection—and in whose faces we sometimes surprise the merest arrogant hint of hatred, the faintest, withdrawn, speculative shadow of contempt—who make us uneasy; whom we cajole, threaten, flatter, fear; who to us remain unknown, though we are not (we feel with both relief and hostility and with bottomless confusion) unknown to them. It is out of our reaction to these hewers of wood and drawers of water that our image of Bigger was created.

It is this image, living yet, which we perpetually seek to evade with good works; and this image which makes of all our good works an intolerable mockery. The "nigger," black, benighted, brutal, consumed with hatred as we are consumed with guilt, cannot be thus blotted out. He stands at our shoulders when we give our maid her wages, it is his hand which we fear we are taking when struggling to communicate with the current "intelligent" Negro, his stench, as it were, which fills our mouths with salt as the monument is unveiled in honor of the latest Negro leader. Each generation has shouted behind him, *Nigger!* as he walked our streets; it is he whom we would rather our sisters did not marry; he is banished into the vast and wailing outer darkness whenever we speak of the "purity" of our women, of the "sanctity" of our homes, of "American" ideals. What is more, he knows it. He is indeed the "native son": he is the "nigger." Let us refrain from inquiring at the moment whether or not he actually exists; for we *believe* that he exists. Whenever we encounter him amongst us in the flesh, our faith is made perfect and his necessary and bloody end is executed with a mystical ferocity of joy.

But there is a complementary faith among the damned which involves their gathering of the stones with which those who walk in the light shall stone them; or there exists among the intolerably degraded the perverse and powerful desire to force into the arena of the actual those fantastic crimes of which they have been accused, achieving their vengeance and their own destruction through making the nightmare real. The American image of the Negro lives also in the Negro's heart; and when he has surrendered to this image life has no other possible reality. Then he, like the white enemy with whom he will be locked one day in mortal struggle, has no means save this of asserting his identity. This is why Bigger's murder of Mary can be referred to as an "act of creation" and why, once this murder has been committed, he can feel for the first time that he is living fully and deeply as a man was meant to live. And there is, I should think, no Negro living in America who has not felt, briefly or for long periods, with anguish sharp or dull, in varying degrees and to varying effect, simple, naked and unanswerable hatred; who has not wanted to smash any white face he may encounter in a day, to violate, out of motives of the cruelest vengeance, their women, to break the bodies of all white people and bring them low, as low as that dust into which he himself has been and is being trampled; no Negro, finally, who has not had to make his own precarious adjustment to the "nigger" who surrounds him and to the "nigger" in himself.

Yet the adjustment must be made—rather, it must be attempted, the tension perpetually sustained—for without this he has surrendered his birthright as a man no less than his birthright as a black man. The entire universe is then peopled only with his enemies, who are not only white men armed with rope and rifle, but his own far-flung and contemptible kinsmen. Their blackness is his degradation and it is their stupid and passive endurance which makes his end inevitable.

Bigger dreams of some black man who will weld all blacks together into a mighty fist, and feels, in relation to his family, that perhaps they had to live as they did precisely because none of them had ever done anything, right or wrong, which mattered very much. It is only he who, by an act of murder, has burst the dungeon cell. He has made it manifest that *he* lives and that his despised blood nourishes the passions of a man. He has forced his oppressors to see the fruit of that oppression: and he feels, when his family and his friends come to visit him in the death cell, that they should not be weeping or frightened, that they should be happy, *proud* that he has dared, through murder and now through his own imminent destruction, to redeem their anger and humiliation, that he has hurled into the spiritless obscurity of their lives the lamp of his passionate life and death. Henceforth, they may remember Bigger—who has died, as we may conclude, for them. But they do not feel this; they only know that he has murdered two women and precipitated a reign of terror; and that now he is to die in the electric chair. They therefore weep and are honestly frightened—for which Bigger despises them and wishes to "blot" them out. What is missing in his situation and in the representation of his psychology—which makes his situation false and his psychology incapable of development—is any revelatory apprehension of Bigger as one of the Negro's realities or as one of the Negro's roles. This failure is part of the previously noted failure to convey any sense of Negro life as a continuing and complex group reality. Bigger, who cannot function therefore as a reflection of the social illness, having, as it were, no society to reflect, likewise refuses to function on the loftier level of the Christ-symbol. His kinsmen are quite right to weep and be frightened, even to be appalled: for it is not his love for them or for himself which causes him to die, but his hatred and his self-hatred; he does not redeem the pains of a despised people, but reveals, on the contrary, nothing more than his own fierce bitterness at having been born one of them. In this also he is the "native son," his progress determinable by the speed with which the distance increases between himself and the auction-block and all that the auction-block implies. To have penetrated this phenomenon, this inward contention of love and hatred, blackness and whiteness, would have given him a stature more nearly human and an end more nearly tragic; and would have given us a document more profoundly and genuinely bitter and less harsh with an anger which is, on the one hand, exhibited and, on the other hand, denied.

Native Son finds itself at length so trapped by the American image of Negro life and by the American necessity to find the ray of hope that it cannot pursue its own implications. This is why Bigger must be at the last redeemed, to be received, if only by rhetoric, into that community of phantoms which is our tenaciously held ideal of the happy social life. It is the socially conscious whites who receive him—the Negroes being capable of no such objectivity—and we have, by way of illustration, that lamentable scene in which Jan, Mary's lover, forgives him for her murder; and, carrying the explicit burden of the novel, Max's long speech to the jury. This speech, which really ends the book, is one of the most desperate performances in American fiction. It is the question of Bigger's humanity which is at stake, the relationship in which he stands to all other Americans—and, by implication, to all people—and it is precisely this question which it cannot clarify, with which it cannot, in fact, come to any coherent terms. He is the monster created by the American republic, the present awful sum of generations of oppression; but to say that he is a monster is to fall into the trap of making him subhuman and he must, therefore, be made representative of a way of life which is real and human in precise ratio to the degree to which it seems to us monstrous and strange. It seems to me that this idea carries, implicitly, a most remarkable confession: that is, that Negro life is in fact as debased and impoverished as our theology claims; and, further, that the use to which Wright puts this idea can only proceed from the assumption—not entirely unsound—that Americans, who evade, so far as possible, all genuine experience, have therefore no way of assessing the experience of others and no way of establishing themselves in relation to any way of life which is not their own. The privacy or obscurity of Negro life makes that life capable, in our imaginations, of producing anything at all; and thus the idea of Bigger's monstrosity can be presented without fear of contradiction, since no American has the knowledge or authority to contest it and no Negro has the voice. It is an idea, which, in the framework of the novel, is dignified by the possibility it promptly affords of presenting Bigger as the herald of disaster, the danger signal of a more bitter time to come when not Bigger alone but all his kindred will rise, in the name of the many thousands who have perished in fire and flood and by rope and torture, to demand their rightful vengeance.

But it is not quite fair, it seems to me, to exploit the national innocence in this way. The idea of Bigger as a warning boomerangs not only because it is quite beyond the limit of probability that Negroes in America will ever achieve the means of wreaking vengeance upon the state but also because it cannot be said that they have any desire to do so. *Native Son* does not convey the altogether savage paradox of the American Negro's situation, of which the social reality which we prefer with such hopeful superficiality to study is but, as it were, the shadow. It is not simply the relationship of oppressed to oppressor, of master to slave, nor is it motivated merely by hatred; it is also, literally and morally, a *blood* relationship, perhaps the most profound reality of the American experience, and we cannot begin to unlock it until we accept how very much it contains of the force and anguish and terror of love.

Negroes are Americans and their destiny is the country's destiny. They have no other experience besides their experience on this continent and it is an experience which cannot be rejected, which yet remains to be embraced. If, as I believe, no American Negro exists who does not have his private Bigger Thomas living in the skull, then what most significantly fails to be illuminated here is the paradoxical adjustment which is perpetually made, the Negro being compelled to accept the fact that this dark and dangerous and unloved stranger is part of himself forever. Only this recognition sets him in any wise free and it is this, this necessary ability to contain and even, in the most honorable sense of the word, to exploit the "nigger," which lends to Negro life its high element of the ironic and which causes the most well-meaning of their American critics to make such exhilarating errors when attempting to understand them. To present Bigger as a warning is simply to reinforce the American guilt and fear concerning him, it is most forcefully to limit him to that previously mentioned social arena in which he has no human validity, it is simply to condemn him to death. For he has always been a warning, he represents the evil, the sin and suffering which we are compelled to reject. It is useless to say to the courtroom in which this heathen sits on trial that he is their responsibility, their creation, and his crimes are theirs; and that they ought, therefore, to allow him to live, to make articulate to himself behind the walls of prison the meaning of his existence. The meaning of his existence has already been most adequately expressed, nor does anyone wish, particularly not in the name of democracy, to think of it any more; as for the possibility of articulation, it is this possibility which above all others we most dread. Moreover, the courtroom, judge, jury, witnesses and spectators, recognize immediately that Bigger is their creation and they recognize this not only with hatred and fear and guilt and the resulting fury of self-righteousness but also with that morbid fullness of pride mixed with horror with which one regards the extent and power of one's wickedness. They know that death is his portion, that he runs to death; coming from darkness and dwelling in darkness, he must be, as often as he rises, banished, lest the entire planet be engulfed. And they know, finally, that they do not wish to forgive him and that he does not wish to be forgiven; that he dies, hating them, scorning that appeal which they cannot make to that irrecoverable humanity of his which cannot hear it; and that he *wants* to die because he glories in his hatred and prefers, like Lucifer, rather to rule in hell than serve in heaven.

For, bearing in mind the premise on which the life of such a man is based, *i.e.*, that black is the color of damnation, this is his only possible end. It is the only death which will allow him a kind of dignity or even, however horribly, a kind of beauty. To tell this story, no more than a single aspect of the story of the "nigger," is inevitably and richly to become involved with the force of life and legend, how each perpetually assumes the guise of the other, creating that dense, many-sided and shifting reality which is the world we live in and the world we make. To tell his story is to begin to liberate us from his image and it is, for the first time, to clothe this phantom with flesh and blood, to deepen, by our understanding of him and his relationship to us, our understanding of ourselves and of all men.

But this is not the story which *Native Son* tells, for we find here merely, repeated in anger, the story which we have told in pride. Nor, since the implications of this anger are evaded, are we ever confronted with the actual or potential significance of our pride; which is why we fall, with such a positive glow of recognition, upon Max's long and bitter summing up. It is addressed to those among us of good will and it seems to say that, though there are whites and blacks among us who hate each other, we will not; there are those who are betrayed by greed, by guilt, by blood lust, but not we; we will set our faces against them and join hands and walk together into that dazzling future when there will be no white or black. This is the dream of all liberal men, a dream not at all dishonorable, but, nevertheless, a dream. For, let us join hands on this mountain as we may, the battle is elsewhere. It proceeds far from us in the heat and horror and pain of life itself where all men are betrayed by greed and guilt and blood lust and where no one's hands are clean. Our good will, from which we yet expect such power to transform us, is thin, passionless, strident: its roots, examined, lead us back to our forebears, whose assumption it was that the black man, to become truly human and acceptable, must first become like us. This assumption once accepted, the Negro in America can only acquiesce in the obliteration of his own personality, the distortion and debasement of his own experience, surrendering to those forces which reduce the person to anonymity and which make themselves manifest daily all over the darkening world.

XIV

MARCUS KLEIN

Ralph Ellison's "Invisible Man"

Ralph Ellison's invisible man speaks first of all for himself, a
Negro whose career, because he is a Negro, has been a search
for a primary, existential sense of himself. The existential question, as a critic says, "lies waiting around the corner for any
introspective person, but it straddles the main highway for a
thoughtful Negro."[1] And despite the statement of faith with
which *Invisible Man* ends, that the hero can accomplish visibility, this invisible man speaks in the conviction of utter failure.

In fact, the only way in which he might exist is in an enormous act of vengeance, a mechanics which Bigger Thomas had
discovered before him. But the world is nothing so simple for
him as it was for Bigger. Simple murder won't do, and anyway
he sees the contradiction in vengeance. He accomplishes revenge and existence only at a remove, in a nightmare underground. He is removed into nightmare not because it may be
that in the ordinary ways of being, men are inevitably determined, nor because there may be no such thing as the existential self, nor because the gratuitous act may be really gratuitous
and without sense except in dreams. That would be certainly
to open the universal theme. And he is condemned not because
of cowardice or lack of maturity—despite the fact Ellison has
once commented on his hero's "refusal to run the risk of his
own humanity, which involves guilt."[2] He is not a coward and

From Marcus Klein, "Ralph Ellison," *After Alienation* (Cleveland and
New York: World Publishing Company, 1964), pp. 71–146. Copyright ©
1964, 1962 by Marcus Klein. Published by arrangement with The World
Publishing Company, Cleveland and New York.

[1] F. Cudworth Flint, "Fiction Chronicle," *Sewanee Review,* LXII (Winter, 1954), 176.

[2] Ralph Ellison in an interview by Alfred Chester and Vilma Howard
in *Paris Review,* No. 8 (Spring, 1955), 68. See also Ellison's statement to
Rochelle Girson ("Sidelights on Invisibility," *Saturday Review,* XXXVI

he is very little guilty. And he is thrust into a nightmare not, despite the fact that Ellison has said it, because the frustration of identity is peculiarly the American theme. He is condemned first of all because he is black. The novel is glued to the fact. . . .

Out of the world and apart from ordinary defined experience is just where, in fact, the hero of the novel always finds himself. The large action of *Invisible Man* is all a circular voyage, consisting of four prominent adventures. It begins with a ritual of the hero's initiation, a test of his bravery, of his knowledge of caste, and of his sexuality, and it ends in failure, with the hero castrated, presented with proofs of his cowardice and ignorance, in a condition prior to his initiation. He is at the end back in the underworld from which he had tried to emerge, with this difference only, that he has illuminated his underworld and he now knows where he is.

That is the great irony the novel deliberately plays on itself—the world moves, the hero tells us in almost the first words of the Prologue, not like an arrow, nor in a spiral, but like a boomerang; his end, he says, is in his beginning. And it should be said immediately, the novel's great fault is in the fact that its end *is* its beginning. The novel is a furious picaresque which plunges the hero forward through a series of violences. Moreover, it is *all* an initiation rite. The hero moves from childhood to the age of manhood, and from the South to the North, and he is one of those heroes who move from the provinces to the capital, to the center of power, from innocence to experience. He moves, moreover, through what seems at all points a linear exploration of the "Negro problem," through ideologies by which it might be approached, and beyond that, through what one of the symbolic structures of the novel suggests is an exploration of some one hundred years of American history. But for all that multiplicity of parallel actions, the novel has no real progress except that at each stage it clarifies and reinforces the hero's dilemma.

[March 14, 1953], 49): "Invisibility has to do with the failure of most of us to regard the individual we contact as a human being. . . . On the other hand, you have the failure of the individual to exert himself to be mature, to run the risk of humanity. . . ."

" 'Ah,' I can hear you say," the hero says in almost the last words of the Epilogue,

"so it was all a build-up to bore us with his buggy jiving. He only wanted us to listen to him rave!" But only partially true: Being invisible and without substance, a disembodied voice, as it were, what else could I do? What else but try to tell you what was really happening when your eyes were looking through?

But the witness is not here being responsive to the witness against him. This appeal is a last-ditch attempt to rescue the book from what must have seemed to Ellison its strategic error. The amount of clarity the novel finally comes to is enormous, and so much clarity is shocking, but still it is a clarity without any further effect. The novel doesn't finally go anywhere.

It is a fault that apparently led Ellison to the desperate, empty, unreasonable, and programmatic optimism of the last few pages of the novel: ". . . we [Negroes] were to affirm the principle on which the country was built. . . ." We "were linked to all others in the loud, clamoring semi-visible world. . . ." ". . . I've overstayed my hibernation, since there's a possibility that even an invisible man has a socially responsible role to play." One asks this hero how he is to come out and be socially responsible? Upon what ground in reality can he affirm *any* positive principle? Just what is he going to do? Everything in the novel has clarified this point: that the bizarre accident that has led him to take up residence in an abandoned coal cellar is no accident at all, that the underworld is his inevitable home, that given the social facts of America, both invisibility and what he now calls his "hibernation" are his permanent condition. And really his only extension into the upper world can be in negative acts and fantasies of vengeance —which do indeed make up another ending to the novel.

And it is just another consequence of its circularity that *Invisible Man* has many endings. The novel sets out to gain clarity but no new discovery. Its ending is in its beginning. Therefore, with every gain in illumination, the novel concludes. There is a constant increase of wattage, but what is to be seen remains the same. And then the consequence of that fact is that —except in the Prologue and the Epilogue to the novel, where the hero speaks in time present and out of all his experience— the hero is fitted with a perceptiveness that is far inferior to

Ellison's. Or, if not always, that becomes a fault. He is sometimes an *ingénu*, sometimes a naive Gulliver when gullibility
should be impossible, sometimes, suddenly, the author. There
is a constant struggle between the two, Ellison straining not to
let his protagonist know too much because that will give the
book away, and sometimes failing. And finally the consequence
of this latter fact is that a great deal of the novel is in a great
density of symbols and puns. They don't, as the danger is, clog
the action. They do contain the material. But they don't always
contribute to the material. Because the hero can't know too
much, because every discovery risks being the last discovery,
because Ellison knows very well what each of his hero's experiences comes to, much of the hero's experience is converted
into tantalizing hieroglyphics. The puns, which should be devices of compression, mount on each other and, like the major
episodes of the novel, they tend each of them to tell the same
and the whole story.

But then if at the end Ellison cops a plea—"what else could
I do? What else but try to tell you what was really happening
when your eyes were looking through?"—his plea is in every
way valid. The novel's task is just the perception of obvious,
repeated facts which no one sees. The task itself must be constantly emphasized and repeated in a great variety of ironic
symbols, because that is a dramatic necessity in the nature of
the task. The repetition is the proof that the task is authentic.
The hero is first a high-school boy in a Southern town, then
a college student at a Negro university, then, briefly, a laborer
in a Northern factory, then a leader in what in the novel is
called the Brotherhood, and finally an underground man. That
is his whole story, all of it devoted to one struggle which is
perpetual and obsessive because all his experience does really
come to the same thing, an unremitting and fruitless attempt
to achieve visibility. The book is filled by a lifetime of events,
all of them leading back to the same meaning.

So in the Prologue, speaking of his invisibility in his coal
cellar, the hero says he needs light because without it he is not
only invisible but formless, and it is part of the joke he intends
that he is, what someone calls him later, a nigger in a coal pile,
that black can't be seen in the dark. The obvious is not obvious.
The need is for illumination. And a series of leaders with whom
the hero becomes engaged and who promise perception turn

out to be blind. A Negro minister at his college, the Reverend Homer (Blind Homer) A. Barbee, preaches a sermon of hope, faith, and endurance, and falls flat on his face. Brother Jack, the local leader of the Brotherhood, sees salvation in the dialectic of historical necessity and can't see a thing because he has a glass eye, just because he has given his eye to the Brotherhood's vision. The Founder of the hero's Negro college, a great leader of his people and a thin disguise for the hero's first hero, Booker T. Washington, is presented to him first in an ambiguous statue in which the Founder is either lifting a veil from the face of a slave or lowering it.

And the task the novel sets for itself, perception of the obvious that is not seen, is reiterated in constant talk and punning, which jumps out everywhere, on eyes, vision, and visions. The hero is troubled by a burning eye within. His one current friend, in the Prologue, time present, is "a junk man I know, a man of vision," who has supplied him with wire and sockets with which to illuminate his underground—the double joke in that being that electricity is light and power and therefore vision, and that a "junk man" is a narcotics peddler, one who has visions to sell. A moment later in a marijuana sleep the hero has his first, this time surreal, vision of the facts of Negro experience. And there is more around every corner. All the novel's purpose is reiterated constantly, in fact, as its basic metaphor is elaborated: the hero is invisible because no one sees him, and it is the function of every episode to confirm the fact that this black man is condemned to a hopeless struggle to be seen.

The hero's end, then, is in his beginning. Quite literally. The novel happens between the Prologue and the Epilogue and those episodes constitute a single dramatic action: the hero, now, in his cellar, is doing sums in his career, writing his memoirs. And except for its burst of optimism, the Epilogue goes nowhere that the Prologue hasn't already been.[3] The novel, apparently, owes much to *Notes from the Underground*, and not least an ending that it does not clearly earn. Moreover, between the Prologue and the Epilogue, the novel moves in a series of circles—concentric planes of meaning, each traveling right back to its beginning, each mode of adventure confirming

[3] Ellison says that he wrote the Prologue after he had finished the action proper of the novel.

the circularity of the hero's voyaging. Each adventure is itself a repetition of each of the others and all the hero's experiences come to the same thing, but from a variety of ways of experiencing. His adventures are of a political order, and then they also have personal significances for him, having to do with his search for a personal identity, and then they are historical, marking a journey through a history of America since Emancipation which comes out where it entered, and finally they are adventures in a metaphysics, and each plane of adventuring rounds back to where it began.

It all began, the hero says, with his grandfather, an odd old guy. He has been told he takes after him. On his deathbed his grandfather had passed on advice which, the hero says, has become a curse.

Son, after I'm gone I want you to keep up the good fight. I never told you, but our life is a war and I have been a traitor all my born days, a spy in the enemy's country ever since I give up my gun back in the Reconstruction. Live with your head in the lion's mouth. I want you to overcome 'em with yesses, undermine 'em with grins, agree 'em to death and destruction, let 'em swoller you till they vomit or bust wide open.

By the end of the novel the hero comes to see in his grandfather's "Yes" a greater affirmation than anything in the novel suggests his grandfather meant. He discovers in it assent to the great principles on which the country was built. But in any event, between the beginning and the ending, his grandfather's riddle defines his every gambit. The grandfather's incantatory phrases contain, Ellison has said, "a rejection of a current code and a denial become metaphysical." The hero is set earnestly to wish his way out of the curse, and the curse composes his being, his actions, and his purpose. He comes to each adventure saying Yes and he learns, or in every adventure but the last he almost learns, at the same time to say No. In the last adventure he goes underground, and it is one of the many puns brought together in that development that his "underground" is a post of constant subversion.

Between, then, his grandfather's curse in the beginning and his acceptance of it in the Epilogue, the novel moves the hero through adventures in the typical ways Negroes and whites manage, or don't manage, to live together in America. He is moved in each case to the point where all relationships disappear in an explosion, from the way of the caste system of a Southern town to that of the subtler caste system of the Negro college created and endowed by whites, the caste inherent in latter-day abolition, to that of the factory in the industrial North, to that of the dogmatic brotherliness of the Brotherhood, finally to the ultimate extension of all these ways: the race riot with which the action proper of the novel ends. And the issue of each of these adventures is a race riot of one dimension or another, and that is the point of them all. An earnest, yea-saying young man reluctant to be a saboteur explores the typical relationships between Negroes and whites and finds them charged with incipient violence, needing but the slightest accident to set them off. The hero moves from one episode to another because in every one an accident happens.

The accident is always just a slight and unavoidable lapse from the propriety he struggles to maintain. In the first episode he delivers his high-school valedictory address. It is a speech on the proper subject—humility is the secret and the essence of progress for the Negro—addressed to the Southern town's most prominent white citizens, who are drunk at this moment and who pay no attention to him. Benumbed by the noise, the smoke, and the reek of the stag dinner for which he is a part of the entertainment, he speaks the words "social equality" for "social responsibility," and by his slip he springs from the crowd a moment of sudden, terrifying silence. In this moment of his triumph, he is crowded suddenly back into the dark, the dark from which, by his academic prowess and his show of humility, he has thought to escape. Humility is not a technique of progress, but the means of his subjugation, and he dare not *not* be humble. That is something his grandfather had known.

At college, next, with all proper respect he chauffeurs a visiting Northern trustee, Mr. Norton. He takes Mr. Norton to a place Mr. Norton wants to visit, the cabin of a local sharecropper, and discovers himself in a double accident. The sharecropper tells a story of incest and Mr. Norton suffers a heart attack. Still properly deferential, the hero takes Mr. Norton to a local saloon, which unfortunately this day is entertaining the Negro veterans from the local madhouse, and he deposits him into the middle of a riot. The adventure ends with his being expelled from college because, so the college president tells him, he has actually obeyed the wishes of a white man and not merely seemed to. Then in the North, as a laborer in a paint factory, he stumbles into a union meeting and, earnest to please everyone, he finds that because he is a Negro, he is a scab, and as such a catalyst to violence. Then as a favored recruit in the Brotherhood, he takes a single step on his own authority: he organizes a public funeral for a Brother shot by the police, which results in the riot in Harlem that is his last adventure. It is his one lucky accident that in that riot he tumbles into an open manhole, leading to his coal cellar.

The lesson in his accidents is, of course, the instability in all typical relationships between Negroes and whites in America, and the impossibility for a Negro of propriety enough. There is always a boomerang somewhere. Beyond that, these accidents function to reveal to the hero that he is not a person in his relations with whites, but a role, and furthermore they serve to reveal to him the kind of role he plays. It is always the same. The end of the novel is finally his ironic acceptance of his role along with his acceptance of his grandfather's curse.

His whole fate is present, though the hero is not allowed to know it, in that first adventure the climax of which is his dreadful slip of the tongue. A great part of the novel, indeed, is in that initial episode. What is revealed here is what is going to be revealed to the hero, in different circumstances, but with not much modification, in his every subsequent adventure.

In fact, in this first adventure he is clearly threatened but not actually punished for his slip of the tongue. The townsmen allow him to continue his speech, on the condition that he never forget his place. But it is his place, precisely, that the episode fixes. The scene of the speech which the hero supposes to be his valediction is itself a race riot. With some of his school-mates, he has been made to participate in a prior entertainment for this town smoker. He and his friends are to stage a battle royal.

We were a small tight group, clustered together, our bare upper bodies touching and shining with anticipatory sweat; while up front the big shots were becoming increasingly excited over something we still could not see. Suddenly I heard the school superintendent, who had told me to come, yell, "Bring up the shines, gentlemen! Bring up the little shines!"

They are herded before a magnificent, stark-naked blonde, and threatened if they look and threatened by the crowd if they don't. They are held there, made to suffer sexual embarrassment becoming sexual torture, and made to participate then vicariously in the lurching obscenities of the town's ranking citizens. They are goaded, threatened, tantalized, tickled, promised money, beaten, degraded and insulted, worked to the hysteria which is that of their audience, and then thrown blindfold into their battle royal where, in blind passion, they punch and kick at each other while the white mob howls around them. After the battle, at the end of their strength, they are forced to another frenzy by being made to scramble for coins on an electrified rug.

It is to this crapulous mob, in this coliseum, that the hero then talks about "social equality." The episode is a sustained orgy. It not only mocks the hero's earnest dogma of pacific humility, and it not only baptizes him in the terror that, he will find, lurks in all adventures of Negroes among American whites. There is no telling what craziness and what brutish violence lie at any next step. More than that, the episode concentrates, brilliantly, and it exposes at the pitch of a ritualistic frenzy the interior facts of caste, not only its mechanism of economic exploitation (the hero tries to make a deal with one of his schoolmates and is rebuffed, division has been effectively imposed upon them), but all its deeper exploitation of the Negro as a ritualistic scapegoat.

The hero is not only discriminated against. The politics of this system goes much deeper. In fact, he is coddled by that white man, the school superintendent, who has most immediate authority over him—the school superintendent presents him for his speech with a pat on the back, a brief case, and a scholarship. He and his schoolmates are not without honor. These whites use them in ways curiously like love. It is the function of this caste system to suppress a great deal more than the Negro, and it is the lesson of this episode that these Negroes incarnate for these whites everything that they suppress. The Negroes are made by them into the bacchants they themselves dare not be. They are made agents of, and at the same time sacrifices to, the forbidden, everything that is dark, their irrational craving for cruelty, their greed and their sex and their itch for self-destruction, the swoon of the id. These Negroes become for them, then, underground men, irrational, sinful, Satanic, the embodiment of the urgent dark, the pressing power of blackness. And beyond that, they act out for them the whole violent struggle for civilization, by first becoming the dark powers and then by exorcising themselves in violent self-punishment. And then again, in a way to triple the irony, in the same moment the Negroes justify the usage that has in the first place made them scapegoats by performing the whole of this ritual for money.

The battle royal is an extraordinarily compressed piece of work, and its one fault is that it is both more intensely maintained and more exhaustive than anything else in the novel, and so the hero's adventures hereafter become more or less adequate echoes of it. But in any event it does contain, both in its significances and in its form, the most of the hero's career. The same chaos of appetites and guilt that is the real, hidden nature of Negro and white relations is exploded at the hero in each of his subsequent accidents.

That same chaos is what is revealed in the double accident of the Mr. Norton episode. The sharecropper, upon command, *lures* Mr. Norton to a heart attack. His story of incest has a truth of blood in it—his name is "Trueblood"—a truth that Mr. Norton, a New England gentleman and a latter-day, declined Calvinist, cannot in any other way accept. He is fascinated, as it were, into a heart attack which is the equivalent of the townsmen's orgiastic smoker. Trueblood plays out the amoral role assigned to the Negro boys of the battle royal. He does what Norton cannot do. His incest has been with his daughter, and Norton, too, has a daughter. " 'You did and are unharmed!' " Norton shouts. " 'You have looked upon chaos and are not destroyed!' " He acts out a scapegoat ritual with Trueblood and then he gives Trueblood money. Trueblood has done him some service. And the saloon episode contains the same implications, only now reversed: the Negroes use Norton for their purposes of vengeance. When he enters, the madmen go mad, and overwhelm him with the madness of blood. . . .

His reconstruction in the South having failed, having in fact collapsed into riot, the hero participates next in that next epochal event of his racial history, the Great Migration—a migration from the South to the North, the traditional road of freedom, from the country to the city, from agrarianism to industry. The Great Migration is to be another promise of progress in freedom which is not redeemed. Its end, too, is chaos bared, because it is just the same promise as that which was implicit in the liberalism of the golden day. Now that liberalism is even more distant from its source, and it has been progressively emasculated.

Fresh from his engagement with Mr. Norton, the hero comes to New York and falls upon the mercies of a young Mr. Emerson, the son of a Mr. Emerson, who has himself now become a rich New York businessman. Young, psychoanalyzed Mr. Emerson, a reader of *Totem and Taboo,* some of whose best friends are Negroes, offers the hero conspicuous kindness. He knows something about tyranny too. He considers himself his father's prisoner. He offers himself up as Huck Finn to the hero's Nigger Jim (a gesture which makes full sense, it happens, only when it is assumed that young Emerson knows about Leslie Fiedler's discovery of a homosexual theme in *Huckleberry Finn*). And young Emerson invites the hero to a party at the Club Calamus—another pale progeny, apparently, of the Golden Day.

When the hero enters industry, his paint factory, it is, as is historically appropriate, by using "Emerson's name without his permission." (Though there would seem as well to be a private joke in the event. Ralph Ellison's middle name is Waldo.) Come to industry, he discovers that the promise in the Great Migration was just a device of industrial capitalism, that he is an unwitting and certainly an unwilling weapon wielded against labor unionism, and he discovers that his coming to terms with this technological society will be nothing if not violent. The industrial war is, so far as he is concerned, just another, though a more complicated, version of the same war. The Great Migration leads him back to chaos. Specifically, the factory explosion sends him to the hospital, into, perhaps, the systematic persecutions that after World War I followed the Great Migration. It is the hospital's intent to put the hero in a glass box and render him docile. He is submitted to the equivalent of a lobotomy, which is in its turn the equivalent of another operation waggishly suggested by one of the doctors—castration. The point of the operation, a doctor explains, is that "society will suffer no traumata on his account."

The operation does not secure the intended results, and the

hero is plunged then into the final one of the great events of his racial career, the Great Depression. He discovers his whereabouts by coming on what may be taken as the Great Depression's most conspicuously typical event, a tenement eviction. It is an event that provides him with another punning metaphor for his history, "dispossession," and it provides him at the same time, as is historically appropriate, with a seeming opportunity. The event is his introduction to the promising radical politics that could flourish because of such events—he makes a speech to the crowd and is on the spot recruited by the Brotherhood. There is seeming opportunity in the Brotherhood, of course, because it seems brotherly, because it is active, because it seems to make the Negro's cause its own. Beyond that, it imposes on the hero a version of his racial history that unites him with the majority, thereby eliminating the war that he has borne in his secret consciousness. The evictees for whom the hero has just spoken are, Brother Jack tells him, "agrarian types" who are being "ground up by industrial conditions," and so, all Brotherhood doctrine would seem to say, the race war is subsumed by and solved by the class war.

To wage the class war instead is not only the way toward freedom, but it is freedom itself. Like other Negro intellectuals during the Great Depression, the hero accepts this unique promise provided by the Great Depression. There is an alternative only in the futile nationalism of Marcus Garvey, for whom, in the novel, Ras the Exhorter-Destroyer stands. But then the Communist Party did not secure its promise, and so neither does the Brotherhood. It abruptly withdraws its concerns for Harlem—and the hero comes on the fact that the race and the class wars are not identical. Furthermore, he discovers that he is bound to maintain the race war within the ranks of the Brotherhood. Brother Jack is one-eyed and cannot see him. The hero, after his first revelation of Jack's duplicity, looks around a corner of his mind and sees "Jack and Norton and Emerson emerge into one single white figure." The Brotherhood's version of history is arbitrary and does not include his history. And therefore the hero is forced back to the version of reality that at bottom he knows—which is, it turns out, Rinehart's, and which is in the image of chaos.

Rinehart is what this history comes to, and he is its hero. He is the climax of the progress up from slavery. Chaos is his freedom. He moves easily in it. He secures his living from it, and if he has been condemned to it, he takes from it also the implements of his revenge. He has made chaos a base of political action. He is a thief, a rascal, an underground man engaged in the subversion of society. Like Melville's hero, he undermines confidence, and thereby the very foundation of society.

The hero's last adventure, in the Epilogue, in his hole in the ground, serves to confirm and to deepen Rinehart, and Rinehart, the underworld man, is the last of a series of puns for the "underground" which now, in a last shift, is to become actual. The hero's progress has been a series of boomeranging reversals, and he returns now to the most final reversal of all. In every instance when he has thought he has been moving upward, he has been moving down. Especially as he has neared his last adventure there has been a play of punning foreshadowings about him all unwary. He attends the Brotherhood's social events at an apartment house named the Chthonian. He attempts to secure secret information about the Brotherhood from a girl named Sybil—as Aeneas consulted the sibyl before he entered the underworld. From the beginning his grandfather had spoken to him from the grave. The technically accommodated Negro of the paint plant had been an underground man. The Brotherhood itself is a secret, underground organization. The hero's progress has all along been a descent.

He has gone out into life repeatedly, he has been frustrated repeatedly, and at the end he descends into death. That is one implication of his drop into his underground. He has looked for definition, and found chaos. He has made a series of voyages into the world which is a white world, and he ends in the pit of darkness. He has sought rationality, and he ends in the heart of the irrational. He has looked for tranquillity, and he ends in hell. There are all these suggestions brought together in his fall. His search for an adequate politics, for a technique of accommodation, his search for a personal identity, his adventuring through his own racial history, have all led him to this complete negation. The hero in his hole in the ground is back to where he began.

But his descent into the underground is the climax to still another set of implications in his adventures, and his return now to his beginnings is a full and stable resolution to all his adventures. With this final reversal, his reverses have come to an end because, like Rinehart before him, he now accepts reversal as the positive law of his being. It is his metaphysics. He is an invisible man in a world without form—but that, his underground adventure, like the Rinehart episode, goes to prove, is something. He does have an identity and a place, only they are contrary. There is a paradox in the fact that the hero's place in the world is underneath the ground, out of the world, but then the paradox is twisted again when the hero converts his hole in the ground into a home. His coal cellar, Ellison has himself pointed out, is not a sewer, but a source of heat and light and power. The hero converts all his losses to assertion. In fact he has found his politics and his person, and he has made sense out of his history, and so in his fall there is finally an ascension—which Ellison ultimately blurs by his promise that the hero will someday rise to do good among men.

His adventures have gone to prove to the hero, simply, that he is black, and, not so simply, that blackness is equivalent to the reverse of things. Now he asserts his blackness, accepting and using all its qualities and associations. The "Blackness of Blackness," the text offered by the preacher of the Prologue, has been, in effect, the text he has had to learn. In the Prologue he had said that he had to illuminate the blackness of his invisibility. Blackness is the cause of his persecution, of the deprivation of his individual humanity, of his apartness. But blackness is also the dark secrets in his persecution, all the totems and taboos that have been thrust upon him. His adventures in light and dark, in what amounts to the Manicheism of the American racial situation, have provided him with the lesson that he is Satan, whose residence should be in the underground, or as he incorporates lawlessness and irrationality he is Dionysus, or he is the darkness just behind consciousness. He is that which is hidden and deceptive and destructive, that which in nature is alien to man, invisible but present, the shadow upon the world. And he is the very principle of the boomerang which scatters all progress, all history, and all the enlightened ethics of civilization.

He embraces the *blackness* of blackness and thereby becomes an underground man—like Dostoevski's hero, an incarnation of that which is just beneath the surface of things, that is treacherous, irresponsible, and mad.[4] He embraces that fate to which he

[4] As important a source of the hero's underground adventure would seem to be a novella by Richard Wright, "The Man Who Lived Under-

was "before of old ordained," and thereby inherits that "power of blackness" which Melville said "derives its force from its appeals to that Calvinistic sense of Innate Depravity and Original Sin, from whose visitations, in some shape or other, no deeply thinking mind is always and wholly free."

The invisible man's end is in the embrace of his diabolism—diabolism is his politics, his identity, his history, and his metaphysics. And his future is be Satan's—treason, violence, revenge. These are the normal activities now of his underground life. Most of the time he walks softly, he says in the Prologue, so as not to awaken the sleeping ones. He restricts himself to the subversion of Monopolated Light & Power. And he dines on his favorite dessert of vanilla ice cream and sloe gin—white, presumably, seeping blood. But once, with little direct provocation, he had beaten and almost killed a white man. An invisible man tries to make himself felt.

And the true end of the invisible man's proper adventures is in a dream of gigantic vengeance. Fallen into his coal cellar, he dreams of Jack and Emerson and Bledsoe and Norton and Ras and the school superintendent. They demand that he return to them, and when he refuses, they castrate him—they do, that is to say, what they have done. They throw his bloody parts over a bridge, but now his sex catches there, beneath the apex of the curving arch of the bridge, and drips blood into the red water. The hero laughs and tells his torturers that it is their own sun hanging there, and their moon and their world, and that dripping upon the water is all the history they are ever going to make. And then the great bridge itself gathers itself together and slowly moves off, "striding like a robot, an iron man, whose iron legs clanged doomfully as it moved." The hero, full of sorrow and pain, shouts that it must be stopped, but that terrifying figure is his own metamorphosis. And the great dark threat in it is his resolution.

---

ground," *Cross Section*, ed. Edwin Seaver (New York: L. B. Fischer, 1944), pp. 58–102. In Wright's novella, too, a Negro protagonist stumbles into an abandoned underground room which he converts to a home. Ellison's hero illuminates his cellar with 1,369 lights and he plans to have in it five radio-phonographs. Wright's hero papers the walls of his cellar with one-hundred-dollar bills, hangs the walls with gold watches and rings, and strews the floor with diamonds. Like Ellison's hero, he arranges for light by stealing electricity. Like Ellison's hero, he finds his freedom underground.

After that all messages would seem to measure Ellison's desperate reluctances. But the hero is turned, in any event, at the very end, to a staccato of abrupt affirmations—of democracy (". . . we, most of all, had to affirm the principle, the plan in whose name we had been brutalized and sacrificed"), of love (". . . in spite of all I find that I love. . . . I *have* to love"), of the mind, of social responsibility, and of the immediate prospect of his emergence. It must be said that Ellison is to be seen at the very last moment trying to take back the book he has written, or at the very least muffling all its severities, and that is unfortunate. But then it should be said as well that lacking some such attempt, there will be nothing more for Ellison ever to say.

The constant technical flaw in *Invisible Man* is that it so frequently comes to an end, and Ellison is put at every point to a greater muscularity to make the next scene more intense, more thoroughly revealing of what has already been largely revealed. It is the concomitant of that flaw that *Invisible Man* is a death-driven novel. Its movement is to confirm again and again that the hero doesn't exist, and Ellison's difficulty, to put it another way, is to resurrect the hero for each subsequent adventure. The novel's series of ironic negations is, after all, a series of negatives. It can and does reach its last possibility. Ellison will be left with only stale repetitions of the act of dying unless he can in fact assert social responsibility and mind and love—and, because the "Negro problem" is entirely an American problem, democracy. That is the only way he can keep possibility open.

That is to say that the end of *Invisible Man* is the beginning of another novel, one that will draw the complicated positive engagement of the hero in this life, specifically this American life. It is the huge achievement of *Invisible Man,* meanwhile, that it has got a vastness of experience as Negroes particularly must know it—there can be very little that it has left out—into a single meaning. The novel creates a negative metaphor, invisibility, that is fully analytic and fully inclusive, that does hold together for a moment the long experience of chaos that has met Ellison's vision.

XV

ROBERT A. BONE

The Novels of James Baldwin

He made me a watchman upon the city wall,
And if I am a Christian, I am the least of all.
*—*NEGRO SPIRITUAL

The most important Negro writer to emerge during the last decade is of course James Baldwin. His publications, which include three books of essays, three novels, and two plays, have had a stunning impact on our cultural life. His political role, as a leading spokesman of the Negro revolt, has been scarcely less effective. Awards and honors, wealth and success, have crowned his career, and Baldwin has become a national celebrity.

Under the circumstances, the separation of the artist from the celebrity is as difficult as it is necessary. For Baldwin is an uneven writer, the quality of whose work can by no means be taken for granted. His achievement in the novel is most open to dispute, and it is that which I propose to discuss in some detail. Meanwhile, it may be possible to narrow the area of controversy by a preliminary assessment of his talent.

I find Baldwin strongest as an essayist, weakest as a playwright, and successful in the novel form on only one occasion. For the three books of essays, *Notes of a Native Son* (1955), *Nobody Knows My Name* (1961), and *The Fire Next Time* (1963), I have nothing but admiration. Baldwin has succeeded in transposing the entire discussion of American race relations to the interior plane; it is a major breakthrough for the American imagination. In the theater, he has written one competent apprentice play, *The Amen Corner*, first produced at Howard University in 1955, and one unspeakably bad propaganda piece, *Blues for Mister Charlie* (1964). In the novel, the impressive achievement of *Go Tell It on the Mountain* (1953) has not been

Reprinted from *The Tri-Quarterly*, No. 2 (Winter, 1965), 3–30, by permission of *Tri-Quarterly* and the author.

matched by his more recent books, *Giovanni's Room* (1956) and *Another Country* (1962). Perhaps a closer acquaintance with the author's life will help us to account for these vicissitudes.

James Baldwin was a product of the Great Migration. His father had come North from New Orleans; his mother, from Maryland. James was born in Harlem in 1924, the first of nine children. His father was a factory worker and lay preacher, and the boy was raised under the twin disciplines of poverty and the store-front church. He experienced a profound religious crisis during the summer of his fourteenth year, entered upon a youthful ministry, and remained in the pulpit for three years. The second crisis of his life was his break with this milieu; that is, with his father's values, hopes, and aspirations for his son. These two crises—the turn into the fold and the turn away—provide the raw material for his first novel and his first play.

Baldwin graduated from De Witt Clinton High School in 1942, having served on the staff of the literary magazine. He had already discovered in this brief encounter a means of transcending his appointed destiny. Shortly after graduation he left home, determined to support himself as best he could while developing his talent as a writer. After six years of frustration and false starts, however, he had two fellowships but no substantial publications to his credit. This initial literary failure, coupled with the pressures of his personal life, drove him into exile. In 1948, at the age of twenty-four, Baldwin left America for Paris, never intending to return.

He remained abroad for nine years. Europe gave him many things. It gave him a world perspective from which to approach the question of his own identity. It gave him a tender love affair which would dominate the pages of his later fiction. But above all, Europe gave him back himself. Some two years after his arrival in Paris, Baldwin suffered a breakdown and went off to Switzerland to recover:

There, in that absolutely alabaster landscape, armed with two Bessie Smith records and a typewriter, I began to try to re-create the life that I had first known as a child and from which I had spent so many years in flight. . . . I had never listened to Bessie Smith in America (in the same way that, for years, I would not touch watermelon), but in Europe she helped to reconcile me to being a "nigger."[1]

The immediate fruit of self-recovery was a great creative outburst. First came two books of reconciliation with his racial heritage. *Go Tell It on the Mountain* and *The Amen Corner* represent a search for roots, a surrender to tradition, an acceptance of the Negro past. Then came a series of essays which probe, deeper than anyone has dared, the psychic history of this nation. They are a moving record of a man's struggle to define the forces that have shaped him, in order that he may accept himself. Last came *Giovanni's Room*, which explores the question of his male identity. Here Baldwin extends the theme of self-acceptance into the sexual realm.

Toward the end of his stay in Paris, Baldwin experienced the first symptoms of a crisis from which he has never recovered. Having exhausted the theme of self-acceptance, he cast about for fresh material, but his third novel stubbornly refused to move. He has described this moment of panic in a later essay: "It is the point at which many artists lose their minds, or commit suicide, or throw themselves into good works, or try to enter politics."[2] Recognizing these dangers to his art, Baldwin has not succeeded in avoiding them. Something like good works and politics has been the recent bent of his career. Unable to grow as an artist, he has fallen back upon a tradition of protest writing which he formerly denounced.

Baldwin returned to America in 1957. The battered self, he must have felt, was ready to confront society. A good many of the essays in *Nobody Knows My Name* record his initial impressions of America, but this is a transitional book, still largely concerned with questions of identity. Protest, however, becomes the dominant theme of his next three books. In *Another Country*, *The Fire Next Time*, and *Blues for Mister Charlie*, he assumes the role of Old Testament prophet, calling down the wrath of history on the heads of the white oppressor.

Baldwin's career may be divided into two distinct periods. His first five books have been concerned with the emotion of shame. The flight from self, the quest for identity, and the sophisticated acceptance of one's "blackness" are the themes that

[1] *Nobody Knows My Name* (New York: Dial Press 1961), p. 5.

[2] *Ibid.*, p. 224.

flow from this emotion. His last three books have been concerned with the emotion of rage. An apocalyptic vision and a new stridency of tone are brought to bear against the racial and the sexual oppressor. The question then arises, why has he avoided the prophetic role until the recent past?

The answer, I believe, lies in Baldwin's relationship to his father, and still more, to his spiritual father, Richard Wright. Baldwin's father died in 1943, and within a year Baldwin met Wright for the first time. It is amply clear from his essays that the twenty-year-old youth adopted the older man as a father-figure. What followed is simplicity itself: Baldwin's habit of defining himself in opposition to his father was transferred to the new relationship. If Wright was committed to protest fiction, Baldwin would launch his own career with a rebellious essay called "Everybody's Protest Novel."[3] So long as Wright remained alive, the prophetic strain in Baldwin was suppressed. But with Wright's death in 1960, Baldwin was free to *become* his father. He has been giving Noah the rainbow sign ever since.

II

Go Tell It on the Mountain (1953) is the best of Baldwin's novels, and the best is very good indeed. It ranks with Jean Toomer's *Cane*, Richard Wright's *Native Son*, and Ralph Ellison's *Invisible Man* as a major contribution to American fiction. For this novel cuts through the walls of the store-front church to the essence of Negro experience in America. This is Baldwin's earliest world, his bright and morning star, and it glows with metaphorical intensity. Its emotions are his emotions; its language, his native tongue. The result is a prose of unusual power and authority. One senses in Baldwin's first novel a confidence, control, and mastery of style which he has not attained again in the novel form.

The central event of *Go Tell It on the Mountain* is the religious conversion of an adolescent boy. In a long autobiographical essay, which forms a part of *The Fire Next Time*,[4] Baldwin leaves no doubt that he was writing of his own experience. During the summer of his fourteenth year, he tells us, he succumbed to the spiritual seduction of a woman evangelist. On

[3] See *Notes of a Native Son* (Boston: Beacon Press, 1955), pp. 13–23.

[4] See *The Fire Next Time* (New York: Dial Press, 1963), pp. 29–61.

the night of his conversion, he suddenly found himself lying on the floor before the altar. He describes his trancelike state, the singing and clapping of the saints, and the all-night prayer vigil which helped to bring him "through." He then recalls the circumstances of his life which prompted so pagan and desperate a journey to the throne of Grace.

The overwhelming fact in Baldwin's childhood was his victimization by the white power structure. At first he experienced white power only indirectly, as refracted through the brutality and degradation of the Harlem ghetto. The world beyond the ghetto seemed remote, and scarcely could be linked in a child's imagination to the harrowing conditions of his daily life. And yet a vague terror, transmitted through his parents to the ghetto child, attested to the power of the white world. Meanwhile, in the forefront of his consciousness was a set of fears by no means vague.

To a young boy growing up in the Harlem ghetto, damnation was a clear and present danger: "For the wages of sin were visible everywhere, in every wine-stained and urine-splashed hallway, in every clanging ambulance bell, in every scar on the faces of the pimps and their whores, in every helpless, newborn baby being brought into this danger, in every knife and pistol fight on the Avenue."[5] To such a boy, the store-front church offered a refuge and a sanctuary from the terrors of the street. God and safety became synonymous, and the church, a part of his survival strategy.

Fear, then, was the principal motive of Baldwin's conversion: "I became, during my fourteenth year, for the first time in my life afraid—afraid of the evil within me and afraid of the evil without."[6] As the twin pressures of sex and race began to mount, the adolescent boy struck a desperate bargain with God. In exchange for sanctuary, he surrendered his sexuality, and abandoned any aspirations which might bring him into conflict with white power. He was safe, but walled off from the world; saved, but isolated from experience. This, to Baldwin, is the historical betrayal of the Negro church. In exchange for the power of the Word, the Negro trades away the personal power of his sex and the social power of his people.

[5] *The Fire Next Time*, p. 34.

[6] *Ibid.*, p. 30.

Life on these terms was unacceptable to Baldwin; he did not care to settle for less than his potential as a man. If his deepest longings were thwarted in the church, he would pursue them through his art. Sexual and racial freedom thus became his constant theme. And yet, even in breaking with the church, he pays tribute to its power: "In spite of everything, there was in the life I fled a zest and a joy and a capacity for facing and surviving disaster that are very moving and very rare."[7] We shall confront, then, in *Go Tell It on the Mountain,* a certain complexity of tone. Baldwin maintains an ironic distance from his material, even as he portrays the spiritual force and emotional appeal of store-front Christianity.

So much for the biographical foundations of the novel. The present action commences on the morning of John Grimes' fourteenth birthday, and before the night is out, he is born again in Christ. Part I, "The Seventh Day," introduces us to the boy and his family, his fears and aspirations, and the Temple of the Fire Baptized which is the center of his life. Part II, "The Prayers of the Saints," contains a series of flashbacks in which we share the inmost thoughts and private histories of his Aunt Florence, his mother, Elizabeth, and his putative father, Gabriel. Part III, "The Threshing-Floor," returns us to the present and completes the story of the boy's conversion.

Parts I and III are set in Harlem in the spring of 1935. The action of Part II, however, takes place for the most part down home. Florence, Elizabeth, and Gabriel belong to a transitional generation, born roughly between 1875 and 1900. *Go Tell It on the Mountain* is thus a novel of the Great Migration. It traces the process of secularization which occurred when the Negro left the land for the Northern ghettos. This theme, to be sure, is handled ironically. Baldwin's protagonist "gets religion," but he is too young, too frightened, and too innocent to grasp the implications of his choice.

It is through the lives of the adults that we achieve perspective on the boy's conversion. His Aunt Florence has been brought to the evening prayer meeting by her fear of death. She is dying of cancer, and in her extremity humbles herself before God, asking forgiveness of her sins. These have consisted of a driving ambition and a ruthless hardening of heart. Early in her adult life, she left her dying mother to come

[7] *Ibid.,* p. 55.

North, in hopes of bettering her lot. Later, she drove from her side a husband whom she loved: "It had not been her fault that Frank was the way he was, determined to live and die a common nigger" (p. 92).[8] All of her deeper feelings have been sacrificed to a futile striving for "whiteness" and respectability. Now she contemplates the wages of her virtue: an agonizing death in a lonely furnished room.

Elizabeth, as she conceives her life, has experienced both the fall and the redemption. Through Richard, she has brought an illegitimate child into the world, but through Gabriel, her error is retrieved. She fell in love with Richard during the last summer of her girlhood, and followed him North to Harlem. There they took jobs as chambermaid and elevator boy, hoping to be married soon. Richard is sensitive, intelligent, and determined to educate himself. Late one evening, however, he is arrested and accused of armed robbery. When he protests his innocence, he is beaten savagely by the police. Ultimately he is released, but half hysterical with rage and shame, he commits suicide. Under the impact of this blow, Elizabeth retreats from life. Her subsequent marriage to Gabriel represents safety, timidity, and atonement for her sin.

As Gabriel prays on the night of John's conversion, his thoughts revert to the events of his twenty-first year: his own conversion and beginning ministry, his joyless marriage to Deborah, and his brief affair with Esther. Deborah has been raped by white men at the age of sixteen. Thin, ugly, sexless, she is treated by the Negroes as a kind of holy fool. Gabriel, who has been a wild and reckless youth, marries her precisely to mortify the flesh. But he cannot master his desire. He commits adultery with Esther, and informed that she is pregnant, refuses all emotional support. Esther dies in childbirth and her son, Royal, who grows to manhood unacknowledged by his father, is killed in a Chicago dive.

Soon after the death of Royal, Deborah dies childless, and Gabriel is left without an heir. When he moves North, however, the Lord sends him a sign in the form of an unwed mother and her fatherless child. He marries Elizabeth and promises to raise Johnny as his own son. In the course of time the second Royal is born, and Gabriel rejoices in the fulfillment of God's promise. But John's half brother, the fruit of the prophet's seed,

[8] All page references are to the Dial Press editions of the novels.

has turned his back on God. Tonight he lies at home with a knife wound, inflicted in a street-fight with some whites. To Gabriel, therefore, John's conversion is a bitter irony: "Only the son of the bondwoman stood where the rightful heir should stand" (p. 128).

Through this allusion, Baldwin alerts us to the metaphorical possibilities of his plot. Gabriel's phrase is from *Genesis* 21, verses 9 and 10: "And Sarah saw the son of Hagar the Egyptian, which she had born unto Abraham, mocking. Wherefore she said unto Abraham, Cast out this bondwoman and her son: for the son of the bondwoman shall not be heir with my son, even with Isaac." Hagar's bastard son is of course Ishmael, the archetypal outcast. Apparently Baldwin wants us to view Gabriel and Johnny in metaphorical relation to Abraham and Ishmael. This tableau of guilty father and rejected child will serve him as an emblem of race relations in America.

Baldwin sees the Negro quite literally as the bastard child of American civilization. In Gabriel's double involvement with bastardy, we have a re-enactment of the white man's historic crime. In Johnny, the innocent victim of Gabriel's hatred, we have an archetypal image of the Negro child. Obliquely, by means of an extended metaphor, Baldwin approaches the very essence of Negro experience. That essence is rejection, and its most destructive consequence is shame. But God, the Heavenly Father, does not reject the Negro utterly. He casts down only to raise up. This is the psychic drama which occurs beneath the surface of John's conversion.

The Negro child, rejected by the whites for reasons that he cannot understand, is afflicted by an overwhelming sense of shame. Something mysterious, he feels, must be wrong with him, that he should be so cruelly ostracized. In time he comes to associate these feelings with the color of his skin—the basis, after all, of his rejection. He feels, and is made to feel, perpetually dirty and unclean:

John hated sweeping this carpet, for dust arose, clogging his nose and sticking to his sweaty skin, and he felt that should he sweep it forever, the clouds of dust would not diminish, the rug would not be clean. It became in his imagination his impossible, lifelong task, his hard trial, like that of a man he had read about somewhere, whose curse it was to push a boulder up a steep hill (p. 27).

This quality of Negro life, unending struggle with one's own blackness, is symbolized by Baldwin in the family name,

Grimes. One can readily understand how such a sense of personal shame might have been inflamed by contact with the Christian tradition and transformed into an obsession with original sin. Gabriel's sermons take off from such texts as "I am a man of unclean lips," or "He which is filthy, let him be filthy still." The Negro's religious ritual, as Baldwin points out in an early essay, is permeated with color symbolism: "Wash me, cried the slave to his Maker, and I shall be whiter, whiter than snow! For black is the color of evil; only the robes of the saved are white."[9]

Given this attack on the core of the self, how can the Negro respond? If he accepts the white man's equation of blackness with evil, he is lost. Hating his true self, he will undertake the construction of a counter-self along the following lines: everything "black" I now disown. To such a man, Christ is a kind of spiritual bleaching cream. Only if the Negro challenges the white man's moral categories can he hope to survive on honorable terms. This involves the sentiment; everything "black" I now embrace, however painfully, as mine. There is, in short, the path of self-hatred and the path of self-acceptance. Both are available to Johnny within the framework of the church, but he is deterred from one by the negative example of his father.

Consider Gabriel. The substance of his life is moral evasion. A preacher of the gospel, and secretly the father of an illegitimate child, he cannot face the evil in himself. In order to preserve his image as the Lord's anointed, he has sacrificed the lives of those around him. His principal victim is Johnny, who is not his natural child. In disowning the bastard, he disowns the "blackness" in himself. Gabriel's psychological mechanisms are, so to say, white. Throughout his work Baldwin has described the scapegoat mechanism which is fundamental to the white man's sense of self. To the question, Who am I?, the white man answers: I am *white*, that is, immaculate, without stain. I am the purified, the saved, the saintly, the elect. It is the *black* who is the embodiment of evil. Let him, the son of the bondwoman, pay the price of my sins.

From self-hatred flows not only self-righteousness but self-glorification as well. From the time of his conversion Gabriel has been living in a world of compensatory fantasy. He sees the Negro race as a chosen people and himself as prophet and

[9] *Notes of a Native Son*, p. 21.

ROBERT A. BONE

founder of a royal line. But if Old Testament materials can be appropriated to buttress such a fantasy world, they also offer a powerful means of grappling with reality. When the Negro preacher compares the lot of his people to that of the children of Israel, he provides his flock with a series of metaphors which correspond to their deepest experience. The church thus offers to the Negro masses a ritual enactment of their daily pain. It is with this poetry of suffering, which Baldwin calls the power of the Word, that the final section of the novel is concerned.

The first fifteen pages of Part III contain some of Baldwin's most effective writing. As John Grimes lies before the altar, a series of visionary states passes through his soul. Dream fragments and Freudian sequences, lively fantasies and Aesopian allegories, combine to produce a generally surrealistic effect. Images of darkness and chaos, silence and emptiness, mist and cold—cumulative patterns developed early in the novel—function now at maximum intensity. These images of damnation express the state of the soul when thrust into outer darkness by a rejecting, punishing, castrating father-figure who is the surrogate of a hostile society. The dominant emotions are shame, despair, guilt, and fear.

At the depth of John's despair, a sound emerges to assuage his pain:

He had heard it all his life, but it was only now that his ears were opened to this sound that came from the darkness, that could only come from darkness, that yet bore such sure witness to the glory of the light. And now in his moaning, and so far from any help, he heard it in himself—it rose from his bleeding, his cracked-open heart. It was a sound of rage and weeping which filled the grave, rage and weeping from time set free, but bound now in eternity; rage that had no language, weeping with no voice—which yet spoke now, to John's startled soul, of boundless melancholy, of the bitterest patience, and the longest night; of the deepest water, the strongest chains, the most cruel lash; of humility most wretched, the dungeon most absolute, of love's bed defiled, and birth dishonored, and most bloody, unspeakable, sudden death. Yes, the darkness hummed with murder: the body in the water, the body in the fire, the body on the tree. John looked down the line of these armies of darkness, army upon army, and his soul whispered, *Who are these?* (p. 228).

This is the sound, though John Grimes doesn't know it, of the blues. It is the sound of Bessie Smith, to which James Bald-

274

win listened as he wrote *Go Tell It on the Mountain*. It is the sound of all Negro art and all Negro religion, for it flows from the cracked-open heart.

On these harsh terms, Baldwin's protagonist discovers his identity. He belongs to those armies of darkness and must forever share their pain. To the question, Who am I?, he can now reply: I am he who suffers, and yet whose suffering on occasion is "from time set free." And thereby he discovers his humanity, for only man can ritualize his pain. We are now very close to that plane of human experience where art and religion intersect. What Baldwin wants us to feel is the emotional pressure exerted on the Negro's cultural forms by his exposure to white oppression. And finally to comprehend that these forms alone, through their power of transforming suffering, have enabled him to survive his terrible ordeal.

III

Give not thyself up, then, to fire, lest it invert thee.

—MOBY DICK

Giovanni's Room (1956) is by far the weakest of Baldwin's novels. There is a tentative, unfinished quality about the book, as if in merely broaching the subject of homosexuality Baldwin had exhausted his creative energy. Viewed in retrospect, it seems less a novel in its own right than a first draft of *Another Country*. The surface of the novel is deliberately opaque, for Baldwin is struggling to articulate the most intimate, the most painful, the most elusive of emotions. The characters are vague and disembodied, the themes half-digested, the colors rather bleached than vivified. We recognize in this sterile psychic landscape the unprocessed raw material of art.

And yet this novel occupies a key position in Baldwin's spiritual development. Links run backward to *Go Tell It on the Mountain* as well as forward to *Another Country*. The very furniture of Baldwin's mind derives from the store-front church of his boyhood and adolescence. When he attempts a novel of homosexual love, with an all-white cast of characters and a European setting, he simply transposes the moral topography of Harlem to the streets of Paris. When he strives toward sexual self-acceptance, he automatically casts the homosexual in a priestly role.

Before supporting this interpretation, let me summarize the

plot. David, an American youth living abroad in Paris, meets a girl from back home and asks her to marry him. Hella is undecided, however, and she goes to Spain to think it over. During her absence, David meets Giovanni, a proud and handsome young Italian. They fall deeply in love and have a passionate affair. When Hella returns, David is forced to choose between his male lover and his American fiancée. He abandons Giovanni to the homosexual underworld which is only too eager to claim him. When Guillaume, whom Baldwin describes as "a disgusting old fairy," inflicts upon the youth a series of humiliations, Giovanni strangles his tormentor. He is tried for murder and executed by the guillotine. Meanwhile David, who has gone with Hella to the south of France, cannot forget Giovanni. Tortured by guilt and self-doubt, he breaks off his engagement by revealing the truth about himself.

At the emotional center of the novel is the relationship between David and Giovanni. It is highly symbolic, and to understand what is at stake, we must turn to Baldwin's essay on André Gide.[10] Published toward the end of 1954, about a year before the appearance of *Giovanni's Room*, this essay is concerned with the two sides of Gide's personality and the precarious balance which was struck between them. On the one side was his sensuality, his lust for the boys on the Piazza d'Espagne, threatening him always with utter degradation. On the other was his Protestantism, his purity, his otherworldliness—that part of him which was not carnal, and which found expression in his Platonic marriage to Madeleine. As Baldwin puts it, "She was his Heaven who would forgive him for his Hell and help him to endure it." It was a drama of salvation, in which the celibate wife, through selfless dedication to the suffering artist, becomes in effect a priest.

In the present novel, Giovanni plays the role of Gide; David, of Madeleine. Giovanni is not merely a sensualist, but a Platonist as well: "I want to escape . . . this dirty world, this dirty body" (p. 35). It is the purity of Giovanni's love for David—its idealized, transcendent quality—that protects him from a kind of homosexual Hell. David is the string connecting him to Heaven, and when David abandons him, he plunges into the abyss.

We can now appreciate the force of David's remark, "The

[10] See *Nobody Knows My Name*, pp. 155–62.

burden of his salvation seemed to be on me and I could not endure it" (p. 168). Possessing the power to save, David rejects the priestly office. Seen in this light, his love affair with Giovanni is a kind of novitiate. The dramatic conflict of the novel can be stated as follows: does David have a true vocation? Is he prepared to renounce the heterosexual world? When David leaves Giovanni for Hella, he betrays his calling, but ironically he has been ruined both for the priesthood and the world.

It is Giovanni, Baldwin's doomed hero, who is the true priest. For a priest is nothing but a journeyman in suffering. Thus Giovanni defies David, the American tourist, even to understand his village: "And you will have no idea of the life there, dripping and bursting and beautiful and terrible, as you have no idea of my life now" (p. 203). It is a crucial distinction for all of Baldwin's work: there are the relatively innocent—the *laity* who are mere apprentices in human suffering—and the fully initiated, the *clergy* who are intimate with pain. Among the laity may be numbered Americans, white folks, heterosexuals, and squares; among the clergy, Europeans, Negroes, homosexuals, hipsters, and jazzmen. The finest statement of this theme, in which the jazzman is portrayed as priest, is Baldwin's moving story, "Sonny's Blues."[11]

Assumption of the priestly role is always preceded by an extraordinary experience of suffering, often symbolized in Baldwin's work by the death of a child. Thus in *The Amen Corner* Sister Margaret becomes a store-front church evangelist after giving birth to a dead child. And in *Giovanni's Room*, the protagonist leaves his wife, his family, and his village after the birth of a still-born child: "When I knew that it was dead I took our crucifix off the wall and I spat on it and threw it on the floor and my mother and my girl screamed and I went out" (p. 205). It is at this point that Giovanni's inverted priesthood begins. Like Gide, he rebels against God, but the priestly impulse persists. He retreats from the heterosexual world, achieves a kind of purity in his relationship with David, is betrayed, and consigned to martyrdom.

The patterns first explored in *Giovanni's Room* are given full expression in *Another Country*. Rufus is a Negro Giovanni—a journeyman in suffering and a martyr to racial oppression. Vivaldo and the other whites are mere apprentices, who cannot

[11] See *Partisan Review*, 24 (Summer, 1957), 327–58.

grasp the beauty and the terror of Negro life. Eric is a David who completes his novitiate, and whose priestly or redemptive role is central to the novel. There has been, however, a crucial change of tone. In *Giovanni's Room*, one part of Baldwin wants David to escape from the male prison, even as another part remains committed to the ideal of homosexual love. In the later novel, this conflict has been resolved. Baldwin seems convinced that homosexuality is a liberating force, and he now brings to the subject a certain proselytizing zeal.

IV

Another Country (1962) is a failure on the grand scale. It is an ambitious novel, rich in thematic possibilities, for Baldwin has at his disposal a body of ideas brilliantly developed in his essays. When he tries to endow these ideas with imaginative life, however, his powers of invention are not equal to the task. The plot consists of little more than a series of occasions for talk and fornication. Since the latter is a limited vehicle for the expression of complex ideas, talk takes over, and the novel drowns in a torrent of rhetoric.

The ideas themselves are impressive enough. At the heart of what Baldwin calls the white problem is a moral cowardice, a refusal to confront the "dark" side of human experience. The white American, at once over-protected and repressed, exhibits an infuriating tendency to deny the reality of pain and suffering, violence and evil, sex and death. He preserves in the teeth of human circumstance what must strike the less protected as a kind of willful innocence.

The American Negro, exposed to the ravages of reality by his status as a slave, has never enjoyed the luxury of innocence. On the contrary, his dark skin has come to be associated, at some buried level of the white psyche, with those forbidden impulses and hidden terrors which the white man is afraid to face. The unremitting daily warfare of American race relations must be understood in these symbolic terms. By projecting the "blackness" of his own being upon the dark skin of his Negro victim, the white man hopes to exorcise the chaotic forces which threaten to destroy him from within.

The psychic cost is of course enormous. The white man loses the experience of "blackness," sacrificing both its beauty and its terror to the illusion of security. In the end, he loses his identity. For a man who cannot acknowledge the dark impulses of his own soul cannot have the vaguest notion of who he is. A stranger to himself and others, the most salient feature of his personality will be a fatal bewilderment.

There are psychic casualties on the Negro side as well. No human personality can escape the effects of prolonged emotional rejection. The victim of this cruelty will defend himself with hatred and with dreams of vengeance, and will lose, perhaps forever, his normal capacity for love. Strictly speaking, this set of defenses, and the threat of self-destruction which they pose, constitutes the Negro problem.

It is up to the whites to break this vicious circle of rejection and hatred. They can do so only by facing the void, by confronting chaos, by making the necessary journey to "another country." What the white folks need is a closer acquaintance with the blues. Then perhaps they will be ready to join the human race. But only if the bloodless learn to bleed will it be possible for the Negro to lay down his burden of hatred and revenge.

So much for the conceptual framework of the novel. What dramatic materials are employed to invest these themes with life? A Greenwich Village setting and a hipster idiom ("Beer, dad, then we'll split"). A square thrown in for laughs. A side trip to Harlem (can we be *slumming?*). A good deal of boozing, and an occasional stick of tea. Some male cheesecake ("He bent down to lift off the scarlet bikini"). Five orgasms (two interracial and two homosexual) or approximately one per eighty pages, a significant increase over the Mailer rate. Distracted by this nonsense, how can one attend to the serious business of the novel?

In one respect only does the setting of *Another Country* succeed. Baldwin's descriptions of New York contain striking images of malaise, scenes and gestures which expose the moral chaos of contemporary urban life. The surface of his prose reflects the aching loneliness of the city with the poignancy of a Hopper painting. Harassed commuters and jostled pedestrians seem to yearn for closer contact. Denizens of a Village bar clutch their drinks with a gesture of buried despair. The whir of cash registers and the blatant glare of neon signs proclaim the harsh ascendancy of the commercial spirit. The tense subway crowds and the ubiquitous police convey a sense of latent violence. The furtive scribblings on lavatory walls provide a chilling commentary, in their mixture of raw lust and ethnic hate, on the scope and depth of our depravity.

Structurally speaking, the novel consists of two articulating parts. Book I is concerned to demonstrate how bad things really are in this America. Books II and III encompass the redemptive movement, the symbolic journey to "another country."

The central figure of Book I is Rufus Scott, a talented jazz drummer who is driven to suicide by the pressures of a racist society. Sensitive, bitter, violent, he sublimates his hatred by pounding on the white skin of his drums. With something of the same malice, he torments his white mistress, ultimately driving her insane. Crushed by this burden of guilt, he throws himself from the George Washington Bridge. Rufus, in short, is a peculiarly passive Bigger Thomas, whose murderous impulses turn back upon himself. Like Bigger, he was created to stir the conscience of the nation. For the underlying cause of Rufus' death is the failure of his white friends to comprehend the depth of his despair.

In the melting pot of Greenwich Village, Baldwin brings together a group of white Americans whose lives are linked to Rufus' fate. His closest friend is Vivaldo Moore, an "Irish wop" who has escaped from the slums of Brooklyn. Cass, a girl of upperclass New England stock, has rebelled against her background to marry an aspiring writer. Eric Jones, having left Alabama for an acting career in New York, has experienced a double exile, and is about to return from a two-year sojourn in France.

Each of these friends has failed Rufus in his hour of need. It is the moral obtuseness of the whites that Baldwin means to stress. Rufus stands in relation to his friends as jazzman to audience: "Now he stood before the misty doors of the jazz joint, peering in, sensing rather than seeing the *frantic* black people on the stand and the *oblivious*, mixed crowd at the bar" (p. 4–5, my emphasis). The audience simply refuses to hear the frantic plea in an insistent riff which seems to ask, "Do you love me?" It is a failure of love, but still more of imagination. Vivaldo and the others fail to transcend their innocence. They are blinded by their fear of self. Meaning well, they acquiesce in Rufus' death.

Having killed off Rufus early in the novel, Baldwin pursues

the theme of vengeance and reconciliation through the character of Ida Scott. Embittered by the death of her brother, on whom she had counted to save her from the streets of Harlem, Ida takes revenge on the nearest white man. She moves in with Vivaldo, ostensibly in love, but actually exploiting the arrangement to advance her career as a blues singer. Toward the end of the novel, however, Vivaldo achieves a new sense of reality. This enables Ida, who has come reluctantly to love him, to confess to her deception. In a gesture of reconciliation, she slips from her finger a ruby-eyed snake ring—a gift from Rufus, and a symbol of her heritage of hate.

Books II and III are dominated by the figure of Eric Jones, the young actor who has gone abroad to find himself. His adolescence in Alabama was marked by a homosexual encounter with a Negro youth. In New York he has a brief, violent, and radically unsatisfying affair with Rufus, from which he flees to France. There he falls in love with Yves, a Paris street boy, and through a chaste and tactful courtship wins his trust and love. As Book II opens, they are enjoying an idyllic holiday in a rented villa on the Côte d'Azur. Eric must soon leave for America, however, where he has accepted a part in a Broadway play. After a suitable interval, Yves will join him in New York.

Since the love affair of Eric and Yves is the turning point of the novel, we must pause to examine its wider implications. Book II commences with a highly charged, symbolic prose:

Eric sat naked in his rented garden. Flies buzzed and boomed in the brilliant heat, and a yellow bee circled his head. Eric remained very still, then reached for the cigarettes beside him and lit one, hoping that the smoke would drive the bee away. Yves' tiny black-and-white kitten stalked the garden as though it were Africa, crouching beneath the mimosas like a panther and leaping into the air (p. 183).

Like Whitman, his spiritual progenitor, Baldwin tends to endow his diffuse sexuality with mythic significance. Here he depicts, in this Mediterranean garden, what appears to be a homosexual Eden. Then, in an attempt to fuse two levels of his own experience, he brings into metaphorical relation the idea of homosexuality and the idea of Africa. Each represents to the "majority" imagination a kind of primal chaos, yet each contains the possibility of liberation. For to be Negro, or to be homosexual, is to be in constant touch with that sensual reality which the white (read: heterosexual) world is at such pains to deny.

The male lovers, naked in the garden, are not to be taken too literally. What Baldwin means to convey through this idyllic episode is the innocence of the unrepressed. He has been reading, one would surmise, Norman Brown's *Life against Death.* "Children," Brown reminds us, "explore in indiscriminate fashion all the erotic potentialities of the human body. In Freudian terms, children are polymorphously perverse."[12] In this episode on the Mediterranean coast, we are back in the cradle of man, back in the sexually and racially undifferentiated human past; back in the lost paradise of the polymorphously perverse.

On these mythic foundations, Baldwin constructs a theory of personality. The primal stuff of human personality is undifferentiated: "He was, briefly and horribly, in a region where there were no definitions of any kind, neither of color nor of male and female" (pp. 301–2). One must face this formlessness, however, before one can hope to achieve form.

At the core of Baldwin's fiction is an existentialist psychology. In a passage whose language is reminiscent of *Genesis,* he describes Vivaldo's struggle to define himself: "And beneath all this was the void where anguish lived and questions crouched, which referred only to Vivaldo and to no one else on earth. Down there, down there, lived the raw unformed substance for the creation of Vivaldo, and only he, Vivaldo alone, could master it" (pp. 305–6). As music depends ultimately on silence, so being is achieved in tension with nothingness. Sexual identity —all identity—emerges from the void. Man, the sole creator of himself, moves alone upon the face of the waters.

We can now account for Eric's pivotal position in the novel. Through his commitment to Yves, he introduces an element of order into the chaos of his personal life. This precarious victory, wrested in anguish from the heart of darkness, is the real subject of *Another Country.* Images of chaos proliferate throughout the novel. Rufus leaps into chaos when he buries himself in the deep black water of the Hudson River. Cass encounters chaos in the strange, pulsating life of Harlem, or in an abstract expressionist canvas at the Museum of Modern Art. To Vivaldo, chaos means a marijuana party in a Village pad; to

[12] Norman Brown, *Life against Death* (Middletown, Conn.: Wesleyan University Press, 1959), p. 27.

Eric, the male demi-monde which threatens to engulf him. Eric is the first of Rufus' friends to face his demons and achieve a sense of self. He in turn emancipates the rest.

From this vantage point, one can envision the novel that Baldwin was trying to write. With the breakdown of traditional standards—even of sexual normality—homosexuality becomes a metaphor of the modern condition. Baldwin says of Eric, "There were no standards for him except those he could make for himself" (p. 212). Forced to create his own values as he goes along, Eric is to serve "as a footnote to the twentieth century torment" (p. 330). The homosexual becomes emblematic of existential man.

What actually happens, however, is that Baldwin's literary aims are deflected by his sexual mystique. Eric returns to America as the high priest of ineffable phallic mysteries. His friends, male and female, dance around the Maypole and, *mirabile dictu*, their sense of reality is restored. Cass commits adultery with Eric, and is thereby reconciled to her faltering marriage. Vivaldo receives at Eric's hands a rectal revelation which prepares him for the bitter truth of Ida's confession. The novel ends as Yves joins Eric in New York, heralding, presumably, a fresh start for all and a new era of sexual and racial freedom.

For most readers of *Another Country*, the difficulty will lie in accepting Eric as a touchstone of reality. Let us consider the over-all design. Rufus is portrayed as the victim of a white society which cannot face unpleasant truths. The redemptive role is then assigned to Eric. But few will concede a sense of reality, at least in the sexual realm, to one who regards heterosexual love as "a kind of superior calisthenics" (p. 336). To most, homosexuality will seem rather an invasion than an affirmation of human truth. Ostensibly the novel summons us to reality. Actually it substitutes for the illusions of white supremacy those of homosexual love.

In any event, it is not the task of a literary critic to debate the merits of homosexuality, but to demonstrate its pressure on the novel. Let us accept Baldwin's postulate that in order to become a man, one must journey to the void. Let us grant that homosexuality is a valid metaphor of this experience. We must now ask of Baldwin's hero: does he face the void and emerge with a new sense of reality, or does he pitch his nomad's tent forever on the shores of the burning lake? The answer hinges, it seems to me, on the strength of Eric's commitment to Yves. Baldwin describes it as total, and yet, within a few weeks' span, while Yves remains behind in France, Eric betrays him with a woman and a man. How can we grant to this lost youth redemptive power?

One senses that Baldwin, in his portrait of Eric, has desired above all to be faithful to his own experience. He will neither falsify nor go beyond it. Central to that experience is a rebellion against the prevailing sexual, as well as racial, mores. But on either plane of experience, Baldwin faces an emotional dilemma. Like Satan and the fallen angels, it is equally painful to persist in his rebellion and to give it up. Total defiance is unthinkable; total reconciliation only less so. These are the poles of Baldwin's psychic life, and the novel vacillates helplessly between them.

The drama of reconciliation is enacted by Ida and Vivaldo. Through their symbolic marriage, Ida is reconciled to whites; Vivaldo to women. This gesture, however, is a mere concession to majority opinion. What Baldwin really feels is dramatized through Rufus and Eric. Rufus can neither be fully reconciled to, nor fully defiant of, white society. No Bigger Thomas, he is incapable of total hate. Pushed to the limits of endurance, he commits suicide. Similarly, Eric can neither be fully reconciled to women, nor can he surrender to the male demi-monde. So he camps on the outskirts of Hell. In the case of Rufus, the suicidal implications are overt. With Eric, as we shall see, Baldwin tries to persuade us that Hell is really Heaven.

In its rhetoric as well, the novel veers between the poles of reconciliation and defiance. At times the butter of brotherhood seems to melt in Baldwin's mouth. But here is Rufus, scoring the first interracial orgasm of the book: "And shortly, nothing could have stopped him, not the white God himself nor a lynch mob arriving on wings. Under his breath he cursed the milk-white bitch and groaned and rode his weapon between her thighs" (p. 22). With what economy of phrase "the milk-white bitch" combines hostility to whites and women! Nowhere is Baldwin's neurotic conflict more nakedly exposed. On one side we have the white God and the lynch mob, determined to suppress sex. On the other, adolescent rebellion and the smashing of taboo, hardening at times into Garveyism.

By Garveyism I mean the emotional and rhetorical excess, and often the extravagant fantasies, to which an embattled minority may resort in promoting its own defense. *Another Country* is doubly susceptible to these temptations, for it was conceived as a joint assault on racial and sexual intolerance. Apparently prejudice encountered in either context will evoke a similar response. The arrogance of the majority has a natural counterpart in exaggerated claims of minority supremacy.

In the racial sphere, Baldwin employs defenses which go well beyond a healthy race pride or a legitimate use of folk material. His portrait of Ida, for example, leans heavily on the exotic, on that stereotype of jungle grace which flourished in the nineteen-twenties. To a touch of primitivism he adds flat assertions of superiority: Negroes are more alive, more colorful, more spontaneous, better dancers, and above all, better lovers than the pale, gray, milk-white, chalk-white, dead-white, ice-hearted, frozen-limbed, stiff-assed zombies from downtown. Well, perhaps. One does not challenge the therapeutic value of these pronouncements, only their artistic relevance.

Coupled with these racial sentiments are manifestations of sexual Garveyism. Throughout the novel, the superiority of homosexual love is affirmed. Here alone can one experience total surrender and full orgastic pleasure; here alone the metaphysical terror of the void. Heterosexual love, by comparison, is a pale—one is tempted to say, white—imitation. In many passages hostility to women reaches savage proportions: "Every time I see a woman wearing her fur coats and her jewels and her gowns, I want to tear all that off her and drag her someplace, to a *pissoir*, and make her smell the smell of many men, the *piss* of many men, and make her know that *that* is what she is for" (p. 210).

It may be argued that these are the sentiments of Yves and not of Baldwin, but that is precisely the point. In *Another Country*, the sharp outlines of character are dissolved by waves of uncontrolled emotion. The novel lacks a proper distancing. One has the impression of Baldwin's recent work that the author does not know where his own psychic life leaves off and that of his characters begins. What is more, he scarcely cares to know, for he is sealed in a narcissism so engrossing that he fails to make emotional contact with his characters. If his people have no otherness, if he repeatedly violates their integrity, how can they achieve the individuality which alone will make them memorable?

In conclusion, I should like to view *Another Country* from

the perspective of the author's spiritual journey. Reduced to its essentials, this journey has carried Baldwin from a store-front church in Harlem to a Greenwich Village pad. His formative years were spent among the saints, in an environment where repressive attitudes toward sex were paramount. As a result, his sexual experience has always contained a metaphysical dimension, bearing inescapably on his relationship to God. To understand the failure of *Another Country*, we must trace the connection between his sexual rebellion, his religious conceptions, and his style.

Baldwin has described the spiritual geography of his adolescence in the opening pages of *The Fire Next Time*. On a little island in the vast sea of Harlem stood the saved, who had fled for their very lives into the church. All around them was the blazing Hell of the Avenue, with its bars and brothels, pimps and junkies, violence and crime. Between God and the Devil an unrelenting contest was waged for the souls of the young, in which the girls of God's party bore a special burden: "They understood that they must act as God's decoys, saving the souls of the boys for Jesus and binding the bodies of the boys in marriage. For this was the beginning of our burning time."[13]

Baldwin's adolescent rebellion began, it seems plain, when his dawning sensuality collided with his youthful ministry. At first he rebelled against the store-front church, then Harlem, seeking to escape at any cost. Ultimately he came to reject the female sex, the white world, and the Christian God. As his rebellion grew, he discovered in his gift for language a means of liberation. Like hundreds of American writers, he fled from the provinces (in his case, Harlem) to Greenwich Village and the Left Bank. There he hoped to find a haven of sexual, racial, and intellectual freedom.

He quickly discovered, however, that he had not left the Avenue behind. In Greenwich Village or its French equivalent, he peered into the abyss, the demi-monde of gay bars, street boys, and male prostitutes. This he recognized as Hell and recoiled in horror. But what alternative does he offer to promiscuity and fleeting physical encounter? He speaks in the rhetoric of commitment and responsibility, but what he has in mind is simply a homosexual version of romantic love. It is a familiar spiritual maneuver. Baldwin has built a palace on the ramparts

[13] *The Fire Next Time*, p. 32.

of Hell and called it Heaven. Its proper name is Pandemonium.

In an effort to make Hell endurable, Baldwin attempts to spiritualize his sexual rebellion. Subjectively, I have no doubt, he is convinced that he has found God. Not the white God of his black father, but a darker deity who dwells in the heart of carnal mystery. One communes with this dark power through what Baldwin calls "the holy and liberating orgasm."[14] The stranger the sex partner, the better for orgasm, for it violates a stronger taboo. Partners of a different race, or the same sex, or preferably both, afford the maximum spiritual opportunities.

Baldwin imagines his new faith to be a complete break with the past, but in fact he has merely inverted the Christian orthodoxy of his youth. Properly regarded, *Another Country* will be seen as the celebration of a Black Mass. The jazzman is Baldwin's priest; the homosexual, his acolyte. The bandstand is his altar; Bessie Smith his choir. God is carnal mystery, and through orgasm, the Word is made flesh. Baldwin's ministry is as vigorous as ever. He summons to the mourners' bench all who remain, so to say, hardened in their innocence. Lose that, he proclaims, and you will be saved. To the truly unregenerate, those stubborn heterosexuals, he offers the prospect of salvation through sodomy. With this novel doctrine, the process of inversion is complete.

These contentions are best supported by a brief discussion of Baldwin's style. Two idioms were available to him from the Negro world: the consecrated and the profane. They derive respectively from the church-oriented and the jazz-oriented segments of the Negro community. To Baldwin, the church idiom signifies submission, reconciliation, brotherhood, and Platonic love. Conversely, the hipster idiom conveys rebellion, defiance, retaliation, and sexual love.

The predominant mode of *Another Country* is the hipster idiom. For Baldwin it is the language of apostasy. In rejecting the God of his youth, he inverts the consecrated language of the saints. The general effect is blasphemous: "What a pain in the ass old Jesus Christ had turned out to be, and it probably wasn't even the poor, doomed, loving, hopheaded old Jew's fault" (p. 308). Baldwin's diction is deliberately shocking; its function is to challenge limits, to transgress. In the sexual realm, it exploits the fascination of the forbidden, like a cheap film aimed at the

14 See *Blues for Mister Charlie* (New York: Dial Press, 1964), p. 105.

teen-age trade. Indeed, if the style proclaims the man, we are dealing with an adolescent: who else gets his kicks from the violation of taboo?

Curiously, however, the language of the store-front church persists. For the hipster idiom is really Baldwin's second language, and in moments of high emotion he reverts to his native tongue. This occurs primarily when he tries to heighten or exalt the moment of sexual union. In the vicinity of orgasm, his diction acquires a religious intensity; his metaphors announce the presence of a new divinity: "When he entered that marvelous wound in her, *rending and tearing! rending and tearing!* was he surrendering, in joy, to the Bridegroom, Lord, and Savior?" (p. 308, emphasis in original).

This sudden shift into the church idiom betrays on Baldwin's part a deep need to spiritualize his sexual revolt. Here he describes Eric's first homosexual encounter: "What had always been *hidden* was to him, that day, *revealed*, and it did not matter that, fifteen years later, he sat in an armchair, overlooking a foreign sea, still struggling to find that *grace* which would allow him to bear that *revelation*" (p. 206, emphasis supplied). This is the language of Pandemonium: evil has become Baldwin's good. The loss of meaning which ensues is both moral and semantic, and the writer who permits it betrays both self and craft.

Another Country is not simply a bad novel, but a dead end. It is symptomatic of a severe crisis in Baldwin's life and art. The author's popular acclaim, his current role as a political celebrity, and the Broadway production of his recent play, have tended to obscure the true state of affairs. But Baldwin must suspect that his hipster phase is coming to a close. He has already devoted two novels to his sexual rebellion. If he persists, he will surely be remembered as the greatest American novelist since Jack Kerouac. The future now depends on his ability to transcend the emotional reflexes of his adolescence. So extraordinary a talent requires of him no less an effort.

BIBLIOGRAPHY

The Negro in American Literature
A Checklist of Criticism and Scholarship

SEYMOUR L. GROSS

This bibliography follows the two-part organization of the book as a whole: In the first part are listed items that deal with the Negro in American literature, as author or subject, in a general, theoretical, or survey fashion. In the second part are listed items that focus on one or two authors or works. Entries have been limited to essays that deal with the Negro substantively and to books that contain at least several consecutive pages on the subject.

A. GENERAL

ABEL, LIONEL. "Theatre of Politics: The Negro," *Nation*, CXCVI (April 27, 1963), 351–54.

ALLEN, SAMUEL. "Negritude and Its Relevance to the American Negro Writer," *The American Negro Writer and His Roots*. New York: American Society of African Culture, 1960. Pp. 8–20.

ANGOFF, ALLAN. "Protest in American Literature since the End of World War II," *CLA Journal*, V (1961), 31–40.

ARDEN, EUGENE. "The Early Harlem Novel," *Phylon*, XX (1959), 25–31.

BALDWIN, JAMES. "Everybody's Protest Novel," *Partisan Review*, XVI (1949), 578–85. Reprinted in *Notes of a Native Son*. Boston: Beacon Press, 1955.

BARKSDALE, RICHARD K. "White Tragedy—Black Comedy," *Phylon*, XXII (1961), 226–33.

BARTON, REBECCA. *Race Consciousness and the American Negro: A Study of the Correlation between the Group Experience and the Fiction of 1900–1930*. Copenhagen: A. Busck, 1934.

"Beginnings of a Negro Drama," *Literary Digest*, XLVIII (1914), 1114.

BEJA, MORRIS. "It Must Be Important: Negroes in Contemporary Fiction," *Antioch Review*, XXIV (1964), 323–36.

BIBLIOGRAPHY

BENNETT, M. W. "Negro Poets," *Negro History Bulletin*, IX (1946), 171–72, 191.

BERGER, ART. "Negroes with Pens," *Mainstream*, XVI (July, 1963), 3–6.

BIRNBAUM, HENRY. "The Poetry of Protest," *Poetry*, XCIV (1959), 408–13.

BLAND, EDWARD. "Racial Bias and Negro Poetry," *Poetry*, LXIII (1944), 328–33.

——. "Social Forces Shaping the Negro Novel," *Negro Quarterly*, I (1945), 241–48.

BOND, FREDERICK W. *The Negro and the Drama*. Washington, D.C.: Associated Publishers, 1940.

BONE, ROBERT A. *The Negro Novel in America*. New Haven: Yale University Press, 1958.

BONTEMPS, ARNA. "The Harlem Renaissance," *Saturday Review of Literature*, XXX (March 22, 1947), 12–13, 44.

——. "Negro Poets, Then and Now," *Phylon*, XI (1950), 355–60.

——, ed. "Introduction," *The Book of Negro Folklore*. New York: Dodd, Mead & Co., 1958.

——. "Introduction," *American Negro Poetry*. New York: Hill and Wang, 1963.

BRADLEY, GERALD. "Goodbye Mr. Bones: The Emergence of Negro Themes and Character in American Drama," *Drama Critique*, VII (1964), 79–86.

BRAITHWAITE, WILLIAM. "The Negro in Literature," *Crisis*, XXVIII (1924), 204–10.

BRAWLEY, BENJAMIN. "The Negro in American Fiction," *Dial*, LX (1916), 445–50.

——. *The Negro in Literature and Art*. New York: Duffield and Company, 1918.

——. "The Negro in American Literature," *Bookman*, LVI (1922), 137–41.

——. "The Negro Literary Renaissance," *Southern Workman*, LVI (1927), 177–80.

——. "The Promise of Negro Literature," *The Journal of Negro History*, XIX (1934), 53–59.

——. *The Negro Genius*. New York: Dodd, Mead & Co., 1937.

BREWER, J. M. "American Negro Folklore," *Phylon*, 6 (1945), 354–61.

BREWSTER, DOROTHY. "From Phillis Wheatley to Richard Wright," *Negro Quarterly*, I (1945), 80–83.

BRONZ, STEPHEN. *Roots of Negro Racial Consciousness: The 1920's: Three Harlem Renaissance Authors*. New York: Libra, 1964. (Johnson, McKay, Cullen.)

BROOKS, RUSSELL. "The Comic Spirit and the Negro's New Look," *CLA Journal,* VI (1962), 35–43.

BROWN, LLOYD. "Which Way for the Negro Writer?" *Masses and Mainstream,* IV (March, 1951), 153–63; (April, 1951), 50–59.

BROWN, STERLING. "Negro Character as Seen by White Authors," *Journal of Negro Education,* II (1933), 179–203.

———. *The Negro in American Fiction.* Washington, D.C.: Associates in Negro Folk Education, 1937.

———. *Negro Poetry and Drama.* Washington, D.C.: Associates in Negro Folk Education, 1937.

———. "The American Race Problem as Reflected in American Literature," *Journal of Negro Education,* VIII (1939), 275–90.

———. "The Negro Author and His Publisher," *Negro Quarterly,* I (1945), 7–20.

———. "Negro Folk Expression," *Phylon,* XI (1950), 318–27.

———. "A Century of Negro Portraiture in American Literature," *Massachusetts Review,* VII (1966), 73–96.

BULLOCK, PENELOPE. "The Mulatto in American Fiction," *Phylon,* VI (1945), 78–82.

BUTCHER, MARGARET. *The Negro in American Culture.* New York: Alfred A. Knopf, Inc., 1956.

BUTCHER, PHILIP. "The Younger Novelists and the Urban Negro," *CLA Journal,* IV (1961), 196–203.

CALVERTON, V. F. "Introduction," *An Anthology of American Negro Literature.* New York: Modern Library, 1929.

———. *The Liberation of American Literature.* New York: Charles Scribner's Sons, 1932.

———. "The Negro and American Culture," *Saturday Review of Literature,* XXII (September 21, 1940), 3–4.

CANTOR, MILTON. "The Image of the Negro in Colonial Literature," *New England Quarterly,* XXXVI (1963), 452–77.

CHAMBERLAIN, JOHN. "The Negro as Writer," *Bookman,* LXX (1930), 603–11.

CHANDLER, G. LEWIS. "Coming of Age: A Note on American Negro Novelists," *Phylon,* IX (1948), 25–29.

———. "A Major Problem of Negro Authors in Their March toward Belles-Lettres," *Phylon,* XI (1950), 383–86.

CLARKE, JOHN HENRIK. "Reclaiming the Lost African Heritage," *The American Negro and His Roots.* New York: American Society of African Culture, 1960. Pp. 21–27.

———. "Transition in the American Short Story," *Phylon,* XXI (1960), 360–66.

CLAY, EDWARD. "The Negro in Recent American Literature," *American Writers Congress.* New York, 1935.

COTTON, L. J. "The Negro in the American Theatre," *Negro History Bulletin*, XXIII (1960), 172–78.

COUCH, WILLIAM, JR. "The Problem of Negro Character and Dramatic Incident," *Phylon*, XI (1950), 127–33.

CULP, D. W. (ed). *Twentieth Century Negro Literature*. Toronto, Naperville, Atlanta, 1902.

DAMON, S. FOSTER. "The Negro in Early American Songsters," *Papers of the Bibliographical Society of America*, XXVIII (1934), 132–63.

DAVID, LEONA KING. "Literary Opinions on Slavery in American Literature from after the American Revolution to the Civil War," *Negro History Bulletin*, XXIII (1960), 99–104.

DAVIS, ARTHUR P. "Integration and Race Literature," *Phylon*, XVII (1956), 141–46.

DAYKIN, WALTER I. "Social Thought in Negro Novels," *Sociology and Social Research*, XIX (1935), 247–52.

———. "Race Consciousness in Negro Poetry," *Sociology and Social Research*, XX (1936), 98–105.

———. "Negro Types in American White Fiction," *Sociology and Social Research*, XXII (1937), 45–52.

DEARMOND, FRED. "A Note on the Sociology of Negro Literature," *Opportunity*, III (1925), 369–71.

DEMPSEY, DAVID. "Uncle Tom's Ghost and the Literary Abolitionists," *Antioch Review*, IV (1946), 442–48.

DRAKE, B. M. *The Negro in Southern Literature since the War*. Nashville: Presbyterian Publishing Co., 1898.

DREER, HERMAN. *American Literature by Negro Authors*. New York: Macmillan Co., 1950.

DUBOIS, W. E. B. "The Negro in Literature and Art," *Annals of the American Academy of Political and Social Science*, XLIX (1913), 233–37.

ECHERUO, M. J. C. "American Negro Poetry," *Phylon*, XXIV (1963), 62–68.

EDMUNDS, RANDOLPH. "Some Reflections on the Negro in American Drama," *Opportunity*, VIII (1930), 303–5.

EGAN, L. H. "The Future of the Negro in Fiction," *Dial*, XVIII (1895), 70.

ELLISON, RALPH. "Recent Negro Fiction," *New Masses*, XL (August 5, 1941), 22–25.

———. *Shadow and Act*. New York: Random House, 1964.

ELLISON, RALPH, and HYMAN, STANLEY EDGAR. "The Negro Writer in America," *Partisan Review*, XXV (1958), 197–211, 212–22.

EMANUEL, JAMES A. "The Invisible Men of American Literature," *Books Abroad*, XXXVI (1963), 391–94.

Bibliography

FIEDLER, LESLIE. *Love and Death in the American Novel*. New York: Criterion Books, 1960.

———. "Negro and Jew: Encounter in America," *No! in Thunder*. Boston: Beacon Press, 1960.

———. "The Jig Is Up," *Waiting for the End*. New York: Stein and Day, 1964.

FORD, NICK AARON. *The Contemporary Negro Novel*. Boston: Meador, 1936.

———. "A Blueprint for Negro Authors," *Phylon*, XI (1950), 374–77.

———. "Four Popular Negro Novelists," *Phylon*, XV (1954), 29–39. (Yerby, Motley, Ellison, Wright.)

———. "Battle of the Books: A Critical Survey of Significant Books by and about Negroes Published in 1960," *Phylon*, XXII (1961), 119–24.

———. "Search for Identity: A Critical Survey of Significant Belles Lettres by and about Negroes Published in 1961," *Phylon*, XXIII (1962), 128–38.

———. "Walls Do a Prison Make: A Critical Survey of Significant Belles Lettres by and about Negroes Published in 1962," *Phylon*, XXIV (1963), 123–34.

———. "The Fire Next Time? A Critical Survey of Belles Lettres by and about Negroes Published in 1963," *Phylon*, XXV (1964), 123–34.

FRANKLIN, JOHN HOPE. "A Harlem Renaissance," *Slavery to Freedom*. 2d ed. New York: Alfred A. Knopf, Inc., 1956.

FULLER, H. W. "The Negro Writer in the United States," *Ebony*, XX (November, 1964), 126–28.

———. "Contemporary Negro Fiction," *Southwest Review*, L (1965), 321–35.

FURNAS, JOSEPH C. *Goodbye to Uncle Tom*. New York: William Sloane, 1956.

GAINES, FRANCIS P. "The Racial Bar Sinister in American Romance," *South Atlantic Quarterly*, XXV (1926), 396–402.

GALE, ZONA. "The Negro Sees Himself," *Survey*, LIV (1925), 300–301.

GÉRARD, ALBERT. "Humanism and Negritude: Notes on the Contemporary Afro-American Novel," *Diogenes*, XXXVII (1962), 115–33.

GIBSON, RICHARD. "A No to Nothing," *Kenyon Review*, XIII (1951), 252–55.

GLICKSBERG, CHARLES I. "The Negro Cult of the Primitive," *Antioch Review*, IV (1944), 47–55.

——. "Negro Fiction in America," *South Atlantic Quarterly*, XLV (1946), 477–88.

——. "Negro Poets and the American Tradition," *Antioch Review*, VI (1946), 243–53.

——. "For Negro Literature: The Catharsis of Laughter," *Forum*, CVII (1947), 45–46.

——. "Race and Revolution in Negro Literature," *Forum*, CVIII (1947), 300–308.

——. "The Furies in Negro Fiction," *Western Review*, XIII (1949), 107–14.

——. "The Alienation of Negro Literature," *Phylon*, XI (1950), 49–58.

——. "Bias, Fiction, and the Negro," *Phylon*, XIII (1952), 127–35.

GLOSTER, H. G. "The Negro Writer and the Southern Scene," *Southern Packet*, IV (1948), 1–3.

GLOSTER, HUGH M. *Negro Voices in American Fiction*. Chapel Hill: University of North Carolina Press, 1948.

——. "Race and the Negro Writer," *Phylon*, XI (1950), 369–71.

GOLDMAN, HANNAH S. "The Tragic Gift: The Serf and Slave Intellectual in Russian and American Fiction," *Phylon*, XXIV (1963), 51–62.

GORDON, EUGENE. "Social and Political Problems of Negro Writers," *American Writers Congress*. New York, 1935. Pp. 145–53.

GRANT, G. C. "The Negro in Dramatic Art," *Journal of Negro History*, XVII (1932), 19–29.

GREEN, ELIZABETH. *The Negro in Contemporary Literature*. Durham: University of North Carolina Press, 1928.

GREEVER, GEORGE. "The Negro in Literature," *Dial*, LX (1916), 531–32.

GREGORY, HORACE, and ZATURENSKA, MARYA. "The Negro Poet in America," *A History of American Poetry, 1900–1940*. New York: Harcourt, Brace & Co., 1946

GRIMER, ALAN, and OWEN, JANET. "Civil Rights and the Race Novel," *Chicago Jewish Forum*, XV (1956), 12–15.

GROSS, THEODORE. "The Negro in the Literature of the Reconstruction," *Phylon*, XXII (1961), 5–14.

HARPER, ALBERT. "Whites Writing Up the Blacks," *Dial*, LXXXVI (1929), 29–30.

HILL, HERBERT (ed.). "Introduction," *Soon, One Morning: New Writing by American Negroes*. New York: Alfred A. Knopf, Inc., 1963.

HILL, LESLIE P. (ed.). "Foreword," *The Wings of Oppression*. Boston: Stratford, 1922.

HOLMES, EUGENE C. "Problems Facing the Negro Writer Today," *New Challenge*, I (1937), 69–75.

HOWE, IRVING. "Black Boys and Native Sons," *A World More Attractive*. New York: Horizon Press, 1963.

HUGGINS, KATHRYN. "Aframerican Fiction," *Southern Literary Messenger*, III (1941), 315–20.

HUGHES, CARL MILTON. *The Negro Novelist*. New York: Citadel Press, 1953.

HUGHES, LANGSTON. "The Negro Artist and the Racial Mountain," *Nation*, CXXII (1926), 692–94.

———. "To Negro Writers," *American Writers Congress*. New York, 1935. Pp. 139–47.

———. "Harlem Literati in the Twenties," *Saturday Review of Literature*, XXII (June 22, 1940), 13–14.

HUGHES, LANGSTON, JONES, LEROI, and WILLIAMS, JOHN A. "Problems of the Negro Writer," *Saturday Review*, XLVI (April 20, 1963), 19–20, 40.

ISAACS, EDITH. *The Negro in the American Theatre*. New York: Theatre Arts Books, 1947.

ISAACS, HAROLD R. "Five Writers and Their African Ancestors," *Phylon*, XXI (1960), 243–65, 317–36. (Baldwin, Ellison, Hansberry, Hughes, Wright.)

ISAACS, J. R. "The Negro in the American Theatre," *Theatre Arts*, XXVI (1942), 492–543.

JACKSON, BLYDEN. "An Essay in Criticism," *Phylon*, XI (1950), 338–43.

———. "Faith without Works in Negro Literature," *Phylan*, XII (1951), 378–88.

———. "The Blithe Newcomers: A Résumé of Negro Literature in 1954," *Phylon*, XVI (1955), 5–12.

———. "The Case for American Negro Literature," *Michigan Alumnus Quarterly Review*, LXI (1955), 161–66.

———. "The Continuing Strain: Résumé of Negro Literature in 1955," *Phylon*, XVII (1956), 35–40.

———. "A Golden Mean for the Negro Novel," *CLA Journal*, III (1959), 81–87.

———. "The Negro's Image of the Universe as Reflected in His Fiction," *CLA Journal*, IV (1960), 22–31.

———. "The Negro's Negro in Negro Literature," *Michigan Quarterly Review*, IV (1965), 290–95.

JACKSON, ESTER MERLE. "The American Negro and the Image of the Absurd," *Phylon*, XXIII (1962), 359–71.

JACKSON, MILES M. "Significant Belles Lettres by and about Negroes Published in 1964," *Phylon*, XXVI (1965), 216–27.

JACOBS, GEORGE W. "Negro Authors Must Eat," *Nation*, CXXVIII (1929), 710–11.

JARRETT, THOMAS. "Toward Unfettered Creativity: A Note on the Negro Novelist's Coming of Age," *Phylon*, XI (1950), 313–17.

———. "Recent Fiction by Negroes," *College English*, XVI (1954), 85–91.

JOHNSON, CHARLES S. "The Negro Enters Literature," *Carolina Magazine*, LVII (May, 1927), 3–9, 44–48.

JOHNSON, JAMES WELDON. "The Dilemma of the Negro Author," *American Mercury*, XV (1928), 477–81.

———. "Race Prejudice and the Negro Artist," *Harper's*, CLVII (1928), 769–76.

———. "Negro Authors and White Publishers," *Crisis*, XXXVI (1929), 313–17.

KAISER, ERNEST. "The Literature of Harlem," *Freedomways*, III (1963), 276–91. Reprinted in *Harlem: A Community in Transition*, J. H. Clarke, ed. New York: Citadel Press, 1964.

———. "The Literature of Negro Revolt," *Freedomways*, III (1963), 36–47. Reprinted in *Harlem: A Community in Transition*, J. H. Clarke, ed. New York: Citadel Press, 1964.

KERLIN, ROBERT. "A Decade of Negro Literature," *Southern Workman*, LIX (1930), 227–29.

KESSLER, S. H. "American Negro Literature: A Bibliographical Guide," *Bulletin of Bibliography*, XXI (1955), 181–85.

LASH, JOHN S. "On Negro Literature," *Phylon*, VI (1945), 240–47.

———. "The American Negro and American Literature," *Bulletin of Bibliography*, XIX (1946), 12–15, 33–36.

———. "The American Negro in American Literature," *Journal of Negro Education*, XV (1946), 722–30.

———. "The Study of Negro Literary Expression," *Negro History Bulletin*, IX (1946), 207–11.

———. "What Is Negro Literature?" *College English*, IX (1947), 37–42.

———. "The Race Consciousness of the American Negro Author," *Social Forces*, XXVIII (October, 1949), 24–34.

———. "A Long Hard Look at the Ghetto: A Critical Summary of Literature by and about Negroes in 1956," *Phylon*, XVIII (1957), 7–24.

———. "The Conditioning of Servitude: A Critical Summary of Literature by and about Negroes in 1957," *Phylon*, XIX (1958), 143–54, 247–57.

———. "Dimension in Racial Experience: A Critical Summary of Literature by and about Negroes in 1958," *Phylon*, XX (1959), 115–31.

———. " 'Expostulation and Reply': A Critical Summary of Literature by and about Negroes in 1959," *Phylon*, XXI (1960), 111–23.

LAWSON, HILDA J. "The Negro in American Drama (Bibliography of Contemporary Negro Drama)," *Bulletin of Bibliography*, XVII (1940), 7–8, 27–30.

LEE, ULYSSES. "Criticism at Mid-Century," *Phylon*, XI (1950), 328–37.

LEVANT, HOWARD. "Aspiraling We Should Go," *Midcontinent American Studies Journal*, IV, ii (1963), 3–20.

LIVELY, ROBERT A. *Fiction Fights the Civil War*. Chapel Hill: University of North Carolina Press, 1957.

LOCKE, ALAIN. "American Literary Tradition and the Negro," *Modern Quarterly*, III (1926), 215–22.

———. "The Drama of Negro Life," *Theatre Arts*, X (1926), 701–6.

———. "The Negro's Contribution to American Art and Literature," *Annals of the American Academy of Political and Social Science*, CXL (1928), 234–47.

———. "Of Native Sons: Real and Otherwise," *Opportunity*, XIX (1941), 4–9, 48–52.

———. "The Negro Minority in American Literature," *English Journal*, XXXV (1946), 315–19.

———. "A Critical Retrospect of the Literature of the Negro for 1947," *Phylon*, IX (1948), 3–12.

———. "Dawn Patrol: A Review of the Literature of the Negro for 1948," *Phylon*, X (1949), 5–13.

———. "Self-criticism: The Third Dimension in Culture," *Phylon*, XI (1950), 391–94.

———. "Wisdom *de Profundis:* The Literature of the Negro, 1949," *Phylon*, XI (1950), 5–14.

———. "Inventory at Mid-Century: A Review of the Literature of the Negro for 1950," *Phylon*, XII (1951), 5–12.

———. "The High Price of Integration: A Review of the Literature of the Negro for 1951," *Phylon*, XIII (1952), 7–18.

———. "The Negro in American Literature," *New World Writing No. 1*. New York: Mentor Books, 1952.

———. "From Native Son to Invisible Man: A Review of the Literature of the Negro for 1952," *Phylon*, XIV (1953), 34–44.

LOGAN, RAYFORD W. "The Negro as Portrayed in the Leading Literary Magazines," *The Negro in American Life and Thought: The Nadir, 1877–1901*. New York: Dial Press, 1954.

LOGGINS, VERNON. *The Negro Author*. New York: Columbia University Press, 1931.

McDONNELL, THOMAS. "The Emergence of the Negro in Literature," *Critic*, XX (December, 1961–January, 1962), 31–34.

McDOWELL, TREMAINE. "The Negro in the Southern Novel Prior to 1850," *Journal of English and Germanic Philology*, XXV (1926), 455–73.

MARCUS, STEVEN. "The American Negro in Search of Identity," *Commentary*, XVI (1953), 456–63.

MARLEY, HAROLD. "The Negro in Recent Southern Literature," *South Atlantic Quarterly*, XXVII (1928), 29–41.

MAUND, ALFRED. "Negro Novelists and the Contemporary American Scene," *Chicago Jewish Forum*, XIII (1954), 28–34.

MAYFIELD, JULIAN. "Into the Mainstream and Oblivion," *The American Negro Writer and His Roots*. New York: American Society of African Culture, 1960. Pp. 29–33.

MAYS, BENJAMIN. *The Negro's God, as Reflected in His Literature*. Boston: Chapman and Grimes, 1938.

MEIER, AUGUST. "Some Reflections on the Negro Novel," *CLA Journal*, II (1959), 168–77.

MITCHELL, LOFTEN. "The Negro Writer and His Materials," *The American Negro Writer and His Roots*. New York: American Society of African Culture, 1960. Pp. 55–60.

———. "The Negro Theatre and the Harlem Community," *Freedomways*, III (1963), 384–94.

———. "Three Writers and a Dream," *Crisis*, LXXII (1965), 219–23. (Childress, Branch, Killens).

MONROE, HARRIET. "Negro Sermon Poetry," *Poetry*, XXX (1923), 291–93.

MORPURGO, J. E. "The American Negro," *Fortnightly*, 168 (July, 1947), 16–24.

MORRIS, LLOYD. "The Negro 'Renaissance,'" *Southern Workman*, LIX (1930), 82–86.

MORSE, GEORGE C. "The Fictitious Negro," *Outlook and Independent*, CLII (1929), 648–49, 678–79.

———. "Broadway Re-discovers the Negro," *Negro History Bulletin*, IX (1946), 173–76, 189–91.

MULDER, ARNOLD. "Wanted: A Negro Novelist," *Independent*, CXII (1924), 341–42.

"The Negro in Art: How Shall He Be Portrayed?" *Crisis*, XXXI (March, April, May, June, August, 1926).

"Negro Minstrelsy—Ancient and Modern," *Putnam's Magazine*, V (1855), 72–79.

The Negro in Print, Part I. Washington, D.C.: The Negro Bibliographic and Research Center, 1965.

NELSON, JOHN H. *The Negro Character in American Literature*. Lawrence, Kansas: University of Kansas Press, 1926.

Bibliography

NICHOLS, CHARLES H., JR. "Slave Narratives and the Plantation Legend," *Phylon*, X (1949), 201–10.

———. "The Forties: A Decade of Growth," *Phylon*, XI (1950), 377–80.

NOLEN, W. "The Colored Child in Contemporary Literature," *Horn Book*, XVIII (1942), 348–55.

OVERSTREET, HARRY. "Images and the Negro," *Saturday Review of Literature*, XXVII (August 26, 1944), 5–6.

———. "The Negro Writer as Spokesman," *Saturday Review of Literature*, XVII (September 2, 1944), 5–6, 26–28.

PATTERSON, CECIL L. "A Different Drum: The Image of the Negro in the Nineteenth Century Songster," *CLA Journal*, VIII (1964), 44–50.

POOL, ROSEY. "The Discovery of American Negro Poetry," *Freedomways*, III (1963), 46–51.

PORTER, DOROTHY B. *North American Negro Poets: A Bibliographical Check List of Their Writings, 1760–1944*. Hattiesburg, Miss.: The Brook Farm, 1945.

RECORD, C. WILSON. "The Negro as Creative Artist," *Crisis*, LXXII (1965), 153–58.

REDDICK, L. D. "No Kafka in the South," *Phylon*, XI, (1950), 380–83.

REDDING, SAUNDERS. *To Make a Poet Black*. Chapel Hill: University of North Carolina Press, 1939.

———. "The Negro Author: His Publisher, His Public, and His Purse," *Publisher's Weekly*, CXLVII (1945), 1284–88.

———. "American Negro Literature," *American Scholar*, XVIII (1949), 137–48.

———. "The Negro Writer—Shadow and Substance," *Phylon*, XI (1950), 371–77.

———. "The Negro Writer and His Relationship to His Roots," *The American Negro Writer and His Roots*. New York: American Society of African Culture, 1960. Pp. 1–8.

———. "Negro Writing in America," *The New Leader*, XLIII (May 16, 1960), 8–10.

———. "The Problems of the Negro Writer," *Massachusetts Review*, VI (1964), 57–70.

REID, IRA. "The Literature of the Negro: A Social Scientist's Appraisal," *Phylon* XI (1950), 388–90.

ROLLINS, H. E. "The Negro in the Southern Short Story," *Sewanee Review*, XXIV (1916), 42–60.

ROURKE, CONSTANCE. "Tradition for a Negro Literature," *Roots of American Culture*. New York: Harcourt, Brace & Co., 1942.

ROUSSÈVE, CHARLES B. *The Negro in Louisiana: Aspects of His*

History and His Literature. New Orleans: Xavier University Press, 1937.

ROVIT, EARL H. "Ralph Ellison and the American Comic Tradition," *Wisconsin Studies in Contemporary Literature*, I (1960), 34–42.

SCALLY, SISTER MAY ANTHONY. *Negro Catholic Writers, 1900–1943*. Detroit: W. Romig, 1945.

SHAPIRO, KARL. "The Decolonization of American Literature," *Wilson Library Bulletin*, XXXIX (June, 1965), 842–53.

SIMMS, H. H. "A Critical Analysis of Abolition Literature, 1830–1840," *Journal of Southern History*, VI (1940), 368–82.

SMITH, WILLIAM GARDNER. "The Negro Writer: Pitfalls and Compensations," *Phylon*, XI (1950), 297–303.

STARKE, JUANITA. "Symbolism of the Negro College in Three Recent Novels," *Phylon*, XVII (1956), 365–73.

TANDY, JEANETTE. "Pro-Slavery Propaganda in American Fiction of the Fifties," *South Atlantic Quarterly*, XXII (1922), 41–50, 170–78.

TANNER, TONY. "Pigment and Ether: A Comment on the American Mind," *British Association for American Studies Bulletin* No. 7 (1963), 40–45.

TAUSSEG, CHARLOTTE E. "The New Negro as Revealed in His Poetry," *Opportunity*, V (1927), 108–11.

THOMPSON, ERA BELL. "Negro Publications and the Writer," *Phylon*, XI (1950), 304–5.

THURMAN, WALLACE. "Negro Artists and the Negro," *New Republic*, LII (1927), 37–39.

———. "Nephews of Uncle Remus," *Independent*, CXIX (1927), 296–98.

———. "Negro Poets and Their Poetry," *Bookman*, LXVII (1928), 555–61.

TILLMAN, N. P. "The Threshold of Maturity," *Phylon*, XI (1950), 387–90.

TURNER, DARWIN. "The Negro Dramatist's Image of the Universe," *CLA Journal*, V (1961), 106–20.

TURNER, LORENZO. "Anti-Slavery Sentiment in American Literature Prior to 1865," *Journal of Negro History*, XIV (1929), 371–492.

TURPIN, WATERS E. "The Contemporary American Negro Playwright," *CLA Journal*, IX (1965), 12–24.

VAN DOREN, CARL. "Negro Renaissance," *Century*, CXI (1926), 635–37.

VILLARD, O. G. "Negro Literature," *Literary Review*, III (1923), 797–98.

WAGNER, JEAN. *Les Poètes nègres des États-Unis*. Paris: Libraire Istra, 1963.

WALKER, MARGARET. "New Poets," *Phylon*, XI (1950), 345–54.

WELSCH, ERWIN K. *The Negro in the United States: A Research Guide.* Bloomington: Indiana University Press, 1965.

WETHERILL, JULIE K. "The Negro as Producer of Literature," *Chautauquan*, XV (1892), 224–25.

WHITE, NEWMAN. "American Negro Poetry," *South Atlantic Quarterly*, XX (1921), 304–22.

———. "Racial Feeling in Negro Poetry," *South Atlantic Quarterly*, XXI (1922), 14–29.

WHITE, WALTER. "Negro Literature," *American Writers on American Literature*, ed. JOHN MACY. New York: Liveright, 1931. Pp. 442–51.

WHITEMAN, MAXWELL. *A Century of Fiction by American Negroes, 1853–1952.* Philadelphia: Maurice Jacobs, 1955.

"Why Not a Negro Drama for Negroes by Negroes?" *Current Opinion*, LXXII (1922), 639–40.

WILLIAMS, JIM. "The Need for a Harlem Theatre," *Freedomways*, III (1963), 307–11.

WILLIAMS, JOHN A. "Negro Literature Today," *Ebony*, XVIII (1963), 73–76.

WILSON, EDMUND. *Patriotic Gore.* New York: Oxford University Press, 1962.

WOODBURN, J. "Resistance Literature," *Saturday Review of Literature*, XXXI (June 5, 1948), 17.

WOOLRIDGE, NANCY. "English Critics and the Negro Writers," *Phylon*, XV (1954), 139–46.

WRIGHT, RICHARD. "Blueprint for Negro Writing," *New Challenge*, I (1937), 53–65.

———. "Littérature noir américain," *Les Temps Modernes*, III (1948), 193–221.

———. *White Man, Listen!* New York: Doubleday & Co., Inc., 1957.

ZANGER, JULES. "The 'Tragic Octoroon' in Pre–Civil War Fiction," *American Quarterly*, XVIII (1966), 63–70.

B. INDIVIDUAL AUTHORS

ALCOTT, LOUISA

HARDEN, J. W. "Louisa Alcott's Contribution to Democracy," *Negro History Bulletin*, VI (1942), 28–32.

TURNER, LORENZO DOW. "Louisa May Alcott's 'M. L.,'" *Journal of Negro History*, XIV (1929), 495–522.

BALDWIN, JAMES

BONE, ROBERT A. "The Novels of James Baldwin," *Tri-Quarterly* (Winter, 1965), 3–20.

BONOSKY, PHILLIP. "The Negro Writer and Commitment," *Mainstream*, XV (1962), 16–22.

CHARNEY, MAURICE. "Baldwin's Quarrel with Richard Wright," *American Quarterly*, XV (1963), 65–75.

COLES, ROBERT. "Baldwin's Burden," *Partisan Review*, XXXI (1964), 409–16.

COX, C. B., and JONES, A. R. "After the Tranquilized Fifties: Notes on Sylvia Plath and James Baldwin," *Critical Quarterly*, VI (1964), 107–22.

FEATHERSTONE, J. "Blues for Mr. Baldwin," *New Republic*, CLIII (November 27, 1965), 34–36.

FINN, JAMES. "The Identity of James Baldwin," *Commonweal*, LXXVII (1962), 113–16, 365–66.

GROSS, THEODORE. "The World of James Baldwin," *Critique*, VII, ii (1965), 139–49.

HAGOPIAN, JOHN V. "James Baldwin: The Black and the Red-White-and-Blue," *CLA Journal*, VII (1963), 133–40.

HASSAN, IHAB. *Radical Innocence*. Princeton, N.J.: Princeton University Press, 1961. (Baldwin and Ellison.)

HEIBERG, INGER. "James Baldwin—negerforfatter og dikter," *Samtiden*, LXXIV (1965), 280–87.

JACOBSON, DAN. "James Baldwin as Spokesman," *Commentary*, XXXII (1961), 497–502.

KENT, GEORGE. "Baldwin and the Problem of Being," *CLA Journal*, VII (1964), 202–14.

KLEIN, MARCUS. "James Baldwin," *After Alienation*. Cleveland: World Publishing Co., 1964.

LASH, JOHN S. "Baldwin Beside Himself: A Study in Modern Phallicism," *CLA Journal*, VIII (1964), 132–40.

LEVIN, DAVID. "Baldwin's Autobiographical Essays: The Problem of Negro Identity," *Massachusetts Review*, V (1964), 239–47.

MACINNES, COLIN "Dark Angel: The Writings of James Baldwin," *Encounter*, XXI, ii (1963), 22–33.

MORRISON, ALLAN. "The Angriest Young Man," *Ebony*, XVI (October, 1961), 23–30.

O'DANIEL, THERMAN B. "James Baldwin: An Interpretive Study," *CLA Journal*, VII (1963), 37–47.

PODHORETZ, NORMAN. "In Defense of Baldwin," *Doings and Undoings*. New York: Farrar, Straus and Co., 1964.

ROTH, PHILLIP. "Channel X: Two Plays on the Race Conflict," *New York Review of Books*, II (May 28, 1964), 10–13. (Baldwin's *Blues for Mr. Charlie* and LeRoi Jones' *The Dutchman*.)

SPENDER, STEPHEN. "James Baldwin: Voice of a Revolution," *Partisan Review*, XXX (1963), 256–60.

Bibliography

BOUCICAULT, DION

FAULKNER, SELDON. "The *Octoroon* War," *Educational Theatre Journal*, XV (1963), 33–38.

KAPLAN, SIDNEY. "*The Octoroon:* Early History of the Drama of Miscegenation," *Journal of Negro Education*, XX (1951), 547–57.

BROOKS, GWENDOLYN

CROCKETT, J. "An Essay on Gwendolyn Brooks," *Negro History Bulletin*, XIX (1955), 37–39.

DAVIS, ARTHUR P. "The Black and Tan Motif in the Poetry of Gwendolyn Brooks, *CLA Journal*, VI (1962), 90–97.

———. "Gwendolyn Brooks: A Poet of the Unheroic," *CLA Journal*, VII (1963), 114–25.

BRYANT, WILLIAM CULLEN

DYKES, E. B. "William Cullen Bryant, Apostle of Freedom," *Negro History Bulletin*, VI (1942), 29–32.

CABLE, GEORGE WASHINGTON

BUTCHER, PHILIP. "George Washington Cable and Booker T. Washington," *Journal of Negro Education*, XVII (1948), 462–68.

———. "George Washington Cable and Negro Education," *Journal of Negro History*, XXXIV (1949), 119–34.

———. *George W. Cable.* New York: Twayne, 1962.

DOHERTY, HERBERT J. "Voices of Protest from the New South," *Mississippi Valley Historical Review*, XLII (1955), 45–66.

TURNER, ARLIN. *George W. Cable: A Biography.* Durham, N.C.: Duke University Press, 1956.

——— (ed.). "Introduction," *The Negro Question: A Selection of Writings on Civil Rights in the South.* Garden City, New York: Doubleday & Co., 1958.

WHIPPLE, JAMES B. "Southern Rebel," *Phylon*, XX (1959), 345–57.

CHESNUTT, CHARLES WADDELL

AMES, RUSSELL. "Social Realism in Charles Chesnutt," *Phylon*, XIV (1953), 199–206.

CHESNUTT, HELEN M. *Charles Waddell Chesnutt: Pioneer of the Color Line.* Chapel Hill: University of North Carolina Press, 1952.

GLOSTER, HUGH M. "Charles W. Chesnutt: Pioneer in the Fiction of Negro Life," *Phylon*, II (1941), 57–66.

HUGLEY, G. "Charles Waddell Chesnutt," *Negro History Bulletin*, XIX (1955), 54–55.

BIBLIOGRAPHY

SILLEN, SAMUEL. "Charles W. Chesnutt: A Pioneer Negro Novelist," *Masses and Mainstream*, VI (1953), 8–14.

SMITH, ROBERT A. "A Note on the Folktales of Charles Chesnutt," *CLA Journal*, V (1962), 229–32.

CONNELLY, MARC

FORD, NICK AARON. "How Genuine Is *The Green Pastures?*" *Phylon*, XX (1959), 67–70.

CULLEN, COUNTEE

DAVIS, ARTHUR P. "The Alien-and-Exile Theme in Countee Cullen's Racial Poems," *Phylon*, XIV (1953), 390–400.

ROBB, IZETTA W. "From the Darker Side," *Opportunity*, IV (1926), 381–82.

SMITH, ROBERT. "The Poetry of Countee Cullen," *Phylon*, XI (1950), 216–21.

WEBSTER, HARVEY. "A Difficult Career," *Poetry*, LXX (1947), 222–25.

WOODRUFF, BERTRAM. "The Poetic Philosophy of Countee Cullen," *Phylon*, I (1940), 213–23.

DIXON, THOMAS

BLOOMFIELD, MAXWELL. "Dixon's *The Leopard's Spots:* A Study in Popular Racism," *American Quarterly*, XVI (1964), 387–401.

CARTER, EVERETT. "Cultural History Written with Lightning: The Significance of *The Birth of a Nation*," *American Quarterly*, XII (1960), 347–57.

PONTE, DURANT DA. " 'The Greatest Play of the South,' " *Tennessee Studies in Literature*, II (1957), 15–24.

DUBOIS, W. E. B.

FINKLESTEIN, SIDNEY. "W. E. B. DuBois' Trilogy: A Literary Triumph," *Mainstream*, XIV (1961), 6–17.

DUNBAR, PAUL LAURENCE

ACHILLE, L. T. "Paul Laurence Dunbar: Poète nègre," *Revue Anglo-Américain*, XII (1934), 504–20.

ARNOLD, EDWARD F. "Some Personal Reminiscences of Paul Laurence Dunbar," *Journal of Negro History*, XVII (1932), 400–408.

BRAWLEY, BENJAMIN. *Paul Laurence Dunbar: Poet of his People.* Chapel Hill: University of North Carolina Press, 1936.

BURCH, CHARLES E. "The Plantation Negro in Dunbar's Poetry," *Southern Workman*, L (1921), 469–73.

BUTCHER, PHILIP. "Mutual Appreciation: Dunbar and Cable," *CLA Journal*, I (1958), 101–2.

Bibliography

CUNNINGHAM, VIRGINIA. *Paul Laurence Dunbar and His Song.* New York: Dodd, Mead & Co., 1947.

DANIEL, T. W. "Paul Laurence Dunbar and the Democratic Ideal," *Negro History Bulletin,* VI (1943), 206–8.

DUNBAR, ALICE M., *et al. Paul Laurence Dunbar: Poet Laureate of the Negro Race.* Philadelphia: A.M.E. Church Review, 1914.

HOWELLS, WILLIAM DEAN. "Paul Laurence Dunbar," *North American Review,* XXIII (1906), 185–86.

LAWSON, VICTOR. *Dunbar Critically Examined.* Washington, D.C.: Associated Publishers, 1941.

ELLISON, RALPH

BAUMBACH, JONATHAN. "Nightmare of a Native Son: Ellison's *Invisible Man," Criticism,* VI (1963), 48–65. Reprinted in *The Landscape of Nightmare.* New York: New York University Press, 1965.

ELLISON, RALPH. "Light on *Invisible Man," Crisis,* LX (1953), 154–56.

GÉRARD, ALBERT. "Ralph Ellison et le dilemme noir (Le roman afro-américain), *Revue générale belge,* XCVII (1961), 89–104.

GLICKSBERG, CHARLES I. "The Symbolism of Vision," *Southwest Review,* XXXIX (1954), 259–65.

HOROWITZ, FLOYD ROSS. "The Enigma of Ellison's Intellectual Man," *CLA Journal,* VII (1963), 126–32.

———. "Ralph Ellison's Modern Version of Brer Bear and Brer Rabbit in *Invisible Man," Midcontinent American Studies Journal,* IV, ii (1963), 21–27.

KLEIN, MARCUS. "Ralph Ellison," *After Alienation.* Cleveland: World Publishing Co., 1964.

RANDALL, JOHN H. "Ralph Ellison: Invisible Man," *Revue des langues vivantes,* XXXI (1965), 24–44.

ROVIT, EARL. "Ralph Ellison and the American Comic Tradition," *Wisconsin Studies in Contemporary Literature,* I (1960), 34–42.

WARREN, ROBERT PENN. "The Unity of Experience," *Commentary,* XXXIX (1965), 91–96.

See also: *Baldwin:* Hassan. *Wright:* Rogge.

EMERSON, RALPH WALDO

BUTCHER, PHILIP. "Emerson and the South," *Phylon,* XVII (1956), 279–85.

MYRTLE, HENRY. "Independence and Freedom as Expressed and Interpreted by Ralph Waldo Emerson," *Negro History Bulletin,* VI (1943), 173–74.

BIBLIOGRAPHY

FAULKNER, WILLIAM

BACKMAN, MELVIN. "The Wilderness and the Negro in Faulkner's *The Bear*," *PMLA*, LXXVI (1961), 595–600.

BECK, WARREN. "Faulkner and the South," *Antioch Review*, I (1941), 82–94.

EDMONDS, IRENE C. "Faulkner and the Black Shadow," *Southern Renascence*, eds. LOUIS D. RUBIN and ROBERT D. JACOBS. Baltimore: Johns Hopkins University Press, 1953. Pp. 192–206.

GEISMAR, MAXWELL. "William Faulkner: The Negro and the Female," *Writers in Crisis*. Boston: Houghton Mifflin, 1942.

GÉRARD, ALBERT. "William Faulkner, ou le fardeau de l'homme noir," *La Revue nouvelle*, XXIV (1956), 331–38.

GLICKSBERG, CHARLES I. "William Faulkner and the Negro Problem," *Phylon*, X (1949), 153–60.

GLOSTER, HUGH M. "Southern Justice," *Phylon*, X (1949), 93–95.

GREER, DOROTHY. "Dilsey and Lucas: Faulkner's Use of the Negro as Gauge of Moral Character," *Emporia State Research Studies*, XI (1962), 43–61.

HOWE, IRVING. "William Faulkner and the Negroes: A Vision of Lost Fraternity," *Commentary*, XII (1951), 359–68.

———. "Faulkner and the Negroes," *William Faulkner: A Critical Study*. New York: Random House, 1962.

HOWE, RUSSELL WARREN. "Prejudice, Superstition, and Economics," *Phylon*, XVII (1956), 215–22.

HOWELL, ELMO. "A Note on Faulkner's Negro Characters," *Mississippi Quarterly*, XI (1958), 201–3.

KAZIN, ALFRED. "The Stillness of *Light in August*," *Partisan Review*, XXIV (1957), 519–38.

NILON, CHARLES. *Faulkner and the Negro*. New York: Citadel Press, 1965.

SEIDEN, MELVIN. "Faulkner's Ambiguous Negro," *Massachusetts Review*, IV (1963), 675–90.

SLABEY, ROBERT M. "Joe Christmas, Faulkner's Marginal Man," *Phylon*, XXI (1960), 266–77.

TAYLOR, WALTER F. "Let My People Go: The White Man's Heritage in *Go Down Moses*," *South Atlantic Quarterly*, LVIII (1959), 20–32.

VICKERY, OLGA. *The Novels of William Faulkner*. 2d ed. Baton Rouge: Louisiana State University Press, 1964.

WARREN, ROBERT PENN. "Faulkner: The South and the Negro," *Southern Review*, n.s., I (1965), 501–27.

———. "William Faulkner," *Selected Essays*. New York: Random House, 1958.

WILSON, EDMUND. "William Faulkner's Reply to the Civil-Rights

Program," *A Literary Chronicle: 1920–1950.* New York: Double-day & Co., 1956.

FAUSET, JESSIE

BRAITHWAITE, WILLIAM. "The Novels of Jessie Fauset," *Opportunity*, XII (1934), 24–28.

STARKEY, MARION L. "Jessie Fauset," *Southern Workman*, LXI (1932), 217–20.

FRANKLIN, BENJAMIN

"Benjamin Franklin and Freedom," *Journal of Negro History*, IV (1919), 41–50.

CRANE, V. W. "Benjamin Franklin on Slavery and American Liberties, *Pennsylvania Magazine of History and Biography*, LXII (1938), 1–11.

PITT, A. S. "Franklin and the Quaker Movement against Slavery," *Bulletin of the Friends Historical Association*, XXXII (September, 1943), 13–31.

GIFT BOOKS

THOMPSON, RALPH. "The Liberty Bell and Other Anti-Slavery Gift Books," *New England Quarterly*, VII (1934), 154–68.

GILMAN, CAROLINE

COHEN, HENNIG. "Caroline Gilman and Negro Boatmen Songs," *Southern Folklore Quarterly*, XX (1956), 116–17.

GREEN, PAUL

MALONE, A. E. "An American Folk-Dramatist: Paul Green," *Dublin Magazine*, n.s., VI (April-June, 1929), 31–42.

GRIGGS, SUTTON E.

GLOSTER, HUGH M. "Sutton E. Griggs, Novelist of the New Negro," *Phylon*, IV (1943), 335–45.

HANSBERRY, LORRAINE

LEWIS, THEOPHILUS. "Social Protest in *A Raisin in the Sun*," *Catholic World*, CXC (1959), 31–35.

HAMMON, JUPITER

WEGELIN, OSCAR. *Jupiter Hammon: American Negro Poet.* New York: Charles Fred Heartman, 1915.

HARRIS, JOEL CHANDLER

PARSONS, ELSIE C. "Joel Chandler Harris and Negro Folklore," *Dial*, LXVI (1919), 491–94.

BIBLIOGRAPHY

HEYWARD, DUBOSE

DURHAM, FRANK M. *DuBose Heyward's Use of Folklore in His Negro Fiction.* Charleston, S.C.: Citadel Monograph Series, No. 2.

———. *DuBose Heyward: The Man Who Wrote Porgy.* Columbia, S.C.: University of South Carolina Press, 1954.

HOWELLS, WILLIAM DEAN

AMACHER, ANNE WARD. "The Genteel Primitivist and the Semi-tragic Octoroon," *New England Quarterly,* XXIX (1956), 216–27.

FORD, THOMAS W. "Howells and the American Negro," *Texas Studies in Literature and Language,* V (1964), 530–37.

HUGHES, LANGSTON

ARVEY, VERNA. "Langston Hughes, Crusader," *Opportunity,* XVIII (1940), 363–64.

DAVIS, ARTHUR P. "The Harlem of Langston Hughes' Poetry," *Phylon,* XIII (1952), 276–83.

———. "Jesse B. Simple: Negro American," *Phylon,* XV (1954), 21–28.

———. "The Tragic Mulatto Theme in Six Works of Langston Hughes," *Phylon,* XVI (1955), 195–204.

LARKIN, MARGARET. "A Poet for the People," *Opportunity,* V (1927), 84–85.

MACLEOD, NORMAN. "The Poetry and Argument of Langston Hughes," *Crisis,* XLV (1938), 358–59.

PETERKIN, JULIA. "Negro Blue and Gold," *Poetry,* XXXI (1927), 44–47.

PRESLEY, JAMES. "The American Dream of Langston Hughes," *Southwest Review,* XLVIII (1963), 380–86.

ROGGE, HEINZ. "Die Figur des Simple im Werke von Langston Hughes," *Die neuren Sprachen,* XII (1955), 555–66.

SCHOELL, FRANK LOUIS. "Un Poète nègre," *Revue politique et littéraire.* XX (1929), 436–38.

HURSTON, ZORA NEALE

BYRD, JAMES W. "Zora Neale Hurston: A Novel Folklorist," *Tennessee Folklore Society Bulletin,* XXI (1955), 37–41.

JACKSON, BLYDEN. "Some Negroes in the Land of Goshen," *Tennessee Folklore Society Bulletin,* XIX (1953), 103–7.

JOHNSON, JAMES WELDON

AUSLANDER, JOSEPH. "Sermon Sagas," *Opportunity,* V (1927), 274–75.

Bibliography

AVERY, WILLIAM A. "James Weldon Johnson: American Negro of Distinction," *School and Society,* XLVIII (1938), 291–94.

COLLIER, EUGENIA W. "James Weldon Johnson: Mirror of Change," *Phylon,* XXI (1960), 351–59.

POTTS, EUNICE B., "J. W. Johnson, His Legacy to Us," *Opportunity,* XVIII (1940), 132–35.

WOHLFORT, ROBERT. "Dark Leader," *New Yorker,* VIII (September 30, 1933), 22–26.

JONES, JAMES

GLICKSBERG, CHARLES I. "Racial Attitudes in *From Here to Eternity,*" *Phylon,* XIV (1953), 384–89.

JONES, LeROI

DENNISON, GEORGE. "The Demagogy of LeRoi Jones," *Commentary,* XXXIX (1965), 67–70.
See also: *Baldwin: Roth.*

LEWIS, SINCLAIR

FADIMAN, CLIFTON. "The American Problem," *Saturday Review of Literature,* XXX (May 24, 1947), 9–10.

McCULLERS, CARSON

GOSSETT, LOUISE Y. "Dispossesed Love: Carson McCullers," *Violence in Recent Southern Fiction.* Durham, N.C.: Duke University Press, 1965.

McGIRT, JAMES EPHRAIM

PARKER, JOHN W. "James Ephraim McGirt: Poet of 'Deferred Hope,'" *Negro History Bulletin,* XVI (1953), 123–27.

McKAY, CLAUDE

BARTON, REBECCA C. "A Long Way from Home: Claude McKay," *Witnesses for Freedom.* New York: Harpers, 1948.

BUTCHER, PHILIP. "Claude McKay—'If We Must Die,'" *Opportunity,* XXVI (1948), 127.

COOPER, WAYNE. "Claude McKay and the New Negro of the 1920's," *Phylon,* XXV (1964), 297–306.

JACKSON, BLYDEN. "The Essential McKay," *Phylon,* XIV (1953), 216–17.

McKAY, CLAUDE. "A Negro to His Critics," *New York Herald Tribune Books* (March 6, 1932).

SMITH, ROBERT A. "Claude McKay: An Essay in Criticism," *Phylon,* IX (1948), 270–73.

BIBLIOGRAPHY

MELVILLE, HERMAN

D'AZEVEDO, WARREN. "Revolt on the *San Dominick*," *Phylon*, XVII (1956), 129–40.

FORREY, ROBERT. "Herman Melville and the Negro Question," *Mainstream*, XV (February, 1962), 28–29.

GLICKSBERG, CHARLES I. "Melville and the Negro Problem," *Phylon*, XI (1950), 207–15.

GUTTMAN, ALLEN. "The Enduring Innocence of Captain Amasa Delano," *Boston University Studies in English*, V (1961), 35–45.

JACKSON, MARGARET Y. "Melville's Use of a Real Slave Mutiny in *Benito Cereno*," *CLA Journal*, IV (1960), 79–93.

KAPLAN, SIDNEY. "Herman Melville and the American National Sin: The Meaning of *Benito Cereno*," *Journal of Negro History*, XLI (1956), 311–38; XLII (1957), 11–37.

SCHIFFMAN, JOSEPH. "Critical Problems in Melville's *Benito Cereno*," *Modern Language Quarterly*, XI (1950), 317–24.

O'NEILL, EUGENE

BROOKS, VAN WYCK. "Eugene O'Neill: Harlem," *The Confident Years: 1885–1915*. New York: Dutton, 1927.

LOWELL, J. "Eugene O'Neill's Darker Brother," *Theatre Arts*, XXXII (1948), 45–48.

PETERKIN, JULIA

LAW, ROBERT A. "Mrs. Peterkin's Negroes," *Southwest Review*, XIV (1929), 455–61.

PETRY, ANN

IVY, J. W. "Mrs. Petry's Harlem," *Crisis*, LIII (1946), 436.

POE, EDGAR ALLAN

CAMPBELL, KILLIS. "Poe's Treatment of the Negro and Negro Dialect," *University of Texas Studies in English*, XVI (1936), 107–14.

KAPLAN, SIDNEY (ed.). "Introduction," *The Narrative of Arthur Gordon Pym*. New York: Hill and Wang, 1960.

LEVIN, HARRY. "Journey to the End of Night," *The Power of Blackness*. New York: Alfred A. Knopf, Inc., 1958.

SIMMS, WILLIAM GILMORE

BURCH, CHARLES E. "Negro Characters in the Novels of William Gilmore Simms," *Southern Workman*, LII (1923), 192–95.

MORRIS, J. A. "Gullah in the Stories and Novels of William Gilmore Simms," *American Speech*, XXII (1947), 46–53.

Bibliography

RIDGLEY, JOSEPH. *"Woodcraft:* Simms' First Answer to *Uncle Tom's Cabin," American Literature,* XXXI (1960), 421–33.

SHELTON, AUSTIN J. "African Realistic Commentary on Culture Hierarchy and Racistic Sentimentalism in *The Yemassee," Phylon,* XXV (1964), 72–78.

SMITH, LILLIAN

DUMBLE, W. R. "A Footnote to Negro Literature," *Negro History Bulletin,* IX (1946), 82–84.

STOWE, HARRIET BEECHER

DOWNS, ROBERT B. *Books That Changed the World.* New York: New American Library, 1956.

DUVALL, SEVERN. *"Uncle Tom's Cabin:* The Sinister Side of the Patriarchy," *New England Quarterly,* XXXVI (1963), 3–22.

HAMBLEN, ABIGAIL. "Uncle Tom and 'Nigger Jim': A Study in Contrasts and Similarities," *Mark Twain Journal,* XI, iii (1961), 13–17.

HUDSON, BENJAMIN F. "Another View of 'Uncle Tom'" *Phylon,* XXIV (1963), 79–87.

LEE, WALLACE et al. "Is *Uncle Tom's Cabin* Anti-Negro?" *Negro Digest,* IV (January, 1946), 68–72.

MURRAY, ALEX L. "Harriet Beecher Stowe on Racial Segregation in the Schools," *American Quarterly,* XII (1960), 518–19.

NICHOLAS, HERBERT G. *"Uncle Tom's Cabin,* 1852–1952," *Georgia Review,* VIII (1954), 140–48.

NICHOLS, CHARLES. "The Origins of *Uncle Tom's Cabin," Phylon,* XIX (1958), 328–34.

OLIVER, EGBERT S. "The Little Cabin of Uncle Tom," *College English,* XXVI (1965), 355–61.

QUINN, ARTHUR HOBSON. "Literature, Politics, and Slavery," *The Literature of the American People,* ed. A. H. QUINN. New York: Appleton-Century-Crofts, 1951.

ROPPOLO, J. P. "Uncle Tom in New Orleans: Three Lost Plays," *New England Quarterly,* XXVII (1954), 213–26.

WILSON, EDMUND. " 'No! No! No! My Soul An't Yours, Mas'r!' " *New Yorker,* XXIV (November 27, 1948), 134–41.

STRIBLING, T. S.

JARRETT, T. D. "Stribling's Novels," *Phylon,* IV (1943), 345–50.

WILSON, J. S. "Poor White and Negro," *Virginia Quarterly Review,* VIII (1932), 621–24.

THOREAU, HENRY DAVID

HARDING, WALTER. "Thoreau and the Negro," *Negro History Bulletin,* X (1946), 29–35.

BIBLIOGRAPHY

TOOMER, JEAN

DuBois, W. E. B., and LOCKE, ALAIN. "The Younger Literary Movement," *Crisis*, XXVII (1924), 161–63.
HOLMES, EUGENE. "Jean Toomer, Apostle of Beauty," *Opportunity*, III (1925), 252–54, 260.
MUNSON, GORHAM. "The Significance of Jean Toomer," *Opportunity*, III (1925), 262–63.
ROSENFELD, PAUL. "Jean Toomer," *Men Seen*. New York: Dial Press, 1925.

TORRENCE, RIDGELY

F. H. "After the Play," *New Republic*, X (1917), 325.

TOURGÉE, ALBION W.

GROSS, THEODORE L. "The Fool's Errand of Albion W. Tourgée," *Phylon*, XXIV (1963), 240–54.
———. *Albion W. Tourgée*. New York: Twayne Publishers, 1963.
KAPLAN, SIDNEY. "Albion Tourgée, Attorney for the Segregated," *Journal of Negro History*, XLIX (1964), 128–33.
OLERICK, M. M. "Albion W. Tourgée, Radical Republican, Spokesman of the Civil War Crusade," *Phylon*, XXIII (1962), 332–45.

TWAIN, MARK

ALTENBERND, LYNN. "Huck Finn, Emancipator," *Criticism*, I (1959), 298–307.
BROWNELL, FRANCIS V. "The Role of Jim in *Huckleberry Finn*," *Boston University Studies in English*, I (1955), 74–83.
BUDD, LOUIS J. *Mark Twain: Social Philosopher*. Bloomington: Indiana University Press, 1962.
BUTCHER, PHILIP. "Mark Twain Sells Roxy Down the River," *CLA Journal*, VIII (1965), 225–33.
CHADWICK, HANSEN. "The Character of Jim and the Ending of *Huckleberry Finn*," *Massachusetts Review*, V (1963), 45–66.
COX, JAMES. "*Pudd'nhead Wilson*: The End of Mark Twain's American Dream," *South Atlantic Quarterly*, LVIII (1959), 351–63.
FIEDLER, LESLIE. " 'Come Back to the Raft Ag'in Huck Honey!' " *Partisan Review*, XV (1948), 664–71. Reprinted in *An End to Innocence*. Boston: Beacon Press, 1955.
FORD, THOMAS W. "The Miscegenation Theme in *Pudd'nhead Wilson*," *Mark Twain Journal*, X (1955), 13–14.
HOFFMAN, DANIEL G. "Jim's Magic: Black or White?" *American Literature*, XXXII (1960), 1–10. Reprinted in *Form and Fable in American Fiction*. New York: Oxford University Press, 1961.

Bibliography

KLAUS, ROSEMARIE. "Mark Twain und die Negerfrage—*Huckleberry Finn*," *Zeitschrift für Anglistik und Amerikanistik* (East Berlin), V (1957), 166–81.

MARX, LEO. "Mr. Eliot, Mr. Trilling, and *Huckleberry Finn*," *American Scholar*, XXII (1953), 423–40.

NOCK, S. A. "The Essential Farce," *Phylon*, XX (1959), 358–63.

REMES, CAROL. "The Heart of *Huckleberry Finn*," *Masses and Mainstream*, XIII (November, 1955), 8–16.

SAKAE, MORIOKA. "*Pudd'nhead Wilson* and the Racial Problem," *Studies in English Literature and Language* (Fukuoka, Japan), No. 12 (1962), 1–11.

TIDWELL, J. N. "Mark Twain's Representation of Negro Speech," *American Speech*, XVII (1942), 174–76.

VAN VECHTEN, CARL

GLOSTER, HUGH M. "The Van Vechten Vogue," *Phylon*, VI (1945), 310–14.

LUEDERS, EDWARD G. *Carl Van Vechten and the Twenties*. Albuquerque: University of New Mexico Press, 1955.

SCHUYLER, GEORGE S. "Carl Van Vechten," *Phylon*, XI (1950), 362–68.

WELTY, EUDORA

ISAACS, NEIL D. "Life for Phoenix," *Sewanee Review*, LXXI (1963), 75–81.

WHEATLEY, PHILLIS

GREGORY, MONTGOMERY. "The Spirit of Phillis Wheatley," *Opportunity*, I (1923), 374–75.

HOLMES, WILFRED. "Phillis Wheatley," *Negro History Bulletin*, VI (1943), 117–18.

RENFRO, HERBERT G. *Life and Works of Phillis Wheatley*. Washington, D.C.: Robert L. Pendleton, 1916.

SLATTERY, J. R. "Phillis Wheatley, the Negro Poetess," *Catholic World*, XXXIX (1884), 484–98.

WHITMAN, WALT

CLARK, LEADIE M. *Walt Whitman's Concept of the American Common Man*. New York: Philosophical Library, 1955.

GLICKSBERG, CHARLES I. "Walt Whitman and the Negro," *Phylon*, IX (1948), 326–31.

TURNER, LORENZO DOW. "Walt Whitman and the Negro," *Chicago Jewish Forum*, XV (1956), 5–11.

WARFEL, HARRY R. "Walt Whitman's *Salut au monde:* The Ideal of Human Brotherhood," *Phylon,* XIX (1958), 154–56.

WHITTIER, JOHN GREENLEAF

FLEMING, B. J. "John Greenleaf Whittier, Abolition Poet," *Negro History Bulletin,* VI (1942), 64–66.

SMALLWOOD, O. T. "The Historical Significance of Whittier's Anti-Slavery Poems," *Journal of Negro History,* XXXV (1950), 150–73.

WILEY, CALVIN

BRAVERMAN, HOWARD. "An Unusual Characterization by a Southern Ante-Bellum Writer," *Phylon,* XIX (1958), 171–79.

WOOLMAN, JOHN

LASH, JOHN S. "John Woolman: Crusader for Freedom," *Phylon,* V (1944), 30–40.

WRIGHT, RICHARD

BALDWIN, JAMES. "Many Thousands Gone," *Partisan Review,* XVII (1951), 665–80. Reprinted in *Notes of a Native Son.* Boston: Beacon Press, 1955.

——. "Richard Wright," *Encounter,* XVI (1961), 58–60.

——. "Ce qui survivra de Richard Wright," *Preuves,* No. 16 (1963), 76–79.

BISOL, GAETANO. "Richard Wright: Drama razziale e narrative negra di protesta," *Letture,* XX (1965), 259–76.

BURGUM, EDWIN BERRY. "The Promise of Democracy in Richard Wright's *Native Son,*" *The Novel and the World's Dilemma.* New York: Oxford University Press, 1947.

COHN, DAVID L. "The Negro Novel: Richard Wright," *Atlantic Monthly,* CLXV (1940), 659–61.

CREEKMORE, HUBERT. "Social Factors in *Native Son,*" *University of Kansas City Review,* VIII (1941), 136–43.

DAVIS, ARTHUR P. "*The Outsider* as a Novel of Race," *Midwest Journal,* VII (1955–56), 320–26.

ELLISON, RALPH. "Richard Wright's Blues," *Antioch Review,* V (1945), 198–211.

FABRE, MICHEL, and MARGOLIES, EDWARD. "Richard Wright (1908–1960)," *Bulletin of Bibliography,* XXIV (1965), 131–33, 137.

FORD, NICK AARON. "The Ordeal of Richard Wright," *College English,* XV (1953), 87–94.

GÉRARD, ALBERT. "Vie et vocation de Richard Wright," *Revue générale belge,* XCVII (1961), 65–78.

Bibliography

LEWIS, T. "Saga of Bigger Thomas," *Catholic World,* CLIII (1941), 201–6.

RASCOE, BURTON. "Negro Novel and White Reviewers: Richard Wright's *Native Son,*" *American Mercury,* L (1940), 113–17.

ROGGE, HEINZ. "Die amerikanische Negerfrage im Lichte der Literatur von Richard Wright und Ralph Ellison," *Die neuren Sprachen,* XV (1958), 56–69, 103–17.

SCOTT, NATHAN A. "Search for Beliefs: The Fiction of Richard Wright," *University of Kansas City Review,* XXIII (1956), 19–24.

SLOCHOWER, HARRY. *No Voice Is Wholly Lost.* New York: Creative Age Press, 1945.

WHICHER, GEORGE F. "The Resurgent South," *The Literature of the American People,* ed. A. H. QUINN. New York: Appleton-Century-Crofts, 1951.

YERBY, FRANK

GLOSTER, HUGH M. "The Significance of Frank Yerby," *Crisis,* LV (1948), 12–13.

JACKSON, BLYDEN. "Full Circle," *Phylon,* IX (1948), 30–35.

INDEX

Index

PHOENIX BOOKS
Literature and Language

PHOENIX BOOKS
in Sociology